Homer
The Iliad

Translated by
Ian Johnston
Malaspina University-College
Nanaimo, BC
Canada

Front Cover Illustration
by Ian Crowe

Richer Resources Publications
Arlington, Virginia

Homer
The Iliad

Reprint requests and requests for additional copies
of this book can be addressed to
Richer Resources Publications
1926 N. Woodrow Street
Arlington, Virginia 22207
or via our website at:
www.RicherResourcesPublications.com

ISBN 978-0-9776269-0-8
Library of Congress Control Number
2006924334

Published by Richer Resources Publications
Arlington, Virginia
Printed in the United States of America

This translation is dedicated to my son
Geoffrey (1974 - 1997)
and to my grandson Fabian (b.1992)

Generations of men are like the leaves.
In winter, winds blow them down to earth,
but then, when spring season comes again,
budding wood grows more. And so with men–
one generation grows, another dies away.

(*Iliad* 6.181-5)

Translator's Note

This text uses the traditional Latinate spellings and common English equivalents for the Greek names, e.g., Achilles, Clytaemnestra, Achaeans, Menelaus, Hecuba, rather than modern renditions which strive to stay more closely to the Greek: Akhilleus, Klytaimnestra, Akhaians, Menelaos, Hekabe, and so on, with the exception of a very few names of gods—Cronos, Ouranos—and a few others (e.g., Idaios). And where there is a common English rendition of the name (e.g., Ajax, Troy, Teucer), I have used that. A dieresis over a vowel indicates that it is pronounced by itself (e.g., Coön rhymes with "go on" not with "goon," Deïphobus is pronounced "Day-ee-phobus" not "Day-phobus" or "Dee-phobus").

In numbering the lines, the translator has usually included a short, indented line with the line above it, so that what looks like two partial lines counts as a single one. These numbers are approximately twenty-five to thirty percent higher than the numbers in the Greek text.

The numbers inserted in the text indicate an explanatory note at the bottom of the page. These have been provided by the translator.

Table of Contents

Book One
The Quarrel by the Ships

*[The invocation to the Muse; Agamemnon insults Apollo; Apollo sends
the plague onto the army; Achilles and Agamemnon quarrel; Calchas
indicates what must be done to appease Apollo; Agamemnon takes
Briseis from Achilles; Achilles prays to Thetis for revenge; Achilles
meets Thetis; Chryseis is returned to her father; Thetis visits Zeus; the
gods converse about the matter on Olympus; the banquet of the gods]*

S ing, Goddess, sing of the rage of Achilles, son of Peleus—
that murderous anger which condemned Achaeans
to countless agonies and threw many warrior souls
deep into Hades, leaving their dead bodies
carrion food for dogs and birds—
all in fulfillment of the will of Zeus.

Start at the point where Agamemnon, son of Atreus,
that king of men, quarreled with noble Achilles.
Which of the gods incited these two men to fight?

That god was Apollo, son of Zeus and Leto.   10
Angry with Agamemnon, he cast plague down
onto the troops—deadly infectious evil.
For Agamemnon had dishonoured the god's priest,
Chryses, who'd come to the ships to find his daughter,
Chryseis, bringing with him a huge ransom.
In his hand he held up on a golden staff
the scarf sacred to archer god Apollo.
He begged Achaeans, above all the army's leaders,
the two sons of Atreus:

       "Menelaus, Agamemnon, sons of Atreus,   20
       all you well-armed Achaeans, may the gods
       on Olympus grant you wipe out Priam's city,
       and then return home safe and sound.
       Release my dear child to me. Take this ransom.
       Honour Apollo, far-shooting son of Zeus."

All the Achaeans roared out their support:

"Respect the priest. Take the generous ransom."

Displeased, Agamemnon dismissed Chryses roughly:

> "Old man,
> don't let me catch you by our hollow ships,
> sneaking back here today or later on.
> Who cares about Apollo's scarf and staff?
> I'll not release the girl to you, no, not before
> she's grown old with me in Argos, far from home,
> working the loom, sharing my bed. Go away.
> If you want to get home safely, don't anger me."

The old man, afraid, obeyed his words, walked off in silence,
along the shore by the tumbling, crashing surf.
Some distance off, he prayed to lord Apollo,
Leto's fair-haired child:

> "God with the silver bow,
> protector of Chryse, sacred Cilla,
> mighty lord of Tenedos, Sminthean Apollo,[1]
> hear my prayer: If I've ever pleased you
> with a holy shrine, or burned bones for you—
> bulls and goats well wrapped in fat—
> grant me my prayer. Force the Danaans
> to pay full price for my tears with your arrows."

So Chryses prayed. Phoebus Apollo heard him.
He came down from Olympus top enraged,
carrying on his shoulders bow and covered quiver,
his arrows rattling in anger against his arm.
So the god swooped down, descending like the night.
He sat some distance from the ships, shot off an arrow—
the silver bow reverberating ominously.

[1] *Sminthean* is a special epithet given to Apollo. It seems to mean something like "killer of field mice." *Chryse* is a small coastal town near Troy, where *Chryses*, the father of *Chryseis*, is a priest of Apollo.

First, the god massacred mules and swift-running dogs,
then loosed sharp arrows in among the troops themselves.
Thick fires burned the corpses ceaselessly.

For nine days Apollo rained death down upon the troops.
On the tenth, Achilles summoned an assembly.
White-armed Hera put that thought into his mind,
concerned for the Danaans, seeing them die.   60
The men gathered. The meeting came to order.
Swift-footed Achilles rose to speak:

> "Son of Atreus,
> I fear we're being beaten back, forced home,
> if we aren't all going to be destroyed right here,
> with war and plague killing off Achaeans.
> Come now, let's ask some prophet, priest,
> interpreter of dreams—for dreams, too, come from Zeus—
> a man who might say why Apollo is so angry,
> whether he faults our prayers and offerings,
> whether somehow he'll welcome sacrificial smoke   70
> from perfect lambs and goats, then rouse himself
> and release us from this plague."

> Achilles spoke and took his seat.
Then Calchas, Thestor's son, stood up before them all,
the most astute interpreter of birds, who understood
present, future, past. His skill in prophecy,
Apollo's gift, had led Achaean ships to Troy.
He addressed the troops, thinking of their common good:

> "Achilles, friend of Zeus, you ask me to explain
> Apollo's anger, the god who shoots from far.
> And I will speak. But first you listen to me.   80
> Swear an oath that you will freely help me
> in word and deed. I think I may provoke
> someone who wields great power over Argives,
> a man who is obeyed by everyone.
> An angry king overpowers lesser men.
> Even if that day his anger is suppressed,

resentment lingers in his chest, until one day
he acts on it. So speak. Will you protect me?"

In response to Calchas, swift-footed Achilles said:

"Take courage. State what your powers tell you.   90
By Apollo, whom Zeus loves, to whom you, Calchas,
pray in prophesy to the Danaans, I swear this—
while I live to look upon the light of day,
no Achaean will raise violent hands against you,
no, not even if you name Agamemnon,
who claims he's by far the best Achaean."

Encouraged, the wise prophet then declared:

"Apollo does not fault us for prayers or offerings,
but for his priest, disgraced by Agamemnon,
who did not free his daughter and take ransom.   100
That's why the archer god has brought disaster,
and will bring still more. He won't remove
this wretched plague from the Danaans,
until we hand back bright-eyed Chryseis,
give her to her beloved father, freely,
without ransom, and offer holy sacrifice
at Chryse. If we will carry out all that,
we may change Apollo's mind, appease him."

So he spoke and sat back down. Then, Atreus' son,
wide-ruling, mighty Agamemnon, stood up before them,   110
incensed, spirit filled with huge black rage.
Eyes blazing fire, he rounded first on Calchas:

"Prophet of evil, when have you ever said
good things to me? You love to predict the worst,
always the worst! You never show good news.
Now, in prophecy to the Danaans,
you say archer Apollo brings us pain
because I was unwilling to accept
fine ransom for Chryses' daughter, Chryseis.

But I have a great desire to take her home.
In fact, I want her more than Clytaemnestra,
the wife I married. Chryseis is just as good
in her shape, physique, intelligence, or work.
Still, I'm prepared to give her back, if that's best.
I want the people safe, not all killed off.
But then you'll owe me another prize.
I won't be the only Argive left without a gift.
That would be entirely unfair to me.
You all can see my spoils are going elsewhere."

At that point, swift-footed Achilles answered the king:

"Noble son of Atreus, most acquisitive of men,
how can brave Achaeans give you a prize now?
There are none left for us to pass around.
We've divided up what we allotted,
loot from captured towns we devastated.
For men to make a common pile again
would be most unfair. Send the girl back now,
as the god demands. Should Zeus ever grant
we pillage Troy, a city rich in goods,
we'll give you three or four times as much."

Mighty Agamemnon then said in reply:

"Achilles, you're a fine man, like a god.
But don't conceal what's in your heart.
You'll not trick me or win me with your words.
You intend to keep your prizes for yourself,
while the army takes my trophy from me.
That's why you tell me to give Chryseis back.
Let Achaeans give me another prize,
equal in value, something I'll enjoy.
If not, then I'll take a prize myself by force,
something from you or Ajax or Odysseus.
The man I visit is going to be enraged.
But let's postpone discussion of all this.
Let's drag a black ship to the sacred sea,

select a crew, load oxen on for sacrifice,
and Chryseis, that fair-complexioned girl.
Let's have as leader some wise counselor—
Idomeneus, Ajax, godlike Odysseus,
or you, Peleus's son, most eminent of all,
so with a sacrifice we may appease   160
the god who shoots from far away."

Scowling grimly, swift-footed Achilles interposed:

"You insatiable creature, quite shameless.
How can any Achaean obey you willingly—
join a raiding party or keep fighting
with full force against an enemy?
I didn't come to battle over here
because of Trojans. I have no fight with them.
They never stole my bulls or horses
or razed my crops in fertile Phthia,   170
where heroes grow. Many shady mountains
and the roaring sea stand there between us.
But you, great shameless man, we came with you,
to please you, to win honour from the Trojans—
for you, dog face, and for Menelaus.
You don't consider this, don't think at all.
You threaten now to confiscate the prize
I worked so hard for, gift from Achaea's sons.
When we Achaeans loot some well-built Trojan town,
my prizes never match the ones you get.   180
The major share of war's fury rests on me.
But when we hand around the battle spoils,
you get much larger trophies. Worn out in war,
I reach my ships with something fine but small.
So I'll return home now to Phthia.
It's far better to sail back in my curved ships.
I don't fancy staying here unvalued,
to pile up riches, treasures just for you."

To that, Agamemnon, king of men, shot back:

"Fly off home then, if that's your heart's desire.   190
I'll not beg you to stay on my account.
I have others around to honour me,
especially all-wise Zeus himself.
Of all the kings Zeus cherishes, it's you
I hate the most. You love constant strife—
war and combat. So what if you're strong?
Some god gave you that. So scurry off home.
Take ships and friends. Go rule your Myrmidons.
I don't like you or care about your rage.
But I'll make this threat: I'll take your prize,   200
fair-cheeked Briseis. I'll fetch her in person.
You'll see just how much I'm the better man.
And others will hate to speak to me as peers,
in public claiming full equality with me."

As Agamemnon spoke, Peleus' son, Achilles,
was overwhelmed with anguish, heart torn two ways,
debating in his shaggy chest what he should do:
Should he draw out the sharp sword on his thigh,
incite the crowd, kill Atreus' son, or suppress his rage,
control his fury? As he argued in his mind and heart,   210
he slid his huge sword part way from its sheath.
At that moment, Athena came down from heaven.
White-armed Hera sent her. She cherished both men,
cared for them equally. Athena stood behind Achilles,
grabbed him by his golden hair, invisible to all
except Achilles. In astonishment he turned.
At once he recognized Pallas Athena,
the dreadful glitter in her eyes. Achilles spoke—
his words had wings.

                    "Child of aegis-bearing Zeus,[1]
        why have you come now? Do you wish to see   220
        how overbearing Agamemnon is?
        I'll tell you where all this is going to lead—
        that arrogance will soon cost him his life."

[1]The *aegis* is Zeus' special shield, the sight of which has the power to terrify men and
make them run away. Zeus sometimes lends it to other gods.

Glittery-eyed Athena then spoke in reply:

  "I came down from heaven to curb your passion,
  if you obey. White-armed Hera sent me.
  She loves you both alike, cares equally.
  Give up this quarrel. Don't draw your sword.
  Fight him with words, so he becomes disgraced.
  For I say to you, and this will happen,   230
  because of Agamemnon's arrogance
  some day gifts three times greater than this girl
  will be set down before you. Control yourself.
  Obey."

      Swift-footed Achilles answered Athena:

  "Goddess, men should follow your instructions,
  though angry in their hearts. It's better so.
  The person who's obedient to the gods,
  the gods attend to all the more."

      Obeying Athena's words,
Achilles relaxed his huge fist on the silver hilt
and pushed the massive sword back in its scabbard. 240
Athena then returned to heaven, home of Zeus,
who bears the aegis, and the other gods.

Achilles turned again on Agamemnon, Atreus' son,
with harsh abuse, his anger still unabated:

  "You drunken sot, dog-eyed, deer-timid coward,
  you're never strong enough within yourself
  to arm for war alongside other comrades,
  or venture with Achaea's bravest on a raid.
  To you that smells too much like death.
  No. You'd much prefer to stroll around   250
  throughout the wide Achaean army,
  to grab gifts from a man who speaks against you.
  A king who gorges on his own people!
  You lord it over worthless men. If not,

son of Atreus, this would be your last offence.
I'll tell you, swear a great oath on this point,
by this sceptre, which will never sprout
leaves and shoots again, since first ripped away
from its mountain stump, nor bloom any more,
now that bronze has sliced off leaf and bark.   260
This sceptre Achaea's sons take in hand
whenever they do justice in Zeus' name.
An oath on this has power. On this I swear—
the time will come when Achaea's sons
all miss Achilles, a time when, in distress,
you'll lack my help, a time when Hector,
that man killer, destroys many warriors.
Then grief will tear your hearts apart,
because you shamed Achaea's finest man."

So the son of Peleus spoke, throwing to the ground   270
the sceptre with the golden studs. Then he sat down,
directly facing furious Agamemnon.

Then Nestor stood up, clear, sweet orator from Pylos.
Sweeter than honey the words flowed from his tongue.
In his own lifetime two generations of mortal men
had come and passed away, all those born and raised
with him so long ago in sacred Pylos.
Now he ruled a third generation of his people.
Concerned about their common good, he said:

"Alas, this is great sorrow for Achaeans.   280
Priam and Priam's children will be glad,
the hearts of other Trojans swell with joy,
should they find out about such quarreling,
a fight between you two, among Danaans
the very best for counsel or combat.
But listen. You are both younger men than I.
And I've been colleague of better men than you,
men who never showed me any disrespect,
men whose like I have not seen again,
and never will—like Peirithous, Dryas,   290

15

a shepherd to his people, Caeneus,
Exadios, god-like Polyphemus,
Theseus, son of Aegeus, all god-like men—
the mightiest earthborn men, the strongest.
And the enemies they fought against were strong,
the most powerful of mountain centaurs.[1]
But they destroyed those creatures totally.
Associate of theirs, I came from Pylos,
a long way from that land, summoned personally.
I fought on my own behalf, by myself.   300
No man alive on earth could now fight them.
Yet they heard me and followed my advice.
So listen, both of you. That's what's best now.
Agamemnon, you're an excellent man,
but do not take Briseis from Achilles.
Let that pass. Achaea's sons gave her to him first.
And you, Peleus' son, don't seek to fight the king,
not as your enemy. The sceptre-bearing king,
whose powerful authority comes from Zeus,
never shares honours equally. Achilles,   310
you may be stronger, since your mother was divine,
but he's more powerful, for he rules more men.
But you, son of Atreus, check your anger.
Set aside, I urge you, your rage against Achilles,
who provides, in the middle of war's evils,
a powerful defence for all Achaeans."

Mighty Agamemnon then replied to Nestor:

"Old man, everything you say is true enough.
But this man wants to put the rest to shame,
rule all of us, lord it over everyone.   320
But some, I think, will not obey him.
So what if the gods, who live forever,
made him a spearman? Is that some reason
we should let him say such shameful things?"

Achilles, interrupting Agamemnon, shouted:

[1] *Centaurs* are creatures with the head and torso of a man and the body of a horse.

"I'd be called a coward, a nobody,
if I held back from any action
because of something you might say.
Order other men about. Don't tell me
what I should do. I'll not obey you any more.   330
But I will tell you this—remember it well—
I'll not raise my hand to fight about that girl,
no, not against you or any other man.
You Achaeans gave her to me, and now,
you seize her back again. But you'll not take
another thing from my swift black ship—
you'll get nothing else with my consent.
If you'd like to see what happens, just try.
My spear will quickly drip with your dark blood."

Thus the pair of them continued arguing.   340
Then they stood up, dissolving the assembly by the ships.
Peleus's son went back to his well-balanced ships and huts,
along with Patroclus, Menoetius' son, and friends.

Agamemnon dragged a swift ship down the shore,
chose twenty sailors, loaded on the oxen,
offerings for the god, and led on fair-cheeked Chryseis.
Shrewd Odysseus shipped on as leader. All aboard,
they set off, carving a pathway through the sea.

Atreus' son ordered troops to cleanse themselves.
The men bathed in the sea, washed off impurities.   350
They then made sacrificial offerings to Apollo—
hundreds of perfect bulls and goats—beside the restless sea.
Savory smells curled up amid the smoke high into heaven.

The men thus occupied, Agamemnon did not forget
the challenge he'd made earlier to Achilles.
He called his heralds, Talthybius and Eurybates:

> "Go to Achilles' tent, Peleus's son,
> take fair-complexioned Briseis by the hand.
> Bring her to me. If he won't surrender her,

I'll come myself in force and take her.

For him that will be a worse disaster."

With these firm orders, he dismissed the men, who moved off,
heavy hearted, along the shore of the restless sea.
They reached the huts and ships of the Myrmidons.
There they found Achilles seated by his hut
and his black ship. As he saw them approach,
Achilles felt no joy. The two heralds, afraid,
just stood in silence, out of deference to the king.
In his heart Achilles sensed their purpose. He called them.

> "Cheer up, heralds, messengers for gods and men. 370
> Come here. I don't blame you, but Agamemnon.
> He sends you both here for the girl Briseis.
> Come, Patroclus, born from Zeus, fetch the girl.
> Give her to these two to take away.
> Let them both witness, before blessed gods,
> mortal men, and that unfeeling king,
> if ever there's a need for me again
> to defend others from a shameful death.
> That man's wits are foolish, disastrously so—
> he's not thinking about past or future, 380
> how Achaeans may fight safely by their ships."

Patroclus did as his dear comrade had requested.
He led out fair-cheeked Briseis from the hut
and gave her up to be led off. The heralds went back,
returning to Achaean ships, Briseis with them,
but against her will.

Achilles then, in tears,
withdrew from his companions, sat by the shore,
staring at the wide gray seas. Stretching out his hands,
he cried aloud, praying repeatedly to Thetis,
his beloved mother.

> "Mother, since you gave me life— 390
> if only for a while—Olympian Zeus,

18

high thunderer, should give me due honour.
But he doesn't grant me even slight respect.
For wide-ruling Agamemnon, Atreus' son,
has shamed me, has taken away my prize,
appropriated it for his own use."

                              As he said this, he wept.
His noble mother heard him from deep within the sea,
where she sat by her old father. Quickly she rose up,
moving above gray waters, like an ocean mist,
and settled down before him, as he wept. She stroked him,   400
then said:

              "My child, why these tears? What sorrows
      weigh down your heart? Tell me, so we'll both know.
      Don't hide from me what's on your mind."

With a deep groan, swift-footed Achilles then replied.

      "You know. Why should I tell you what you know?
      We came to Thebe, Eëtion's sacred city,
      sacked it, taking everything the city had.
      Achaea's sons apportioned it all fairly
      amongst themselves. Agamemnon's share
      was fair-skinned Chryseis. Then Chryses arrived   410
      at the swift ships of bronze-armed Achaeans.
      Archer god Apollo's priest sought out his daughter.
      He brought with him an enormous ransom,
      carried in his hands the sacred golden staff
      with the shawl of archer god Apollo.
      He begged Achaeans, above all Atreus' two sons,
      the people's leaders. All Achaeans called on them
      to respect the priest, accept the splendid ransom.
      But that didn't please Agamemnon in his heart.
      He sent him roughly off with harsh abusive orders   420
      The old man went away again, enraged.
      He prayed to Apollo, who loved him well.
      The god heard him and sent his deadly arrows
      against the Argives. The troops kept dying,

19

one by one, as the god rained arrows down
throughout the wide Achaean army.
The prophet Calchas, understanding all,
told us Apollo's will. At once I was the first
to recommend we all appease the god.
But anger got control of Agamemnon.   430
He stood up on the spot and made that threat
which he's just carried out. So quick-eyed Achaeans
are sending Chryseis in fast ships back to Chryse,
transporting gifts for lord Apollo, and heralds came
to take away Briseis from my huts,
the girl who is my gift from Achaea's sons.
So now, if you can, protect your son.
Go to Mount Olympus, implore Zeus,
if ever you in word or deed have pleased him.
For often I have heard you boast in father's house   440
that you alone of all the deathless gods
saved Zeus of the dark clouds from disgraceful ruin,
when other Olympians came to tie him up,
Hera, Pallas Athena, and Poseidon.
But you, goddess, came and set him free,
by quickly calling up to high Olympus
that hundred-handed monster gods call Briareos,
and men all name Aigaion, a creature
whose strength was greater than his father's.
He sat down beside the son of Cronos,   450
exulting in his glory. The sacred gods, afraid,
stopped tying up Zeus. So sit down right by Zeus,
clasp his knee, remind him of all that,
so he'll want to help the Trojans somehow,
corner Achaeans by the sea, by their ships' prows,
have them destroyed, so they all enjoy their king,
so the son of Atreus, wide-ruling Agamemnon,
himself may see his foolishness, dishonouring
Achilles, the best of the Achaeans."

Thetis, shedding tears, answered her son, Achilles: 460

"Oh my child, why did I rear you,

20

since I brought you up to so much pain?
Would you were safely by your ships dry-eyed.
Your life is fated to be short—you'll not live long.
Now, faced with a quick doom, you're in distress,
more so than any other man. At home,
I gave you life marked by an evil fate.
But I'll tell these things to thunder-loving Zeus.
I'll go myself to snow-topped Mount Olympus,
to see if he will undertake all this.   470
Meanwhile, you should sit by your swift ships,
angry at Achaeans. Take no part in war.
For yesterday Zeus went to Oceanus,
to banquet with the worthy Ethiopians.
The gods all journeyed with him. In twelve days,
when he returns and comes home to Olympus,
I'll go to Zeus' bronze-floored house, clasp his knee.
I think I'll get him to consent."

                                                Thetis spoke.
Then she went away, leaving Achilles there,
angry at heart for lovely girdled Briseis,   480
taken from him by force against his will.

Odysseus sailed to Chryse, bringing with him
the sacrificial animals as sacred offerings.
When they had sailed into deep anchorage,
they took in the sails and stowed them in the ship.
With forestays they soon set the mast down in its notch,
then rowed the ship in to its mooring place.
They threw out anchor stones, lashed stern cables,
and clambered out into the ocean surf.
They brought off the offerings to archer god Apollo.   490
Then Chryseis disembarked from the ocean ship.
Resourceful Odysseus led her to the altar,
placed her in her beloved father's hands, then said:

      "Chryses, I have been sent by Agamemnon,
      ruler of men, to bring your daughter to you,
      and then, on behalf of the Danaans,

to make an offering to lord Apollo—
all these sacrificial beasts—to placate the god,
who now inflicts such dismal evil on us."

After saying this, he handed the girl over.   500
Chryses gave his daughter a joyful welcome back.
And then around the well-built altar, they arranged
the splendid sacrifice. They washed their hands,
and picked up the barley grain for sprinkling.
Raising his arms, Chryses prayed out loud on their behalf:

"Hear me, god of the silver bow, protector
of Chryse, mighty lord of holy Cilla,
sacred Tenedos. You heard me earlier,
when I prayed to you. Just as you honoured me,
striking hard against Achaeans then, so now,   510
grant me what I pray for—remove disaster,
this wretched evil, from the Danaans."

So Chryses spoke. Phoebus Apollo heard him.
Once they had prayed and scattered barley grain,
they pulled back the heads of sacrificial beasts,
slit their throats, flayed them, sliced the thigh bones out,
and hid them in twin layers of fat, with raw meat on top.
Old Chryses burned them on split wood, poured wine on them.
Young men beside him held out five-pronged forks.
Once the thighs were well burned, they sampled entrails,   520
then sliced up all the rest, skewered the meat on spits,
roasted it carefully, and drew off every piece.
That work complete, they then prepared a meal and ate.
No heart was left unsatisfied. All feasted equally.
And when the men had had their fill of food and drink,
young boys filled the mixing bowl with wine up to the brim,
and served it, pouring libations into every cup.
Then all day long young Achaean lads played music,
singing to the god a lovely hymn of praise,
honouring in dance and song the god who shoots from far.   530
Hearing them, Apollo felt joy fill his heart. At sunset,
as dusk came on, by the ship's stern they went to sleep.

22

But when early born, rose-fingered Dawn appeared,
they set off, once more back to the wide Achaean camp.
Far-shooting Apollo sent them favourable winds.
They raised the mast and then the sails. The wind blew,
filling out the body of the sail—on both sides of the prow
the purple waves hissed loudly as the ship sped on its way,
its motion carving a path through the ocean swell.
When they reached the broad Achaean army,   540
they hauled the black ship high up on the sand,
pushed long props tight beneath it, then dispersed,
each man returning to his own huts and ships.

Meanwhile, Achilles, divinely born son of Peleus,
sat down in anger alongside his swift ships. Not once
did he attend assembly where men win glory
or go out to fight. But he pined away at heart,
remaining idle by his ships, yearning
for the hue and cry and clash of battle.

Twelve days later, the company of gods came back   550
together to Olympus, with Zeus in the lead.
Thetis did not forget the promise to her son.
She rose up through the ocean waves at daybreak,
then moved high up to great Olympus. She found Zeus,
wide-seeing son of Cronos, some distance from the rest,
seated on the highest peak of many-ridged Olympus.
She sat down right in front of him. With her left hand,
she clutched his knees, with her right she cupped his chin,
in supplication to lord Zeus, son of Cronos:

> "Father Zeus, if, among the deathless gods,   560
> I've ever served you well in word or deed,
> then grant my prayer will be fulfilled.
> Bring honour to my son, who, of all men
> will be fate's quickest victim. For just now,
> Agamemnon, king of men, has shamed him.
> He seized his prize, robbing him in person,
> and kept it for himself. But honour him,
> Zeus, all-wise Olympian. Give the Trojans

23

the upper hand, until Achaeans respect my son,
until they multiply his honours."

Thetis finished. Cloud gatherer Zeus did not respond.
He sat a long time silent. Thetis held his knees,
clinging close, repeating her request once more:

> "Promise me truly, nod your head, or deny me—
> since there's nothing here for you to fear—
> so I'll clearly see how among all gods
> I enjoy the least respect."

Cloud gatherer Zeus, greatly troubled, said:

> "A nasty business.
> What you say will set Hera against me.
> She provokes me so with her abuse. Even now, 580
> in the assembly of immortal gods,
> she's always insulting me, accusing me
> of favouring the Trojans in the war.
> But go away for now, in case Hera catches on.
> I'll take care of this, make sure it comes to pass.
> Come, to convince you, I'll nod my head.
> Among gods that's the strongest pledge I make.
> Once I nod my assent, nothing I say
> can be revoked, denied, or unfulfilled."

Zeus, son of Cronos, nodded his dark brows. 590
The divine hair on the king of gods fell forward,
down over his immortal head, shaking Olympus
to its very base. The conference over, the two parted.
Thetis plunged from bright Olympus back into the sea.

Zeus went inside his house. Their father present,
all the gods at once stood up from their seats.
No one dared stay put as he came in—all rose together.
Zeus seated himself upon his throne. Looking at him,
Hera sensed he'd made some deal with Thetis,
silver-footed daughter of the Old Man of the Sea. 600

24

At once she spoke up accusingly:

"Which god has been scheming with you, you crafty one?
You always love to work on things in secret,
without involving me. You never want
to tell me openly what you intend."

The father of gods and men replied:

"Hera,
don't hope to understand my every plan.
Even for my own wife that's dangerous.
What's appropriate for you to hear about,
no one, god or man, will know before you.   610
But when I wish to hide my thoughts from gods,
don't you go digging after them,
or pestering me for every detail."

Ox-eyed queen Hera then replied to Zeus:

"Most dread son of Cronos, what are you saying?
I have not been overzealous before now,
in questioning you or seeking answers.
Surely you're quite at liberty to plan
anything you wish. But now, in my mind,
I've got this dreadful fear that Thetis,   620
silver-footed daughter of the Old Man of the Sea,
has won you over, for this morning early,
she sat down beside you, held your knees.
I think you surely nodded your agreement
to honour Achilles, killing many soldiers,
slaughtering them by the Achaean ships."

Zeus, the cloud gatherer, spoke out in response:

"My dear lady, you're always fancying things.
Your attention picks up every detail.
But you can't do anything about it,   630
except push yourself still further from my heart,

25

making matters so much worse for you.
If things are as they are, then that's the way
I want them. So sit down quietly.
Do as I say. If not, then all the gods
here on Olympus won't be any help,
when I reach out to set my hands on you,
for they're invincible."

Zeus finished speaking. Ox-eyed queen Hera sat down,
in fear, silently suppressing what her heart desired.   640
In Zeus' home the Olympian gods began to quarrel.
Then that famous artisan, Hephaestus, concerned
about his mother, white-armed Hera, spoke to them:

"A troublesome matter this will prove—
unendurable—if you two start fighting
over mortal men like this, inciting gods to quarrel.
If we start bickering, we can't enjoy the meal,
our excellent banquet. So I'm urging mother,
though she's more than willing, to humour Zeus,
our dear father, so he won't get angry once again,   650
disturb the feast for us. For if Zeus,
the Olympian lord of lightning, was of a mind
to hurl us from our seats, his strength's too great.
But if you talk to him with soothing words,
at once Olympian Zeus will treat us well."

Hephaestus spoke, then stood up, passed a double goblet
across to his dear mother, saying:

"Stay calm, mother, even though you are upset.
If not, then, as beloved as you are,
I may see you beaten up before my eyes,   660
with me incapable of helping out,
though the sight would make me most unhappy.
It's hard to take a stand opposing Zeus.
Once, when I was eager to assist you,
Zeus seized me by the feet and threw me out,
down from heaven's heights. The entire day

I fell and then, right at sunset, dropped
on Lemnos, almost dead. After that fall,
men of Sintes helped me to recover."

As he spoke, the white-armed goddess Hera smiled.   670
She reached for her son's goblet. He poured the drink,
going from right to left, for all the other gods,
drawing off sweet nectar from the mixing bowl.
Then their laughter broke out irrepressibly,
as the sacred gods saw Hephaestus bustling around,
concerned about the feast. All that day they dined,
until sunset. No one's heart went unsatisfied.
All feasted equally. They heard exquisite music,
from Apollo's lyre and the Muses' beautiful song
and counter-song. When the sun's bright light had set,   680
the gods all went to their own homes. Hephaestus,
the famous lame god, with his resourceful skill,
had made each god a place to live. Olympian Zeus,
god of lightning, went home to his own bed,
where he usually reclined whenever sweet sleep
came over him. He went inside and lay down there,
with Hera of the golden throne stretched out beside him.

Book Two
Agamemnon's Dream and The Catalogue of Ships

[Zeus sends a false dream to Agamemnon; Agamemnon reports the dream to his advisors and outlines a test of the army; Agamemnon urges his troops to go home; Odysseus restores order; Thersites insults Agamemnon; Odysseus deals with Thersites, reminds the men of Calchas' original prophecy; Nestor suggests a display of the troops; the Catalogue of Ships (list of the Achaean, Trojan, and allied forces)]

Gods and warriors slept through the entire night.
But sweet Sleep did not visit Zeus, tossing and turning
over in his mind some way to honour Achilles,
by slaughtering many soldiers by the Achaean ships.
In Zeus' heart the best idea seemed to be
to send out a wicked Dream to Agamemnon.
Calling the Dream, Zeus said these winged words to him:

> "Evil Dream, fly quickly to Achaea's men,
> by their swift ships. Go to Agamemnon's hut,   10
> Atreus' son. Report my words precisely.
> Bid him quickly arm long-haired Achaean troops,
> for now they'll capture Troy, city of wide streets.
> Immortal gods who dwell on Mount Olympus
> no longer disagree about all this.
> Hera's entreaties have persuaded them.
> Trojans can expect more sorrows, more disasters."

Zeus spoke. With these instructions, Dream set off,
quickly reaching Achaea's fast ships and Atreus's son.
He found Agamemnon resting in his hut,
wrapped up in the sweet divinity of Sleep.   20
Dream stood above his head, looking just like Nestor,
son of Neleus, of all the more senior men
the one Agamemnon held in special honour.
In that shape, divine Dream spoke to Agamemnon:

"You are sleeping, son of fiery Atreus,
tamer of horses. But a prudent man,
one to whom people have given their trust,
who has so many things to think about,
shouldn't sleep all night. So pay attention.
Hear what I have to say. I come to you   30
as Zeus' messenger, with his orders.
He's far off, but pities and cares for you.
He bids you quickly arm long-haired Achaeans,
for now you can take Troy, city of wide streets.
The immortal gods who dwell on Mount Olympus
no longer disagree about all this.
Hera's entreaties have persuaded them.
Trojans can expect from Zeus more sorrows,
more disasters. Remember what I've said.
Don't let forgetfulness seize your mind,   40
when honey Sleep has loosed his sweet grip on you."

This said, Dream went off, leaving the king imagining things
which would not come to pass. He thought he'd take Troy,
Priam's city, that very day. Fool! He had no clue
of what Zeus really meant, his plan to load on them,
Trojans and Danaans both, still more suffering,
more cries of sorrow, through war's brutality.

Agamemnon roused himself from sleep, the divine voice
all round him still. He sat up, pulled on a supple tunic,
new and finely made. On top he threw a large cloak.   50
He laced up lovely sandals over his sleek feet
and slung a silver-studded sword around both shoulders.
He took with him the royal staff of his ancestors,
eternal and imperishable. Gripping this,
he approached the ships of the bronze-armed Achaeans.
When goddess Dawn rose high up on Olympus,
bringing light to Zeus and the immortals,
Agamemnon bid the loud-voiced heralds summon
all the long-haired Achaeans to assembly.
Such a call went out. Men answered on the run.   60
But first, Agamemnon convened a meeting

29

of all his great-hearted senior counselors.
They met by Nestor's ships, king born on Pylos.
To the assembled group Agamemnon then sketched out
a plan he had conceived—a devious one.

                       "My friends, listen.
A divine Dream has just come to me,
through the sacred night, as I lay asleep,
in form, size, and voice just like worthy Nestor.
He stood above my head and spoke these words:
'You are sleeping, son of fiery Atreus,   70
tamer of horses. But a prudent man,
one to whom people have given their trust,
who has so many things to think about,
shouldn't sleep all night. So pay attention.
Hear what I have to say. I come to you
as Zeus' messenger, with his orders.
He's far off, but pities and cares for you.
He bids you quickly arm long-haired Achaeans,
for now you can take Troy, city of wide streets.
Immortal gods who dwell on Mount Olympus   80
no longer disagree about all this.
Hera's entreaties have persuaded them.
The Trojans can expect from Zeus more sorrows,
more disasters. Remember what I've said.'
With that, Dream flew off, sweet Sleep released me.
Come, then, let's get long-haired Achaeans
somehow armed for battle. But first,
it's only right I test the men, ordering them
to go home in their ships with many oars.
You hold them back with your commands,   90
each one working from his own position."

Agamemnon finished speaking and sat back down.
Nestor stood up before them, king of sandy Pylos.
With a wise sense of their common cause, he addressed them:

           "My friends, chiefs and leaders of the Argives,
if any other Achaean had told us such a dream,

we would declare it quite false, dismiss it.
But now the man who has a claim to be
the greatest of Achaeans has witnessed it.
So come, let's find a way to arm Achaea's sons." 100

So Nestor spoke. Then he began to make his way back,
leaving the council meeting. The others stood up,
all sceptre-bearing kings, following Nestor's lead,
his people's shepherd. Troops came streaming out to them.
Just as dense clouds of bees pour out in endless swarms
from hollow rocks, in clusters flying to spring flowers,
charging off in all directions, so from ships and huts
the many clans rushed out to meet, group after group.
Among the troops Rumour blazed, Zeus' messenger,
igniting them. The assembly was in uproar. 110
Beneath the men, as they sat amid the din, earth groaned.
Nine heralds shouted out instructions, attempting
to control the noise, so men could hear their leaders,
god's chosen ones. Gradually men settled down,
kept quiet in their places. The noise subsided.
King Agamemnon stood up, hands gripping his staff,
one fashioned by Hephaestus' careful craftsmanship.
That god had given it to lord Zeus, son of Cronos.
Later Zeus had presented it to Hermes,
the guide, killer of Argus.[1] Hermes, in his turn, 120
gave it to king Pelops, the chariot racer,
who passed the staff to Atreus, the people's leader.
This man, as he lay dying, left it for Thyestes,
who owned many flocks. Thyestes, in his turn,
passed it onto Agamemnon, who held it
as ruler of all Argos and many islands.
With this staff as his support, Agamemnon spoke:

> "You Danaan warriors, comrades,
> companions of Ares, god of war,
> Zeus, son of Cronos, has entangled me 130
> in some really serious foolishness.

[1]Argus was a monster sent by Hera to guard Io, because she didn't want Zeus to seduce Io. Hermes killed Argus on Zeus' orders.

Perverse Zeus! He promised me, he agreed—
I'd have devastated well-built Troy
before going home. Now he plans a cruel trick,
tells me to return to Argos dishonoured,
after I've lost so many warriors.
This is apparently what high Zeus desires,
he who has smashed so many city heights,
and will destroy still more, such is his power,
the greatest power of all. This is a great disgrace,   140
which people will learn about in years to come—
how an Achaean force of such quality and size
vainly sailed off to fight a lesser force,
and failed to get what they set out to take.
For if we Achaeans and the Trojans wished,
in good faith, to draw up a treaty,
to tally up the numbers on both sides,
with Trojans counting each inhabitant of Troy,
and if we Achaeans set ourselves in groups of ten,
then chose, for every group, a Trojan man   150
to pour our wine, then of our groups of ten
many would lack a man to act as steward.
That, I tell you, indicates just how much
Achaea's sons outnumber Trojans,
those who live in Troy. But all their allies,
warrior spearmen from many cities,
are a huge problem for me. They thwart my wish
to smash down those sturdy walls of Troy.
Nine of great Zeus' years have rolled on past.
Ships' planks have rotted, their ropes have frayed.   160
Back home our wives and children wait for us.
The work for which we came remains undone.
So come, let's all agree to what I say.
Let's go back to our own dear country in our ships.
For we'll not capture Troy with its broad streets."

So Agamemnon spoke. Among the soldiers,
all those with no idea of what he'd planned,
men's feelings quickened. The assembly was aroused.
Just like huge ocean waves on the Icarian Sea,

when East Wind and South Wind rush down together   170
from Father Zeus' clouds to whip up the sea,
the whole assembly rippled, like a large grain field,
undulating under the fury of the storm,
as West Wind roars in with force, all ears of corn
ducking down under the power of the gusts—
that's how the shouting men stampeded to their ships.
From underneath their feet a dust cloud rose.
They yelled orders to each other to grab the ships,
drag them to the sacred sea, clear out channels
for launching boats, knock out props from underneath,   180
frantic to get home. Heaven echoed with the din.
At that point, the Argives might well have gone back—
contravening what Fate had proposed for them—
if Hera had not spoken to Athena:

> "Alas, unconquerable child of Zeus,
> who bears the aegis, the Argives will flee,
> go back home to their dear native land,
> cross the wide sea, abandoning Helen,
> an Argive woman, leaving in triumph
> Priam and his Trojans. On her account,   190
> many Achaeans have perished here in Troy,
> far from the homes they love. So now, come on,
> go down to the bronze-clad Achaean troops,
> use your persuasive power to stop the men
> hauling their curved ships down into the sea."

So Hera spoke. Bright-eyed goddess Athena obeyed.
She sped off, raced down from Mount Olympus' crest,
quickly reached Achaea's swift ships, rushing to the spot
Odysseus, a man as wise as Zeus, was standing.
He'd laid no hand on his fast, black, well-decked ship.   200
His stout heart was filled with pain. Standing close to him,
bright-eyed Athena spoke to him:

> "Odysseus,
> divinely bred, Laertes' resourceful son,
> so you are going to fly back home,

sail off to your own dear country.
You'll leap into your ships with many oars,
and leave in triumph Priam and the Trojans,
abandoning Argive Helen, for whose sake
so many Achaeans have died here in Troy,
far from the homes they love. But come now,   210
move around among Achaean soldiers.
Don't hesitate. Persuade each man to stop
dragging the curved ships down into the sea."

So Athena spoke. Odysseus knew her from her voice,
as she talked. Then he ran, shrugging off his cloak—
Eurybates, the herald, later picked it up,
a man from Ithaca, aide to Odysseus.
Odysseus went straight to Agamemnon, Atreus' son,
took from him his imperishable ancestral staff.
Grasping this, he ran to the bronze-clad Achaeans' ships.   220
When he came across some king or prominent leader,
he'd confront him, telling him to hold his ground:

"Friend, it's not suitable for you to panic,
as if you're worthless. Take your seat instead.
Get other soldiers to remain in place.
You've no clear sense of Agamemnon's plan.
Right now he's testing all the army.
Soon enough he'll punish Achaea's sons.
Didn't we all hear what he said in council?
In his rage he may harm Achaean troops—   230
passions run high in kings whom Zeus supports.
Their honour comes from Zeus the Counselor,
who loves them."

                    By contrast, when Odysseus
came across some common soldier yelling out,
he'd beat him with the staff, admonishing him:

"My friend, take your place in silence. Stay put.
Listen to what others say, your betters,
you puny coward, useless in war or council.

Achaeans can't all rule here as kings.
No good comes from having many leaders.   240
Let there be one in charge, one ruler,
who receives from crooked-minded Cronos
sceptre and laws, so he may rule his people."

Odysseus moved throughout the army, calming things.
From ships and huts, soldiers rushed to reassemble,
echoing like waves of the roaring sea crashing on shore,
as Ocean thunders on. Men sat calmly in their places.
But a single man kept on yelling out abuse—
scurrilous Thersites, expert in various insults,
vulgar terms for inappropriate attacks on kings,   250
whatever he thought would make the Argives laugh.
Of all the men who came to Troy, he was the ugliest—
bow legged, one crippled foot, rounded shoulders
curving in toward his chest. On top, his pointed head
sprouted thin, scraggly tufts of hair. Achilles hated him,
as did Odysseus, too, both subject to his taunts.
But now Agamemnon was the target of his gibes.
The Achaeans, despising Thersites in their hearts,
were furious at him. But he kept shouting out,
aiming noisy insults right at Agamemnon: 260

        "Son of Atreus, what's your problem now?
        What do you lack? Your huts are stuffed with bronze,
        plenty of choice women, too—all presents
        we Achaeans give you as our leader,
        whenever we ransack some city.
        Or are you in need of still more gold,
        a ransom fetched by some horse-taming Trojan
        for his son tied up and delivered here
        by me or by some other Achaean?
        Or do you want a young girl to stash away,   270
        so you're the only one who gets to screw her?
        It's just not fair that you, our leader,
        have botched things up so badly for us,
        Achaea's sons. But you men, you soldiers,
        cowardly comrades, disgraceful people,

you're Achaean women, not warriors.
Let's sail home in our ships, leave this man,
our king, in Troy here to enjoy his loot.
That way he might come to recognize
whether or not we're of some use to him.   280
Now Agamemnon has even shamed Achilles,
a much finer warrior than himself,
stealing a prize, keeping it for his own use.
Then there's Achilles, no heart's anger there,
who lets it all just happen. If he didn't,
this bullying of yours, son of Atreus,
would be your last."

        Thersites yelled out these insults
right at Agamemnon, the people's shepherd,
abusing him. Noble Odysseus stood up quickly,
confronting Thersites. Scowling, he lashed out sternly: 290

"Shut up, chatterbox. You're a champion talker.
But don't try to have it out with kings,
all by yourself. Let me tell you something—
of all those who came to Troy with Atreus' sons,
you're the most disgraceful. So shut your mouth.
No more words from you abusing our kings,
seeking to sneak back home. How this war will end,
we've no idea—whether Achaea's sons
will go back home successful or will fail.
You sit here, railing at Agamemnon,   300
Atreus' son, leader of his people,
because Danaan heroes have given him
so many gifts—but that's a cheap insult.
So I'll tell you how things are going to be.
If I find you being so foolish any more,
then let Odysseus' head no longer stay
upon his shoulders, let him no longer
be called the father of Telemachus,
if I don't grab you, rip off all your clothes,
cloak and tunic, down to your cock and balls,   310
and beat you back to the fast ships in tears,

whipping you in shame from our assembly."

Saying this, Odysseus lashed out with the sceptre,
hitting Thersites hard across his back and shoulders.
He doubled up in pain, shedding many tears.
In the middle of Thersites' back sprang up
bloody welts beneath the golden sceptre.
He sat down, afraid and hurt, peering around,
like an idiot, and rubbing away his tears.
The soldiers, though discontent, laughed uproariously,   320
saying to one another:

                          "Comrades,
before now Odysseus has done good things,
thinking up fine plans and leading us in war.
But that's the best thing he's done by far
to help the Argives, shutting up that rabble-rouser.
Thersites' bold spirit won't urge him on
to trash our kings again with his abuse."

That's how the soldiers talked together. Then Odysseus,
destroyer of cities, rose up, grasping the sceptre.
At his side, bright-eyed Athena, looking like a herald,   330
silenced troops, so Achaeans close by and far away
could hear him and follow his advice. Odysseus,
bearing in mind their common good, spoke out:

                       "Son of Atreus,
now the Achaeans wish to disgrace you,
their king, shame you before all mortal men.
They're refusing now to keep their promise,
the one they all swore to while sailing here,
still on their way from horse-breeding Argos,
that oath that they'd return after we'd destroyed
Troy's strong walls. Like widows or small children,   340
they're whining to each other to go home.
But going back demoralized is bad.
A man who spends one month aboard his ship,
away from his wife, becomes downhearted

when winter gusts and stormy seas confine him.
This is now the ninth revolving year
we've been waiting here, on this very spot.
So I don't think that badly of Achaeans
in their frustration here by their curved ships.
Still, it's shameful to go home with nothing.   350
My friends, be patient, give us all more time,
until Calchas' prophecy comes true or not.
We all have kept in mind what he foretold.
You all are witnesses, the ones whom Fate
has not yet visited to carry off in death.
Not long ago, when our Achaean ships
gathered at Aulis, bringing disaster
for Priam and his Trojans, we sacrificed
on holy altars placed around a spring
hundreds of perfect creatures to the gods,   360
the immortals—underneath that tree,
a lovely plane tree, where bright water flowed.
And then a great omen appeared, a snake,
blood-red along its back, a dreadful sight,
a thing sent out by Zeus into the daylight.
Out from under the altar that snake slithered,
darting for the plane tree, where there lay
tiny, new-born sparrows, eight fledglings,
huddled under foliage at the very top.
The ninth one was the mother of the batch.   370
The serpent ate the infants, who screamed with fear.
The mother fluttered around here and there,
lamenting her dear chicks. The coiled serpent
snatched the crying mother by the wing.
Once the beast had gobbled up the sparrow
and her chicks, the god who'd made the snake appear
did something to it there for all to see.
Crooked Cronos' son changed that snake to stone!
We stood there astounded at what we'd seen—
a horror desecrating the gods' sacrifice.   380
Calchas at once spoke out in prophecy:
'Long-haired Achaeans, why stand there so mute?
Counselor Zeus has made manifest to us

38

a tremendous omen. It has come late,
and will take many years to be fulfilled,
but its fame will never die. Just as that snake
swallowed the sparrow's brood, eight in all,
with the mother who bore them the ninth one killed,
so that's how long we'll fight them over there.
In the tenth year we'll take Troy, wide streets and all.'   390
That's what Calchas said. Now it's coming true.
So come on, all you well-armed Achaeans,
let's stay, until we seize Priam's great city."

At this speech Argives gave out an enormous cheer.
The ships on all sides resounded ominously,
as Achaeans roared out their endorsement of his words.
Then Nestor, the Geranian horseman, cried out:

"Alas! In our assembly you're all infants,
silly children, with no sense of war's events.
What will happen to our agreements,   400
the oaths we made? Let fire consume
our strategies, men's plans, our treaties,
ratified with wine and handshakes, those things
we used to trust. For now we fight ourselves,
arguing like this. We can't find any remedy,
though we've been sitting here for years.
Son of Atreus, you must maintain with force
your previous plan to lead the Argive troops
directly to the harsh demands of war.
And let those one or two be damned,   410
the men who don't think like Achaeans,
the few of them who yearn to go back home—
something they'll find impossible to do—
before we learn the truth or falsehood
of what was promised by aegis-bearing Zeus.
For I assure you mighty Zeus nodded assent
on that very day the Argives put to sea,
bearing Troy's destructive fate in their swift ships.
On our right hand, Zeus hurled down lightning bolts,
signs manifesting his good will to us.   420

So let no man run off to get back home—
not before he's had sex with some Trojan's wife,
payment for Helen's miseries, her cries of pain.
If any man is really keen to get back home,
let him just set hand to his well-benched ship,
he'll come face to face, in plain view of all,
with death, his fate. You, my lord, think carefully—
think about what someone else suggests.
Don't simply throw out what I say to you.
Agamemnon, set men in groups by tribes and clans,   430
so clans encourage clans, tribes bolster tribes.
If you do that, if Achaeans all obey,
you'll then recognize who's good and bad
among your leaders and your men. Ranged like that,
the two groups will stand against each other.
You'll then know whether failure to take Troy
stems from divine will or craven soldiers
or ineptitude in managing the war."

Mighty Agamemnon then answered Nestor:

"Old man, in our assembly once again   440
you win out over all Achaea's sons.
O Father Zeus, Athena, and Apollo—
if I only had ten such counselors
among Achaeans, king Priam's city
would soon fall, be taken, sacked at our hands.
But aegis-bearing Zeus, son of Cronos,
keeps showering me with grievous troubles.
He throws me into pointless bitter fights.
So Achilles and I fought for that girl,
yelling at each other. The first offence was mine.   450
But if we two agreed, were of one mind,
then Troy's fate would be sealed without delay,
without a moment's pause. But let's go off to eat,
so we can resume the fight. Every one of you,
get your spears and shields prepared for action.
Feed your swift-footed horses properly.
Inspect the chariots with a careful eye,

40

so we can stand all day and battle Ares,
hateful god of war. We'll get no respite,
not even for a moment, except at dusk, 460
when nightfall separates the frenzied soldiers.
Chest straps on our protective body shields
will be soaked through with sweat. Around our spears
hands will grow numb. Horses, too, will sweat,
under the strain of hauling polished chariots.
But if I see a man coming out to fight
reluctantly, hanging back by our curved ships,
he'll not escape being food for dogs and birds."

Argives answered Agamemnon with a mighty roar,
like waves by a steep cliff crashing on the rock face, 470
lashed by South Wind's blasts, always foaming on the rock,
whipped on by every wind gusting here and there.
The men leapt up, moved off, scattering to ships,
set fires by their huts, and each man ate his dinner.
Every man then sacrificed to the immortal gods,
praying to escape death and war's killing zone.
Agamemnon, king of men, sacrificed an ox,
a fat one, five years old, to Zeus, exalted son of Cronos.
He summoned the best senior men of all Achaeans—
first, Nestor and Idomeneus, then both Ajaxes, 480
then Diomedes, Tydeus' son. Seventh came Odysseus.
Warrior Menelaus arrived without a summons,
knowing in his heart all Agamemnon's worries.
They stood by the ox, with barley grains for sprinkling.
Then Agamemnon prayed on their behalf:

"Most powerful Zeus,
exalted lord of thunder clouds, Zeus,
who dwells in heaven, grant my prayer—
May the sun not go down, nor darkness come,
before I have cast down Priam's palace,
covered it with dust, destroyed its doors 490
in all-consuming fire, and with my bronze sword
sliced to shreds the tunic on Hector's chest.
May many of his comrades lie beside him,

41

face down on the ground, teeth grinding dirt."

So he prayed. But Cronos' son did not grant his wish.
Zeus took the offering but increased their suffering.

Once the men had prayed, scattering barley grain,
they pulled back the beast's head, slit its throat, flayed it,
sliced thigh bones out and hid them in twin layers of fat,
with raw meat on top. They cooked these on split wood,   500
then placed the innards on spits in Hephaestus' fire.
When the wrapped-up thigh bones were completely cooked,
and they'd tasted samples of the inner organs,
they chopped up the rest, arranged the meat on spits,
cooked it carefully, then drew it from the fire.
This work finished, the men prepared a meal and ate.
Each soldier's appetite was fully satisfied—
all dined equally. When every man had eaten
as much food and drink as anyone could wish,
Geranian horseman Nestor was the first to speak.   510

    "Lord Agamemnon, son of Atreus,
king of men, let's end our discussions now
and not postpone work given by the gods.
Come, let heralds of bronze-clad Achaeans
summon all the soldiers to assembly.
Let's move together across the wide front,
rouse Achaea's men with blood-lust for war."

Agamemnon, king of men, agreed with Nestor.
He ordered clear-voiced heralds immediately
to sound the battle call to long-haired Achaeans.   520
The call went out. Troops assembled on the run.
Around Agamemnon, kings nurtured by the gods
rushed to establish order. With them strode Athena,
her eyes glittering, holding up the aegis—
her priceless, ageless, eternal aegis,
its hundred golden tassels quivering,
each finely woven, valued at a hundred oxen.
With this, she sped on through Achaean ranks,

42

like lightning, firing soldiers' hearts for war.
As she passed, she roused in men that hot desire   530
to fight, to kill. At once she made each man feel war
far sweeter than returning home, finer than sailing
in the hollow ships back to his dear native land.
Just as an all-consuming fire burns through huge forests
on a mountain top, and men far off can see its light,
so, as soldiers marched out, their glittering bronze
blazed through the sky to heaven, an amazing sight.
As many birds in flight—geese, cranes, and long-necked swans—
in an Asian meadow by the flowing river Caystrios,
fly here and there, proud of their strong wings, and call,   540
as they settle, the meadow resounding with the noise,
so the many groups of soldiers moved out then
from ships and huts onto Scamander's plain.
Under men's and horses' feet the earth rang ominously.
Then they stood there, in that flowered meadow,
by the Scamander, an immense array,
as numerous as leaves and flowers in springtime.
Like flies swarming around shepherds' pens in spring,
when pails fill up with milk, so the Achaeans,
a huge long-haired host, marched out onto that plain   550
against the Trojans, eager to destroy them.
Just as goatherds sort out with ease the wandering beasts,
all mixed up in the pasture, so through all the army,
the leaders organized the troops for battle.
Among them powerful Agamemnon roamed,
eyes and head like Zeus, who loves the thunder,
waist like Ares, god of war, chest like Poseidon.
Just as in cattle herds the bull stands out above the rest,
by far the most conspicuous amid the cows,
so on that day Zeus made Agamemnon stand   560
pre-eminent among the troops, first of heroes.

Now, you Muses living on Olympus, tell me—
for you are goddesses and know everything,
while we hear only stories, knowing nothing certain—
tell me the leaders of Danaans, the rulers.
It would be impossible for me to tell

the story of or name those in the common mass,
not even with ten tongues, ten mouths, an untiring voice,
a heart of bronze, unless the Olympian Muses,
daughters of aegis-bearing Zeus, could sing of the men,   570
all those who came to Troy. But I shall list the leaders,
commanders of the ships, and all the ships in full.

Peneleus, Leitus, and Arcesilaus
led the Boeotians, with Clonius and Prothoenor.
Their men came from Hyria, rocky Aulis,
Schoenus, Scolus, mountainous Eteonus,
Thespeia, Graia, spacious Mycalassus,
men holding Harma, Eilesium, Erythrae;
men holding Eleon, Hyle, Peteon,
Ocalea, the well-built fortress Medeon,   580
Copae, Eutresis, Thisbe, city full of doves;
men from Coronea, grassy Haliartus;
men from Plataea, Glisas, those who held
fortified Lower Thebe and sacred Onchestus,
with Poseidon's splendid grove; men from Arne,
land rich in grapes, Midea, sacred Nisa,
and distant Anthedon. Fifty ships came with these men,
each with one hundred and twenty young Boeotians.

Men from Aspledon and Minyan Orchomenus
were led by Ascalaphus and Ialmenus,   590
Ares' sons. Astyoche bore them in Actor's house,
Azeus' son, to mighty Ares. She, a modest virgin,
went upstairs, where the god lay with her in secret.
These men brought with them a fleet of thirty ships.

Schedius and Epistrophus, sons of Iphitus,
the son of great-hearted Naubolus,
commanded Phoceans—men from Cyparissus,
rocky Pytho, holy Crisa, Daulis, and Panopeus;
men from Anemorea and Hyampolis;
from around the sacred river Cephisus,   600
from Lilaea, beside Cephissus' springs.
Forty black ships these two leaders brought with them.

44

Moving around, as soldiers armed themselves,
they set Phocean ranks by the Boeotians, on their left.

The Locrians were led by swift Ajax, son of Oileus,
the lesser Ajax, not the greater Ajax,
son of Telamon, but a much smaller man.
Though he was short and wore cloth armour,
among all Hellenes and Achaeans he excelled
in fighting with his spear. Locrians came from Cynus,   610
Opous, Calliarus, Bessa, Scarphe,
lovely Aegeiae, Tarphe, Thronion,
and from around the river Boagrius.
Ajax brought forty black ships of Locrians
living across from sacred Euboea.

Elephenor, offspring of Ares, son of Chalcodon,
great-hearted leader, commanded the Abantes,
who live to breathe war's fury, soldiers from Euboea,
Chalcis, Eretria, wine-rich Histiaea, Cerinthus by the sea,
men from the steep fortress Dium, Carystus, and Styra.   620
These swift Abantes came with Elephenor,
their hair grown long behind, warrior spearmen,
filled with fierce desire to tear apart their enemies,
to pierce armed bodies with their long ash spears.
Forty black ships came with Elephenor.

Soldiers came from that well-built fortress Athens,
land of proud Erechtheus, whom Athena raised,
after he was born out of the harvest land.
She placed him in Athens, at her own rich shrine.
To him Athenian youth make sacrificial offerings,   630
with bulls and rams as each year comes around.
Menestheus, son of Peteos, led these men.
In tactics no one alive on earth could match him
in deploying chariots or shield-bearing men.
Nestor, from a previous age, was his only rival.
Menestheus brought with him fifty black ships.

From Salamis Ajax commanded twelve ships.

He organized his men in their positions,
so they stood adjacent to Athenian ranks.

Warriors from Argos, fortified Tiryns, Hermione,   640
Asine, both with deep bays, Troezene, Eionae,
vine-rich Epidaurus, Achaean youth from Aegina, Mases—
all these were led by mighty fighter Diomedes,
skilled in war cries, and by Sthenelus, dear son
of famous Capaneus. There was a third leader,
god-like Euryalus, Mecisteus' son, son of lord Talaus.
But warlike Diomedes was the main commander.
These men brought with them eighty black ships.

Troops from the strong fortress Mycenae, rich Corinth,
well-built Cleonae, Orneae, lovely Araethyrea,   650
Sicyon, whose first king was Adrestus,
with men from Hyperesia, lofty Gonoessa,
Pellene, from Aegium, men from coastal regions,
and wide Helice—of these men Agamemnon,
son of Atreus, led one hundred ships.
The most troops came with him, the finest men by far.
In their midst, Agamemnon put on a proud display,
dressed in gleaming armour, prominent among all heroes.
He was the best of all, because he had most men.

Men from Lacedaemon, land of ravines, Pharis,   660
Sparta, Messe, where doves congregate,
men living in Bryseae, beautiful Augeiae,
Amyclae, coastal Helos, men from Laäs,
from around Oetylus—all these in sixty ships
were led by powerful, warlike Menelaus,
Agamemnon's brother. Among these warriors,
as they armed themselves some distance off,
Menelaus strode—confident, courageous—
rousing his troops for war, his heart passionate
to avenge Helen's struggles, her cries of pain.   670

Men came from Pylos, lovely Arene, Thryum,
by Alpheus ford, well-built Aipy, Cyparisseis,

Amphigenea, Pteleum, Helos, Dorium,
where the Muses met the Thracian Thamyris,
and stopped his singing. He was coming back
from Oechalia, from the court of Eurytus the king.
He'd boasted his singing would surpass the Muses,
daughters of aegis-bearing Zeus, should they compete.
In their anger the Muses mutilated Thamyris,
taking away his godlike power of song,   680
and making him forget his skill in playing the lyre.
Geranian horseman Nestor led these men
in a flotilla of ninety hollow ships.

Men from Arcadia, from below steep mount Cyllene,
near Aepytus' tomb, where men excel in combat
hand to hand, troops from Pheneus, Orchomenus,
rich in flocks, Rhipe, Stratie, windy Enispe,
Tegea, lovely Mantinea, Stymphelus,
Parrhasia—mighty Agapenor led these men,
Ancaeus' son, in sixty ships. Many Arcadians   690
came in every ship, skilled fighters. Agamemnon,
king of men, had himself provided well-decked ships
for them to sail across the wine-dark ocean,
for these men lacked expertise in matters of the sea.

Soldiers from Bouprasium, fair Elis, those parts
bounded by Hyrmine, coastal Myrsinus,
the rock of Olene, and Alesium—these troops
had four commanders, each with ten swift ships.
The many Epeians on board were commanded
by Amphimachus, son of Cteatus, and Thalpius,   700
son of Eurytus, descended both from Actor.
Third leader was Diores, son of Amarynces.
Fourth was Polyxeinus, son of Agasthenes, Augeas' son.

Men from Doulichium, sacred Echinean islands,
living across the sea from Elis, were commanded
by warlike Meges, son of Phyleus, the horseman,
loved of Zeus. Phyleus, angry with his father,
moved to Doulichium. Meges brought with him

47

forty black ships in his flotilla.

Odysseus led on
the Cephallenians, soldiers from Ithaca, 710
well wooded Neritum, Crocylea,
rugged Aegilips, from Zacynthus, Samos,
both those inhabiting the mainland
and those from cities on the facing shore.
Odysseus, as wise as Zeus, led these troops,
who came with him in twelve black ships.

Thoas, son of Andraemon, led the Aetolians,
men from Pleuron, Olenus, Pylene,
coastal Chalchis, and rocky Calydon.
Proud king Oeneus had no living sons, 720
and he himself was dead, as was fair-haired Meleager.
Thus, Thoas ruled alone. He brought forty black ships.

Famous spearman Idomeneus led the Cretans
from Cnossus, fortified Gortyn, Lyctus, Miletus,
chalky Lycastus, Phaestus, Rhytium,
both populous towns, with other warriors
from Crete's one hundred cities. Idomeneus,
famous for fighting with a spear, led these troops,
along with Meriones, as skilled at killing men
as Ares, god of war. They brought eighty black ships. 730

Tlepolemus, son of Hercules, a huge brave man,
led nine ships of courageous troops, men from Rhodes,
split into three divisions—from Lindus, Ialysus,
and chalky Cameirus—all led by Tlepolemus,
famous spearman, born to Astyocheia
and mighty Hercules, who'd taken her from Ephyra,
by the river Selleis, after razing many towns
full of vital warriors. Once he'd grown up
in their well-furnished home, Tlepolemus killed
his father's uncle, Licymnius, a well-loved old man, 740
a great fighter, too. At once Tlepolemus built a fleet,
assembled many men, and fled away. Other sons

and grandsons of great Hercules had threatened him.
He suffered badly, until he came to Rhodes,
whose people live in three groups split by tribes.
Zeus, who governs gods and men, loved them,
and so the son of Cronos blessed them with great wealth.

Nireus brought three well-balanced ships from Syme.
The son of Aglaea and lord Charopus,
the handsomest of all Danaans who sailed to Troy,   750
after Achilles, who had no equal. But he was weak,
because he had few troops.

                             Men from Nisyrus,
Crapathus, Casus, Cos, Eurypylus' city,
the Calydnian islands had Pheidippus and Antiphus,
sons of lord Thessalus, Hercules' son, as leaders.
With them came thirty hollow ships.

All the troops from Pelasgian Argos, Alos,
men living in Alope, Trachis, from Phthia,
and Hellas, where lovely women live, men called
Myrmidons, Hellenes, Achaeans—these troops   760
Achilles led in fifty ships. But their minds weren't set
on the grim clash of war. They had no one to lead them.
Godlike Achilles, swift of foot, sat by his ships,
still angry over fair-complexioned Briseis, seized
from Lyrnessus after heavy fighting.
Achilles had laid waste Lyrnessus and Thebe's walls,
overthrown the spearmen Mynes and Epistrophus,
sons of lord Euenus, son of king Selepius
Because of her, Achilles sat still grieving.
But soon enough he'd rouse himself again.   770

Troops from Phylace, flowering Pyrasus,
shrine of Demeter, Iton, where flocks breed,
Antrum by the sea, and grassy Pteleum—
brave Protesilaus had led these men, while still alive.
Now the black earth held him. In Phylace,
he left behind a wife to tear her cheeks in grief,

home half complete. Some Dardanian killed him,
as he jumped on Trojan soil, the first on shore,
far ahead of all Achaeans. His soldiers lamented
the loss of their chief, but didn't lack a leader.   780
Warlike Podarces, son of Iphicles, led them—
the man owned many flocks and was a young blood brother
to Protesilaus. But that great-hearted warlike soldier
was an older, better man. So these troops had a leader,
though they missed the noble one they'd lost.
Podarces brought forty black ships along with him.

Troops from Pherae by Lake Boebea, from Boebeïs,
Glaphyrae, well-built Iolcus—these came
in eleven ships, commanded by Eumelus,
Admetus' well-loved son, born to him by Alcestis,   790
loveliest of Pelias' daughters.

Troops from Methone, Thaumacia, Meliboea,
and rugged Olizon, were led by Philoctetes,
the skilled archer, in seven ships, each with fifty men,
expert archers. But Philoctetes stayed behind on Lemnos,
the sacred island, in horrific pain, abandoned.
Achaea's sons had left him there in agony,
wounded by a snake bite. He lay there in torment.
But soon the Argives by their ships would have reason
to remember him. These soldiers missed their chief,   800
but were now led by Medon, Oïleus' bastard son,
whom Rhene bore to Oïleus, destroyer of cities.
So Medon was the one who set their ranks in order.

Men from Tricca, rocky Ithome, Oechalia,
city of Eurytus, the Oechalian,
were commanded by two sons of Asclepius,
skilled healers, Podaleirus and Machaon.
They brought thirty hollow ships with them.
Troops from Ormenius, from the fount of Hyperea,
from Asterius, from Titanus with its white hilltops—   810
these men were commanded by Eurypylus,
fine son of Euaemon, in forty black ships.

50

Men from Argissa, Gyrtone, Orthe, Elone,
the white city Oloösson—these troops were led
by Polypoetes, a steadfast soldier,
son of Perithous, himself son to immortal Zeus.
That famous lady Hippodameia bore
Polypoetes to Perithous on that very day
he took revenge out on those hairy monsters,
and beat them from mount Pelion towards the Aithices.   820
But Polypoetes was not the sole commander.
With him was Leonteus, a warlike man,
son of proud-hearted Coronus, Caeneus' son.
With them they brought forty black ships.

Gouneus brought twenty-two ships from Cyphus.
With him sailed the Enienes and Peraebians,
reliable fighting men from cold Dodona,
who work by the lovely river Titaressus,
which empties its beautiful, flowing waters
into the Peneus. These do not intermingle   830
with the silver stream of the Peneus,
but flow along on top of them, like oil.
For the Titaressus is a branch of the river Styx,
dread waters by which the most solemn oaths are sealed.

Prothous, son of Tenthredon, led the Magnetes,
from the region round Peneus and mount Pelion,
where leaves are always trembling in the wind.
With him swift Prothous brought forty black ships.

These men were leaders, rulers of the Danaans.
Muse, tell me this—Which of them were the very best   840
of those who came over with the sons of Atreus?

The best horses were those of Admetus, son of Pheres.
Eumelus drove them. As fast as birds, they matched
each other in colour, age, and height along the back.
Bred by Apollo of the silver bow in Perea,
both mares, they carried terror with them.
Of the men, by far the best was Ajax, son of Telamon,

51

but only while Achilles didn't join in battle.
For Achilles was the better man by far.
The horses carrying Peleus' son, man without equal,   850
were much better, too. But he stayed behind,
by his curved seaworthy ships, still enraged
at Agamemnon, Atreus' son, the people's shepherd.
His soldiers amused themselves beside the breaking sea
by throwing spears and discus or with archery.
Their horses stood near their chariots, browsing on lotus
and parsley from the marsh. Their masters' chariots,
fully covered, remained stationed in the huts.
Missing their warlike leader, these troops strolled
here and there throughout the camp and did not fight.   860

The soldiers, like a fire consuming all the land,
moved on out. Earth groaned under them, just as it does
when Zeus, who loves thunder, in his anger lashes
the land around Typhoeus, among the Arimi,
where people say Typhoeus has his lair.
That's how the earth groaned loudly under marching feet.

Then wind-swift Iris came to Troy as messenger
from aegis-bearing Zeus carrying grim news.
Trojans had summoned an assembly by Priam's palace gates.
There all had gathered, young and old. Standing by Priam,   870
swift-footed Iris spoke, sounding like Polites, Priam's son.
He'd been stationed as a scout—fully confident
of his skill at running—at old Aesyetes' tomb,[1]
right at the top, waiting for the moment
Achaeans moved out from their ships.
Looking just like Polites, swift-footed Iris said:

> "Priam, old man, you always love to talk
> about irrelevant things, as you did earlier
> in peacetime. But now this war continues
> relentlessly. I've gone to battle many times.   880
> I've never seen an army like this one, so many men,

[1] *Aesyetes' tomb* is a prominent landmark outside the walls of Troy, a convenient
place for a lookout.

as numerous as leaves or grains of sand,
coming across the plain to assault our city.
Hector, I call on you, on you above all, to follow
my instructions—the numerous allies here
in Priam's great city all speak different languages
from far-scattered regions. So let each man
issue orders to the ones he leads,
let him now organize his countrymen,
then lead them out to battle."   890

Iris spoke. Hector understood her words.
Immediately he ended the assembly.
Men rushed to arm themselves. They opened up the gates.
Troops streamed out, infantry and horses. A huge din arose.
In the plain, some distance off, a high hill stood by itself,
right before the city. People call it Batieia,
but the gods know it as the tomb of agile Myrine.
Here the Trojans and their allies marshaled forces.

Hector of the flashing helmet, Priam's son,
led out the Trojans. With him marched in arms   900
the largest contingent, the finest men by far,
eager to get working with their spears.

Aeneas, Anchises' worthy son, led the Dardanians.
Goddess Aphrodite had borne him to Anchises.
She had lain with him on the slopes of Ida.
But Aeneas was not their sole commander.
With him were Antenor's two sons, Archelochus
and Acamas, extremely skilled in every form of war.

Men from Zeleia, on mount Ida's lowest slope,
wealthy Trojans, men who drink dark waters   910
of the river Aesepus were led by Pandarus,
Lycaon's worthy son, whom Apollo had taught archery.
Soldiers from Adresteia, Apaesus, Pityeia,
steep Mount Tereia were commanded by Adrestus
and Amphius in cloth armour, Merops' sons from Percote,
who knew more of prophecy than anyone.

53

He gave his children orders to stay away from war,
which eats men up. They did not obey him.
Deadly black fates had called them on to battle.

Troops from Percote, Practius, Sestos, Abydos,   920
holy Arisbe—these troops were led by Asius,
son of Hyrtacus, an important ruler.
Arius's huge, tawny horses brought him
from Arisbe, from the river Selleïs.

Hippothous led tribes of spearmen from Pelasgia,
fertile Larisa, along with Pylaeus, offshoots of Ares,
sons of Pelasgian Lethus, Teutamus's son.

Acamas and warlike Peirous led the Thracians,
those men bounded by the Hellespont's strong flow.

Euphemus, son of god-nurtured Troezenus,   930
son of Ceos, led Ciconian spearmen.

Pyraechmes led archers from Paeonia,
from far off Amydon, by the Axius,
a broad flowing river, whose moving waters
are the loveliest on earth.

                Pylaemenes,
a brave soldier, commanded Paphlagonians
from Enetae, where herds of mules run wild,
men from Cytorus, from around Sesamus,
those with fine homes by the stream Parthenius,
from Cromna, Aegialus, high Erithini.   940
Odius and Epistrophus led the Halizoni
from distant Alybe, where men mine silver.
Chromis and prophet Ennomus led the Mysians.
But Ennomus' great skill in prophecy
did not allow him to evade his deadly fate.
Swift Achilles, descendant of Aeacus, killed him
in the river where he slaughtered other Trojans.
Phorcys and noble Ascanius led up Phrygians

from far-off Ascania, men keen for war.

Mesthles and Antiphus commanded the Maeonians.   950
Sons of Talaemenes, born to Gygaea,
a water nymph, they led Maeonians
from around the foot of Mount Tmolus.

Nastes led the Carians, men with a strange language,
from Miletus, Phthires, with its wooded mountain,
Maeander's waters and high peaks of Mount Mycale.
Nastes and Amphimachus, noble sons of Nomion
were their leaders. Nastes went to war carrying gold,
like a girl. What a fool! His gold did not spare him
a wretched death. He died in the river,   960
at the hand of swift Achilles, descended from Aeacus.
Fiery Achilles carried off his gold.

Sarpedon and noble Glaucus commanded Lycians,
from distant Lycia, by the swirling river Xanthus.

Book Three
Paris, Menelaus and Helen

[The armies move together; Paris volunteers to fight Menelaus in single combat; both sides prepare make a truce; Iris visits Helen; Helen goes to the Scaean Gate, looks at the Achaean troops with Priam; Priam leaves Troy to visit the armies and administer the treaty oath; Agamemnon utters the prayer for the treaty; Paris and Menelaus fight in single combat; Aphrodite rescues Paris; Paris and Helen meet back in Troy; Agamemnon demands compensation from the Trojans]

Once troops had formed in ranks under their own leaders,
Trojans marched out, clamouring like birds, like cranes
screeching overhead, when winter's harsh storms drive them off,
screaming as they move over the flowing Ocean,
bearing death and destruction to the Pygmies,
launching their savage attack on them at dawn.
Achaeans came on in silence, breathing ferocity,
determined to stand by each other in the fight.
Just as South Wind spreads mist around the mountain peak,
something shepherds hate, but thieves prefer to night,   10
for one can see only a stone's throw up ahead,
so, as men marched, dense dust clouds rose from underfoot.
They advanced at full speed out across the plain.
The two armies moved in close towards each other.
Then godlike Paris stepped out, as Trojan champion,
on his shoulders a leopard skin. He had bow and sword.
Brandishing two bronze-tipped spears, he challenged
the best men in the whole Achaean force to fight—
a single combat, to the death. War-loving Menelaus
noticed Alexander striding there,[1] his troops   20
bunched up in ranks behind him, and he rejoiced,
like a famished lion finding a large carcass—
antlered stag or wild goat—and devouring it at once,
though fierce young hunters and swift dogs attack.
So Menelaus was pleased to see Paris there,
right before his eyes. Menelaus had in mind

[1]Alexander is another name for Paris.

taking revenge on the man who'd injured him.
At once Menelaus jumped from his chariot,
down to the ground, his weapons in his fists.
When godlike Alexander saw Menelaus there,   30
among the fighters at the front, his heart sank.
He moved back into the ranks, among his comrades,
avoiding death. Just as a man stumbles on a snake
in some mountainous ravine and gives way, jumping back,
his limbs trembling, his cheeks pale, so godlike Paris,
afraid of Atreus' son, slid back into proud Trojan ranks.
Seeing this, Hector went at Alexander, insulting him:

     "Despicable Paris, handsomest of men,
     but woman-mad seducer. How I wish
     you never had been born or died unmarried.   40
     That's what I'd prefer, so much better
     than to live in shame, hated by others.
     Now long-haired Achaeans are mocking us,
     saying we've put forward as a champion
     one who looks good, but lacks a strong brave mind.
     Was this what you were like back on that day
     you gathered up your faithful comrades,
     sailed sea-worthy ships across the ocean,
     went out among a foreign people,
     and carried back from that far-off land   50
     a lovely woman linked by marriage
     to warrior spearmen, thus bringing on
     great suffering for your father and your city,
     all your people—joy to your enemies
     and to yourself disgrace? And can you now
     not face Menelaus? If so, you'd learn
     the kind of man he is whose wife you took.
     You'd get no help then from your lyre, long hair,
     good looks—Aphrodite's gifts—once face down,
     lying in the dirt. Trojans must be timid men.   60
     If not, for all the evil things you've done
     by now you'd wear a garment made of stones."

To Hector godlike Alexander then replied:

"Hector, you're right in what you say against me.
Those complaints of yours are not unjustified.
Your heart is tireless, like a wood-chopping axe
wielded by a craftsman cutting timber for a ship.
The axe makes his force stronger. Your mind's like that—
the spirit in your chest is fearless. But don't blame me
for golden Aphrodite's lovely gifts.   70
Men can't reject fine presents from the gods,
those gifts they personally bestow on us,
though no man would take them of his own free will.
You want me now to go to battle.
Get others to sit down—Trojans and Achaeans.
Put me and war-loving Menelaus
in their midst to fight it out for Helen,
all her property. The one who triumphs,
comes off victorious, the better man,
let him take all the goods and lead her home,   80
as his wife. Let others swear a solemn oath,
as friends, either to live on in fertile Troy
or to return to horse-breeding Argos,
land of the lovely women of Achaea."

So Paris spoke. Hearing those words, Hector felt great joy.
He went to the middle ground, between the armies,
halted Trojan troops, grasping the centre of his spear shaft.
The men sat. But long-haired Achaeans kept on shooting,
attempting to hit Hector with rocks and arrows.
Then Agamemnon, king of men, roared out at them: 90

      "Argives, Achaean lads, stop hurling things.
      Hector of the flashing helmet wants to talk to us."

Once Agamemnon spoke, the men stopped fighting,
quickly falling silent. Hector then addressed both sides:

      "You Trojans, you well-armed Achaeans,
      listen now to what Paris has to say,
      the man whose actions brought about our fight.
      He bids the other Trojans, all Achaeans,

set their weapons on the fertile ground.
He and war-loving Menelaus here   110
will fight it out alone between the armies
for Helen and for all her property.
Whichever one comes out victorious,
the stronger man, let him seize all the goods,
and take the woman as his wife back home.
Let others swear a solemn oath as friends."

So Hector spoke. The soldiers all grew silent.
Then Menelaus, loud in war, answered Hector:

> "Listen now to me. More than anyone,
> my heart has suffered pain. So now I think   110
> Argives and Trojans should part company,
> since you have suffered many hardships,
> thanks to the fight between myself and Paris,
> a fight that he began. Whichever one of us
> death takes, our fate, let that man perish.
> You others quickly go your separate ways.
> So bring two lambs here—white male, black female—
> for earth and sun. We'll bring one more for Zeus.
> Lead out great Priam to administer the oath
> in person, for his sons are over-proud,   120
> untrustworthy. No man should transgress
> by violence oaths sworn in Zeus' name.
> Young men's minds are fickle. An older man
> who joins them thinks of past and future,
> so for both groups things happen for the best."

Achaeans and Trojans were elated, full of hope
that wretched war would end. They pulled the chariots back
into the ranks, climbed out, disarmed, and placed their weapons
next to each other on the ground, with little room
between both groups. Hector sent two heralds to the city,   130
to fetch the lambs with speed and summon Priam.
Agamemnon sent Talthybius to the hollow ships,
instructing him to bring a sacrificial lamb.
Talthybius obeyed god-like Agamemnon's orders.

Then Iris came as messenger to white-armed Helen,
taking on the image of her sister-in-law,
wife of Antenor's son, fine Helicaon.
Her name was Laodice, of all Priam's daughters
the most beautiful. She found Helen in her room,
weaving a large cloth, a double purple cloak,   140
creating pictures of the many battle scenes
between horse-taming Trojans and bronze-clad Achaeans,
wars they suffered for her sake at the hands of Ares.
Standing near by, swift-footed Iris said:

                              "Come here, dear girl.
        Look at the amazing things going on.
        Horse-taming Trojans and bronze-clad Achaeans,
        men who earlier were fighting one another
        in wretched war out there on the plain,
        both keen for war's destruction, are sitting still.
        Alexander and war-loving Menelaus   150
        are going to fight for you with their long spears.
        The man who triumphs will call you his dear wife."

With these words the goddess set in Helen's heart
sweet longing for her former husband, city, parents.
Covering herself with a white shawl, she left the house,
shedding tears. She did not go alone, but took with her
two attendants, Aethrae, daughter of Pittheus,
and ox-eyed Clymene. They soon reached the Scaean Gates.
Oucalegaon and Antenor, both prudent men,
elder statesmen, sat at the Scaean Gates,   160
with Priam and his entourage—Panthous, Thymoetes,
Lampus, Clytius, and warlike Hicataeon. Old men now,
their fighting days were finished, but they all spoke well.
They sat there, on the tower, these Trojan elders,
like cicadas perched up on a forest branch, chirping
soft, delicate sounds. Seeing Helen approach the tower,
they commented softly to each other—their words had wings:

        "There's nothing shameful about the fact
        that Trojans and well-armed Achaeans

have endured great suffering a long time   170
over such a woman—just like a goddess,
immortal, awe-inspiring. She's beautiful.
But nonetheless let her go back with the ships.
Let her not stay here, a blight on us, our children."

So they talked. Priam then called out to Helen.

"Come here, dear child. Sit down in front of me,
so you can see your first husband, your friends,
your relatives. As far as I'm concerned,
it's not your fault. For I blame the gods.
They drove me to wage this wretched war   180
against Achaeans. Tell me, who's that large man,
over there, that impressive, strong Achaean?
Others may be taller by a head than him,
but I've never seen with my own eyes
such a striking man, so noble, so like a king."

Then Helen, goddess among women, said to Priam:

"My dear father-in-law, whom I respect and honour,
how I wish I'd chosen evil death
when I came here with your son, leaving behind
my married home, companions, darling child,   190
and friends my age. But things didn't work that way.
So I weep all the time. But to answer you,
that man is wide-ruling Agamemnon,
son of Atreus, a good king, fine fighter,
and once he was my brother-in-law,
if that life was ever real. I'm such a whore."

Priam gazed in wonder at Agamemnon, saying:

"Son of Atreus, blessed by the gods, fortune's child,
divinely favoured, many long-haired Achaeans
serve under you. Once I went to Phrygia,   200
that vine-rich land, where I saw Phrygian troops
with all their horses, thousands of them,
soldiers of Otreus, godlike Mygdon,

camped by the banks of the Sangarius river.
I was their ally, part of their army,
the day the Amazons, men's peers in war,
came on against them. But those forces then
were fewer than these bright-eyed Achaeans."

The old man then spied Odysseus and asked:

"Dear child, come tell me who this man is,   210
shorter by a head than Agamemnon,
son of Atreus. But he looks broader
in his shoulders and his chest. His armour's stacked
there on the fertile earth, but he strides on,
marching through men's ranks just like a ram
moving through large white multitudes of sheep.
Yes, a woolly ram, that's what he seems to me."

Helen, child of Zeus, then answered Priam:

"That man is Laertes' son, crafty Odysseus,
raised in rocky Ithaca. He's well versed   220
in all sorts of tricks, deceptive strategies."

At that point, wise Antenor said to Helen:

"Lady, what you say is true. Once lord Odysseus
came here with war-loving Menelaus,
as an ambassador in your affairs.
I received them both in my residence
and entertained them. I got to know them—
from their appearance and their wise advice.
When they mingled with us Trojans
in our meeting and Menelaus rose,   230
his broad shoulders were higher than the other's.
But once they sat, Odysseus seemed more regal.
When the time came for them to speak to us,
setting out their thoughts quite formally,
Menelaus spoke with fluency—few words,
but very clear—no chatter, no digressions—

62

although he was the younger of the two.
But when wise Odysseus got up to speak,
he just stood, eyes downcast, staring at the ground.
He didn't move the sceptre to and fro,   240
but gripped it tightly, like some ignoramus—
a bumpkin or someone idiotic.
But when that great voice issued from his chest,
with words like winter snowflakes, no man alive
could match Odysseus. We were no longer
disconcerted at witnessing his style."

Priam, the old man, saw a third figure, Ajax, and asked:

"Who is that other man? He's over there—
that huge, burly Achaean—his head and shoulders
tower over the Achaeans."   250

                    Then Helen,
long-robed goddess among women, answered:

"That's massive Ajax, Achaea's bulwark.
Across from him stands Idomeneus,
surrounded by his Cretans, like a god.
Around him there stand the Cretan leaders.
Often war-loving Menelaus welcomed him
in our house, whenever he arrived from Crete.
Now I see all the bright-eyed Achaeans
whom I know well, whose names I could recite.
But I can't see two of the men's leaders,   260
Castor, tamer of horses, and Pollux,
the fine boxer—they are both my brothers,
whom my mother bore along with me.
Either they did not come with the contingent
from lovely Lacedaemon, or they sailed here
in their seaworthy ships, but have no wish
to join men's battles, fearing the disgrace,
the many slurs, which are justly mine."

Helen spoke. But the life-nourishing earth

already held her brothers in Lacedaemon,
in their own dear native land.

                                        Through Troy,
heralds brought offerings to seal the binding oaths,
two lambs and in a goatskin sack some sparkling wine,
fruit of the earth. Idaios, the herald, brought in
the gleaming mixing bowl and golden cups.
Standing close by Priam, he encouraged him.

          "Son of Laomedon, the leading officers
          among horse-taming Trojans and bronze-clad Achaeans
          are calling you to come down to the plain,
          to administer their binding promises.   280
          Paris and war-loving Menelaus
          are going to fight it out with their long spears
          over the woman. The man who wins,
          who comes off the victor, gets the woman
          and her property. The others will all swear
          an oath of friendship, a binding one—
          we will live in fertile Troy, they in Argos,
          where horses breed, and in Achaea,
          land of lovely women."

                                        Idaios finished.
The old man trembled, then ordered his attendants   290
to prepare his chariot. They obeyed at once.
Priam climbed in and pulled back on the reins.
Antenor climbed in the fine chariot beside him.
The two men led swift horses through the Scaean Gate,
out to the plain. Once they reached the Trojans and Achaeans,
they climbed out of the chariot onto fertile ground,
in the space between the Trojan and Achaean troops.
At once, Agamemnon and crafty Odysseus
stood up to greet them. Noble heralds fetched the offerings,
to ratify their solemn oaths pledged to the gods.   300
They prepared wine in the mixing bowl, then poured water
over the kings' hands. Atreus' son drew out the dagger
which always hung beside his sword's huge scabbard,

then sliced hairs off lambs' heads. Attendants passed these hairs
among the leaders of the Trojans and Achaeans.
Raising his hands, Agamemnon then intoned
a mighty prayer on their behalf:

> "Father Zeus,
> ruling from Mount Ida, most glorious,
> most powerful, and you, too, god of the sun,
> who sees everything, hears everything,   310
> you rivers, earth, you gods below the earth,
> who punish the dead when men swear false oaths,
> you gods are witnesses. Keep this oath firm.
> If Alexander slays Menelaus,
> let him keep Helen, all her property.
> Let us return in our sea-worthy ships.
> But if fair-haired Menelaus kills Alexander,
> then let the Trojans hand back Helen,
> with all her property, and compensate
> Achaeans with something suitable,   320
> which future ages will remember.
> If Alexander's killed and Priam
> and Priam's children are unwilling
> to reimburse me, then I'll remain here,
> fight on until I'm fully satisfied,
> until I end this war appropriately."

So Agamemnon prayed. With his bronze dagger,
he slit the lambs' throats, placed them on the ground,
gasping in their death throes as their life ebbed out,
their spirit sliced away by Agamemnon's knife.   330
Next from the mixing bowl, they drew off wine in cups,
poured out libations to the deathless gods.
Then Trojans and Achaeans all spoke out this prayer:

> "Most powerful, mighty Zeus, and you others,
> you immortal gods, may you make sure
> the men who first violate these oaths
> will have their brains spill out onto the ground,
> just like this wine, they and their children.

May their wives be carried off by other men."

So they prayed. But the son of Cronos didn't grant their wish.　340
Then Priam, descendant of Dardanus, addressed them all:

"Hear me, you Trojans, you well-armed Achaeans.
I am returning now to windy Troy.
I have no wish to see with my own eyes
my dear son fight war-loving Menelaus.
Zeus and other immortal gods know well
which of them is fated to end up dead."

So Priam spoke. He placed the lambs in his chariot.
The god-like man climbed in, held back the reins.
Antenor climbed in the fine chariot by Priam.　350
Then both men set off, moving back toward Troy.

Then Hector, Priam's son, and lord Odysseus
first measured out the ground, took lots, and shook them up
in a bronze helmet, to see who'd throw his bronze spear first.
Then every Trojan and Achaean held up his hands,
praying to the gods:

"Father Zeus, ruling from Mount Ida,
mighty, all-powerful, of these two men,
let the one who brought this war to both sides
be killed and then go down to Hades' house.
And grant our oath of friendship will hold firm."　360

So they prayed. Hector of the flashing helmet
turned his eyes to one side and shook out the lots.
Alexander's token fell out immediately.
The troops sat down in their respective places,
by their high-stepping horses and their inlaid armour.
Paris, husband to Helen with the lovely hair,
hoisted his fine armour on his shoulders. On his shins,
he clipped leg armour fitted with silver ankle clasps.
Then he put around his chest the body armour
belonging to his brother Lycaon. It fit him well.　370

66

On his shoulder he looped his bronze, silver-studded sword,
his huge strong shield. On his handsome head he put
a fine helmet with nodding horse-hair plumes on top,
full of menace. Then he picked out a brave spear
which fit his grip. Menelaus prepared himself as well.
When the two men, standing on each side with their troops,
had armed themselves, they strode out to the open space
between the Trojans and Achaeans, staring ferociously.
As horse-taming Trojans and well-armed Achaeans
gazed at the two men, they were overcome with wonder.   380
The two men approached each other over measured ground,
brandishing their spears in mutual fury.
Alexander was the first to hurl his spear.
It struck Menelaus' shield, a perfect circle,
but the bronze did not break through, the point deflected
by the powerful shield. Then Menelaus, Atreus' son,
threw in his turn. First he made this prayer to Zeus:

> "Lord Zeus, grant I may be revenged on this man,
> who first committed crimes against me,
> lord Alexander. Let him die at my hands,   390
> so generations of men yet to come
> will dread doing wrong to anyone
> who welcomes them into his home as friends."

Menelaus then drew back his long-shadowed spear,
and hurled it. It hit the son of Priam's shield,
a perfect circle. The heavy spear pierced through it,
went straight through the fine body armour, through the shirt
which covered Alexander's naked flesh.
But Paris twisted to the side, evading a black fate.
Pulling out his silver-studded sword, the son of Atreus   400
raised it and struck the crest of Paris' helmet.
But the sword shattered into three or four pieces,
falling from his hand. The son of Atreus, in vexation,
looked up into wide heaven, crying out:

> "Father Zeus,
> what god brings us more trouble than you do?

I thought I was paying Alexander
for his wickedness, but now my sword
has shattered in my fist, while from my hand
my spear has flown in vain. I haven't hit him."

As Menelaus said these words, he sprang forward,   410
grabbing the horse hair crest on Paris' helmet,
twisting him around. He began dragging Paris off,
back in the direction of well-armed Achaeans.
The fine leather strap stretched round Paris' soft neck,
right below his chin, was strangling him to death.
At that point Menelaus would've hauled back Paris
and won unending fame, if Aphrodite, Zeus' daughter,
had not had sharp eyes. Her force broke the ox-hide strap,
leaving Menelaus clutching in his massive hands
an empty helmet. Whipping it around, Menelaus   420
hurled the helmet in among well-armed Achaeans.
His loyal companions retrieved it. He charged back,
with his bronze spear, intent on killing Alexander.
But Aphrodite had snatched Paris up—for a god
an easy feat—concealed him in a heavy mist,
and placed him in his own sweetly scented bedroom.

Then Aphrodite went to summon Helen.
She found her on the high tower, in a crowd
among the Trojan women. She clutched Helen
by her perfumed dress, twitched it, then addressed her,   430
in the form of an old woman, a wool carder,
someone who used to live in Lacedaemon,
producing fine wool, a woman Helen really liked.
In this shape, divine Aphrodite spoke to Helen:

> "Alexander is asking you to come back home.
> He's in the bedroom, on the carved-out bed,
> his beauty and his garments glistening.
> You wouldn't think he's just come from some fight.
> He looks as if he's going to a dance,
> or if he's sitting down right after dancing."   440

Aphrodite spoke, stirring emotion in Helen's heart.

Noticing the goddess' lovely neck, enticing breasts,
her glittering eyes, Helen was astonished.

"Goddess, why do you wish to deceive me so?
Are you going to take me still further off,
to some well-populated city somewhere
in Phrygia or beautiful Maeonia,
because you're in love with some mortal man
and Menelaus has just beaten Paris
and wants to take me, a despised woman,   450
back home with him? Is that why you're here,
you and your devious trickery?
Why don't you go with Paris by yourself,
stop walking around here like a goddess,
stop guiding your feet toward Olympus,
and lead a miserable life with him,
caring for him, until he makes you his wife
or slave. I won't go to him in there—
that would be shameful, serving him in bed.
Every Trojan woman would revile me afterwards.   460
Besides, my heart is hurt enough already."

Divine Aphrodite, angry at Helen, answered her:

"Don't provoke me, you obstinate girl.
I might lose my temper, abandon you,
and hate you just as much as I have loved you.
I could make Trojans and Danaans hate you, too.
Then you'd suffer death in misery."

Aphrodite spoke. Helen, born from Zeus, was too afraid.
She covered herself in her soft white linen shawl,
went off in silence, unnoticed by all the Trojan women.   470
With goddess Aphrodite in the lead,
they came to Alexander's lovely house.
There the attendants quickly set about their work.
Helen, goddess among women, went to her room upstairs,
where laughter-loving goddess Aphrodite
picked up a chair and carried it for Helen.

She placed it facing Paris. Helen, child of Zeus,
who bears the aegis, sat down. With eyes averted,
she began to criticize her husband:

> "You've come back from the fight. How I wish   480
> you'd died there, killed by that strong warrior
> who was my husband once. You used to boast
> you were stronger than warlike Menelaus,
> more strength in your hands, more power in your spear.
> So go now, challenge war-loving Menelaus
> to fight again in single combat.
> I'd suggest you stay away. Don't fight it out
> man to man with fair-haired Menelaus,
> without further thought. You might well die,
> come to a quick end on his spear."   490

Replying to Helen, Paris said:

>   "Wife,
> don't mock my courage with your insults.
> Yes, Menelaus has just defeated me,
> but with Athena's help. Next time I'll beat him.
> For we have gods on our side, too. But come,
> let's enjoy our love together on the bed.
> Never has desire so filled my mind as now,
> not even when I first took you away
> from lovely Lacedaemon, sailing off
> in our sea-worthy ships, or when I lay with you   500
> in our lover's bed on the isle of Cranae.
> That's how sweet passion has seized hold of me,
> how much I want you now."

>   Paris finished speaking.
He led the way to bed. His wife went, too.
The two lay down together on the bed.

Atreus' son paced through the crowd, like a wild beast,
searching for some glimpse of godlike Alexander.
But no Trojan nor any of their famous allies

could reveal Alexander to warlike Menelaus.
If they'd seen him, they had no desire to hide him. 510
For they all hated Paris, as they hated gloomy death.
Agamemnon, king of men, addressed them:

> "Listen to me, Trojans, Dardanians, allies—
> victory clearly falls to war-loving Menelaus.
> So give back Argive Helen and her property,
> compensate us with a suitable amount,
> something future ages will all talk about."

As he finished speaking, the other Achaeans cheered.

Book Four
The Armies Clash

[The Council of the Gods on Olympus; Zeus sends Athena to break the truce; Athena persuades Pandarus to fire an arrow at Menelaus; Menelaus is wounded; Machaon tends to Menelaus; Agamemnon tours the battlefield rallying his troops; the battle starts again]

The gods all sat assembled in the golden courtyard,
with Zeus there, too. Gracious Hebe went among them,
pouring nectar. They toasted each other in golden cups,
as they looked out on Troy. Then Zeus, son of Cronos,
wishing to irk Hera with a sarcastic speech,
addressed them in deviously provoking words:

  "Menelaus has two goddesses
  assisting him, Hera of Argos
  and Athena of Alalcomene.
  But they sit far away, looking on,   10
  enjoying themselves, while Aphrodite,
  who loves laughter, helps Paris all the time,
  protecting him from death. Now, for instance,
  she's just rescued him from certain death.
  For war-loving Menelaus was the victor,
  no doubt of that. But why don't we discuss
  how this warfare is going to finish up—
  whether we should re-ignite harsh combat,
  this horrific strife, or make both sides friends.
  If this second option pleases all of us,   20
  if we find it sweet, then king Priam's city
  remains inhabited, and Menelaus
  takes Argive Helen home with him."

Athena and Hera sat together muttering,
plotting trouble for the Trojans. Angry at Zeus,
her father, Athena sat there silently,
so enraged she didn't say a word. But Hera,
unable to contain her anger, burst out:

"Most fearful son of Cronos, what are you saying?
How can you wish to undermine my efforts,   30
prevent them from achieving anything?
What about the sweat which dripped from me,
as I worked so hard, wearing my horses out,
gathering men to wipe out Priam and his children.
Go ahead then. But all we other gods
do not approve of what you're doing."

Then cloud-gatherer Zeus, irritated, said to her:

"Dear wife, what sort of crimes have Priam
or Priam's children committed against you,
that you should be so vehemently keen   40
to destroy that well-built city Ilion?
If you went through its gates or its huge walls,
you'd gorge on Priam and his children,
other Trojans, too, swallow their flesh raw.
That's what you'd do to slake your anger.
Do as you wish. We shouldn't make this matter
something you and I later squabble over,
a source of major disagreements.
But I'll tell you this—keep it in mind.
Whenever I get the urge to wipe out   50
some city whose inhabitants you love,
don't try to thwart me. Let me have my way.
I'll give in to you freely, though unwillingly.
For of all towns inhabited by earth's peoples,
under the sun, beneath the heavenly stars,
sacred Ilion, with Priam and his people,
expert spearmen, stands dearest in my heart.
My altar there has always shared their feasts,
with libations and sacrificial smoke,
offerings we get as honours due to us "   60

Ox-eyed Hera then said in reply to Zeus:

"The three cities I love the best by far
are Argos, Sparta, and Mycenae,

73

city of wide streets. Destroy them utterly,
if you ever hate them in your heart.
I won't deny you or get in your way.
If I tried disagreeing with such destruction,
my hostile stance would be quite useless.
For you are far more powerful than me.
But my own work must not be wasted,   70
worth nothing. I'm a god, the same race as you—
I'm crooked-minded Cronos' eldest daughter.
Another thing—in addition to my birth—
I'm called your wife, and you rule all immortals.
In this matter, then, let's both support
each other's wishes—you mine, I yours.
Other gods will follow our example.
Instruct Athena to go immediately
where Trojans and Achaeans carry on
their bitter conflict. There she should try   80
to get the Trojans to break their oaths first,
by harming the glorious Achaeans."

Hera spoke. The father of gods and men agreed.
He spoke up to Athena—his words had wings.

"Go quickly to the Trojan and Achaean troops.
Try to get the Trojans to break their oaths first,
by injuring the glorious Achaeans."

Zeus' words stirred up Athena's earlier desires.
She darted from Olympus summit, sped off,
like a comet sent by crooked-minded Cronos' son,   90
a beacon for sailors and the wide race of men,
showering sparks behind her as she flew.
That's how Pallas Athena shot to earth, then dropped
right down into the middle of the soldiers.
Horse-taming Trojans looked on in amazement,
well-armed Achaeans, too. As they saw her,
each man said to the person next to him:

"There's going to be more war, more wretched combat,

74

or else great Zeus, who serves up war to men,
will make the troops on both sides friends."

That's what troops muttered, both Trojan and Achaean.
Athena went down into the Trojan crowd,
looking like Laodocus, Antenor's son,
a strong spearman, seeking godlike Pandarus.
She met Pandarus, Lycaon's powerful son,
a fine man, standing there with his sturdy regiment,
shield-bearing troops who'd come from the river Aesopus.
Standing near him, Athena spoke. Her words had wings.

    "Fiery hearted son of Lycaon,
why not do as I suggest? Prepare yourself   110
to shoot a swift arrow at Menelaus.
You'd earn thanks and glory from all Trojans,
most of all from prince Alexander.
He'd be the very first to bring fine gifts,
if he could see warlike Menelaus,
son of Atreus, mounted on his bier,
his bitter funeral pyre, killed by your arrow.
So come, then, shoot an arrow at him—
at splendid Menelaus. Promise Apollo,
illustrious archer born in Lycia,   120
you'll make fine sacrifice, some new-born lambs,
once you get back to your city, holy Zeleia."

Athena spoke and thus swayed his foolish wits.
Pandarus took up his bow of polished horn,
made from a nimble wild goat he himself once shot
under the chest, as it leapt down from a rock.
He'd waited in an ambush and hit it in the front.
The goat fell down onto the rocks, landing on its back.
Horns on its head were sixteen palm widths long.
A man skilled in shaping horn had worked on them,   130
to fit the horns together to create a bow.
He'd polished it all over, adding gold caps
snugly fitted on the tips. Pandarus stooped down,
strung the bow, then set it on the ground.

His brave companions held their shields before him,
just in case Achaea's warlike sons attacked them,
before he could shoot Menelaus, Atreus' warrior son.
Then, removing the cover from his quiver,
Pandarus took out an arrow, a fresh-winged courier
bearing dark agony. Next he quickly set   140
the keen arrow on the string, swearing an oath
to the archer god, Lycian-born Apollo,
that he would make splendid sacrifice, first-born lambs,
when he got back to his city, holy Zaleia.
Gripping the arrow notch, the ox-gut bowstring,
he pulled back, drawing the string right to his nipple,
iron arrow head against the bow. Once he'd bent
that great bow into a circle, the bow twanged,
the string sang out, the sharp-pointed arrow flew away,
eager to bury itself in crowds of men.   150
But, Menelaus, the immortal sacred gods
did not forget you. Athena, Zeus' daughter,
goddess of war's spoils, was first to stand before you,
to ward off the piercing arrow—she brushed it from your skin,
just as a mother brushes a fly off her child
while he lies sweetly sleeping. Athena led the arrow
to the spot where the gold buckles on the belt
rest on the joint in the double body armour.
The keen arrow dug into the leather strap,
passed right through the finely decorated belt,   160
through the richly embossed armour, the body mail,
his most powerful guard, worn to protect his flesh,
by blocking spears and arrows. The arrow pierced it,
going through that mail, and grazed the skin of Menelaus.
Dark blood at once came flowing from the wound.
Just as when some woman of Meonia or Caria
stains white ivory with purple dye, making a cheek piece
for a horse, and leaves it in her room—an object
many riders covet for themselves, a king's treasure
with double value—horse's ornament and rider's glory—   170
that's how, Menelaus, your strong thighs, shins and ankles
were stained with your own blood below the wound.
When Agamemnon saw dark blood flowing from the wound,

that king of men shuddered. And Menelaus,
who loved war, shuddered, too. But when he saw
barbs of the arrow head, its binding, still outside,
not underneath the skin, his spirits rose, and courage
flowed back into his chest. Mighty Agamemnon,
taking Menelaus by the hand, with a bitter groan,
spoke to his companions, all grieving with him: 180

"Dear brother, that oath I swore to was your death—
letting you step forward to fight Trojans,
as Achaea's champion. For now the Trojans
have shot you, walking roughshod on their oaths,
that treaty they swore to in good faith. But still,
the oath, lambs' blood, unmixed libations,
handshakes, things in which we placed our trust—
all these will not go in vain. For if Zeus,
the Olympian, does not fulfill them now,
later on he will. Trojans will pay much—   190
with their heads, their wives, their children.
I know in my mind and heart that day will come
when holy Troy, Priam, and his people,
fine spearmen, will be annihilated,
when high-ruling Zeus, son of Cronos,
who dwells in the sky, angry at their lies,
will shake his dark aegis against them all.
These things will be fulfilled. But, Menelaus,
I'll be in dreadful pain on your account,
if you die, if Fate now ends your life,   200
if I return to arid Argos totally disgraced.
For Achaeans immediately will think of home,
leaving Priam and his Trojans here in triumph,
abandoning Helen, an Argive woman.
Your bones will lie rotting here in Trojan soil,
recalling the work we failed to finish.
Then some arrogant Trojan, leaping up
onto the tomb of famous Menelaus,
will shout: 'May Agamemnon's anger
always end like this. His Achaean army   210
he brought here in vain. He returned home,

back to his native land in empty ships,
abandoning courageous Menelaus.'
That's what he'll say. Before that day
I hope the broad earth will lie over me!"

Then Menelaus, to cheer up Agamemnon, said:

"Take courage. Don't upset Achaeans.
This sharp arrow is not a fatal hit.
My gleaming belt protected me on top,
as did my body chain mail underneath,   220
forged in bronze."

                   Mighty Agamemnon answered:

"My dear Menelaus, I hope that's true.
But a healer must inspect your wound,
apply his medicine to relieve black pain."

Agamemnon ordered Talthybius, his godlike herald:

"Talthybius, as quickly as you can,
get Machaon here, son of Asclepius,
healer without equal, to look over
warlike Menelaus, son of Atreus,
shot by someone's arrow, a skilled archer,   230
Trojan or Lycian—to his glory and our grief."

Hearing his orders, Talthybius obeyed.
He set off among bronze-clad Achaeans,
seeking heroic Machaon. He saw him there,
standing among the ranks of his strong warriors,
shield-bearing men who'd come with him from Tricca,
land where horses breed. Standing close to him,
Talthybius spoke. His words had wings.

"Son of Asclepius, rouse yourself.
For mighty Agamemnon calls for you   240
to look at warrior Menelaus, Achaea's leader,

shot by someone's arrow, a skilled archer,
Trojan or Lycian—to his glory and our grief."

At Talthybius' words Machaon's spirits
were stirred up in his chest. They set off together,
through the wide Achaean army's crowded ranks.
They came where wounded fair-haired Menelaus lay.
Around him all the noblest men had gathered in a circle.
Machaon, godlike man, strode into the middle,
drew the arrow from the belt without delay,   250
twisting back the sharp barbs as he pulled the arrow out.
He undid the finely decorated belt and armour,
then, under that, the chain mail forged in bronze.
Next, he inspected the wound the keen arrow made,
sucked out the blood, then skillfully applied his potions,
soothing medicines which Cheiron gave his father.

While the Achaeans were looking after Menelaus,
lord of the loud war shout, Trojan ranks advanced,
shields ready, once more armed with all their weapons,
fully charged with passionate desire for battle.   260
Then you'd not have seen lord Agamemnon sleeping,
hiding, or not keen to fight. Quite the reverse,
he was moving out to combat, to man-ennobling war.
He left his horses and ornate bronze chariot
with his aide Eurymedon, son of Ptolemaeus,
son of Peiraeus, who held the panting horses at a distance.
For Agamemnon had ordered him repeatedly
to keep the horses ready for the time his limbs
grew tired from moving through so many soldiers.
He went around on foot, inspecting warrior ranks.   270
When he saw Danaans coming up with horses,
he'd approach them, shouting words of encouragement:

"Argives, don't lose your warlike spirit.
Father Zeus will never help those liars.
By attacking us, these Trojans were the first
to violate their oaths. Vultures will gnaw away
their tender flesh, while we lead off their wives

and their dear delicate children to our ships,
when we've destroyed their city."

But when Agamemnon saw soldiers holding back   280
from hateful war, he'd lash out at them in anger

"You cowards, disgraceful Argives, aren't you ashamed?
What are you doing just standing here,
like dazed fawns exhausted after running
over a large plain, now motionless,
hearts drained of spirit—that's how you stand,
in a trance, not marching up to battle.
Are you waiting for Trojans to come closer,
up to the fine sterns of our ships beached here,
on the gray sea shore, so you can see   290
if the hand of Cronos' son will shield you?"

In this way, Agamemnon moved around the army,
exerting his authority throughout the ranks.
Going past crowds of men, he met the troops from Crete,
as they armed themselves round Idomeneus,
their fiery-hearted leader at the front,
fierce as a wild boar. In the rear, Meriones
roused the ranks for action. Looking at these two,
Agamemnon, king of men, rejoiced. He spoke out,
talking straight to Idomeneus in a friendly tone: 300

"Idomeneus, above all Danaans,
with their swift horses, I value you in war,
in all other things, and at banquets,
when Achaea's finest prepare gleaming wine,
the kind reserved for kings, in mixing bowls.
Other long-haired Achaeans drink their portion,
the amount allotted to them, but your cup
always stands full of wine, as does mine,
so you can drink any time your heart desires.
Set off to battle, then—show you're a man,   310
the fine man you claimed to be before."

Idomeneus, Cretan leader, answered Agamemnon:

"Son of Atreus, indeed I'll prove myself
a loyal comrade to you, as I promised
that first time long ago. But you should rouse
other long-haired Achaean men to action,
so we may fight at once, without delay.
Since Trojans have broken their sworn promises,
death and sorrow will come to them at last,
for they attacked us first, breaking their oaths."   320

At these words, the son of Atreus felt joy fill his heart.
Then he moved off. As he continued on his way,
he met both men called Ajax, arming themselves
among the hordes of troops, with crowds of men on foot.
Just as a goatherd high on a lookout sees a cloud
coming down across the sea, driven by West Wind's force—
something which at a distance seems pitch black
as it moves across the sea, driving a huge storm,
and, shuddering at the sight, he takes his flocks
into a cave—that's how the dense ranks of young men,   330
gods' favourites, marched around both Ajaxes,
ready for war, all dressed in black, with shields and spears,
Seeing them, powerful Agamemnon felt great joy—
he shouted out to them in words with wings:

                    "You two Ajaxes,
leaders of the Argives armed in bronze,
for you I have no orders. It's not right
for me to urge you forward—both of you
are rousing men to fight with all their force.
By Father Zeus, Athena, and Apollo,
I wish such spirit would fill each man's chest.   340
Then king Priam's city would soon fall,
we'd capture it, destroy it utterly."

With these words, he left them there, going on to others.
He met Nestor, clear-voiced orator from Pylos,
setting his troops in order, urging them to fight

under huge Pelagon, Alastor, Chromius,
Haemon, and mighty Bias, his people's shepherd.
Nestor set horses, chariots, and charioteers in front.
In the rear, he placed his many brave foot soldiers,
a battle wall. In the middle he placed his poorer troops,   350
to force them to keep fighting on against their will.
First, he told the charioteers to control their horses,
to avoid confusing the entire battle line:

    "In your eagerness to engage the Trojans,
    don't any of you charge ahead of others,
    trusting in your strength and horsemanship.
    And don't lag behind. That will hurt our charge.
    Any man whose chariot confronts an enemy's
    should thrust with his spear at him from there.
    That's the most effective tactic, the way   360
    men wiped out city strongholds long ago—
    their chests full of that style and spirit."

Thus that old man, skilled in war's traditions, roused his men.
Seeing him, mighty Agamemnon was elated.
He spoke to Nestor. His words had wings.

                              "Old man,
    how I wish the power in those knees of yours
    could match the spirit in your chest, your strength
    remain unbowed. But old age, our common enemy,
    has worn you down. If only that had happened
    to some other man and left you in place,   370
    among the ranks of younger warriors."

To these words Geranian horseman Nestor said:

    "Son of Atreus, yes, indeed, I wish
    I were the man I used to be back then,
    when I cut down lord Ereuthalion.
    But gods don't give men everything at once.
    Then I was young. Now old age follows me.
    But I'll be with my horsemen, advising them,

giving them their orders, an old man's right.
Fighting with spears is for the younger men 380
born after me, men who rely on strength."

Nestor spoke. Filled with joy, Atreus' son moved on.
Next, he came upon Menestheus, Peteos' son,
a charioteer, standing still among Athenians,
famous for their battle cries. Close by them,
resourceful Odysseus stood among his troops,
Cephallenian soldiers, powerful fighting men.
These men had not yet heard the call to battle.
For the armies of horse-taming Trojans
and Achaeans had only just begun to march 390
against each other. So Odysseus' soldiers
stood waiting for the rest of the Achaeans
to charge against the Trojans and begin the fight.
Seeing this, Agamemnon, king of men, spoke out,
rebuking them. His words had wings.

"Son of Peteos, god-given king, and you,
Odysseus, skilled in sly deception,
crafty minded, why are you holding back,
standing apart? Are you waiting for the rest?
By rights you two should be with those in front, 400
sharing the heat of battle. At banquets,
when we Achaeans feast our senior men,
you hear me call your name out first.
Then you like to have roast meat and cups of wine,
honey sweet, to your heart's content.
But now you'd be quite happy looking on
if ten Achaean groups were fighting here
with ruthless bronze before your very eyes."

Resourceful Odysseus, scowling grimly, then replied:

"Son of Atreus, how can you say such things? 410
How can you claim I'm hanging back from battle
each time we Achaeans rouse ourselves for war
against horse-taming Trojans? If you want,

83

        if it's of interest to you, then you'll see
        Telemachus' dear father battling
        horse-taming Trojans at the very front.
        What you've been saying is clearly nonsense."

Mighty Agamemnon saw the anger in Odysseus.
He smiled at him and took back what he'd just said:

        "Odysseus, you resourceful man,   420
        divinely born son of Laertes,
        I'm not finding serious fault with you.
        I'm issuing no orders to you.
        I know that spirit in your loyal chest
        is well disposed. We both are of one mind.
        If I've said something bad we'll make it good.
        May the gods bring all of this to nothing."

With these words, Agamemnon left Odysseus there,
moving on to other men. He met Diomedes,
Tydeus' high-spirited son, standing by his horses   430
and his well-made chariot. Beside him stood Sthenelus,
son of Capaneus. Seeing them, Agamemnon
spoke out in rebuke. His words had wings.

                        "Alas, Diomedes,
        son of fiery-hearted, horse-taming Tydeus,
        why are you hiding, just watching battle lanes?
        Tydeus was not a man to shirk like this.
        He fought his enemies in front of his companions.
        That's what they say, those who saw him work.
        I never saw him for myself. People claim
        he ranked above the rest. Once he came to Mycenae   440
        as a peaceful guest with godlike Polyneices,
        mustering men to assault the sacred walls of Thebes.
        They begged us to give them worthy comrades.
        Mycenaeans, willing to comply, agreed.
        But then Zeus later changed their minds,
        revealing an unlucky omen to them.
        So Tydeus and Polyneices left.

On their way, they reached the river Asopus,
its lush grassy meadows full of reeds.
Sent by Achaeans as envoy to Thebes,   450
Tydeus went there. He found Cadmeans[1]
feasting in large numbers in the palace,
home of great Eteocles. Though a stranger,
all by himself in that Cadmean crowd,
chariot fighter Tydeus was not afraid.
He challenged them in various contests.
Athena helped, so he won them all with ease.
Horse-breaking Cadmeans were upset with him.
They organized a strong ambush against him
as he returned—fifty young men, with two leaders,   460
that godlike hero Maeon, Haemon's son,
and warlike Polyphontes, son of Autophonus.
But these men came to fatal shameful ends.
For Tydeus killed them, all but one.
He let Maeon go home, sent him away,
in obedience to an omen from the gods.
That's the man Aetolian Tydeus was.
But his son is a lesser man than he,
though better when it comes to talking."

Mighty Diomedes did not reply to Agamemnon's words,   470
shamed at the rebuke from a king whom he respected.
But Sthenelus, son of famous Capaneus, answered:

"Son of Atreus, don't spread lies. You know the truth.
We claim we're far better than our fathers.
We captured Thebes, city of seven gates,
leading smaller forces over stronger walls,
trusting signs sent by the gods and Zeus' aid.
The others died through their own foolishness.
So don't give our fathers honours high as mine."

Powerful Diomedes, frowning, spoke to Sthenelus: 480

[1]Citizens of Thebes were commonly called *Cadmeans* after Cadmus, the founder of
the city.

"My friend. Stay quiet. Follow my advice.
For I'm not hurt that Agamemnon,
the army's shepherd, urges armed Achaeans
on to battle. For he will get the glory,
if Achaeans annihilate the Trojans
and capture sacred Ilion. And he'll get
great sorrow, if Achaeans are wiped out.
But come, let's get our two minds working
to rouse our spirits for this coming fight."

Diomedes spoke. Then with his weapons he jumped   490
from his chariot down to the ground. Around his chest
the bronze rang fearfully, as he moved into action,
a sound to make even brave warriors afraid.

Just as thundering ocean surf crashes on the sand,
wave after wave, driven by the West Wind's power,
one wave rising at sea, then booming down on shore,
arching in crests and crashing down among the rocks,
spewing salt foam, so then Danaan ranks,
row after row, moved out, spirits firmly set on war.
Each leader issued his own orders to his men.   500
The rest marched on in silence. You'd never think
such a huge army could move out with its voice
buried in those chests, in silent fear of their commanders.
As they marched, the polished armour on them glittered.

As for the Trojans, they were like thousands of ewes
standing in a rich man's farm, bleating constantly,
waiting for someone to come and collect white milk,
as they hear lambs call. Just like that, the din rose up
throughout the widespread Trojan force. They shared no words—
they had no common language, but mixtures of tongues,   510
with men from many lands. Ares urged the Trojans on,
while bright-eyed Athena kept rousing the Achaeans.
With them came Terror, Fear, and tireless Strife,
sister and companion of man-destroying Ares—
at first small in stature, she later grows enormous,
head reaching heaven, as she strides across the earth.

Strife went through crowds of soldiers, casting hatred
on both sides equally, multiplying human miseries.

When the two armies came to one common ground,
they smashed into each other—shields, spears, fierce angry men   520
encased in bronze. Studded shields bashed one another.
A huge din arose—human cries of grief and triumph,
those killing and those killed. Earth flowed with blood.
Just as streams swollen with melting snows pour out,
flow down the hill into a pool, and meet some torrent
from a great spring in a hollow gully there,
and the shepherd in the distant hills hears the roar—
so the shouts and turmoil resounded then from warriors,
as they collided.

     Antilochus was the first to kill a man—
a well-armed Trojan warrior, Echepolus,   530
son of Thalysius, a courageous man,
who fought in the front ranks. He hit his helmet crest,
topped with horsehair plumes, spearing his forehead.
The bronze point smashed straight through the frontal bone.
Darkness hid his eyes and he collapsed, like a tower,
falling down into that frenzied battle. As he fell,
powerful Elephenor, son of Chalcodon,
courageous leader of the Abantes, seized his feet,
and started pulling him beyond the range of weapons,
eager to strip him of his armour quickly.   540
But Elephenor's attempt did not go on for long.
Great-hearted Agenor saw him drag the dead man.
He stabbed Elephenor with his bronze spear,
right in his exposed side, where his shield left him
vulnerable as he bent down. His limbs gave way,
as his spirit left him. Over his dead body,
Trojans and Achaeans kept fighting grimly on,
attacking like wolves, man whirling against man.

Then Ajax, son of Telamon, hit Simoeisius,
Anthemion's son, a fine young warrior.   550
He was born on the banks of the river Simoeis,

while his mother was coming down Mount Ida,
accompanying her parents to watch their flocks.
That's why the people called him Simoeisius.
But he did not repay his fond parents for raising him.
His life was cut short on great Ajax's deadly spear.
As he was moving forward with the men in front,
Ajax struck him in the chest, by the right nipple.
The bronze spear went clean through his shoulder.
He collapsed in the dust, like a poplar tree,   560
one growing in a large well-watered meadow,
from whose smooth trunk the branches grow up to the top,
until a chariot builder's bright axe topples it,
bends the wood, to make wheel rims for a splendid chariot,
letting the wood season by the riverbank.
That's how godlike Ajax chopped down Simoeisius,
son of Anthemion.

                    Then Antiphus, Priam's son,
with his shining helmet, hurled his sharp spear at Ajax
through a crowd of men. He missed Ajax, but hit Leucus,
a brave companion of Odysseus, in the groin,   570
as he was dragging Simoeisius away.
His hands let go. He fell down on the corpse.
Enraged at Leucus' slaughter, Odysseus strode up,
through the front ranks, armed in gleaming bronze. Going in close,
he took his stand. Looking round, he hurled his glittering spear.
As he threw, Trojans moved back, but the spear found a mark.
It hit Democoön, Priam's bastard son, who'd come
from Abydos, where he bred horses for their speed.
Angry for his friend, Odysseus speared him in the temple.
The sharp bronze pressed on through the other side,   580
coming out his forehead. Darkness fell on his eyes,
and he collapsed with a crash. The armour on him echoed.
Trojans in the front ranks, among them noble Hector,
backed away. Raising a huge shout, the Argives
hauled off the corpses and charged ahead much further.

Looking down from Pergamus, Apollo grew annoyed.

He called out to the Trojans, shouting:

"Charge ahead, you horse-taming Trojans.
Don't make Argives happy. Their skin's not made
of stone or iron. Once you strike at them   590
it can't stop flesh-ripping bronze. And Achilles,
son of lovely Thetis, isn't in this fight.
He's sitting by his ships, nursing his anger."

So the fearsome god spoke out from the city.
Athena Tritogeneia, mighty Zeus' daughter,
rushed among Achaeans, urging companies on,
if she saw men holding back, hesitant to fight.

Death then came to Diores, son of Amarynceus.
He was hit by a jagged rock on his right shin,
beside the ankle. It was thrown by Peirous,   600
son of Imbrasus, captain of the Thracians,
who'd come from Aenus. The cruel rock crushed both tendons
and the bone. He fell onto his back down in the dust.
There he reached out with both hands for his companions.
His spirit left his body with each gasp he took.
Peirous, who'd thrown the rock, ran up and speared his gut.
His bowels spilled out onto the ground. Darkness hid his eyes.
As Peirous moved off, Thoas, an Aetolian, hit him,
his spear striking him above the nipple. The bronze spear point
bit into his lungs. Thoas moved in to close quarters,   610
pulled the heavy spear out from his chest, drew his sharp sword,
then drove it straight into the middle of his belly,
destroying Peirous' life. But Thoas couldn't strip
the armour off. For Peirous' companions,
Thracian men whose hair is piled atop their heads,
rallied round, holding out long spears, forcing Thoas
away from them. Thoas was big, strong, and brave,
but he fell back, shaken. And so those two warriors
lay stretched out in the dirt beside each other—
one Thracian chief, one captain of bronze-clad Epeians.   620
And many other men lay dead around them.

At that point, no man who joined in the battle there
could take it lightly, not even one who strolled unhurt
through the middle of the fight, untouched by that sharp bronze,
with Pallas Athena escorting him by hand,
shielding him from flying weapons. For on that day,
many Trojans and Achaeans lay there side by side,
stretched out together, face down in the dust.

Book Five
Diomedes Goes to Battle

[Athena inspires Diomedes with special powers; Athena takes Ares from the battle; Achaean leaders kill many Trojans; Diomedes' special glory on the field; Pandarus hits Diomedes with an arrow; Athena restores Diomedes, who continues his battle frenzy; Aeneas and Pandarus move out against Diomedes; Diomedes kills Pandarus, wounds Aeneas; Aphrodite saves Aeneas; Sthenelus captures Aeneas' horses; Diomedes attacks and wounds Aphrodite, who returns to Olympus; Diomedes threatens Apollo; Apollo heals Aeneas; Sarpedon complains to Hector; the battle continues; Sarpedon kills Tlepolemus, but is wounded; Athena and Hera go down to the battlefield; Athena and Diomedes attack and wound Ares; Ares returns to Olympus]

Then Pallas Athena gave Diomedes, son of Tydeus,
strength and courage, so among all Argives,
he'd stand out and win heroic glory.
She made his helmet blaze with tireless flames,
his shield as well—like a late star in summer
which shines especially bright, newly risen from its bath
in Ocean's streams. Around his head and shoulders
the goddess put a fiery glow, then drove him forward,
right into the middle of the strife, the killing zone,
where most warriors fight.

               Among the Trojans   10
was a rich and honorable man called Dares,
priest of Hephaestus. He had two sons—Phegeus
and Idaios—both very skilled in all aspects of war.
Moving forward in their chariot to the front,
these two charged Diomedes, who was on foot,
staying on the ground. When they were at close range,
Phegeus was the first to hurl his long-shadowed spear.
The spear point flew by Diomedes' left shoulder—
it missed him. Tydeus' son then threw his spear.
The weapon did not leave his hand and miss the target.   20

It hit Phegeus right between the nipples
and knocked him from his splendid chariot.
Idaios jumped out and ran off from his horses.
He didn't dare protect his slaughtered brother's corpse.
Even so, he wouldn't have escaped black doom,
but Hephaestus saved him with a dark cloud cover,
so his aged father wouldn't waste away with grief.
Tydeus' son, great Diomedes, drove the horses off,
then gave them to his comrades to take back to the ships.
When great-hearted Trojans saw those two sons of Dares—   30
one shunning battle, one dead beside his chariot—
all their hearts were stirred.

Then Athena, eyes glittering,
took her brother, headstrong Ares, by the hand,
and said to him:

"Ares, Ares, insatiable man-killer,
destroyer of cities, why don't we leave
Trojans and Achaeans to fight it out?
Father Zeus will make one group victorious.
Let's withdraw, avoiding Zeus' anger."

With these words, she led headstrong Ares from the battle,
then sat him down by Scamander river bank.   40

Danaans then began to push the Trojans back.
Each leader killed his enemy. First, Agamemnon,
king of men, threw huge Odius, chief of the Halizoni,
from his chariot. His spear first struck him in the back,
between the shoulder blades, as he turned to flee.
It drove clean through his chest. Odius pitched forward
with a thud, his armour rattling round him as he fell.
Idomeneus slaughtered Phaestus, son of Borus,
a Meonian, who'd come from fertile Tarne.
With his long spear, skillful Idomeneus struck him   50
in his right shoulder, as he climbed in his chariot.
Dreadful darkness came and gathered Phaestus in.
Those attending Idomeneus stripped the armour.

Then with his sharp spear Menelaus, son of Atreus,
killed Scamandrius, son of Strophius, a huntsman.
Artemis herself had taught him how to shoot
every animal raised in the mountain forests.
But archer Artemis was no help to him then,
no more than was his expertise in archery,
at which he'd been pre-eminent in former times.   60
For fine spearman Menelaus, son of Atreus,
caught him as he ran away in front of him,
hitting him in the back between his shoulder blades,
forcing the spear right through Scamandrius' chest.
He fell head first. His armour rattled round him.

Meriones then killed Phereclus, son of Tecton,
Harmon's son, whose hands could make fine objects of all sorts.
Pallas Athena had a special love for him.
He was the one who'd made well-balanced ships
for Paris at the start of all the trouble,   70
bringing disaster on the Trojans and on Paris, too,
for he was ignorant of what gods had decreed.
Meriones went after Phereclus as he ran off,
hurled his spear straight into his right buttock.
The spear point pushed on through, below the bone,
piercing his bladder. He fell down on his knees,
screaming. Then death carried him into its shadows.

Then Meges killed Pedaeus, Antenor's bastard son.
Theano had raised him with all care, loving him
as one of her own children, to please her husband.   80
That famous spearman Meges, son of Phyleus,
coming up close, drove a sharp spear in his neck,
into the nape behind his head. The bronze point,
slicing under his tongue, smashed through his teeth.
He fell into the dust, jaws locked on the cold bronze.

Eurypylus, Euaemon's son, killed lord Hypsenor,
son of proud Dolopion, Scamander's priest,
a man honoured by his people as a god.
Eurypylus, Euaemon's splendid son, caught him

as he ran off in front of him. Going quickly after him,   90
Eurypylus struck at Hypsenor's shoulder—
his sharp sword sliced off Hypsenor's brawny arm.
The bloody limb fell on the ground. Then death's black night,
all-powerful fate, moved in and stole away his sight.

Thus these men kept toiling in the battle frenzy.
As for Diomedes, you couldn't tell where he belonged,
whether among the Trojans or Achaeans.
For he rushed across the plain like a swollen river,
like a swift winter torrent bursting dikes—
no dam put in its way can hold it back,   100
no barrier of fruitful vineyards check its current,
as all at once it floods when storms from Zeus roar down.
It knocks aside all fine things built by farmers,
hard-working men. That's how the son of Tydeus
drove the dense ranks of Trojans into mass confusion.
For all their numbers they could not contain him.

Lycaon's fine son saw Diomedes moving fast
along the plain, pushing Trojan ranks in front of him,
in complete disorder. He quickly bent his bow,
taking aim at Diomedes. He shot an arrow   110
and hit him on his sculpted body armour,
in the right shoulder. The sharp arrow went in there,
kept going, and splattered blood down on the curving metal.
At this Lycaon's noble son gave out a noisy shout:

>   "Come on, you brave horse-lashing Trojans.
>   For the finest of Achaeans has been hurt.
>   I don't think he'll long survive my arrow's force,
>   if Apollo, son of Zeus, really was the one
>   who put it in my heart to leave Lycia."

That's what Lycaon's son cried out, boasting aloud.   120
But his sharp arrow hadn't killed Diomedes,
who moved back to stand beside his chariot and horses.
He called to Sthenelus, son of Capaneus.

"My friend, son of Capaneus, come on,
get down from the chariot, so you can pull
this sharp arrow from my shoulder for me."

Diomedes spoke. Sthenelus jumped down on the ground.
Standing beside him, he pulled out the sharp arrow
stuck in his shoulder. Blood seeped through the woven shirt.
Diomedes, expert in war cries, then spoke this prayer: 130

"Hear me, Athena, unwearied daughter
of aegis-bearing Zeus. If you've ever
loved my father, stood by his side
in murderous combat, be my friend now.
Grant that I kill this man, that I come
a spear's throw from the one who hit me
unexpectedly and now boasts about it,
saying I won't see daylight for much longer."

As Diomedes prayed, Pallas Athena heard.
She put fresh strength into his legs and upper arms.   140
Standing close by, she spoke. Her words had wings.

"Take courage, Diomedes, in this fight with Trojans.
I've put your father's strength into your chest,
that shield-bearing horseman's fearless power.
And I've removed the filter from your eyes
which covered them before, so now,
you'll easily distinguish gods from men.
If a god comes here and stands against you,
don't offer to fight any deathless one,
except for Aphrodite, Zeus' daughter.   150
If she fights, cut her with your sharp bronze."

Bright-eyed Athena left. Diomedes charged off,
joining at once those soldiers fighting in the front,
his spirit on fire to battle Trojans, seized by frenzy
three times greater than before. He was like a lion
slightly hurt by a shepherd guarding his sheep flock
out in the wilds, when it jumps the wall into the pen.

But he's not killed it. The wound rouses the beast's strength.
The shepherd can't keep the charging lion from his sheep,
who, left unguarded, panic. Huddled in a mass, 160
they crowd in on one another. So the lion,
in his hot rage, leaps over the wide sheep-fold wall.
That's how strong Diomedes went to fight the Trojans
in his angry fury.

        First he killed Astynous,
and then Hypeiron, a shepherd of his people.
His bronze spear hit one right above the nipple.
His huge sword struck the other on the collar,
by the shoulder, slicing through the shoulder bone,
severing it from Hypeiron's neck and back.
He left them there, to chase Abas and Polyidus, 170
sons of old Eurydamas, interpreter of dreams.
The old man didn't visit them to explain their dreams,
for mighty Diomedes slaughtered both of them.
Then Diomedes went after Xanthus and Thoön,
two sons of Phaenops, both of whom he loved.
Worn down by sad old age, he'd have no other child,
no person to inherit all his property.
Diomedes killed them, took the life they loved,
leaving bitter grief and anguish for their father,
who wouldn't welcome them back home from war alive. 180
His next of kin thus divided up his assets.
Diomedes then challenged two sons of Priam,
son of Dardanus, both in a single chariot—
Echemmon and Chromius. Just as a lion
leaps onto cattle and snaps necks on the cows,
some heifer grazing in the bushes, so Tydeus's son
knocked them out of their chariot viciously,
against their will. Then he stripped their armour.
His companions took the horses to the ships.

Aeneas saw Diomedes cutting his way 190
through ranks of soldiers. He charged on through the fight,
the clash of spears, looking for Pandarus.
He met Lycaon's son, a fine and powerful man.

Standing close by, Aeneas said to him:

                                   "Pandarus,
where's your bow, your feathered arrows,
your reputation as a splendid archer?
No man can match your expertise in that.
No one in Lycia can claim to be your better.
Come, raise your hands in prayer to Zeus,
then shoot an arrow at that man, whose force   200
now dominates the field, hurting Trojans badly,
hacking limbs from many fine young men,
unless, of course, it is some angry god,
displeased with Trojans' sacrificial gifts.
It's hard to stand against a raging god."

To Aeneas Lycaon's fine son then replied:

    "Aeneas, counselor to bronze-armed Trojans,
from all I see, I think that man must be
the warlike son of Tydeus. I know him
by his shield, the visor on his helmet,   210
and by looking at his horses. I'm not sure
he's not a god. But if he's the man
I think he is, the fierce son of Tydeus,
he could not be charging at us in this way
without help from some god beside him,
an immortal with a covering cloud
around his shoulders, the god who pushed aside
that sharp arrow which struck Diomedes.
For I've already shot an arrow at him,
hit his shoulder through that moulded armour.   220
I thought I'd shipped him straight to Hades.
But I didn't kill him. The man must be
some angry god. But we've no horses here,
no chariot for me to chase him in.
In storage in Lycaon's house somewhere
there are eleven chariots, new ones, too.
They're beautiful and made just recently,
but covered up with drapes. Beside each one

stand pairs of horses, munching wheat and barley.
When I was coming here, old soldier Lycaon,   230
in his well-built home, gave me much advice.
He told me to take chariots and horses
when I lead Trojans into the hot heart of war.
But I didn't follow his advice. If I had,
things would have been much better for me.
But I worried about the horses—they'd lack forage
with so many men all crammed together,
and they were used to eating very well.
I left them and came to Troy to fight on foot,
relying on my expertise in archery.   240
But that skill is apparently of little use.
For already I've hit two of their best men,
Tydeus' son and the son of Atreus.
I've drawn blood from both of them, it's true,
but that just made them much more dangerous.
It was a evil time, that day I took
my curved bow off its peg to lead my Lycians
to lovely Troy, a favour for prince Hector.
If I get home and see with my own eyes
my native land, my wife, my large and lofty home,   250
let someone chop my head off on the spot,
if I don't smash this bow with my own hands
and throw the pieces in the blazing fire.
For me it's been completely useless."

Aeneas, leader of the Trojans, then replied:

"Don't talk like that. Things won't change at all
until the two of us go out to challenge
Diomedes with a chariot and horses,
until we confront him with our weapons.
Come, get in my chariot. Then you'll see   260
how good these horses are from Troas' stock,
skilled in rapid movement on the plain,
in all directions, in pursuit or in retreat.
This pair will take us safely to the city,
should Zeus give victory to Diomedes.

Let's go. Take the whip and glistening reins.
I'll leave you the horses, so I can fight.
Or if you fight him, I'll control the horses."

Lycaon's fine son then said in reply:

> "Aeneas, you should take the reins yourself,   270
> guide your own horses—for they will pull
> your curving chariot that much better
> with a driver they're accustomed to,
> if we must flee Tydeus' son this time.
> If they miss your voice, they may shy or panic,
> or refuse to charge straight into battle.
> Then the son of great-hearted Tydeus
> in his attack may kill us both, and lead
> these swift horses off. You drive the chariot,
> guide your horses. I'll do battle with him—   280
> my spear will give him a sharp welcome."

They finished talking, climbed up together, and set off,
riding out in a fine chariot, both keen to kill,
driving the swift horses against Tydeus' son.
Seeing them coming, Sthenelus, Capaneus' brave son,
at once spoke up to Diomedes—his words had wings.

> "Diomedes, son of Tydeus, my heart's
> true friend, I see two men approaching,
> eager to attack you, two powerful men,
> an outstanding team. One's Pandarus,   290
> the skillful archer, who boasts he's Lycaon's son.
> The other is Aeneas, proud Anchises' son,
> that's his claim. His mother's Aphrodite.
> So come, let's retire with the horses,
> in case our quick charge through front lines
> ends up costing you your precious life."

Strong Diomedes, with a scowl, answered Sthenelus:

> "Don't talk of moving back. For I know well

you won't persuade me. By birth it's not in me
to shirk war or seek refuge. My spirit's strong.
Nor am I keen to climb up in the chariot.
I'll go to fight them as I am, on foot.
Pallas Athena does not allow me
to withdraw in fear. Their horses may be fast,
but they'll not carry them both back again,
away from us, even if one escapes.
But I will tell you this—keep it in mind—
if Athena, that clever schemer, gives me
great glory and I do kill them both,
then you must hold our swift horses here,
tying these reins up to the chariot rail.
Remember to run down Aeneas' team,
then drive those horses from the Trojans
to well-armed Achaeans. For those horses
come from the stock that wide-seeing Zeus
gave Tros, payment for Ganymede, his son.
They're the finest horses under the sun,
beneath the light of day. Anchises,
king of men, got some of that line by stealth,
putting his mares into Laomedon's herd
without his knowledge. Six of those horses
became the breeding stock on his estate.
He kept four of them in his own stable
and gave Aeneas two, horses so fierce,
they scatter men before them. If we can,
we'll catch these two, win ourselves great glory."

As they talked to each other of their strategy,
the fast horses quickly brought the two men closer.
Lycaon's worthy son spoke first, shouting out:

> "Great spirited, warlike son of Tydeus,
> that noble man, I see that my sharp arrow,
> a bitter shaft, did not destroy you.
> So now I'll try to hit you with my spear."

He spoke, balanced his long-shadowed spear, and threw it.

The spear hit the son of Tydeus on his shield.
The bronze point pierced it, but stopped at the body armour.
Seeing that, Lycaon's fine son let out a mighty cheer:

> "You're hit, right in the ribs. You won't last long.
> I think you've given me a glorious triumph."

Unperturbed, powerful Diomedes said to him: 340

> "You're wrong. You haven't hit me. In my view,
> this matter won't end for the two of you,
> until one of you falls dead, and his blood
> satisfies in full hard warlike Ares."

That said, he threw his spear. Athena guided it
straight to Pandarus' nose, directly by the eyes.
It smashed through his white teeth. The tireless bronze
sliced through his tongue at its root, coming out his chin,
right at the tip. Pandarus fell from the chariot,
his brightly shining armour rattling round him.   350
The swiftly running horses swerved aside.
Then and there his life-force, his spirit, left him.
Aeneas then leapt down with his long spear and shield,
fearing Achaeans would somehow haul away the corpse.
He made a stand by Pandarus, like a lion,
confident of its strength. He held his spear in front,
his round shield, too, with fearful shouts, fiercely eager
to kill anyone who came up to confront him.
The son of Tydeus picked up a stone, a massive rock
which no two men now alive could lift. He threw it   360
all by himself with ease. It hit Aeneas' hip,
where thigh meets pelvis, what people call the hip joint.
The boulder smashed the socket and both tendons round it.
The rough edges on the rock scraped off his skin.
Falling to his knees, warlike Aeneas stayed down,
supporting himself with his strong hand on the ground.
Black night came down and covered both his eyes.
Aeneas, king of men, would have perished there,
if Aphrodite, Zeus' daughter, hadn't seen him right away.

She was his mother—she'd conceived him with Anchises,
while he was tending cattle. Wrapping her white arms
around the son she loved, she hid him in the folds
of her bright gown, to ward off any spears,
should some Danaan driving with swift horses
hurl a spear into his chest and take his life.
She then began to carry her dear son from the fight.

Meanwhile, Sthenelus, son of Capaneus,
did not forget what Diomedes, skilled in war cries,
told him. He pulled his sure-footed horses to one side,
beyond the fight, tying the reins onto the rail,
and then went after those fine-maned horses of Aeneas.
He drove the animals away from Trojan lines
towards well-armed Achaeans. There he gave them
to his dear companion Deïpylus, whom he esteemed
above all others the same age as himself,
since they both thought alike. He instructed him
to take them to the hollow ships. Then brave Sthenelus
climbed back into his chariot, grabbed the shining reins,
and raced the strong horses back, keen to rejoin Diomedes.

But Diomedes with his ruthless bronze had gone
to run down Aphrodite—knowing she was not a god
who could do much in battle, not one of those
who control men's wars. She was no Athena,
no goddess Strife, who destroys whole cities.
He chased her through the crowded battle zone.
When he met her, great-hearted Tydeus' son
charged, lunging with his sharp spear at Aphrodite.
His weapon wounded her slim wrist, piercing the skin
above her hand, right through her godlike robe,
a garment the Graces had made for her themselves.[1]
Immortal divine fluid then flowed out, ichor,
which circulates only in the blessed gods.
They don't eat food or drink down gleaming wine.
Hence, they lack blood, and men call them immortal.

[1]The *Graces* are the divine daughters of Zeus, goddesses of charm and grace,
usually three in number.

Aphrodite screamed wildly and let go of her son.
But Phoebus Apollo caught him in his hands,
then shielded him with a dark cloud, just in case
some fast-riding Danaan threw a spear into his chest
and took away his life. Then Diomedes,
expert in war cries, shouted loudly:

>"Daughter of Zeus,   410
>leave war and fights alone. Isn't it enough
>for you to fool around with feeble women?
>If you start loitering on the battlefield,
>I think the war will make you shake with terror,
>even though you learn about it from a distance."

Diomedes spoke. Aphrodite left in agony,
distressed and fearful. Wind-swift Iris came to her,
led her off, out of the crowd, moaning in pain,
her fair skin stained with blood. She came across
fierce Ares, seated on the left flank of the fight,   420
his spear and his fast horses resting on a cloud.
Falling on her knees, she implored her dear brother,
pleading hard for his golden-bridled horses:

>"Dear brother, save me. Give me your horses,
>so I may go back up to Mount Olympus,
>the immortals' home. My wound pains me a lot.
>A mortal man inflicted this wound on me,
>Tydeus' son, who'd now fight Father Zeus himself."

At this, Ares gave her his golden-bridled horses.
She climbed up in the chariot, her fond heart suffering.   430
Getting in beside her, Iris picked up the reins,
then lashed the horses forward. They flew on willingly.
At once they reached the gods' home, steep Olympus.
There wind-swift Iris stopped the horses, untied them
from the chariot, and gave them heavenly fodder.
Aphrodite threw herself into her mother's lap,
divine Dione, who took her daughter in her arms,
caressed her with her hand, then said:

"My dear child,
which of the heavenly gods has done this,
acted so brazenly against you, as if   440
you'd done something evil in broad daylight?"

Laughter-loving Aphrodite answered her:

"Proud Diomedes, son of Tydeus,
wounded me, for I was carrying off
Aeneas, my dear son, away from battle.
Of all men, he's the one I love the most.
Now grim war is not just Trojans and Achaeans,
for Danaans fight against immortals, too."

Dione, queen among the goddesses, replied:

"Be brave, my child, hold on, though you're in pain.   450
Many of us living on Olympus
have been hurt by men in our attempts
to bring harsh troubles on each other.
Ares suffered, too, when mighty Otus
and Ephialtes, children of Aloëus,
tied him up in powerful manacles,
then kept him prisoner in a brass jar
for thirteen months. Ares would've died there,
with all his war-lust, if their step-mother,
fair Eëriboea, had not told Hermes.   460
He stole Ares secretly. Ares was exhausted.
That harsh imprisonment was breaking him.
Hera suffered, as well, when Hercules,
the powerful son of Amphitryon,
hit her right breast with a three-barbed arrow.
She was wracked by pain beyond all cure.
With them huge Hades also suffered
from a sharp arrow, when this same man,
this Hercules, a son of aegis-bearing Zeus,
shot him in Pylos, among the corpses there,   470
inflicting pain. Hades went straight to Zeus
at home on Olympus—his heart enraged,

104

in agony, the arrow buried deep
in his strong shoulder. He was incensed.
Paeëon healed him with pain-killing herbs
smeared on the wound, for Hades was immortal.
What a wretch he was, that Hercules,
a trouble maker. He didn't hesitate
to commit bad acts with that bow of his
against the gods who dwell on Mount Olympus.   480
But Athena, the bright-eyed goddess,
prompted Tydeus' son to go at you.
Still, he's a fool for not remembering
the man who fights wars against immortals
does not live long. His children have no chance
to prattle to their father at his knee,
once he comes home from war's grim butchery.
Diomedes is surely powerful—
but he should take care. A greater power than you
may come against him. Then Aegialeia,   490
wise daughter of Adrestus, brave wife
of horse-taming Diomedes, with cries of sorrow
will rouse all her dear household from their sleep,
lamenting the husband whom she married,
the best of the Achaeans."

           As she said this,
with her hand Dione cleaned away the ichor
on Aphrodite's wrist, healing the hand,
curing Aphrodite of her pain. Looking on,
Athena and Hera teased Zeus, son of Cronos:

       "Father Zeus, you won't get angry with me   500
       for what I say, will you? Aphrodite,
       trying to coax some new Achaean woman
       into running off with one of those Trojans
       she loves so much, must have been caressing
       some well-dressed Achaean lady and scratched
       her delicate hand on a golden brooch."

When they spoke, the father of gods and men smiled,

called for golden Aphrodite, and then said to her:

> "My child, this warfare is not your business.
> You should concern yourself with your own work— 510
> love, especially erotic love in marriage.
> Swift Ares and Athena will take care of this."

As the gods talked the matter over with each other,
Diomedes, expert at war cries, sought out Aeneas.
Though he knew Apollo himself was shielding him,
he had no fear at all of that great god, pushing on
to kill Aeneas, then strip his fine armour from him.
Three times he charged forward, in a frenzy for the kill.
Three times Apollo pushed back his shining shield.
But when for the fourth time he came on like a god, 520
Apollo, the far shooter, in a terrifying voice, cried out:

> "Take care, son of Tydeus. Go back.
> Don't think you're equal to the gods.
> The race of men who walk upon the ground
> can never match the race of deathless gods."

At these words, the son of Tydeus drew back somewhat,
avoiding the anger of Apollo, the far shooter.
Apollo put Aeneas some distance from the fight,
on sacred Pergamus, where his temple stood.[1]
There, in the large shrine, Leto and Artemis, 530
the archer goddess, healed Aeneas, restoring him
to his former power and magnificence.
Apollo of the silver bow then made an image,
a copy of Aeneas, with matching armour,
around which Trojans and brave Achaeans fought,
hacking away at ox-hide covering their chests,
at the round shields or smaller shields with fringes.
Phoebus Apollo then called to foolhardy Ares:

> "Ares, Ares, you bloodstained man-killer,
> can't you return to Diomedes 540

[1] Pergamus is the high citadel of Troy, inside the city.

and remove him from the battle? Right now,
he'd stand and fight with Father Zeus himself.
First, he wounded Aphrodite on the wrist,
fighting at close quarters. Then he flung himself,
like some god, at me."

After saying this,
Apollo took a seat high up on Pergamus.
Murderous Ares went in among the Trojan ranks,
inspiring the troops. In the shape of Acamas,
Thracian leader, he yelled at Priam's royal sons:

"You sons of Priam, that god-nurtured king,   550
why are you still allowing the Achaeans
to keep slaughtering your troops? Are you waiting
until they fight by the well-built city gates?
There lies great-hearted Anchises' son,
Aeneas, whom we honour as we do prince Hector.
Come, let's save our brave comrade from the battle roar."

Ares' words gave each man courage and blood-zest for war.
Then Sarpedon spoke to Hector, bitterly complaining:

"Hector, where's that courage you used to have?
You kept claiming you could guard the city   560
on your own, without your people or your allies,
using your own family and relatives.
Looking round now, I can't see them here,
any of them. They've all taken refuge,
like dogs around a lion. Those of us
who've come as allies, we do all the fighting.
I marched here as an ally, traveling far,
for Lycia is a long, long way from here,
by the swirling river Xanthus, where I left
my dear wife, my infant son, much property,   570
something poor men covet. But for all that,
I urge my Lycian troops to action,
I stand and fight all comers on my own,
when I've nothing for the enemy to take.

107

But you stand around, without urging men
to fight back or defend their wives. Watch out.
You may become a prize yourself—a trophy
for your enemies. You'll be like a fish
snared in the meshes of a fatal net.
They'll quickly smash your well-built city.   580
You should be thinking of this day and night,
imploring leaders of your famous allies
to hold on staunchly, thus preventing them
from mounting any serious complaints."

Sarpedon's speech stung Hector's heart. Fully armed,
he quickly jumped down from his chariot to the ground.
Waving two sharp spears, he roamed through all the army,
rousing men to fight, steeling hearts for dreadful war.
Troops rallied once more and turned to face Achaeans.
Argives, too, stood firm. The men did not withdraw.   590
As on the sacred threshing floor wind blows the chaff,
while men stand winnowing the crop, when Demeter,
with her golden hair, separates the grain from chaff
in the rushing breeze, and piles of chaff grow whiter,
so then Achaean troops grew white, covered with dust
stirred up by horses' hooves. It coloured the sky bronze.
So the chariots came on to battle once again,
wheeled round by drivers' strong ferocious hands.
Headstrong Ares assisted Trojans in the battle,
concealing them in darkness, roaming everywhere,   600
carrying out his orders from Phoebus Apollo,
god with the golden sword, who'd told him to arouse
the Trojans' spirits when he saw Pallas Athena
leave the fighting, for she was helping the Danaans.

Apollo then sent Aeneas from his costly shrine,
putting fighting strength into this warrior's heart,
his people's shepherd. Aeneas rejoined his friends,
who were overjoyed to see him safe and sound—alive—
approaching with brave spirits. They didn't question him.
They had too much other work at hand to do.   610
For Apollo, god with the silver bow, and Ares,

the man killer, along with insatiable Strife,
had stirred things up there on the battlefield.

Then the two Ajaxes, Odysseus, and Diomedes
roused Danaans, urging them to battle.
They did not fear the Trojans' powerful attack
and stood their ground like clouds set in place by Zeus,
son of Cronos, above a range of mountain peaks
on a windless day, quite motionless, while the force
of North Wind and other raging blasts is sound asleep.   620
When these storm winds blow, they scatter shadowy clouds.
That's the way Danaans held their positions then,
without flinching, without fear. The son of Atreus
moved through the troops and gave out many orders.

"My friends, be men. Let courage fill your hearts.
In the heat of battle remember honour,
each man's reputation. When men recall
their honour, more troops are saved than slaughtered.
Those who run away lose life and fame."

Agamemnon spoke, then quickly hurled his spear.   630
He hit a good fighting man, comrade to Aeneas,
great-hearted Deïcoön, son of Pergasus,
whom Trojans honoured as they did king Priam's sons,
for he was quick to take his place among the best,
the men who do their fighting at the very front.
Mighty Agamemnon's spear struck against his shield,
but the shield could not hold out—the bronze went through,
piercing Deïcoön's belt and sinking in his gut.
He fell with a thud, his armour rattling round him.

Then Aeneas killed two of the best Danaans,   640
Crethon and Orsilochus, whose father lived
in well-built Phere, a man of property,
descended from the river Alpheus, whose broad streams
flow through Pylian land. The river bore Orsilochus,
king of many men, and Orsilochus fathered
great-hearted Diocles, to whom were born twin sons,

Crethon and Orsilochus, experts in all aspects of war.
These two, once grown, came with Argives in black ships
to Troy, city rich in horses, to win honour
for Agamemnon and Menelaus, sons of Atreus.   650
Death's final moment took them in. As two lions,
cared for by their mother in a deep thick forest
on a mountain peak, steal stout sheep and cattle
and plunder people's farmsteads, until they perish,
killed by sharp bronze in the hands of men, so these two died,
cut down by Aeneas. They fell like lofty pines.

War-loving Menelaus felt pity for these two,
seeing them die. He made his way through the men's front ranks,
armed in glittering bronze, brandishing his spear.
Ares stirred his battle spirit, planning his death   660
at Aeneas' hand. But then Antilochus,
son of great-hearted Nestor, saw Menelaus.
He hurried through the foremost ranks, in his concern
for this shepherd of the people, that if he came to grief,
all their efforts would be completely futile.
Menelaus and Aeneas, now faced each other,
with eager hands and spears, ready to begin the fight.
But when Antilochus stood by Menelaus,
Aeneas, though a swift fighter, started to withdraw,
seeing these two men standing their ground together.   670
So Menelaus and Antilochus dragged the corpses
of Crethon and Orsilochus to Achaean troops,
placed the two dead heroes in the hands of friends,
then turned back to fight with those in the front ranks.

Antilochus and Menelaus then killed Pylaemenes,
a man like Ares, leader of the Paphlagonians,
great-hearted, shield-bearing men. The son of Atreus,
famous spearman Menelaus, struck him,
as he stood up in his chariot, hitting him
right on his collar bone. Antilochus hit Mydon,   680
Atymnius' noble son, the attendant driver,
as he was wheeling his sure-footed horses round.
He struck him with a rock square on the elbow.

110

The reins, decorated with rich ivory,
fell from his hands onto the dusty ground.
Antilochus sprang out and with his sword struck Mydon
on the temple. Gasping with pain, Mydon pitched over,
and tumbled from the well-made chariot headfirst,
his head and shoulders disappearing in the dirt.
For some time he stayed stuck, buried in deep sand,   690
until his horses kicked him flat, level with the dust,
stamping him into the ground, as Antilochus
whipped them on, leading them back to Achaean troops.

Hector saw this from the lines. He ran against them,
shouting wildly, with strong Trojan soldiers in support.
Leading these men came Ares along with fearful Strife,
bringing war's pitiless and murderous confusion.
Ares worked with a huge spear in his hands, moving round,
sometimes behind Hector, sometimes in front of him.
When Diomedes, skilled in war cries, noticed Ares,   700
he shuddered—just a man crossing a large plain
stops at a raging river rushing to the sea,
looks helplessly at swirling foam, and moves away—
so Tydeus' son backed off then, saying to his men:

> "My friends, we're so amazed prince Hector
> is such a spearman, so courageous, warlike.
> But he's always got some god beside him,
> to ward off destruction. Right now, it's Ares
> he's has with him, looking like a mortal man.
> Stay turned towards the Trojans, but fall back.   710
> Don't try to fight it out with gods."

Diomedes spoke. Trojans then approached much closer.
Hector killed two men, keen warriors—Menesthes
and Anchialus—both riding in a single chariot.
Seeing them fall, great Telamonian Ajax felt pity.
He approached, stood firm, then threw his shining spear.
The spear struck Amphion, son of Selagus,
who owned much property in Paesus, with many crops.
Fate led him to become allied with Priam and his sons.

Ajax, son of Telamon, hit Amphion in the belt.   720
The long-shadowed spear struck hard, low in his gut.
He collapsed with a crash. Noble Ajax ran up
to strip the armour off, but Trojans showered him
with bright, sharp spears. His shield took many hits.
He pushed his heel into the corpse and yanked out his bronze spear.
But the hail of weapons stopped him stripping off
Amphion's fine armour from his shoulders.
He feared the fierce brave Trojans standing by the corpse,
for many spearmen crowded him and forced him back.
And Ajax, for all his massive size and strength,   730
for all his courage, had to withdraw, shaken.

As these men toiled in frantic battle, powerful fate
drove strong, brave Tlepolemus, son of Hercules,
against godlike Sarpedon. These two men approached,
facing each other at close quarters, son and grandson
of cloud-gathering Zeus. Tlepolemus called out first:

> "Sarpedon, counselor to the Lycians,
> what forces you to cower down right here,
> quite ignorant in battle? Those who say
> you're aegis-bearing Zeus' son are liars.   740
> You're far inferior to those men born of Zeus
> in times long past. Consider mighty Hercules,
> my father. He was quite different, they say—
> steadfast, brave, his spirit like a lion.
> He came here once for Laomedon's horses.
> With fewer men and only six ships, he sacked
> the Trojan city and emptied all its streets.
> But you've a paltry spirit, your troops
> are withering away. And it's impossible
> you'll help the Trojans by coming here   750
> from Lycia, even if you're powerful.
> I'll kill you, and you'll pass through Hades' gate."

Sarpedon, Lycian leader, then said in reply:

> "Yes, Tlepolemus, Hercules did destroy

sacred Ilion, but through the foolishness
of the city's king, high-born Laomedon,
who deceived the man who'd worked so well for him.
He didn't offer Hercules the horses
he'd come so far to get.[1] As for you,
I'll now see to your death, that fatal blackness.   760
You'll give me great glory, and your life
you'll give to famous horseman Hades."

Sarpedon spoke. Tlepolemus raised his ash spear high.
Then two long spears flew from their hands together.
Sarpedon's spear hit Tlepolemus right in the neck.
The cruel point kept going. Dark night covered up his eyes.
Tlepolemus' long spear struck Sarpedon in his left thigh.
Its bloodthirsty point pierced him, aiming for the bone.
On this occasion, Father Zeus held off his fate.
His brave companions carried off godlike Sarpedon,   770
pulled down by the long spear's weight, as it dragged behind.
No one thought to pull the ash spear from his thigh,
so he could walk. They were in such a rush to shift him.

On the opposing side, well-armed Achaeans
carried Tlepolemus away from battle.
Godlike Odysseus noticed them, his spirit steady,
but his fond heart was burning, as he turned over
in his mind, whether to chase after that son of Zeus,
loud thunderer, or stay to kill more Lycians.
But Fate did not decree that brave Odysseus   780
should kill Zeus' mighty son with his sharp bronze.
Athena turned his heart against that Lycian crowd.
So he killed Coeranus, Alastor, Chromius,
Alcandrus, Halius, Noëmon, and Prytanis.
Lord Odysseus would have killed still more Lycians,
if Hector of the flashing helmet had not seen him,
then gone through the ranks in front, armed in shining bronze,
terrifying Danaans. Sarpedon, son of Zeus,

---

[1]Hercules killed a monster to help Laomedon, king of Troy. But Laomedon did not
give Hercules the promised reward of horses. So Hercules raised an army and
captured Troy.

113

was glad to see him coming. He implored Hector:

> "Son of Priam, don't let me lie here,   790
> a trophy for Danaans. Rescue me.
> Let me remain forever in your city,
> since it seems I'll not be going home
> to cheer up my dear wife and infant son."

Hector of the flashing helmet made no reply.
He charged on, eager to force the Argives quickly back,
to massacre large numbers of their soldiers.
God-like Sarpedon's noble comrades placed him
by a fine oak tree, sacred to aegis-bearing Zeus.
Pelagon, his strong, well-loved attendant, then pushed   800
the ash spear straight out through his thigh. Sarpedon fainted.
A mist fell, clouding his eyes, but soon he breathed again.
North Wind's breeze revived him, blowing air into his heart,
as his spirit panted, gasping his life away.

Argives weren't driven back to their black ships by Ares
or by bronze-armed Hector. Nor did they wheel about
to battle Trojans face to face. They kept moving back,
once they realized Ares was with the Trojans.

Among the Argives, who were the first and last men killed
by Hector, son of Priam, and brazen Ares?   810
They were godlike Teuthras, Orestes the charioteer,
Trechus, an Aetolian spearman, Oenomaus,
Helenus, son of Oenops, and Oresbius,
with his glittering belt, a man who lived in Hyle
and kept himself preoccupied with wealth
along the shores of lake Cephisia. Beside him
lived even more Boeotians, owners of rich lands.

White-armed goddess Hera saw Argives being slaughtered
in the thick of battle. She spoke out to Athena.

> "Alas, Athena, child of aegis-bearing Zeus,   820
> tireless one, we've made an empty promise

to Menelaus, that he'd wipe out Troy,
that well-built city, before going home,
if we let murderous Ares rage on like this.
Come, let's both recall our fighting power."

Athena, the bright-eyed goddess, agreed with Hera's words.
So that revered goddess Hera, daughter of great Cronos,
went to prepare her horses with their golden bridles.
Then Hebe quickly checked the chariot's curved wheels,
bronze with eight spokes each, on axles made of iron,   830
wheel rims made out of imperishable gold,
edged with tires of close-fitted bronze, an amazing sight.
Silver axle boxes revolve on either side.
The body of the chariot has gold and silver strips.
Two rails run round it. The pole is made of silver.
On its end Hebe tied the cross-piece, lovely gold,
then fixed the golden collar straps. Hera, keen for war,
led her swift-footed horses out into their yoke.
Then Athena, daughter of aegis-bearing Zeus,
threw on her father's porch the embroidered gown   840
which she had made herself with her own hands.
She then put on the robe of cloud-gatherer Zeus
and armed herself with weapons for that wretched war.
She slung across her shoulders the fearsome tasseled aegis,
its borders woven with Fear, Strife, Force, terrorizing Panic,
with the chilling, horrifying and monstrous Gorgon's head—
the horrifying emblem of aegis-bearing Zeus.
On her head she placed a double-ridged gold helmet,
men from a hundred cities etched upon its four-part crest.
She set foot in her blazing chariot, grasping   850
her huge, strong, heavy spear, with which she kills men,
heroes who annoy her, goddess with a mighty father.
Hera quickly lashed the horses with her whip.
The gates of heaven scraped open on their own.
The Seasons supervise them, for they're in charge
of great heavenly Olympus, opening up
the dense packed clouds or closing them again.
Through these gates the goddesses led out their horses,
Hera lashing them ahead. They met the son of Cronos,

sitting some distance from the other gods,
on the highest crest of many-ridged Olympus.
Hera, white-armed goddess, reined in the horses,
then spoke to Zeus, most high son of Cronos:

> "Father Zeus, aren't you angry with Ares
> for killing off those warriors? He's wiped out
> so many Achaean men, good ones, too,
> and so rashly. It's not right. It pains me.
> Meanwhile, Aphrodite and Apollo,
> with his silver bow, are enjoying themselves,
> happy about this madman they've unleashed,
> who has no sense of what's appropriate.
> Father Zeus, would I annoy you very much
> if I hurt Ares and chased him from this fight?"

Cloud gatherer Zeus smiled and then said in reply:

> "All right, then, do that. But set Athena,
> goddess of the battle spoils, against him.
> For she's the one who's most accustomed
> to inflicting nasty pains on Ares."

White-armed goddess Hera agreed with what Zeus said.
She whipped the horses on. They flew off willingly,
mid-way between the starry heaven and earth.
As far as a man on a height can see in the distant haze
as he looks out across the wine-dark sea, that's how far
gods' snorting horses vault in just one stride.
When they came to Troy's two flowing rivers,
where the Simoeis and the Scamander meet,
white-armed goddess Hera stopped the horses,
loosed them from the chariot and hid them in thick cloud.
Simoeis produced ambrosia for them to eat.
The goddesses moved stealthily, like wild pigeons,
eager to assist the Argive troops. They reached that place
where most of the bravest men were fighting, in a crowd
by mighty Diomedes, tamer of horses,
like lions who eat raw meat or wild boars whose strength

is not easily exhausted. In that place Hera,
white-armed goddess, stood up, looking just like Stentor,
a great-hearted, loud-throated man, whose voice could shout
with the strength of fifty men. Hera cried out:

> "Shame on you, you Argive warriors.
> You're a disgrace, good only for display.   900
> When lord Achilles used to go to battle,
> the Trojans didn't dare to venture out
> beyond the Dardanian gates. They feared
> his mighty spear. But now they're fighting
> well outside the city, by our hollow ships."

With these words, she roused each man's heart and spirit.
Bright-eyed Athena quickly moved to Diomedes.
She found that king beside his chariot and horses,
recovering from the wound from Pandarus' arrow.
The sweat under the wide strap of his round shield   910
was bothering him. The chafing made his arms grow tired.
He was lifting up the strap, wiping off dark blood.
Setting her hand on the chariot yoke, the goddess said:

> "Tydeus had a son not much like his father.
> He may have been short, but he was a fighter.
> When I would not allow him into battle
> or to display himself, that time he came
> to Thebes alone, far from his Achaeans,
> in the middle of all those Cadmeans,
> I told him to be quiet at the palace feast.   920
> But he possessed a powerful spirit
> always active in him. So he challenged
> Cadmean young men and beat them easily.
> That's how much I helped him. Now I stand here,
> beside you, taking care of you, your friend.
> And I'm telling you to fight the Trojans.
> But you're either weary after so much action,
> your limbs worn out, or fear has made you timid.
> If so, then you're no son of Tydeus,
> the son of warlike Oeneus."   930

In answer to Athena, mighty Diomedes said:

"I recognize you, goddess daughter
of aegis-bearing Zeus. I'll speak to you
quite openly, concealing nothing. It's not
that fear has made me hesitant or anxious.
But I'm remembering your own instructions,
what you laid down. You told me not to fight
face to face with any immortal god,
unless Zeus' daughter Aphrodite
should come to battle. With my sharp bronze,   940
I was to wound her. I've pulled myself back,
and told the other Argives to stay here,
since I see Ares dominates the fight."

Bright-eyed goddess Athena answered him:

"Diomedes, son of Tydeus,
you fill my heart with joy. Don't fear Ares
or any other immortal deity.
For I'll give you all the help you need.
But come, first let your sure-footed horses
charge at Ares. Hit him up close. Have no fear   950
of headstrong Ares, that madman, born evil,
that fickle god. Just now he gave his word
to me and Hera too that he would fight
the Trojans and assist the Argives. But now,
he's forgotten that and helps the Trojans."

Saying this, Athena grabbed Sthenelus' hand
and hauled him from the chariot to the ground.
He jumped up at once. The goddess climbed up eagerly
beside lord Diomedes in the chariot.
The oaken axle groaned aloud, weighed down,   960
bearing the fearful goddess and the finest man.
Pallas Athena took up the reins and whip.
First, she led the sure-footed horses against Ares.
He was removing armour from huge Periphas,
Ochesius' fine son, by far the best of the Aetolians.

Blood-stained Ares was stripping him of all his weapons.
Then Athena put Hades' helmet on her head,
so she was invisible to mighty Ares.
But man-killing Ares did see Diomedes.
He let the body of huge Periphas lie there,   970
where he'd first killed him and ripped out his spirit.
He strode straight up to horse-taming Diomedes.
When the two came to close quarters and faced each other,
Ares thrust his bronze spear first, over the yoke
and horses' reins, eager to take Diomedes' life.
Athena, bright-eyed goddess, hands gripping the reins,
shoved the spear aside, so its thrust was harmless,
above the chariot. Diomedes, skilled in war cries,
then made the second thrust with his bronze spear.
Pallas Athena guided the weapon right to Ares' gut,   980
the lower part where his waist band went around him.
Diomedes wounded Ares, piercing his fair skin,
then pulled back on his spear. Brazen Ares roared
as loud as the screams of nine or ten thousand men
when they clash in war. Fear seized Achaeans—Trojans, too.
They shuddered. That's how strong that cry sounded
as it came from Ares, insatiable for war.
Just as a dark mist moves upward from the clouds,
when in hot weather a strong wind arises,
so brazen Ares looked to Tydeus' son, Diomedes,   990
as the god at once soared up into the clouds,
ascending to wide heaven. Ares, in a rush,
went to the gods' home, steep Olympus, sat by Zeus,
distressed at heart. He showed Zeus where he'd been wounded,
dripping with immortal blood, then made his complaint.
His words had wings.

                    "Father Zeus,
          aren't you incensed at this barbarity?
          We gods are always suffering dreadfully
          at each other's hands, when we bring men help.
          We all lay the blame for this on you.   1000
          For you gave birth to that insane young girl,
          your destructive daughter, always busy

119

with some nastiness. All the other gods,
all those on Mount Olympus, do what you say.
And each of us is subject to your will.
But you never punish her in word or deed.
You do nothing, because you gave birth to her
yourself, to Athena, your vicious daughter.[1]
Just now she urged proud Diomedes,
son of Tydeus, to charge insanely   1010
against deathless gods. First he attacked
Aphrodite and struck her on the wrist.
Then he charged me, even me, like a god.
But my quick feet took me away. If not,
I'd be in lasting pain with the fearful dead,
or have barely lived, wounded by bronze spears."

Scowling at him, cloud-gatherer Zeus replied:

"You hypocrite, don't sit there whining at me.
Among the gods who live on Mount Olympus,
you're the one I hate the most. For you love war,   1020
constant strife and battle. Your mother, Hera,
has an implacable, unyielding spirit.
It's hard for me to control how she reacts
to what I say. You're suffering because of her,
through her conniving, that's what I think.
But I'll leave you in pain no longer.
You're my child—your mother and I made you.
But if you'd been born from any other god,
by now you'd be lower than the sons
of Ouranos—you're so destructive."[2]   1030

Zeus spoke. He instructed Paeëon to heal Ares.
Paeëon cured him by spreading pain-killing herbs,
for Ares wasn't born to die. Just as fig juice
added quickly to white milk clots it at once,

[1]Athena sprung from Zeus' head and therefore had no mother.
[2]Ouranos was the original god who was overthrown by his son Cronos. Zeus fought
against Cronos and the other children of Ouranos and imprisoned them deep in the
earth.

as it's stirred, that's how fast headstrong Ares healed.
Hebe washed him and clothed him in fine garments.
He sat beside Zeus, son of Cronos, enjoying his splendour.

Athena of Alalcomenae and Argive Hera
returned once more to mighty Zeus' house,
now they'd stopped man-killing Ares' slaughter.

Book Six
Hector and Andromache

*[The battle continues; Menelaus captures Adrestus; Agamemnon
refuses ransom; Helenus gives advice to Hector; Glaucus and Diomedes
prepare to fight; Glaucus tells the story of Bellerophon; Glaucus and
Diomedes exchange armour in friendship; Hector goes to Troy, talks to
his mother; Hector talks to Paris and Helen; Hector goes home, talks to
his housekeeper; Hector meets Andromache and Astyanax; Hector
prays for his son's future; Paris rejoins Hector at the gates]*

Now the grim war between Trojans and Achaeans
was left to run its course. The battle raged,
this way and that, across the entire plain,
as warriors hurled bronze-tipped spears at one another,
between the Simoeis and Xanthus rivers.

Ajax, son of Telamon, Achaea's tower of strength,
was the first to break through ranks of Trojans,
punching out some breathing room for his companions.
He hit Acamas, son of Eussorus, a strong brave soldier,
best of the Thracians. Ajax's spear struck him first   10
on the peak of his horse-plumed helmet. The sharp bronze
drove right into his forehead—dead in the centre—
straight through bone into the brain. Darkness fell on his eyes.

Diomedes, expert in war cries, killed Axylus,
son of Teuthras, a rich man, from well-built Arisbe.
People really loved him, for he lived beside a road
and welcomed all passers-by into his home.
But not one of those men he'd entertained now stood
in front of him, protecting him from wretched death.
Diomedes took the lives of two men—Axylus   20
and his attendant charioteer, Calesius.
So both men went down into the underworld.

Euryalus killed Dresus and Opheltius,
then charged after Aesepus and Pedasus,

whom the naiad nymph Abarbarea bore
to noble Boucolion, son of high-born Laomedon,
his eldest son. His mother bore Pedasus in secret.
Bucolion had had sex with the nymph
while tending to his flock. She became pregnant,
then gave birth to two twin sons. Euryalus,   30
son of Mecistus, slaughtered both of them,
destroying their strength and splendid bodies.
Then he stripped the armour from their shoulders.

Next, fierce warrior Polypoetes killed Astyalus.
With his bronze spear Odysseus killed Pidytes from Percote.
Teucer slaughtered lord Aretaon, and Antilochus,
Nestor's son, with his glittering spear killed Ableros.
Agamemnon, king of men, killed Elatus,
who lived in high Pedasus, beside the banks
of the fair-flowing river Satnioeis.   40
Heroic Leitus knocked down Phylacus, as he was fleeing.
And Eurypylus then slaughtered Melanthus.

Menelaus, skilled in war cries, took Adrestus still alive.
His horses had panicked and bolted off across the plain.
They charged into a tamarisk bush and snapped the pole
on the curved chariot, right at the very end.
The horses then ran off towards the city, where others,
panic stricken, were headed, too. Adrestus
rolled out of the chariot beside the wheel,
face down in the dirt. Menelaus, son of Atreus,   50
stood there over him, holding his long-shadowed spear.
Adrestus clutched Menelaus by the knees and begged:

> "Take me alive, son of Atreus—you'll get
> good ransom. My father is a wealthy man,
> owns lots of things—bronze, silver, well-worked iron.
> So he'll give you a splendid ransom,
> if he learns I'm by Achaean ships, alive."

Adrestus pleaded. Menelaus' heart in his chest was moved.
He was about to hand Adrestus to his attendant,

to take back captive to the fast Achaean ships.
But then Agamemnon came running up to him,
sharply criticizing Menelaus:

> "Menelaus, you soft-hearted man,
> why are you sparing men's lives like this?
> In your own home, Trojans treated you
> exceptionally well, did they not?
> So don't let any one of them evade
> a terrible destruction at our hands—
> not even the young child still carried
> in his mother's belly. Let no one escape.
> Let everyone in Troy be slaughtered,
> without pity, without leaving any trace."

With these words, by this appeal to justice,
he changed his brother's mind. So Menelaus
shoved heroic Adrestus away from him.
Mighty Agamemnon then speared him in the side.
Adrestus fell onto his back. The son of Atreus
placed his heel down on his chest and pulled the ash spear out.

Then Nestor addressed the Argives, shouting:

>   "My friends,
> Danaan heroes, comrades of Ares,
> let no one lag behind to pick up loot,
> seeking to reach our ships with all you can.
> Let's kill the enemy instead. Later,
> with the corpses on the plain, you'll have time
> to strip off bodies of the slaughtered men."

With this Nestor stirred each man's strength and spirit.
Then Achaeans, filled with love of war, would once more
have beaten Trojans, broken by cowardice,
back in flight to Troy, if Helenus, a son of Priam,
by far the best at reading omens, had not spoken out.
Standing by Hector and Aeneas, Helenus said:

"Aeneas, Hector, among Trojans and Lycians,
the main weight falls particularly on you,
for you are, in all attacks, the best at fighting,
at strategy. Make a stand right here.
Rally the men before the city gates.
Move around through the entire army,
before men run and fall into their women's arms.
How that would make our enemies rejoice!
Then, once you've restored the spirits   100
in all our ranks, we'll stand right here
and fight Danaans, no matter how hard pressed.
For then we'll have no other option.
And you, Hector, go into the city.
Speak to our mother, yours and mine.
Tell her to assemble the old women
at the temple of bright-eyed Athena,
on the city heights. She should take the key,
open the doors of the sacred building,
then place in the lap of the goddess there,   110
fair-haired Athena, the garment she thinks
loveliest, the greatest in the palace,
the one she likes far above the others.
Tell her to promise Athena she'll give
twelve heifers in a temple sacrifice,
yearlings, as yet untouched by any goad,
if she will pity Troy, pity the wives
and Trojan children, if she will keep
Tydeus' son away from sacred Ilion,
that fierce spearman, that mighty warrior,   120
who makes men afraid—in my opinion,
the most powerful of all Achaeans.
We didn't fear Achilles, chief of men,
like this, although they say a goddess
was his mother. But this man's fighting rage
has no equal. We can't match his power."

Helenus spoke. Hector was convinced by his advice.
At once he jumped down from his chariot to the ground,
clutching his weapons. Brandishing two sharp spears,

he moved through all the army, urging men to fight, 130
rousing their spirits for the harsh brutality of war.
So men wheeled around and faced Achaean soldiers.
Argives then drew back and stopped the slaughter,
thinking that one of the immortal gods had come,
descending from star-lit heaven to help the Trojans,
enabling them to turn themselves around and fight.
Hector issued orders to the Trojans, shouting:

> "You proud Trojans, wide-renowned allies,
> friends, be men, summon up your fighting strength,
> while I go to Troy in person, to instruct 140
> the old men of the council and our wives
> to pray to the gods and promise sacrifice."

With these words, Hector of the shining helmet moved away.
As he went, black leather running round the outer edge
on his studded shield struck his neck and ankles.

Then Glaucus, son of Hippolochus, and Diomedes
moved out together between the armies, keen to fight.
When they'd come to close quarters, facing one another,
Diomedes, expert in war cries, was the first to speak:

> "Who are you, my dear man, among mortal men? 150
> For I've never clapped eyes on you before
> in those fights where men win glory.
> But now you've stepped out well beyond the ranks,
> showing more courage here than anyone,
> standing up to my long-shadowed spear.
> Men who face me end up with grieving parents.
> If you're one of the immortal gods
> come down from heaven, I won't fight you.
> Even mighty Lycurgus, son of Dryas,
> did not live long, once he started battling 160
> heavenly gods. He was the one who chased
> attendants of the frenzied Dionysus,
> forcing them to run by sacred Nysa.
> They all threw their holy wands onto the ground,

as murderous Lycurgus with his ox whip
kept beating them. Even Dionysus,
terrified, jumped in the ocean waves.
Thetis embraced him, as he shook with fear,
intimidated by Lycurgus' threats.
He angered the gods, who live without a care,   170
so the son of Cronos blinded him.
He didn't live much longer, not once he'd made
all the deathless gods displeased with him.
So I don't want to battle sacred gods.
But if you're a mortal man, someone
who eats earth's fruit, come closer to me,
so you can meet your death more quickly."

Glaucus, fine son of Hippolochus, replied:

"Son of Tydeus, great-hearted Diomedes,
why ask me about my ancestry?   180
Generations of men are like the leaves.
In winter, winds blow them down to earth,
but then, when spring season comes again,
the budding wood grows more. And so with men—
one generation grows, another dies away.
But if you wish to learn about my family,
so you're familiar with my lineage,
well, many people know the details.
There is a city in a part of Argos,
land where horses breed—it's called Ephyra.   190
There Sisyphus lived, craftiest man ever born,
Sisyphus, Aeolus' son. He had a son,
Glaucus, father of handsome Bellerophon.
The gods made Bellerophon so beautiful
and gave him the best qualities of men.
But Proetus, in his heart, plotted against him,
driving him from Argos, being much stronger,
for Zeus had given royal power to Proetus.
Now, Proetus' wife, lady Anteia,
desperate to have sex with Bellerophon,   200
wanted him to lie with her in secret.

But fiery Bellerophon refused,
for he possessed an honourable heart.
So Anteia made up lies, telling Proetus,
the king, 'You'll be murdered, Proetus,
unless you assassinate Bellerophon,
who wants to have sex with me against my will.'
Proetus was overcome with anger
at what he'd heard, but was reluctant
to kill Bellerophon—in his heart   210
he shrank from such an evil act.
He sent Bellerophon to Lycia,
with a lethal message, coded symbols
written on a folded tablet.[1] These told
many lies about Bellerophon.
Proetus told him to give the message
to his father-in-law, so he'd be killed.
Bellerophon went off to Lycia,
under safe conduct from the gods.
In Lycia he reached the river Xanthus,   220
and was honoured fully by the Lycian king,
with nine days of welcome entertainment,
nine sacrificial oxen. The tenth day,
when rose-fingered early Dawn appeared,
the Lycian king questioned Bellerophon,
asking to see the message he had brought
from Proetus, his son-in-law.
Once he'd received the evil message
from his son-in-law, he told Bellerophon,
first of all, to kill the Chimera,   230
an invincible inhuman monster,
but divine in origin. Its front part was a lion,
its rear a snake's tail, and in between a goat.
She breathed deadly rage in searing fire.
But Bellerophon killed the Chimera,
putting his trust in omens from the gods.
Next, he battled the Solymi, the worst fight,
they say, he ever had with mortal beings.

---

[1]This detail has been much discussed, since it is the only explicit reference in the
Iliad to some form of writing.

Then, third, he massacred the Amazons,
women who rival men. The king planned   240
one more devious evil trick against him,
as he was returning from the Amazons.
He set Lycia's best men in ambush.
But not a single one of them came back—
worthy Bellerophon had killed them all.
Then the king knew he must be divinely born.
So he kept him with him there in Lycia,
gave him his daughter's hand in marriage,
and half the honours in the entire kingdom.
The Lycians then gave him an estate   250
far better than the rest, rich in vineyards,
wheat-growing farmland, for him to keep.
The king's daughter bore him three children—
Isander, Hippolochus, and Laodamia.
Counselor Zeus then had sex with the girl.
She bore great Sarpedon, bronze-armed warrior.
But then Bellerophon angered all the gods.
He wandered out alone on the Aleian plain—
depressed in spirit, roaming there and shunning all.
Ares, insatiable in war, killed his son Isander,   260
while he was fighting the famous Solymi.
Artemis, goddess with the golden reins,
in anger killed the daughter of Bellerophon.
My father was Hippolochus. I claim
my descent from him. He sent me to Troy,
telling me repeatedly to strive always
to be the best, to outdo other warriors,
so I do not shame my father's family,
the finest men by far in Ephyra,
in spacious Lycia. That's my lineage,   270
the blood ancestry I claim as mine."

Glaucus spoke. Diomedes, skilled at war cries, rejoiced.
He jabbed his spear into the life-giving earth,
and then spoke to that shepherd of his people as a friend:

"In that case, you're an old friend of my father.

129

For Oeneus once entertained Bellerophon,
that worthy man, in his home for twenty days.
The two of them exchanged fine presents.
Oeneus gave a shining purple belt,
Bellerophon a gold two-handled cup,   280
which I left in my house when I came here.
I have no memory of Tydeus,
for he died while far away from me,
killed at Thebes with the Achaean army.
Now I'll be your kind host in middle Argos,
you'll be mine in Lycia, when I visit you.
Let's make sure we avoid each other's spears,
even in the thick of all the fighting.
For there are many famous Trojans and allies
for me to kill, any warrior the gods provide,   290
whom I can run after and catch on foot.
For you there are many Argives to destroy,
all you can manage. So let's trade armour.
Then those warriors here will all recognize
that we acknowledge our father's bonds as friends."

With these words, the two men jumped out of their chariots,
clasped hands and pledged their mutual friendship.
Then Zeus, son of Cronos, stole Glaucus' wits,
for he gave Tydeus' son his golden armour,
worth one hundred oxen, exchanging that   300
for armour made of bronze, worth only nine.

Meanwhile, Hector reached the Scaean Gates and oak tree.
The Trojans' wives and daughters ran up round him,
asking after children, brothers, relatives, and husbands.
Addressing each of them in turn, he ordered them
to pray to all the gods. For many were to face great grief.
He came to Priam's splendid palace, with porticos
of well-ground stone. It had fifty private bed rooms,
all of polished rock, built close to one another,
where Priam's sons slept with the wives they married.   310
On the opposite side, within the courtyard,
were twelve roofed rooms, all made of polished stone,

for Priam's daughters, built near one another,
where Priam's sons-in-law slept with their married wives.
It was here Hector's gracious mother, Hecuba,
met him, as she was going to the palace,
with Laodice, loveliest of all her daughters.
Taking his hand, she spoke to Hector:

                          "My child,
why have you left hard battle to come here?
The sons of Achaea—may gods curse them!—   320
press us hard, eager to fight around our city.
Your spirit has led you here to lift your hands
in prayers to Zeus from our city heights.
But wait. I can fetch some sweet wine for you,
so you can start by pouring a libation
to father Zeus and other deathless gods.
Then you may enjoy some, too, if you'll drink.
Wine restores strength well in a weary man,
and you've grown tired guarding your own family."

Great Hector of the shining helmet then replied: 330

"My dear mother, don't bring me some sweet wine,
for you'll weaken me. I'll lose my battle strength.
And I'm ashamed to offer up to Zeus
libations of bright wine with unwashed hands.
It's not at all appropriate for a man
spattered with blood and dirt to offer prayers
to the son of Cronos, lord of the black clouds.
But you must go to Athena's temple,
goddess of battle spoils, with burnt offerings.
First assemble the old women all together,   340
then place in Athena's lap, that fair-haired goddess,
the garment which you think is loveliest,
the very finest you keep here at home,
the one you like far better than the rest.
You must promise you will give Athena
twelve heifers in a temple sacrifice,
yearlings, as yet untouched by any goad,

if she will pity Troy, pity the wives
and Trojan children, if she will keep
Tydeus' son away from sacred Ilion,   350
that fierce spearman, that mighty warrior,
who makes men so afraid. You must leave now—
go straight to the temple of Athena,
goddess of battle spoils. I'll find Paris
and call him back, if he will to listen to me.
If only the earth would open under him,
swallow him up! Olympian Zeus raised him
as trouble for the Trojans, for brave Priam,
for his children. If I could see Paris die,
heading down to Hades, then I could say   360
my heart's sorrows were over and forgotten."

Hector spoke. His mother went into the house,
calling her attendants, who brought together
the matrons from the city. Then she went down
into the sweet-smelling room which stored their gowns,
fine embroidered work of women from Sidonia,
which godlike Paris brought with him from Sidon,
when he sailed across the broad sea, on that voyage
where he carried high-born Helen off. Hecuba took out
one of the gowns, the finest embroidery, the largest.   370
Glittering like a star, it lay at the bottom of the chest.
Taking that as Athena's gift, she walked away.
The old ladies followed her. At Athena's temple
fair-cheeked Theano, daughter of Cisseus,
wife of horse-taming Antenor, let them in.
Trojans had appointed her Athena's priestess.
All the women raised their hands, praying to Athena,
while Theano took that lovely robe and placed it
in Athena's lap, the goddess with the lovely hair,
then spoke out this prayer to great Zeus' daughter: 380

"Blessed Athena, sacred goddess,
defender of our city, break the spear
of Diomedes. Let him fall face down
before the Scaean Gates. If so, right now

132

we'll sacrifice twelve heifers in your temple,
beasts untouched by any goad, if you'll pity
our city, Trojans' wives and children."

The women prayed. But Pallas Athena refused their prayer.

As they made their plea to great Zeus' daughter,
Hector went to the fine house of Alexander.   390
He'd built it himself with fertile Troy's best craftsmen.
They'd made a bedroom, living quarters, and a yard
close to Priam and to Hector, on the city height.
Hector, loved by Zeus, went in the house, holding his spear,
sixteen feet long, bronze point glittering in front of him,
a gold band running round it. He met Alexander,
busy in his room with his fine weapons—shield
and body armour—polishing his curving bow.
Argive Helen sat there, too, with her attendant ladies,
directing servants in their famous handicrafts.   400
Seeing Paris, Hector spoke some sharp words to him:

"Paris, you're a worthless man.
It's quite wrong of you to nurse that anger
in your heart, while men are being destroyed,
fighting round the city, its steep walls.
It's because of you the sounds of warfare
catch fire round our city. You would fight
any man you saw avoiding battle,
fleeing war's brutality. So up with you,
or soon our city will go up in smoke,   410
with fire consuming everything."

Godlike Alexander then replied:

"Hector, your rebuke is not unfair,
without reason. So I'll speak plainly.
Listen and remember what I'm saying.
I'm not sitting in my bedroom here
out of spite or anger with the Trojans.
I want to grieve. Just now my wife urged me,

133

using gentle words, to rouse myself to fight.
And personally I think that would be best.
Winning shifts from one man to another. 420
Now, wait here, while I put on my armour.
Or go, and I'll come later, catch up with you."

Hector of the shining helmet did not answer.
So Helen spoke to Hector with these soothing words:

"O Hector, you're my brother, and me,
I'm a horrible, conniving bitch.
I wish that on that day my mother bore me
some evil wind had come, carried me away,
and swept me off, up into the mountains,
or to the waves of the tumbling, crashing sea. 430
Then I would've died before this happened.
But since gods have ordained these evil things,
I wish I'd been wife to a better man,
someone sensitive to others' insults,
with feeling for his many shameful acts.
This husband of mine has no sense now
and won't acquire any in the future.
I expect he'll get from that what he deserves.
But come in, sit on this chair, my brother,
since this trouble really weighs upon your mind— 440
all because I was a bitch—because of that
and Paris' folly, Zeus gives us an evil fate,
so we may be subjects for men's songs
in human generations yet to come."

Great Hector of the shining helmet answered Helen:

"Don't ask me to sit down, Helen. You're kind,
but you won't persuade me. For my heart's on fire
to help Trojans, who really miss me when I'm gone.
But you must rouse Paris, and he should hurry,
so he can catch me here in the city. 450
I'm going home, to visit my dear wife
and infant son, for I've no idea

134

if I'll be coming back to them again,
or if the gods will kill me at Achaean hands."

Saying this, Hector of the shining helmet went away.
Soon afterwards he reached his well-built house.
He didn't find white-armed Andromache at home,
for she'd left with the infant child, going to the walls
with a finely dressed attendant, in tears, lamenting.
When Hector didn't meet his fair wife in the house,   460
he went and, standing in the doorway, asked his servant:

> "Woman, tell me the truth. Where's Andromache?
> At one of my sisters? With a well-dressed wife
> of one of my brothers? Or is she at Athena's temple,
> where the other fine-haired Trojan women
> are praying to that fearful goddess?"

His busy housekeeper then answered him:

> "Hector, you asked me to tell you the truth.
> She didn't go to one of your sisters,
> or one of your brothers' well-dressed wives,   470
> nor did she go to Athena's temple,
> where other fine-haired Trojan women
> are praying to that fearful goddess.
> No. She went to Ilion's great tower,
> for she'd heard the Trojans were hard pressed,
> the power of Achaeans was so great.
> So she's hurrying off up to the walls,
> like someone in a fit. A nurse went, too,
> carrying the child."

Once the housekeeper spoke,
Hector left the house by the same route he'd come,   480
through the well-built streets, across the mighty city,
and reached the Scaean Gates, beyond which he'd go
out onto the plain. There his wife ran up to meet him,
Andromache, daughter of great-hearted Eëtion,
who'd included a large dowry with her.

135

Eëtion had lived below forested Mount Placus,
in Thebe, king of the Cilician people. She'd become
married wife to Hector of the shining helmet.
Now she met him there. With her came the nurse,
holding at her breast their happy infant child,   490
well-loved son of Hector, like a beautiful star.
Hector had named him Scamandrius, but others
called him Astyanax, lord of the city,
because Hector was Troy's only guardian.
Hector looked at his son in silence, with a smile.
Andromache stood close to him, weeping.
Taking Hector by the hand, she spoke to him.

    "My dear husband, your warlike spirit
    will be your death. You've no compassion
    for your infant child, for me, your sad wife,   500
    who before long will be your widow.
    For soon the Achaeans will attack you,
    all together, and cut you down. As for me,
    it would be better, if I'm to lose you,
    to be buried in the ground. For then I'll have
    no other comfort, once you meet your death,
    except my sorrow. I have no father,
    no dear mother. For lord Achilles killed
    my father, when he wiped out Thebe,
    city with high gates, slaying Eëtion.   510
    But he didn't strip his corpse—his heart
    felt too much shame for that. So he burned him
    in his finely decorated armour
    and raised a burial mound above the ashes.
    Mountain nymphs, daughters of aegis-bearing Zeus,
    planted elm trees all around his body.
    I had seven brothers in my home.
    All went down to Hades in a single day,
    for swift-footed lord Achilles killed them all,
    while they were guarding their shambling oxen   520
    and their white shining sheep. As for my mother,
    who ruled wooded Thebe-under-Placus,
    he brought her here with all his other spoils.

Then he released her for a massive ransom.
But archer goddess Artemis then killed her
in her father's house. So, Hector, you are now
my father, noble mother, brother,
and my protecting husband. So pity me.
Stay here in this tower. Don't orphan your child
and make me a widow. Place men by the fig tree,   530
for there the city is most vulnerable,
the wall most easily scaled. Three times
their best men have come there to attack,
led by the two Ajaxes, the sons of Atreus,
famous Idomeneus, and Diomedes,
Tydeus' courageous son, incited to it
by someone well versed in prophecy
or by their own hearts' inclination."

Great Hector of the shining helmet answered her:

                                          "Wife,
all this concerns me, too. But I'd be disgraced,   540
dreadfully shamed among Trojan men
and Trojan women in their trailing gowns,
if I should, like a coward, slink away from war.
My heart will never prompt me to do that,
for I have learned always to be brave,
to fight alongside Trojans at the front,
striving to win fame for father and myself.
My heart and mind know well the day is coming
when sacred Ilion will be destroyed,
along with Priam of the fine ash spear   550
and Priam's people. But what pains me most
about these future sorrows is not so much
the Trojans, Hecuba, or king Priam,
or even my many noble brothers,
who'll fall down in the dust, slaughtered
by their enemies. My pain focuses on you,
when one of those bronze-clad Achaeans
leads you off in tears, ends your days of freedom.
If then you come to Argos as a slave,

137

working the loom for some other woman,   560
fetching water from Hypereia or Messeis,
against your will, forced by powerful Fate,
then someone seeing you as you weep
may well say: 'That woman is Hector's wife.
He was the finest warrior in battle
of all horse-taming Trojans in that war
when they fought for Troy.' Someone will say that,
and it will bring still more grief to you,
to be without a man like that to save you
from days of servitude. May I lie dead,   570
hidden deep under a burial mound,
before I hear about your screaming,
as you are dragged away."

                          With these words,
glorious Hector stretched his hands out for his son.
The boy immediately shrank back against the breast
of the finely girdled nurse, crying out in terror
to see his own dear father, scared at the sight of bronze,
the horse-hair plume nodding fearfully from his helmet top.
The child's loving father laughed, his noble mother, too.
Glorious Hector pulled the glittering helmet off   580
and set it on the ground. Then he kissed his dear son
and held him in his arms. He prayed aloud to Zeus
and the rest of the immortals.

                          "Zeus, all you other gods,
grant that this child, my son, may become,
like me, pre-eminent among the Trojans,
as strong and brave as me. Grant that he may rule
Troy with strength. May people someday say,
as he returns from war, 'This man is far better
than his father.' May he carry back
bloody spoils from his slaughtered enemy,   590
making his mother's heart rejoice."

He placed his son in the hands of his dear wife.
She embraced the child on her sweet breast, smiling

through her tears. Observing her, Hector felt compassion.
He took her hand, then spoke to her.

       "My dearest wife,
don't let your heart be sad on my account.
No man will throw me down to Hades
before my destined time. I tell you this—
no one escapes his fate, not the coward,
nor the brave man, from the moment of his birth.   600
So you should go into the house, keep busy
with your proper work, with your loom and wool,
telling your servants to set about their tasks.
War will be every man's concern, especially mine,
of all those who live in Troy."

      Having said these words,
glorious Hector took his plumed helmet in his hands.
His beloved wife went home, often looking back,
as she went, crying bitterly. She quickly reached
the spacious home of Hector, killer of men.
Inside she met her many servants and bid them all lament. 610
So they mourned for Hector in his own house,
though he was still alive—they thought he'd not come back,
he'd not escape the battle fury of Achaean hands.

Paris did not wait for long in his high-roofed home.
Once he'd pulled on his famous armour, ornate bronze,
he hurried off on foot quickly through the city.
Just as some stalled stallion, well fed in the barn,
breaks his restraints, then gallops at top speed
across the plain, off to bathe in a fair-flowing river,
something he does habitually, proud of his strength, 620
holding his head high, mane streaming on his shoulders,
legs taking him swiftly to the grazing mares—
that's how Paris, son of Priam, hurried then,
rushing down from the heights of Pergamus,
gleaming like a ray of sunshine in his armour,
laughing with joy as his feet carried him so fast.
He soon met his brother Hector, turning away

from where he'd had his conversation with his wife.
Godlike Paris was the first to speak:

> "My dear brother, you're in a hurry.   630
> I'm holding you back with my delay,
> not coming as quickly as you asked."

Hector of the shining helmet answered Paris:

> "Brother, no one could justly criticize
> your work in battle, for you fight bravely.
> But you deliberately hold back
> and do not wish to fight. It pains my heart,
> when I hear shameful things about you
> from Trojans, who are suffering much distress
> because of you. But let's be on our way.   640
> We'll sort all this out later, if Zeus ever grants
> we arrange in place inside our homes
> bowls of wine to celebrate our freedom,
> in thanks to the eternal, heavenly gods,
> once we have driven away from Troy
> all these well-armed Achaeans."

Book Seven

Hector and Ajax

[Hector and Paris leave Troy, rejoin the fighting; Athena and Apollo plan to halt the battle; Helenus suggests Hector issue a challenge for single combat; Hector issues his challenge; no one responds; Nestor shames the Achaeans; Achaeans draw lots to see who will fight Hector; Ajax's lot falls out; Ajax's shield is described; Ajax and Hector fight; heralds intervene to stop them; Nestor suggests collecting the dead and building a defensive wall and ditch; in Troy Antenor suggests the return of Helen; Paris refuses but offers to return all the goods he took away; Idaios goes to the Argives to suggest a truce to bury the dead, repeats Paris' offer; the Achaeans refuse the offer; the armies collect and cremate the dead; the Achaeans build the wall; Poseidon objects to Zeus; both sides feast after the funeral rites]

After glorious Hector had talked with Paris,
he and his brother hurried through the gates,
both of them with hearts on fire to fight in battle.
Just as some god sends a breeze to sailors in distress,
when they work themselves too hard rowing out at sea,
bodies broken with fatigue at their polished oars—
that's how these two looked to the long-suffering Trojans.

Paris then killed Menesthius, king Areithous' son.
He lived in Arne, born from Areithous,
a mace fighter, and ox-eyed Phylomedusa.   10
Hector hit Eioneus with his sharp spear
in the neck, just under his bronze helmet rim.
His legs collapsed. Glaucus, son of Hippolochus,
leader of Lycians, amid the battle din,
struck Iphinous, son of Dexius, in the shoulder,
just as he was jumping in behind fast horses.
He fell out of his chariot down on the ground.
Then his limbs went limp and lifeless.

When goddess Athena with her glittering eyes
saw Argives being slaughtered in the battle frenzy,   20
she rushed down from Olympus heights to sacred Ilion.

141

Apollo, keeping watch from Pergamus,
came to confront her. He wanted victory
for Trojans. The two met one another by the oak tree.
Lord Apollo, son of Zeus, addressed Athena first:

> "Daughter of great-hearted Zeus, why has your spirit
> pushed you so eagerly down from Olympus?
> You want to change the tide of battle,
> giving victory to the Danaans.
> You don't pity Trojans as they're butchered.   30
> But it would be much better if you'd follow
> what I say—let's put an end to battle
> and the killing, for today. They'll fight again,
> later on, until they reach their goal in Troy,
> since the demolition of that city
> is what you goddesses desire in your hearts."

Bright-eyed Athena then said to Apollo:

> "God who works from far away, I agree—
> that's what I myself intended, coming
> from Olympus down to mingle here   40
> with Trojans and Achaeans. How will you get
> these troops to end this present battle?"

Lord Apollo, son of Zeus, answered Athena:

> "Let's rouse the powerful fighting spirit
> of horse-taming Hector, so he challenges
> one of the Danaans to fight him alone,
> in a grim single combat, one on one.
> Bronze-armed Achaeans, in admiration,
> may incite someone to fight lord Hector."

Apollo spoke, and bright-eyed Athena then agreed.   50

Helenus, Priam's much-loved son, in his heart
well understood the scheme the gods had planned.
So he went to Hector, stood by him, and said:

"Hector, son of Priam, wise as Zeus,
why not be persuaded by what I suggest,
since I'm your brother? Let other Trojans
and Achaeans sit. You should challenge
the best of the Achaeans to fight you,
a personal single combat, a grim fight.
I've heard the voices of eternal gods—   60
now is not your fated time to die."

Helenus spoke. Hector was elated with the plan.
He went into the middle of the Trojan ranks
gripping the centre of his spear and pushed men back.
The men sat down. Agamemnon, on his side,
got well-armed Achaeans to stop fighting, too.
Athena, with Apollo of the silver bow,
perched in the lofty oak tree sacred to Zeus,
who bears the aegis, looking like two vultures,
set to enjoy the unfolding human action.   70
Ranks of men were closely packed, bristling with shields,
with spears and helmets. As West Wind, when it starts to blow,
ruffles the sea, and waters under it grow black—
that's what ranks of Trojans and Achaeans looked like
out there on the plain. Hector then addressed both armies:

"Listen to me, you Trojans, you well-armed Achaeans,
so I may speak what my heart prompts.
High-ruling son of Cronos has quashed our pact,
intending to bring both of us bad things,
until you capture well-built Troy or else   80
are conquered at your seaworthy ships.
Achaea's finest men are here among you.
Let the one whose heart now drives him
to fight with me step out as champion,
your representative against lord Hector.
That's what I propose—let Zeus be my witness.
If your man kills me with his sharpened bronze,
let him strip my armour, take it away,
off to your hollow ships, but give my body
back to my house, so Trojans and their wives   90

may give me ritual burning once I'm dead.
If I kill your champion, if Apollo
grants me that triumph, I'll strip his armour,
take it to sacred Ilion and hang it
in the temple of Apollo, the far shooter.
I'll give up the body to be taken back
to well-decked ships, so long-haired Achaeans
can bury him and build his funeral mound
on the banks of the broad Hellespont.
Then people born in years to come who sail   100
their ships with many oars on the wine-dark sea
will say, 'This is the funeral mound of some man
who died long ago, the best of warriors,
killed by glorious Hector.' That's what they'll say.
And then my glory will never fade away."

Hector finished. The Achaeans all grew silent,
ashamed to duck the challenge, afraid to answer it.
At last Menelaus, sick at heart, stood up to speak,
reproaching them with bitter words of shame:

    "Alas, you boasters, you're Achaean women,   110
not men. This shame will mean total disgrace,
unless some Danaan now stands up to Hector.
All of you sitting here, without heart,
disgraced like this, may all of you dissolve,
disintegrate to earth and water.
I'll personally take up arms myself.
I'll fight Hector. The rope that's tied
to victory comes from heaven above,
from the hands of the immortal gods."

This said, Menelaus pulled his fine armour on.   120
And then, Menelaus, they would've seen you die
at Hector's hands—he was by far the stronger man—
if wide-ruling Agamemnon, son of Atreus,
king of the Achaeans, had not hurried up,
grabbed you by your right hand, and said these words:

"Lord Menelaus, have you lost your mind?
There's no need for you to act so foolishly.
Be patient, even though you're disappointed.
Don't volunteer from mere love of battle
to fight someone better than yourself,   130
for Hector, son of Priam, is a man
whom other men avoid. Even Achilles,
a far better man than you, was hesitant
to meet Hector in fights where men win fame.
So go now, sit down with your companions.
Achaeans will send out another man
as champion against Hector. Though he's fearless,
with boundless appetite for battle,
I think he'll be content to take a rest,
if he survives this combat, this grim fight."   140

Agamemnon's prudent speech changed his brother's mind.
Menelaus was convinced, and his attendants
gladly pulled the armour off his shoulders.

Then Nestor, standing up before the Argives, said:

"Alas, what great sorrow for Achaea!
Old horseman Peleus would cry with grief,
noble counselor of the Myrmidons.
When I was in his house, he loved to talk with me,
asking questions about men's families,
the ancestry of all Achaeans. If he knew   150
these warriors were all afraid of Hector,
he'd keep lifting up his dear hands in prayer
to the immortal gods that his spirit
leave his body and go down to Hades' home.
By father Zeus, Athena, and Apollo,
would I were as young as when the Pylian
and Arcadian spearmen gathered to fight
by the walls of Pheia, beside the banks
of the fast-flowing river Celadon.
Ereuthalion then stepped forward   160
as their champion, a godlike soldier,

145

wearing on his shoulders the armour
of king Areithous—that noble Areithous,
whom men and well-dressed women gave
the name of Mace-man, because he fought,
not with long spear or bow, but with an iron mace.
With that he smashed down ranks of warriors.
Lycurgus killed him, not in a fair fight,
but by a trick, in a narrow place,
where the iron mace could not protect him   170
from destruction. Lycurgus anticipated
Areithous' blow and struck him first
a spear thrust in the belly. He fell down,
dropping to the ground upon his back.
Lycurgus then stripped off the armour
which brazen Ares had given Areithous.
Lycurgus himself wore it in later fights.
And then, when he'd grown old in his own home,
he gave the armour to Ereuthalion,
his loyal attendant, who wore it as his own.   180
That's the armour he had on at that time,
when he challenged all our finest men.
They held back, afraid, not daring to accept.
But my spirit, full of fighting confidence,
incited me to take him on in battle.
By birth I was the youngest of them all.
I fought him, and Athena gave me glory.
I killed their biggest and most powerful man,
left his huge body sprawling on the ground.
Would I were that young now, my strength as firm.   190
Hector of the shining helmet would soon have
a man to fight. But now you warriors here,
although the finest of Achaean men,
aren't keen at all to face up to Hector."

Old man Nestor shamed them. Nine men in all stood up.
First to rise, well before the rest, was Agamemnon,
king of men. Strong Diomedes, son of Tydeus,
jumped up after him. Next came the two Ajaxes,
men clothed in an impetuous ferocity.

146

Then Idomeneus, his comrade Meriones, 200
and Eurypylus, Eumaeon's fine son, then Thoas,
son of Andraemon, then lord Odysseus.
They were all willing volunteers to fight with Hector.
Geranian horseman Nestor spoke out once again:

> "To choose, you must cast lots. Shake them well.
> The chosen man will greatly benefit
> well-armed Achaeans and his own heart, too—
> if he comes away from this grim fight,
> this dangerous combat."

Nestor spoke. The nine men
marked their lots and threw them in Agamemnon's helmet. 210
Troops held up their hands, praying to the gods, saying,
as they gazed up at wide heaven:

> "Father Zeus,
> let the choice fall on Ajax, or Tydeus' son,
> or on Mycenae's king, rich in gold."

Geranian horseman Nestor shook the helmet.
From it fell out the very lot men were hoping for,
the one for Ajax. A herald carried round the lot,
showing it to all the best Achaeans in the throng,
moving from left to right. But no one took it.
Each man declined. But when, in passing through the crowd, 220
the herald came to the one who'd scratched his mark
upon the lot and thrown it in the helmet,
noble Ajax held out his hand. Approaching Ajax,
the herald dropped the token in his palm.
Ajax looked at the mark and saw that it was his.
His heart was happy. Throwing the lot down on the ground
beside his feet, he said:

> "Friends, this marker here
> belongs to me. And I'm happy in my heart,
> for I think I'll overcome lord Hector.
> But come, while I put on my battle armour, 230

you should pray to lord Zeus, son of Cronos,
but silently, so Trojans don't find out—
or do it aloud, since we fear no one.
No man is going to force me to move off
through his power or will, if I don't consent,
or through his fighting skill. For I was born
and raised in Salamis, so I'm no novice."

Ajax spoke. Men prayed to lord Zeus, son of Cronos.
Gazing up to heaven, they uttered words like these:

"Father Zeus, ruling from Mount Ida,   240
most glorious one, most powerful—
grant Ajax victory, the winner's triumph.
But if you love Hector and look out for him,
grant them both equal strength, equal glory."

So men prayed. Ajax armed himself in glittering bronze.
When all his armour was in place around his body,
he moved forward, like some gigantic Ares
when he sets off to battle among warriors
whom Zeus, son of Cronos, has stirred up for war,
to fight with that war frenzy which consumes men's hearts.   250
That's how huge Ajax, bulwark of Achaeans,
came up then, a grim smile on his face, moving his feet
with giant strides. He clutched a long-shadowed spear.
When Argives looked at him, they felt great joy,
while the limbs of all the Trojans shook with fear.
Even in Hector's chest the heart beat rapidly.
But there was nothing he could do to pull back now,
retreat into the ranks. For he had made the challenge,
made it eagerly. Ajax approached bearing his shield.
It was like a tower made of bronze, with seven layers,   260
each one of ox-hide, a weapon made by Tychius,
the best of leather workers, who lived in Hyle.
He'd made the glittering shield for Ajax from the hides
of seven well-fed bulls. On top of these, he'd set
an eighth layer made of bronze. Telamonian Ajax
carried this shield in front of him. He came up,

stood quite close to Hector, then spoke out grimly:

> "Hector, now you'll come to recognize,
> one against one, just what the finest men
> are like among Danaans, not counting   270
> Achilles, breaker of men, with his lion's heart.
> He now lies by his curved sea-worthy ships,
> angry at Agamemnon, his people's shepherd.
> But there are lots of us who'll stand against you.
> So come on then. Let's start this fight."

Great Hector of the shining helmet then replied:

> "Noble Ajax, son of Telamon,
> leader of your people. Don't play with me,
> as if I were a witless child or woman
> who knows nothing of what war requires.   280
> For I understand well how to fight,
> how to kill men. I know how to shift
> my tanned leather shield to right or left,
> to me a crucial skill in fighting battles.
> I know how to charge into the frenzy
> of fast chariots, and I know how to dance
> to Ares' tune in the grim killing zone.
> I don't want to hit you with a sneaky shot,
> not a man like you, but in open combat,
> if I can manage it."

                         Once Hector spoke,   290
he balanced his long-shadowed spear and hurled it.
He hit Ajax's fearful seven-layered shield
on the outer covering of bronze, its eighth layer.
The tireless spear tore its way through six layers.
But it stopped at the seventh. Then noble Ajax,
in his turn, threw his long-shadowed spear at Hector.
His spear hit the even circle of Hector's shield,
broke through the glittering shield, and forced its way
through the breast plate and tunic covering his ribs.
Hector twisted to one side, evading a black fate.   300

The two men then both pulled the long spears from their shields
and charged each other, like flesh-eating lions
or savage boars, whose strength is inexhaustible.
With his spear Hector struck the centre of Ajax's shield,
but the bronze did not break through—its point bent aside.
Then Ajax charged ahead and speared Hector's shield,
breaking clean through and striking Hector as he lunged.
Its motion slashed at Hector's neck. Dark blood seeped out.
But Hector of the shining helmet didn't stop the fight.
He stepped back, picked up in his powerful hand a rock   310
lying there on the plain, a huge black jagged stone.
With this he hit Ajax's seven-layered shield
on its central boss, making the bronze ring out.
Then Ajax, in his turn, seized a much bigger stone,
swung it round and threw it with terrific force.
The rock, like a millstone, hit Hector's shield and smashed it.
Strength drained from Hector's limbs. He was thrown on his back,
with his shield pressing him on top, weighing him down.
At once Apollo raised him up. Now they would've fought
hand to hand with swords, if heralds, those messengers   320
of gods and men, had not stepped in, one from Trojans,
one from bronze-clad Achaeans—two trusted men,
Talthybius and Idaios. They held out their staffs,
symbols of their herald's office, between the two.
Then herald Idaios, a wise prudent man, spoke out:

> "You dear lads, fight no more. End this combat.
> Cloud-gatherer Zeus cares for you both.
> You're both fine fighters. We all know that.
> But night already is approaching.
> And it's good to be persuaded by the night."   330

Telamonian Ajax then said in reply:

> "Idaios, tell Hector here to give the word.
> For he was keen to challenge our best men.
> Let him speak first. I'll gladly follow what he says."

Great Hector of the shining helmet answered Ajax:

"Ajax, god has given you size, power,
judgment, and you're the strongest with the spear,
among Achaeans. For today let's end
our battle combat. We'll fight once again,
later on, until god decides between us,   340
awarding one of us the victory.
For night already is approaching,
and it's good to be persuaded by the night.
So you can bring joy to all Achaeans
by their ships, especially your clansmen,
your companions. And I can bring joy
to the mighty city of king Priam,
to Trojans and women in their trailing gowns.
They'll gather in holy processions now,
giving thanks on my behalf in prayer.   350
But come, let's exchange noteworthy presents
with each other, so Trojans and Achaeans
may say, 'These men fought in life-destroying war
but were reconciled and parted friends.'"

This said, Hector gave Ajax a silver-studded sword,
along with a scabbard and a well-cut sword belt.
Ajax gave Hector a shining purple belt.
Then they parted, Ajax going to Achaean troops,
Hector rejoining Trojans, who were overjoyed
to see him return alive, safe and sound,   360
surviving Ajax's fury, his unconquerable hands.
They'd given up all hope for Hector's safety.
Now they took him back with them into the city.

Well-armed Achaeans, for their part, led Ajax,
elated by his victory, to lord Agamemnon.
When they all came inside the son of Atreus' hut,
Agamemnon, king of men, sacrificed an ox,
a male five years old, to the exalted son of Cronos.
They flayed the beast, prepared and carved it up,
chopping it skillfully into tiny pieces.   370
They skewered these on spits, cooked them carefully,
and drew them off. This done, they prepared a meal and ate.

151

No one went unsatisfied. All feasted equally.
Wide-ruling Agamemnon, heroic son of Atreus,
acknowledged Ajax with the whole back cut of meat.
When everyone had had his fill of food and drink,
old Nestor spoke up first, outlining for them
a plan he had. Earlier his advice had seemed the best.
Keeping in mind their common good, he said:

> "Son of Atreus, you other Argive leaders,   380
> many long-haired Achaeans have been killed.
> Fierce Ares has scattered their dark blood
> beside the fair-flowing Scamander river.
> Their souls have departed down to Hades.
> So tomorrow you should call a halt.
> Stop Achaeans fighting. We should all assemble,
> then carry off the bodies of the dead
> with mules and oxen. Then we'll burn them
> a short distance from our ships, so each of us,
> when we return, may carry back the bones.   390
> Let's set up one single common funeral mound
> close by the fire and angled on the plain.
> Then with all speed from that mound we'll build
> some high walls with turrets, to guard us and our ships.
> In those walls we'll construct tight-fitting gates,
> so there's a path to drive our chariots through.
> Outside we'll dig a deep trench close by it,
> to enclose the walls and hold out chariots—
> soldiers, too, if those impetuous Trojans
> should ever drive us back in battle."   400

So Nestor spoke. All the kings approved his plan.

Meanwhile the Trojans were meeting on the city heights,
by Priam's palace doors—they were confused and fearful.
Antenor, a wise counselor, was the first to speak:

> "Listen to me, you Trojans, Dardan allies,
> so I may say what the heart in my chest prompts.
> Come now, let's give back Argive Helen

and her possessions to the sons of Atreus
for them to keep. We've broken the truce
and are fighting once again, so I don't see   410
how things will work out very well for us,
unless we carry out what I propose."

Antenor spoke, then sat down. Before them all,
lord Alexander, husband of fair-haired Helen,
stood up to reply. His words had wings:

                         "Antenor,
I'm not pleased with what you've said.
You know very well how to think up
some alternative, some better plan.
But if you truly mean what you've just said,
the gods themselves have muddled up your wits.   420
Now I'll speak to horse-taming Trojans.
I flatly refuse. I won't give up my wife.
But I will surrender all the goods
I carried back from Argos to our home.
I'm willing to give up all of it,
even to add to it things of my own."

Paris spoke, then sat back down. Priam stood up,
descendant of Dardanus, wise as the gods.
Thinking of their common cause, he spoke out:

       "Listen to me, Trojans, Dardan allies,   430
so I may state what the heart in my chest prompts.
You should prepare your dinner and then eat,
here in the city, as before. But remember—
keep sentries posted. Each man should stay awake.
Tomorrow morning Idaios should go
to the hollow ships, to tell the sons of Atreus,
both Agamemnon and Menelaus,
what Alexander has just now proposed,
the very man whose cause launched this dispute.
Idaios should propose this wise suggestion—   440
if they'll consent to postpone grim warfare,

153

so we can burn our dead, we'll fight later,
until god adjudicates between us
and awards one side the victory."

They heard what Priam said and readily agreed.
Throughout the army, in the ranks, they ate their dinner.

At dawn Idaios went out to the hollow ships.
There he found Danaans, companions of Ares,
assembled by the stern of Agamemnon's ship.
The loud-voiced herald, standing in their midst, spoke out: 450

"Son of Atreus, other Achaean leaders,
Priam and other noble Trojans asked me
to tell you what Alexander has proposed,
if that meets with your approval, an offer
you will want to hear. That man began our strife.
All the property which Paris brought here
in his hollow ships to Troy—how I wish
he'd died before that day!—he'll hand over
and add more goods from his own home.
But he says he'll not return that noble lady,   460
wife of Menelaus, though the Trojans wish
he'd do that. There's more. My orders tell me
to speak to you to see if you are willing
to put a stop to the harsh clash of war,
until such time as we have burned our dead.
We will fight later, until god chooses
between us, makes one of us the victors."

Idaios spoke. They all remained silent, speechless.
At last Diomedes, skilled at war shouts, cried out:

"Let no man now accept Alexander's stuff,   470
nor Helen. For it's quite clear, even to a fool,
the Trojans are tied down to lethal fate."

Diomedes spoke. All Achaea's sons roared out,
approving what horse-taming Diomedes said.

154

Mighty Agamemnon then addressed Idaios:

"Idaios, you yourself have heard our answer,
what Achaeans think of what you offer.
And I agree with them. But I don't object
to burning corpses, for when men die,
one should not deny the bodies of the dead   480
a swift propitiation in the flames.
So let Zeus, Hera's loud-thundering husband,
stand as witness here to our pledged word."

Saying this, Agamemnon held up his sceptre,
invoking all the gods. Idaios then returned,
going back to sacred Ilion. There the Trojans
and Dardanians were seated in a meeting,
a general assembly, awaiting his return.
He came, stood in their midst, and delivered his report.
Then they quickly organized two working parties—   490
some to gather bodies, others to get firewood.

Argives also moved swiftly from their well-decked ships.
Some hurried to bring in the dead, others to find wood.
Just as the sun began to shine down on the fields,
rising from the gently flowing Ocean depths,
climbing in the sky, the two groups met each other.
At that point it was hard to recognize each dead man.
They washed blood off with water and piled them onto carts,
shedding hot tears. Great Priam did not permit
his Trojans to lament. So they heaped the corpses   500
on the pyre in silence, hearts full of anguish.
Once they'd burned the bodies, they went back to sacred Troy.
Opposite them, in the same way, well-armed Achaeans
heaped their dead up on a pyre, sick at heart, burned them,
and then returned back to their hollow ships.

Next day, just before dawn, still at night, in half light,
a chosen group of Achaeans was awake around the pyre.
Beside it, on an angle, they made a common grave,
back from the plain. From that mound they built a wall,

155

with high towers, to defend them and their ships.
Inside the rampart they set close-fitting gates,
to make a passage so chariots could pass through.
Outside the wall they dug a big ditch, wide and deep,
close to the rampart, setting stakes down in the trench.

As long-haired Achaeans worked, gods sitting beside Zeus,
lord of lightning, gazed down on the huge construction,
the project undertaken by bronze-armed Achaeans.
Earthshaker Poseidon was the first to speak:

> "Father Zeus, will any mortal man
> on boundless earth, after this event,   520
> inform gods of his plans, of his intentions?
> Don't you see that long-haired Achaeans
> have built a new wall to protect their ships,
> dug a ditch around it, and yet have made
> no splendid sacrifice to us, the gods?
> The fame of this wall will reach everywhere,
> as far as light of dawn. People will forget
> that wall which Phoebus Apollo and myself
> worked hard to build for heroic Laomedon."

Cloud-gatherer Zeus, quite irked, answered Poseidon: 530

> "Such talk from you, mighty Earthshaker, is silly.
> Another god might well fear this design,
> some god with a far less powerful hand,
> a weaker spirit than your own. Your fame
> will reach as far as the shining light of dawn.
> Come now, when the long-haired Achaeans leave,
> sailing their ships to their dear native land,
> you can smash their wall, take it out to sea,
> bury the great shore under sand, and so erase
> that great Achaean wall completely."   540

As the gods discussed these things amongst themselves,
the sun went down and Achaeans finished working.
They slaughtered oxen by their huts and ate their dinner.

Many ships had come, bringing wine from Lemnos,
sent by Jason's son Euneus—born to Jason,
his people's shepherd, from Hypsipyle.
Euneus had donated wine, a thousand measures,
to go to Agamemnon and Menelaus.
From these ships long-haired Achaeans bought their wine.
Some bartered with bronze, some with shiny iron,   550
others with hides, live oxen, or with slaves.
And then the men prepared a sumptuous banquet.
Long-haired Achaeans feasted all night long,
as did Trojans and their allies in the city,
while throughout the night, Counselor Zeus,
thundering ominously, plotted bad things for them.
Pale fear gripped men. They kept pouring wine from goblets
onto the ground. No one dared to drink before he made
an offering to Zeus, almighty son of Cronos.
Then they went to bed, to receive the gift of sleep.

Book Eight
The Trojans Have Success

[At a council on Olympus Zeus decides to favour the Trojans, leaves for Ida, and holds up the golden scales; Diomedes comes to Nestor's help; Diomedes confronts Hector; Zeus stops Diomedes with a lightning bolt; Hera tries to get Poseidon to plot against Zeus; Agamemnon's speech to rally the troops; Zeus sends an omen to encourage the Argives; the Argives rally; Teucer's success against the Trojans; Hector wounds Teucer, drives him from the battle; Hera and Athena set out to help the Achaeans; Zeus sends Iris to stop them; Hector's speech to his troops the night before the big battle; Trojans sacrifice to the gods]

As Dawn first spread her yellow robe across the earth,
thunder-loving Zeus summoned an assembly of the gods
on the highest crest of many-ridged Olympus.
Zeus himself addressed them. The other deities,
those ranked below him, listened carefully.

    "Hear me, all you gods and goddesses,
I'll speak what the spirit in my chest prompts.
And let no female god, no male one either,
seek to thwart my plan. Let's get agreement
from all of you to end this matter quickly.   10
If I see any of you breaking ranks of gods,
keen to assist the Trojans or Danaans,
that god I'll beat up ignominiously
and send back to Olympus. Or I'll seize him
and pitch him into black Tartarus, way down,
into the deepest pit below the earth,
where the gates are iron, the threshold bronze,
as far below Hades as heaven lies
above the earth. Then he'll acknowledge
just how strong I am, the strongest of all gods.   20
Come on, try it—then everyone will know.
Take a golden cord, hang it from heaven.
Let gods and goddesses, all together,
grab hold of one end of it and pull.

You'd not drag Zeus, the highest counselor,
down from heaven to the ground, never,
no matter how hard you tried to do it.
But when I wished to pull in earnest,
I'd yank up earth itself, the sea as well.
I'd loop that cord round some Olympian peak   30
and hang it in mid-air—the whole of it.
I'm that much stronger than the gods and men."

Zeus finished. All the gods were speechless, shocked
at what Zeus had said, at the power of his tone.
At last Athena, the bright-eyed goddess, spoke up:

> "Son of Cronos, you're the father of us all,
> highest ruling force. We well know your strength.
> It's invincible. Still, we're sorry for the troops,
> Danaan spearmen dying, suffering dreadful fates.
> But we'll stand apart from battle, as you wish,   40
> although we'll give the Argives our advice,
> help them, to prevent destruction of them all,
> just to answer your displeasure."

Cloud-gatherer Zeus, smiling at Athena, said:

> "My dear child Tritogeneia, have no fears.
> I wasn't speaking all that seriously.
> I want to treat you in a friendly way."

Zeus harnessed his two horses, swift-flying animals,
with hooves of bronze and flowing golden manes.
He encased his body all in gold, took up his whip,   50
a gold one, finely crafted, climbed in his chariot,
then lashed the horses onward. They flew off eagerly.
Midway between the earth and starry heaven,
Zeus reached Mount Ida with its many springs,
mother of wild beasts. He reached Gargaros,
site of his grove and temple, fragrant with sacrifice.
There, the father of gods and men reined in his horses,
untied them from the chariot, and hid them in thick cloud.

Then he sat on the mountain peak, proud and splendid,
gazing down on the Trojan city, the Achaean ships. 60

Long-haired Achaeans gulped a quick meal by their huts.
Then they armed themselves. On the other side, in town,
Trojans, too, prepared for war, fewer in number,
but keen to fight on in the killing zone, a grim necessity,
for wives and children. They threw open all the gates.
The army streamed out, foot soldiers and charioteers,
making a huge din. As the two groups moved out
to the same spot, they crashed together, smashing shields
and spears, the battle frenzy of bronze-armed warriors.
Embossed shields collided one against the other, 70
a tremendous noise. Screams of pain and triumph
came from soldiers—those killing, those being killed—
and the earth was saturated with their blood.

In early morning, as that sacred day grew stronger,
weapons hurled by both sides grimly took their toll—
men kept on dying. But when the sun was at its height,
Father Zeus set up his golden balance, placed on it
two fatal destinies, one for horse-taming Trojans,
one for bronze-armed Achaeans. Gripping the scales,
he raised them by the centre. One scale sank down, 80
the one which held the Achaeans' fate that day—
it moved down to the all-sustaining earth,
while the Trojans' fate rose up toward wide heaven.
From Mount Ida, Zeus sent out a loud thunder clap
and hurled a lighting bolt down on Achaean troops.
Men looked and were astounded. Pale fear gripped them all.
At that, Idomeneus did not dare to stand his ground,
nor did Agamemnon, nor the two men named Ajax,
companions of the war god Ares. Only Nestor,
the Geranian, guardian of Achaeans, 90
kept his place, but not because he wanted to.
One of his horses had been hurt, hit by an arrow
on its head, right on top, that spot where on a horse
hairs begin to grow out from the skull, a deadly place.
The arrow had been loosed by Alexander,

lovely Helen's mate. The beast reared up in agony,
as the arrow pierced its brain. Skewered by the shaft,
the beast's convulsions confused the other horses.
While old Nestor with his sword was hacking feverishly
to cut the traces holding the animal in place,   100
Hector's fast horses came through the fighting men,
bearing Hector with them and their bold charioteer.
Nestor would have died right there, if Diomedes,
skilled in war cries, hadn't seen him right away.
He let out a loud shout to Odysseus, urging him
to come to Nestor's help.

             "Noble Odysseus, Laertes' son,
you resourceful man, why move away,
turning your back on all these flying weapons,
like a coward? Watch someone doesn't spear you
right in the back as you run off. Come on,   110
let's save old man Nestor from wild Hector."

Diomedes' words missed godlike, firm Odysseus,
who moved off to the Achaeans' hollow ships.
Diomedes, though left alone, charged straight ahead,
back into the fight. He made a stand right there,
in front of old Nestor's chariot, calling out to Nestor,
son of Neleus—his words had wings.

                   "Old man, in this fight
these young men are pressing you too hard.
Your strength is waning. Old age weighs you down.
Your attendant's weak, your horses slow.   120
So come on, climb up into my chariot.
You'll see how these Trojan horses do,
experts in moving to and fro across the plain,
in pursuit or flight. I took them from Aeneas.
These horses would fill any man with terror.
So turn your team over to subordinates.
With my two let's charge against the Trojans.
Let Hector see how my hand wields a spear."

Geranian horseman Nestor followed this suggestion.
At once, the two strong officers, Sthelenus   130
and noble Eurymedon, took Nestor's horses.
The two men climbed up in Diomedes' chariot.
Nestor grabbed the shining reins and lashed the horses.
They closed in on Hector quickly. Then he, in turn,
eager to fight, charged them impetuously.
The son of Tydeus threw his spear at Hector.
He missed, but struck Hector's companion charioteer,
Eniopeus, son of proud Thebaios, in the chest,
right by the nipple, as Eniopeus held the reins.
He tumbled from the chariot. The swift horses swerved.   140
Then strength and spirit left him as he lay there.
Savage grief seized Hector for his charioteer,
but he left him lying there, for all the pain he felt
for his companion. He went to find a substitute,
a second driver full of courage. Before long,
those horses had another charioteer,
for Hector soon ran into Archeptolemos,
son of Iphitus, and placed him in the chariot
behind swift horses, then handed him the reins.

At that point irrevocable disaster might have struck   150
the people all penned up in Troy like sheep,
if the father of gods and men hadn't kept sharp watch.
Sounding a dreadful thunder clap, he loosed his lightning,
a dazzling fiery bolt which hit the ground
immediately in front of Diomedes' horses.
A dreadful flash came from the blazing sulphur.
In terror, both horses reared up in their harnesses.
Nestor let the shining reins drop from his hands.
Feeling fear inside his chest, he cried:

                              "Son of Tydeus,
          wheel your sure-footed horses round. Go back.   160
     Don't you see Zeus is not protecting you?
     Today the son of Cronos grants Hector glory.
     Tomorrow he'll give victory to us,
     if that's his will. No man stops Zeus' plans,

no one, not even the mightiest warrior.
Zeus' force is more powerful by far."

Diomedes, expert in war cries, then replied:

"Everything you say, old man, is true enough.
But this brings fearful pain into my heart and chest.
For Hector then will speak out in Troy.   170
He'll say, 'The son of Tydeus, in fear of me,
scurried off, back to his ships.' That's what he'll boast.
Then let the wide earth open up for me."

Geranian horseman Nestor answered Diomedes:

"Son of fiery-hearted Tydeus, why talk like that?
Even if he slanders you and calls you coward,
he'll not convince the Trojans or Dardanians,
or Trojan wives, married partners of brave men
you've thrown into the dirt, still in their prime."

With these words he turned the sure-footed horses back,   180
fleeing through the battle zone. Hector and the Trojans,
with a shout, threw volleys of lethal weapons at them.
Hector with his glittering helmet then yelled out:

"Son of Tydeus,
fast-riding Danaans at their banquets
have awarded you a place of honour,
with lots of meat, a wine cup always full.
Now they're ashamed of you. You've turned out
no better than a woman. Run off then,
you coward girl. I'll not back away,
let you climb our walls, or take our women.   190
Before that happens, I'll send you to your death."

At Hector's words, the son of Tydeus was torn two ways,
debating whether to wheel the horses round and fight,
face Hector man to man. Three times he thought it through
in his mind and heart, and three times counselor Zeus

163

pealed thunder from Mount Ida, signaling to Trojans
that victory now would shift to them. Then Hector,
with a great shout, cried out to his Trojan warriors:

> "You Trojans, Lycians, and Dardanians—
> soldiers who fight in the killing zone—   200
> my friends, be men. Summon your warlike spirit.
> I see the son of Cronos grants us victory,
> great glory, a disaster for Danaans.
> What fools they were to build this feeble wall,
> a puny hazard—it will not check me,
> my warlike spirit. As for the trench they dug,
> my horses will jump over that with ease.
> When I reach their hollow ships, don't forget the fire,
> which wipes out everything—I'll burn their fleet,
> slaughter them, those Argives by their ships,   210
> as they suffocate, choking on the smoke."

With these words, Hector urged his horses on:

> "Xanthus, and you Podargus, Aithus,
> noble Lampus! Now's the time to pay me back
> for all my care, all the sweet grain you've had
> from Andromache, great Eëtion's daughter,
> for the wine she's mixed for you to drink,
> whenever you desired. She took care of you,
> even before me, her own fine husband.
> Come on then, go after them with speed,   220
> so we may capture Nestor's shield, whose fame
> extends right up to heaven—it's all gold—
> the shield itself, cross braces, too.
> From horse-taming Diomedes' shoulders
> we'll strip the decorated body armour,
> a work created by Hephaestus.
> I think if we could capture these two things,
> Achaeans would climb aboard their ships tonight."

So Hector bragged. That made queen Hera angry.
She shook with fury, sitting on her throne,   230

making high Olympus tremble. Then she spoke out
to great god Poseidon:

> "Alas, great Earthshaker,
> don't you feel any anguish in your heart,
> as Danaans are destroyed? After all,
> they bring you presents, many pleasing gifts,
> to Helice and Aegae. Don't you want them to win?
> Now, if all those of us who protect Danaans
> were to agree to drive the Trojans back,
> we'd leave wide-seeing Zeus up there by himself,
> sulking where he sits alone on Ida"   240

Mighty Earthshaker Poseidon, very angry,
answered Hera:

> "Hera, you fearless talker,
> What are you saying? That's not what I want,
> the rest of us to war on Zeus, son of Cronos.
> For he is much more powerful than us."

As the two gods talked together in this way,
horses and shield-bearing troops were jammed together,
crammed into the space encircled by the ditch,
from ships to wall, pinned down there by Hector, Priam's son,
like swift Ares, now that Zeus was giving him the glory.   250
And then he would've burned those well-balanced ships
with searing fire on the spot, if queen Hera
had not set a plan in Agamemnon's mind
to rouse Achaeans with all speed on his own.
He strode through Achaean huts and ships,
holding a huge purple cloak in his large fists.
He took up a position by Odysseus' ship,
a black vessel, broad in the beam, whose place,
in the middle of the row, allowed his voice
to reach both ends of the line, from the huts of Ajax,   260
son of Telamon, to those belonging to Achilles,
for these two men had placed their balanced ships

165

at either end, relying on their courage and strong hands.[1]
Agamemnon, from that spot, then shouted out,
making himself heard to all Danaans:

> "You Argives! What a shameful bunch of men!
> Splendid to look at, but a sour disgrace!
> What's happened to our sworn oaths, when we claimed
> we were the best, the bravest? Idle boasters!
> There in Lemnos, as you stuffed yourselves with meat   270
> from straight-horned cattle and drank bowls of wine,
> foaming to the brim, you talked of how you'd stand,
> each and every one of you, firm in battle
> against a hundred or two hundred Trojans.
> Now we're matched by Hector, just one man,
> who'll quickly set our ships alight with fire.
> Father Zeus, have you ever so deluded
> a high-minded king and stolen his glory?
> While sailing well-decked ships to this disaster,
> I say I never overlooked your lovely altars.   280
> On every one I burned fat and thighs of oxen—
> I was so keen to conquer Troy, its well-made walls.
> But Zeus, grant me now at least this prayer—
> let us get out of here alive, in safety.
> Don't let Trojans kill Achaeans off like this."

As Agamemnon spoke, tears streaming down his face,
Father Zeus pitied him and nodded his assent—
the army would be saved and not demolished.
At once Zeus sent the surest of all bird omens,
an eagle, gripping in its talons a young fawn,   290
child of some swift deer. The eagle released the fawn,
dropping it right beside that splendid altar
where Achaeans sacrificed to all-knowing Zeus.
Seeing that Zeus had sent the bird, men resumed the fight,
attacking Trojans eagerly, their battle spirits roused.

Then none of those many Danaans there could claim

[1]The ends of the line are the most vulnerable. So the two best fighters, Achilles and
the Greater Ajax, are encamped there.

he was quicker with his horses than Diomedes,
driving them ahead and charging through the ditch,
to confront their enemies face to face and fight.
Well ahead of all the rest, Diomedes killed his man,   300
a well-armed Trojan, Agelaus, son of Phradmon.
He'd turned his team around to get away.
But once he showed his back, Diomedes speared him
between his shoulder blades, driving through his chest.
He fell from the chariot, armour rattling round him.
After Diomedes, the sons of Atreus came charging in,
Agamemnon and Menelaus, and after them
both Ajaxes, encased in war's ferocity,
followed by Idomeneus and his attendant,
Meriones, the equal of man-killing Ares.   310
Then came Eurypylus, brave son of Euaemon.
Ninth came Teucer, stretching his curved bow.
He stood beneath the shield of Ajax, son of Telamon.
As Ajax cautiously pulled his shield aside,
Teucer would peer out quickly, shoot off an arrow,
hit someone in the crowd, dropping that soldier
right where he stood, ending his life—then he'd duck back,
crouching down by Ajax, like a child beside its mother.
Ajax would then conceal him with his shining shield.
Who were the first Trojans skillful Teucer killed?   320
Orsilochus died first, then Ormenus, Ophelestes,
Daitor, Chromius, godlike Lycophontes,
Amopaon, son of Polyaimon, and Melanippus—
all these Teucer dropped one by one on fertile earth.
Watching him cause havoc with his bow in Trojan ranks,
Agamemnon, king of men, was overjoyed.
He went up, stood beside him, then spoke out:

        "Teucer, son of Telamon, master of your people,
        my dear comrade, keep on shooting as you're doing.
        You'll be a saving light to the Danaans,   330
        and to your father Telamon, who raised you,
        took care of you, a bastard, in his own home.
        Though he's far off, cover him with glory now.
        For I'll tell you something—and this will happen—

if Athena and aegis-bearing Zeus permit me
to devastate that well-built city Ilion,
you'll be the first to take the prize of honour,
after me, of course—a tripod, two horses,
their chariot as well, or some woman
to climb up into your bed with you."   340

Skillful Teucer then replied to Agamemnon:

"Mighty son of Atreus, why urge me on?
I'm eager to continue shooting.
Since we first drove them back to Ilion,
I've not stopped fighting as hard as I know how,
cutting men down with my bow and killing them.
I've shot off eight long-barbed arrows. Each one
has sunk itself deep inside a soldier's flesh,
some strong, swift warrior. But this man,
Hector, I can't hit. He's like some crazy dog."   350

With that, Teucer launched another arrow from his bowstring,
directly facing Hector, eager to hit him.
The arrow missed, but struck handsome Gorgythion,
son of Priam, in the chest, a man whose mother,
lovely Castianeira, divinely beautiful,
went from Aisyme to become a wife to Priam.
Just as the head on a garden poppy leans aslant,
loaded down with heavy seed and spring rain showers,
so Gorgythion's head sagged under his helmet's weight.
Teucer loosed yet another arrow from his bowstring,   360
straight at Hector, his spirit still keen to hit him.
Again he missed, for Apollo deflected it.
But the arrow did hit Archeptolemos,
Hector's bold driver, as he was coming to the fight.
It struck him in the chest, right by the nipple.
He fell from the chariot. The fast horses swerved.
Then and there his strength and spirit abandoned him.
In his heart Hector felt sharp pain for his charioteer,
but he left him there, though grieving for his comrade.

He called out to his brother Cebriones, 370
who was near by, to take up the chariot reins.
Cebriones heard him and willingly agreed.
Hector jumped down from his glittering chariot
with a fearful yell. Picking up a boulder
lying on the ground, he went straight at Teucer,
his heart aroused to hit him with it. At that moment,
Teucer had just taken a sharp arrow from his quiver,
set it on the bowstring, and was drawing back the bow,
once again desperately eager to hit Hector.
But Hector struck him with that jagged rock 380
right on the shoulder, where collar bones divide
neck from chest, an especially vulnerable spot.
The rock broke the bowstring and numbed his hands and wrists.
Teucer fell forward on his knees and stayed there,
letting his bow fall from his hand. Seeing his brother down,
Ajax quickly hurried up and straddled Teucer,
covering him with his shield. Two loyal attendants,
Mecisteus, son of Echios, and noble Alastor,
hoisted Teucer up—he was groaning heavily—
then took him with them back to the hollow ships. 390

Once more Olympian Zeus put force into the Trojans.
They drove Achaeans back, right back to their deep trench,
Hector at the front, proudly showing off his strength.
Just as some hunting dog in a swift-footed chase
gets a grip on a wild boar or lion from the back,
on the flank or rump, and watches that beast's every move,
that's how Hector harried the long-haired Achaeans,
always killing off the stragglers as they fled.
By the time Achaeans had rushed through the stakes,
as they crossed the ditch, many had died at Trojan hands. 400
At last they halted by the ships and stayed there,
calling out to one another. Raising their hands,
each man prayed fervently to all the gods.
Hector drove his fine-maned horses back and forth,
his eyes glaring like a Gorgon or man-killing Ares.[1]

[1]The Gorgons are dreadful monsters. The most famous, Medusa, could turn people
to stone.

169

Seeing all this, white-armed Hera pitied the Achaeans.
She quickly spoke these winged words to Athena:

"Alas, child of aegis-bearing Zeus,
Achaeans are being massacred. It's their last stand.
Aren't we concerned about them any more,   410
as their evil fate accomplishes its purpose?
They're being destroyed by one man's charging frenzy.
Hector, son of Priam, is on a rampage.
He can't be stopped. He's already done great harm."

Bright-eyed goddess Athena answered Hera:

"I wish Hector somehow would lose his strength
and die, killed in his own native land
at Argive hands. But my father, too,
is in a rage, destruction on his mind.
What a wretch he is, always in the way,   420
wrecking my plans. He does not remember
how many times I saved Hercules, his son,
worn down by work he got from Eurystheus.
If I'd had the foresight to anticipate
what Zeus is doing now when Eurystheus
sent Hercules down to the house of Hades,
the Gate Keeper, to fetch back from Erebus
Hades' dreadful hound, he'd never have escaped
the deep rushing waters of the river Styx.
Now Zeus dislikes me. He's carrying out   430
what Thetis wants. She kissed his knee, cupped his chin,
begged him to grant due honour to Achilles,
destroyer of cities. But the day will come
when Zeus calls me dear bright eyes once more.
Now harness your sure-footed horses for us,
while I go to aegis-bearing Zeus' home
and arm myself with weapons for this battle,
so I may see whether this son of Priam,
this Hector of the shining helmet, is pleased
when we two show up in the battle lanes,   440
or whether some Trojan will make a meal

for dogs and birds with flesh and body fat,
as he falls there beside Achaean ships."

Athena finished. White-armed Hera agreed with her.
Then Hera, honoured goddess, great Cronos' daughter,
went off and started harnessing her horses
with their golden headpieces. Meanwhile, Athena,
daughter of aegis-bearing Zeus, threw her dress
down on the floor of her father's house, a soft robe,
richly embroidered, which she'd made with her own hands.   450
She pulled on the tunic of cloud-gatherer Zeus
and armed herself with weapons for destructive war.
Then she stepped up into the flaming chariot,
grasping the huge thick strong spear she used to break
heroic warrior ranks which had provoked her,
making the daughter of a mighty father angry.
Hera immediately whipped the horses forward.
With a groan, the gates of heaven opened on their own,
those gates which the Seasons, custodians of Olympus
and great heaven, too, look after, pushing open   460
the heavy cloud, then pushing it shut once more.
Through these gates the goddesses lashed on their horses.

Father Zeus noticed them from Ida. In a huge rage,
he sent down gold-winged Iris with a message for them.

"Off with you, swift Iris. Turn them back again.
Don't permit them to come into my presence.
For if we come to blows, then we'll have trouble.
But I do say this—and it will surely happen—
I'll cripple their fast horses in their traces,
throw them from the chariot, smash it in pieces.   470
Ten revolving years won't be sufficient
to cure the wounds my lightning will inflict,
so the bright-eyed goddess knows what it means
to fight against her father. As for Hera,
I'm not so angry or upset with her,
for no matter what I say, she undermines it."

Zeus spoke. Then Iris, swift as a storm, rushed off,
taking his message. She came down from Mount Ida
and made for high Olympus. She met the goddesses
at the outer gate of many-ridged Olympus.   480
She stopped them and reported Zeus' message:

> "Where are you rushing off? Have you lost your wits?
> The son of Cronos has forbidden anyone
> to assist the Argives. And he's made this threat—
> which he intends to carry out—he'll maim
> your swift horses in their traces, throw you both
> out of the chariot, smash it in pieces.
> Ten revolving years won't be sufficient
> to cure the wounds his lightning will inflict,
> so that you'll understand, bright-eyed goddess,   490
> what it means to fight against your father.
> With Hera's he's not so angry or upset.
> For no matter what he says, she undermines it.
> But as for you, you shameless schemer,
> are you daring to fight Zeus with one large spear?"

Having said this, swift-footed Iris went away.
Hera then said to Athena:

>   "What a mess,
> child of aegis-bearing Zeus! I'm not keen,
> not now, that two of us should take on Zeus
> for the sake of mortal men. Let some die   500
> and others live, as chance will work it out.
> Let Zeus judge between Trojans and Achaeans,
> as his heart desires. That's how it should be."

With these words, she turned her sure-footed horses back.
The Seasons unyoked the horses with the lovely manes,
led them to their heavenly stalls, and leaned the chariot
against the courtyard's luminescent inner wall.
The goddesses then sat down on their golden thrones,
among the other gods, with anger in their hearts.
Father Zeus drove his fine-wheeled chariot and horses   510

from Ida to Olympus, to the place where gods
were all assembled. The famous Earthshaker,
Poseidon, loosed his horses from their harness for him,
put the chariot on its stand, and covered it with cloth.
Then wide-seeing Zeus himself sat on his golden throne.
Underneath his feet great Olympus trembled.
Athena and Hera were sitting by themselves,
away from Zeus, not saying anything to him
or asking questions. Knowing what was in their hearts,
Zeus spoke:

> "Why are you so irritated,   520
> Hera and Athena? Surely you're not tired
> from those fights where men win glory,
> exhausted after killing off the Trojans,
> for whom you feel such deadly hatred?
> Be that as it may, such is my power,
> the strength in my own hands, it's impossible
> for all the Olympian gods combined
> to turn me from my purposes. As for you,
> you both were trembling in your shining limbs
> even before you looked on any fight   530
> or witnessed first-hand war's destructiveness.
> But I'll tell you what would've taken place—
> neither of you would've come back to Olympus,
> the immortals' home, riding in your chariot.
> My lightning would have blasted both of you."

Zeus finished speaking. Hera and Athena muttered,
sitting together, plotting trouble for the Trojans.
Athena sat in silence, not saying anything,
angry with her father, consumed with rage.
But Hera couldn't hold the fury in her chest. She said: 540

> "Dread son of Cronos, what are you saying?
> We know well enough how strong you are—
> invincible. But nonetheless, we pity
> Danaan spearmen who are being destroyed,
> suffering a dreadful fate. But we'll hold back,

173

refrain from fighting, if that's your order.
We'll provide useful advice to Argives,
so they don't all die from your displeasure."

In response to Hera, cloud-gatherer Zeus then said:

"Ox-eyed queen Hera, if you're so inclined,   550
tomorrow morning you can witness
the exalted son of Cronos, as he kills
many Achaean spearmen in their army.
For warlike Hector won't stop fighting,
until beside the ships he stirs to action
swift Achilles, son of Peleus, on that day
they fight with bloody desperation
by the ships' sterns—they'll be battling over
the body of Patroclus. That's been decreed.
I don't care at all if this annoys you.   560
Even if you descend to the lowest place
beneath the earth and sea, where Iapetus
and Cronos live, where they get no pleasure
in any sunlight from Hyperion,
or any breeze, in the depths of Tartarus—
even if you went as far away as that
in your wandering, I'd still pay no attention
to your displeasure. For you've no rival
when it comes to behaving like a bitch."

Zeus spoke. White-armed Hera didn't answer him.   570

Now the sun's bright light sank down into the ocean,
dragging black night over fertile crop lands.
The end of daylight made the Trojans sorrowful,
but Achaeans welcomed the arrival of black night,
something they'd been praying for constantly.

Then glorious Hector assembled all the Trojans
some distance from the ships, by the swirling river,
in open ground where there were no corpses in plain view.
Jumping from their chariots to the ground, warriors

174

listened for what Hector, loved by Zeus, would say.
In his hand, he gripped a spear eighteen feet long,
its bronze point glittering there in front of them,
a golden ring around it. Leaning on this spear,
Hector then addressed his Trojans:

                              "Listen to me,
you Trojans, Dardanians, you allies.
Just now I stated we'd go back to Troy today,
once we'd destroyed the ships and slaughtered
all Achaeans. But darkness intervened.
That's the only thing that spared the Argives
and saved their ships beached on the shore. Come then,   590
let's do what black night demands—prepare a meal.
So from your chariots take out of harness
those horses with their lovely manes, feed them,
then quickly bring here from the city
cattle and stout sheep. Bring sweet wine as well,
and bread from your own homes. Get lots of wood,
so all night long, until first light of dawn,
we can burn many fires, lighting up the sky.
Some time in the night, long-haired Achaeans
may make their move to get away by sea.   600
We must not let them embark easily,
without a fight. Let some of them be hit,
take something home they need to nurse with care—
an arrow wound, a slash from some sharp spear
as they jump in their ships—so someone else
will think twice about bringing wretched war
upon horse-taming Trojans. Let the call go out
from heralds, whom Zeus loves, through all the city,
for growing boys and gray-haired men to camp
up on the city's walls, built by the gods.   610
Let each grown woman get ready a large fire
in her home. Let all keep a sharp lookout,
to stop a group from entering our city
while the army is elsewhere. Do all this,
you great-hearted Trojans, just as I've said.
That's all I have to tell you at this time.

I've more orders for horse-taming Trojans
for tomorrow. I hope and pray to Zeus,
to other gods as well, I'll drive away
these death-infected dogs, conducted here   620
in their black ships by mortal fates. Right now,
let's watch out for ourselves tonight. At dawn,
let's arm ourselves with weapons and re-ignite
this bitter warfare by the hollow ships.
Then I'll know if mighty Diomedes,
son of Tydeus, will repel me from the ships,
or whether with my bronze I'll slaughter him
and take away the spoils all stained with blood.
Tomorrow he'll understand how good he is,
whether he can stand against my spear,   630
as it comes after him. I think he'll fall.
He'll be among the first men speared to death,
with many of his comrades round him,
at tomorrow's sunrise. I wish I were as sure
I were immortal, ageless for all time,
that I'd be worshiped as Athena is,
and Apollo, too, as I am that this day
will bring destruction to the Argives."

Hector finished speaking. Trojans gave a shout.
They untied their sweaty horses from their yokes,   640
tethered them with straps, each by its chariot.
From the city they soon brought cattle and stout sheep,
sweet wine and bread from home. They gathered piles of wood
and made perfect sacrificial offerings to the gods.
From the plain, the wind carried the sweet-smelling smoke
right up to heaven. But the blessed gods weren't willing
to accept it, for sacred Ilion, and Priam,
and Priam's people, rich in sheep, did not please them.
So all night long men sat there in the battle lanes,
with high expectations, burning many fires.   650
Just as those times when the stars shine bright in heaven,
clustered around the glowing moon, with no wind at all,
and every peak and jutting headland, every forest glade
is clearly visible, when every star shines out,

and the shepherd's heart rejoices—that's the way
the many Trojan fires looked, as they burned there
in front of Ilion, between the river Xanthus
and the ships, a thousand fires burning on the plain.
By each sat fifty men in the glow of firelight.
Horses munched on wheat and barley, standing there   660
by their chariots, awaiting the regal splendour of the dawn.

Book Nine
Peace Offerings to Achilles

*[The Argives in despair; Agamemnon proposes they go home; Diomedes
responds, rebuking Agamemnon; Nestor proposes a reconciliation with
Achilles; Agamemnon agrees, outlines his offer; Phoenix, Odysseus, and
Ajax go to Achilles with the offer; he welcomes them with a meal;
Odysseus outlines Agamemnon's offer; Achilles refuses; Phoenix urges
Achilles to accept, tells the story of Meleager; Achilles refuses Phoenix;
Ajax speaks last; Achilles makes a slight concession; the envoys return
with Achilles' answer; Achaeans retire for the night.]*

Meanwhile, as the Trojans maintained their careful watch,
Panic, chilling Fear's dread comrade, gripped Achaeans,
their best men suffering unendurable anguish.
Just like those times two winds blow in from Thrace—
North Wind and West Wind suddenly spring up
and lash the fish-filled seas—black waves at once rise up,
then fling seaweed in piles along the shoreline—
so spirits in Achaean chests were now cast down.
Atreus' son, heart overwhelmed with painful sorrow,
went to give out orders for clear-voiced heralds   10
to summon all the warriors to assembly,
calling them one by one, not with a general shout.
He himself, with his heralds, carried out the task.
The counselors sat heart sick. Agamemnon stood,
his face shedding tears like a black water spring
whose dark stream flows down a sheer rock precipice.
With a sigh, Agamemnon addressed the Argives:

"My friends, leaders, Argive counselors,
Zeus, son of Cronos, has snared me badly
in grievous folly. Deceptive god,   20
he promised me—he nodded his assent—
that I'd lay waste to well-built Ilion,
before I went back home. Now he tricks me.
He's devised a cruel deceit for me,
telling me to return to Argos in disgrace,
after the deaths of so many warriors.

That's what now delights all-powerful Zeus,
who has hurled down so many lofty towns,
and who'll still demolish many more—
such is his power, irresistible.   30
But come, let's all follow what I propose—
let's sail back to our dear native land.
For we're never going to capture Troy."

He finished. All those there stayed silent, stunned.
Achaea's sons just sat there, speechless with grief.
At last Diomedes, skilled in battle cries, spoke out:

    "Son of Atreus, I'll be the first to challenge
your foolishness, as is my right, my lord,
in our assembly. So don't be angry.
First of all, you slighted my bravery   40
in front of all Danaans, when you claimed
I was no soldier, an unwarlike man.
Achaeans, young and old, all know this.
The son of crooked-minded Cronos gave you
a two-edged gift—he gave you honour
to govern all men with your sceptre,
but he didn't give the strongest power,
courage. My misguided king, do you think
Achaea's sons are really fearful cowards,
as you state? If your heart wishes to go home,   50
then go. The road lies there in front of you.
The many ships which sailed here with you
from Mycenae stand ready by the sea.
But the rest of the long-haired Achaeans
will stay here, until we demolish Troy.
If they flee back to their dear native land
in their ships, too, then Sthenelus and I
will fight on to our goal, to take Ilion.
For the gods were with us when we came."

With a roar, all Achaea's sons endorsed his words,   60
pleased with the speech made by horse-taming Diomedes.
Then horseman Nestor, standing up before them, said:

"Son of Tydeus, you're excellent in battle
and the best Achaean of your age in council.
No Achaean will fault what you've just said
or oppose it. But your speech is incomplete.
You are still young—you might well be my son,
my youngest born. Still, you spoke sensibly,
in what you said to the Achaean king.
For you spoke justly and kept to the point.   70
But come, I can claim to be your senior,
so I shall explain this matter fully.
Let no one take issue now with what I say,
not even mighty Agamemnon.
Any man who's keen on civil war
is an evil outlaw, without a heart,
without a home. So for the time being,
now that night has come, let's do what we must.
Let's get dinner ready, something to eat.
And let's have sentries camp beside that trench   80
we dug outside the wall. I'm saying young men
should do this. Then, issue your instructions,
son of Atreus, for you are chief king here.
Prepare a meal for senior counselors—
that's the right and proper thing to do.
You've got lots of wine stockpiled in your huts,
which Achaea's sons bring here each day
over the wide sea from Thrace—you've got
all you need to show such hospitality,
for you are ruler over many men.   90
Once many people have assembled there,
you should follow whoever offers you
the best advice. All we Achaeans need
good practical advice, especially now,
when enemies are burning many fires
right beside our ships. Who finds that pleasant?
This night saves our army or destroys it."

Nestor spoke. Those present listened carefully,
then followed his advice. Armed sentinels went out,
led by Thrasymedes, Nestor's son, his people's shepherd,   100

180

with Ascalaphus and Ialmenus, strong fighters,
and Meriones, Aphareus, and Deïpyrus,
along with noble Lycomedes, Creion's son.
These seven were captains of the sentinels.
A hundred young men, all armed with their long spears,
went with each of them. They marched off and took positions
half way between the ditch and wall. Then the men lit fires
and prepared their meals. Atreus' son led his advisors
to his hut and gave all of them a generous meal.
They ate the food prepared and set before them,   110
and each man ate and drank to his full heart's content.
Old Nestor, whose previous advice had seemed the best,
was the first to begin explaining what he thought.
Keeping in mind their common good, he spoke out:

> "Mighty son of Atreus, Agamemnon,
> king of men, I'll begin and end my speech
> with you, for you are lord of many men.
> Zeus gave you sceptre and laws to rule them.
> Thus, you, above all, should speak and listen,
> then act upon what other men may say,   120
> if their spirit prompts them to speak well.
> You'll get the credit for what they begin.
> So I'll say what seems to me the best advice.
> No one else has set out a better scheme
> than the one which I've been mulling over
> a long time now, ever since you, my lord,
> made Achilles angry by taking back
> that young girl Briseis from his hut,
> against my judgment. Repeatedly,
> I urged you not to do it. But then you,   130
> surrendering to your arrogant spirit,
> shamed our strongest man, honoured by the gods.
> You still have that prize you took. So now let's think
> how we may make amends, win him back with gifts
> and gracious speeches, and be friends once more."

Agamemnon, king of men, then answered Nestor:

"Old man, you expose my folly justly.
I was deluded. I don't deny that.
The man whom Zeus loves in his heart is worth
whole armies. And this man Zeus now honours   140
by destroying an army of Achaeans.
Since my delusion made me follow
my mistaken feelings, I'm now willing
to make amends, to give in recompense
immense treasures. I'll list these rich gifts
in presence of you all—seven tripods
which fire has not yet touched, ten gold talents,
twenty shining cauldrons, twelve strong horses
whose speed has triumphed and earned them prizes.
A man who has as much as I have won   150
from racing these sure-footed animals
would not be poor, or lack possessions,
or need precious gold. And then I'll give him
seven women of Lesbos, skilled in crafts,
whom I chose for myself when he captured
well-built Lesbos. They surpass all women
for their beauty. These I shall present to him.
With them the one I seized from him, Briseis,
daughter of Briseus. I'll solemnly swear
I never once went up into her bed   160
or had sex with her, as is men's custom,
where men and women are concerned.
All these things he will receive immediately.
If gods grant we destroy Priam's great city,
when we Achaeans allocate the spoils,
let him come and load his ship with gold,
with bronze, as much as he desires. He may choose
twenty Trojan women for himself,
the loveliest after Argive Helen.
If we get back to the rich land of Argos,   170
he can then become my son-in-law.
I'll honour him just as I do Orestes,
my son, whom I dearly love. He's being raised
in great prosperity. In my well-built home,
I have three daughters—Chrysothemis,

Iphianessa and Laodice.
He can take whichever one he chooses
back home as his wife to Peleus' house
and pay no bridal gift. I'll give much more
to bring about our reconciliation,   180
a dowry bigger than any man so far
has ever handed over with his daughter.
I'll give him seven populous cities,
Cardamyle, Enope, grassy Hire,
holy Pherae, fertile Antheia,
lovely Aepea, and vine-rich Pedasus,
all near the sea, beside sandy Pylos.
People living in these places own a lot,
many sheep and cattle. They will honour him
and give him gifts, as if he were a god.   190
Under his laws and sceptre they'll do well.
I shall give all this if he will abate
his anger. Let him concede. Only Hades
is totally relentless and unyielding.
That's why of all the gods, he's the one
men hate the most. And let him acknowledge
my authority, for I'm the greater king.
In age I can claim to be his senior."

Geranian horseman Nestor then said in reply:

"Mighty son of Atreus, Agamemnon,   200
king of men, the gifts you're offering
to lord Achilles can't be criticized.
But come, let's send out hand-picked men
to go with all speed to Achilles' hut,
Peleus' son. And may those I select
agree to do it. First, let Phoenix,
whom Zeus loves, be leader, then great Ajax,
and lord Odysseus. Let herald Odius
accompany them, along with Eurybates.
Bring some water for our hands. Let's observe   210
a holy silence, so we may pray to Zeus,
son of Cronos, to take pity on us."

Nestor spoke. All present approved of what he'd said.
Attendants then poured water on their hands.
Young men filled mixing bowls with wine up to the brim
and passed them round. With every cup they made libations.
Once they'd made offerings and drunk their fill of wine,
they left the hut of Agamemnon, son of Atreus.
Geranian horseman Nestor, looking at each man,
especially at Odysseus, kept encouraging them   220
to persuade Achilles, Peleus' excellent son.

Along the shore of the tumbling, crashing sea,
the envoys made their way, offering up their prayers
to world-circling Earthshaker Poseidon to help them
more easily convince the great heart of Achilles.
They came to the ships and huts of the Myrmidons.
There they found Achilles. He was easing his spirit
with a tuneful finely decorated lyre.
It had a silver cross-piece. He'd seized it as a prize
when he'd destroyed the city of Eëtion.   230
With the lyre he was bringing pleasure to his heart,
singing about the celebrated deeds of men.
Patroclus, his sole companion, sat there facing him,
waiting in silence until Achilles finished singing.
The envoys approached, lord Odysseus in the lead.
They stood in front of him. In astonishment,
Achilles got up off his chair and stood up quickly,
still holding the lyre. Patroclus did the same,
standing up as soon as he saw the embassy.
Swift-footed Achilles greeted them and said:

                                        "Welcome.   240
        My dear friends have come. I must be needed.
        Among Achaeans you're the men I love the most,
        even in my anger."

                    With these words,
lord Achilles conducted them inside his hut
and seated them on chairs covered with purple rugs.
Moving up close to Patroclus, Achilles said:

"Son of Menoetius, set out for us
a larger wine bowl, and mix stronger wine.
Prepare a cup for everyone. These men,
my closest friends, are under my own roof."   250

Achilles spoke. Patroclus obeyed his dear companion.
Then in the firelight he set down a large chopping block,
placed on it slabs of mutton, goat, and the chine
of a plump hog, swimming in fat. Achilles carved,
while Automedon held the meat. He sliced up
small pieces, then got them ready on the spits.
The son of Menoetius, godlike man, stoked the fire,
a huge one. Once the blaze died down and flames subsided,
Patroclus spread the glowing embers, laid the spits
lengthwise on top, setting them in place on stones   260
and sprinkling on the sacred salt. When the meat was cooked,
he laid it out on platters. Patroclus took the bread,
then passed it in fine baskets round the table.
Achilles served the meat and sat down by the wall,
directly opposite godlike Odysseus.
Achilles told Patroclus, his companion,
to sacrifice to all the gods. Patroclus threw the offerings
into the fire. Then each man helped himself,
eating the food prepared and set before him.
They all ate and drank to their full heart's content.   270
Then Ajax gave a nod to Phoenix. Seeing that,
lord Odysseus filled up his cup with wine
and proposed a toast:

                    "Good health, Achilles.
We have not had to go without our share
of feasts, either in Agamemnon's hut,
Atreus' son, or here, for you've prepared
a richly satisfying meal. But now
our business is not pleasant banqueting.
For we are staring at a great disaster.
And, my lord, we are afraid, in a quandary,   280
whether we can save our well-decked ships,
or whether they will be destroyed, unless

185

you put on your warlike power once again.
For haughty Trojans and their famous allies
have camped close to the ships and barricade
and lit many fires throughout their army.
They claim nothing can prevent them now
from attacking our black ships. And Zeus,
son of Cronos, has sent them his signal,
on their right a lightning flash. Hector,   290
exulting hugely in his power,
in a terrifying manic frenzy,
puts his faith in Zeus, fears neither man nor god.
A killing passion now possesses him.
He prays for holy dawn to come quickly,
vowing he'll hack apart the high sterns
of our ships, burn them in destructive fire,
and by those very ships kill the Achaeans
driven out in desperation by the smoke.
I have a dreadful fear deep in my heart   300
that the gods will make good all his boasting,
seal our fate, to perish here in Troy,
far away from Argos, where horses breed.
So rouse yourself, late though it may be,
if you've a mind to save Achaeans
from their suffering at this Trojan onslaught.
If not, you'll suffer future agonies.
You won't find any cure for such despair.
Before that happens, you should think about
how to help Argives at this evil hour.   310
My friend, that day your father, Peleus,
sent you off, away from Phthia,
to join Agamemnon, didn't he say this,
'My son, Athena and Hera will give you
power, if they so wish, but you must check
that overbearing spirit in your chest.
It's better to show good will, to give up
malicious quarreling. Then Achaeans,
young and old, will respect you all the more'?
That's what your old father said, advice   320
which you've forgotten. So even now

you should stop, cease this heart-corroding rage.
For if you will mitigate your anger,
Agamemnon will give you worthy gifts.
If you will hear the list, then I'll repeat
what Agamemnon has promised to you.
All gifts are in his huts—seven tripods
which fire has not yet touched, ten gold talents,
twenty shining cauldrons, twelve strong horses
whose speed has triumphed, earned them prizes—   330
a man who's won as much as Agamemnon
from racing these sure-footed animals
would not be poor or lack possessions
or precious gold. Then he will add to this
seven women of Lesbos, skilled in crafts,
whom he chose for himself when you captured
well-built Lesbos. They surpass all women
for their beauty. These he will present to you,
with them the one he seized from you, Briseis,
daughter of Briseus. He'll solemnly swear   340
he never once went up into her bed
or had sex with her, as is men's custom,
where men and women are concerned.
All these things you will receive immediately.
If gods grant that we destroy Priam's great city,
when we Achaeans allocate the spoils,
you may come and load your ship with gold,
with bronze, as much as you desire. You may choose
twenty Trojan women for yourself,
the loveliest after Argive Helen.   350
If we get back to the rich land of Argos,
you can then become his son-in-law.
He'll honour you just as he does Orestes,
his son, whom he dearly loves. He's being raised
in great prosperity. In his well-built home
he has three daughters—Chrysothemis,
Iphianessa, and Laodice.
You can take whichever one you choose
back home as your wife to Peleus' house
and pay no bridal gift. He'll give much more   360

187

to bring about your reconciliation,
a dowry bigger than any man so far
has ever handed over with his daughter.
He'll give you seven populous cities,
Cardamyle, Enope, grassy Hire,
holy Pherae, fertile Antheia,
lovely Aepea, and vine-rich Pedasus,
all near the sea, beside sandy Pylos.
People living in these places possess
many sheep and cattle and will honour you   370
and give you gifts, as if you were a god.
Under your laws and sceptre they'll do well.
He will give all this, if you will abate
your anger. But if your heart still resents
Atreus' son and his gifts, then take pity
on all Achaeans, our exhausted soldiers.
They will pay you honours like a god.
Among them you'll earn enormous glory,
for now you might kill Hector, who may well
approach you—he's so obsessed with slaughter,   380
he thinks there's not a warrior his equal
among Danaans brought here in our ships."

Swift-footed Achilles then answered Odysseus:

"Divinely born son of Laertes,
resourceful Odysseus. I must be blunt
about what I think, where all this will lead,
so you do not sit there and, one by one,
try to entice me with sweet promises.
I hate like the gates of Hell any man
who says one thing while thinking something else   390
which stays hidden in his mind. So I'll declare
what, in my view, it's best for me to say—
I don't believe that Agamemnon,
Atreus' son, or any other Argive
will persuade me, for no thanks are given
to the man who always fights without rest
against the enemy. Whether one fights

188

or stays behind, the shares are still the same.
Coward and brave man both get equal honour.
Death treats idle and active men alike.   400
I've won nothing for all I've suffered,
battling on, pain in my heart, with my life
always under threat. Just as a bird
takes scraps of food, whatever she can find,
to her fledglings, but herself eats little,
so have I lain without sleep many nights,
persevered through bloody days of fighting,
in battling men in wars about their wives.
With ships, I've seized twelve towns and killed their men.
On land, in the area of fertile Troy,   410
I claim eleven more. From all these,
I took fine treasure, lots of it, brought it
to Agamemnon, Atreus' son—I gave it
all to him. He stayed back, at the swift ships.
He shared very little of what he got,
keeping most of it for his own use.
He gave prizes to the best of men, the kings,
and they hung on to them. From me alone
he stole away a prize, a woman I love.
Let him have his pleasure in bed with her.   420
Why must Argives fight against the Trojans?
Why did Atreus' son collect an army
and lead it here if not for fair-haired Helen?
Are Atreus' sons the only mortal men
who love their wives? Every good and prudent man
loves his wife and cares for her, as my heart
loved that girl, though captured with my spear.
Since he's taken my prize out of my hands
and cheated me, let him not try to take
another thing from me. I know him too well.   430
He'll never persuade me to agree.
But, Odysseus, let him rely on you
and other kings as well to save his ships
from fiery destruction. He has done much
without me already. He's built a wall,
constructed a large wide ditch around it,

and fixed stakes inside. But for all these things,
he's not been able to check the power
of man-killing Hector. When I fought
beside Achaeans, Hector wasn't eager 440
to push the battle far from his own walls.
He came out only to the Scaean Gates
and to the oak tree. Once he met me there
alone. He barely got away from my attack.
But now I don't want to fight lord Hector.
Tomorrow I'll make holy sacrifice
to Zeus, to all the gods, and load my ships,
once I've dragged them down into the sea.
You'll see, if you wish, if you're interested,
tomorrow my ships will be sailing off, 450
on the fish-filled Hellespont, men rowing
with great eagerness. And if Poseidon,
famous Earthshaker, gives us fair sailing,
in three days I'll reach fertile Phthia.
There I own many things I left behind
when I made this disastrous trip to Troy.
I'll take back from here more gold, red bronze,
fair women, and gray iron—all I captured.
But mighty Agamemnon, Atreus' son,
in his arrogance, seized back from me 460
the prize which he awarded. Tell him that.
Repeat in public everything I say,
so other Achaeans will grow angry,
if he, still clothed in shamelessness, hopes
at any time to deceive some Argive.
Cur that he is, he doesn't dare confront me
face to face. I'll discuss no plans with him,
no actions. He cheated me, betrayed me.
His words will cheat no more. To hell with him!
Let him march to his death by his own road, 470
for Counselor Zeus has stolen his wits.
I hate his gifts. And he's not worth a damn.
Not even if he gave me ten times, no,
twenty times more than all he owns right now,
or will possess in future, not even

all the wealth amassed in Orchomenus,
or Egyptian Thebes, where huge treasures sit
piled up in houses—that city of gates,
one hundred of them, through each can ride
two hundred men, horses and chariots 480
all together—not even if he gave me
gifts as numerous as grains of sand
beside the sea or particles of dust,
not for all that would Agamemnon win
my heart, not until he satisfies me
in full for all my heartfelt bitter pain.
I'll never take as wife any daughter
of Agamemnon, son of Atreus,
not even if her beauty rivals that
of golden Aphrodite, or her skill 490
in crafts equals bright-eyed Athena's.
I will not marry her. Let him select
another Achaean, someone like himself,
a more prestigious king than me. For me,
if the gods keep me safe and I get home,
Peleus himself will find me a wife.
There are plenty of Achaean women
in Hellas and in Phthia—daughters of lords,
men who govern cities. From them I'll choose
the one I want to make my cherished wife. 500
My heart has often felt a strong desire
to take a woman there as my own wife,
someone suitable for marriage, to enjoy
the riches which old Peleus has acquired.
Life is worth more to me than all the wealth
they say was stored in well-built Ilion
some time ago, when they were still at peace,
before the sons of Achaea came,
more than all the treasures of the archer,
Phoebus Apollo, stacked on the stone floor 510
in rocky Pytho. Men can steal cattle,
fat sheep, get tripods, herds of sorrel horses.
But no man gets his life back, not by theft
or plunder, once it has flown out from him,

191

passed beyond the barrier of his teeth.
My goddess mother, silver-footed Thetis,
has said two fates may bring about my death.
If I remain here, continuing the fight
against the Trojans' city, that means
I won't be going home, but my glory   520
will never die. But if I go back home,
my fame will die, though my life will last
a long time—death will not end it quickly.
And so I encourage all the rest of you
to sail back home. You'll not attain your goal,
steep Ilion, because far-seeing Zeus
shields that city with his hand. Its people
have confidence in that. Thus, you should go.
Report this message to Achaean leaders—
that's the privilege of senior men—   530
their minds must come up with some better plan
to save the Achaean fleet and army
beside the hollow ships. The one they've got
won't work, since anger still keeps me away.
Let Phoenix stay here with me, sleep here,
so tomorrow he may join our voyage
to his dear native land, if that's his wish.
For I will not take him back by force."

Achilles spoke. Astounded by his speech, they all sat there,
in silence, stunned by the sheer force of his refusal.   540
After a pause, old horseman Phoenix spoke:

"Glorious Achilles, if your mind
is really set on going back, if you
are totally unwilling to protect
our swift ships from destructive fire,
because that anger has consumed your heart,
how can I remain here, dear lad, alone,
away from you? Old horseman Peleus
sent me with you, on that day he shipped you
from Phthia to join Agamemnon.   550
You were young, knowing nothing about war,

which levels men, or about public debates,
where men acquire distinction. Thus Peleus
sent me to teach you all these things,
so you could speak and carry out great actions.
Given all this, dear lad, how can I wish
to be alone and separated from you?
No, not even if god himself promised
to cast off my old age, to make me young,
the man I was when I first left Hellas,   560
land of beautiful women, running off
from my angry father, Amyntor,
Ormenus' son. He was incensed with me
about his fair-haired mistress. He loved her,
thus dishonouring his wife, my mother,
who begged me constantly—on her knees—
to have sex with that mistress, so she'd hate
my father. I obeyed, did what she asked.
My father soon found out what I had done—
he cursed me many times repeatedly,   570
praying to dread Furies that no dear son
born from me would ever sit upon his knees.
The gods made sure his curses took effect,
underworld Zeus and dread Persephone.
I planned to murder him with my sharp bronze.
Some god checked my anger, putting in my heart
what men would say, their great contempt—
how among all Achaeans I'd be called
the man who'd slaughtered his own father.
My heart no longer felt the slightest wish   580
to stay in my father's house with him so angry.
My friends and relatives who lived around me
begged me repeatedly to stay right there.
And then they butchered many well-fed sheep,
shuffling cattle with crumpled horns, and laid out
many hogs, swimming in fat, to be singed
in Hephaestus' flames. They drank many jugs
of the old man's wine. For nine nights,
they kept watch over me throughout the night,
taking turns as guards. Fires always burned,   590

one underneath the enclosed portico,
another in the hallway right outside
my bedroom doors. Ten nights later, as night fell,
I broke through the tight-closed bedroom doors,
went out, and jumped with ease across the wall
around the outer court, without being seen
by men and women checking up on me.
I ran away through all of spacious Hellas,
then came a suppliant to fertile Phthia,
where flocks are bred, to king Peleus.   600
He received me hospitably, loved me,
as a father dearly loves his only son,
heir to all his goods. He made me wealthy,
assigning me to govern many people.
I lived in the borderlands of Phthia,
reigning as king over the Dolopes.
And I was the one, godlike Achilles,
who raised you up to be the man you are.
You would refuse to attend a banquet
with anyone or eat in your own home,   610
unless I set you on my knees, fed you,
cut the meat, and held the wine cup for you.
Many times you soaked the shirt on my chest,
slobbering your wine, a helpless baby.
I've gone through a lot for you, worked hard,
bearing in mind that gods had taken care
I'd never have some children of my own.
Godlike Achilles, I made you my son,
so that if I ever met disaster,
you'd protect me. So, Achilles, subdue   620
your giant passion. It's not right for you
to have an unyielding heart. Gods themselves
are flexible, and they have more honour
than we possess, more power, too. Men pray
when they go wrong or make mistakes,
propitiating gods with offerings,
gentle prayers, libations, sacrifice.
Prayers are the daughters of almighty Zeus.
Lame, wrinkled, cross-eyed, they try to follow

behind Folly, who, because she's strong and quick, 630
runs far in front of them, appearing
all over the world, bringing harm to men.
Far behind, Prayers carry on their healing.
If a man honours these daughters of Zeus
as they come near, they will help him greatly,
paying attention to him as he prays.
If someone spurns them, rudely rejecting them,
they go to Zeus, son of Cronos, begging
for Folly to pursue that man, who then
harms himself and suffers punishment. 640
For that reason, Achilles, you should give
Zeus' daughters your respect. They have changed
the minds of other men, even great ones.
If Agamemnon were not bringing gifts—
and naming more to come—but persisting,
inflexibly angry, I wouldn't tell you
to cast aside your rage and help the Argives,
no matter how painful their distress.
But he's giving plenty now, more later.
He has sent out his greatest warriors, 650
selected from the whole Achaean army,
your finest friends among the Argives.
Don't show contempt for what they have to say
or insult their coming here. Up to now,
your resentment has been justified.
But we learn this from previous actions
of heroic men—when furious anger
came over some of them, they were swayed
by gifts and by persuasive speeches.
I recall an old tale from long ago. 660
Since you are all my friends, I'll tell it.
The Curetes and staunch Aetolians
were fighting and killing one another,
around Calydon, with the Aetolians
defending Calydon and the Curetes
eager to destroy the place in war.
Golden-throned Artemis had driven them to fight,
in her rage that Oeneus hadn't given her

a harvest-offering, first fruits of his orchard.
Other gods had received their sacrifices,   670
but he'd failed to offer anything to her,
a daughter of great Zeus. He forgot, or else
grew careless, a lapse within his foolish heart.
The archer goddess, in her rage, incited
a savage white-tusked wild boar against him.
This beast from the gods reached Oeneus' orchard
and was causing serious damage there,
knocking tall plants to the ground, entire trees,
including roots and flowering apples.
Meleager, Oeneus' son, killed the beast.   680
First he gathered huntsmen and hunting dogs
from many cities, for a small group
could not subdue such an enormous boar.
It had killed many men and sent them off
to their funeral pyres in agony.
Artemis began a war about this beast,
that battle between the Curetes
and the Aetolians, courageous men
fighting for the boar's head and bristly hide.
So long as war-loving Meleager   690
was in the fight, the Curetes did not do well.
For all their numbers, they could not hold
their ground outside the city walls.
But then anger swept through Meleager,
just as it forcibly swells up in chests
of other men, including wise ones, too.
His heart was angry with his dear mother,
Althea. So he stayed home with his wife,
Cleopatra, the attractive daughter
of the lady with the lovely ankles,   700
Maripessa, daughter of Euenus
and Ides, strongest of all men then alive.
He was the one who took his bow to make
a stand against a god, Phoebus Apollo,
fighting for the girl with lovely ankles.
Cleopatra's father and noble mother
at home called her by the name Alcyone.

Her mother shared the same fate as that bird,
the mournful halcyon, for she cried
when Apollo, the far shooter, seized her.   710
Beside this Cleopatra Meleager lay,
brooding on the rage that pained his heart,
infuriated by his mother's curses.
In her grief over her brothers' killing,
she prayed to the gods, beating fertile earth
with her hands over and over, kneeling down,
her breasts wet from crying, begging Hades
and fearful Persephone to kill her son.[1]
The night-walking Furies, with their stone hearts,
listened to her prayers from Erebus.   720
Then around the gates of Calydon
the battle din grew loud, war's turmoil.
The gates were being demolished. The old men
of the Aetolians begged Meleager
to come to their assistance. They sent
their gods' most important holy priests.
They promised him great gifts, telling him
he could take for himself, from anywhere
on the richest plain of lovely Calydon
fifty acres of the finest farm land,   730
half for a vineyard and half for farming,
open fields for ploughing. Oeneus,
the old horseman, kept imploring him,
standing at the threshold of his high room,
beating on the firmly bolted doors,
begging his son. His sisters and his mother
often entreated him. But he refused.
His companions, those most faithful to him,
his closest friends of all, added their prayers.
But they could not overcome those passions   740
in his chest, not until his own room
was under fierce attack, once the Curetes
had scaled the tower and begun to burn
that great city. Then his lovely wife,

[1]In a quarrel over who should get credit for first wounding the great wild boar,
Meleager had killed his mother's brothers.

in her grief, implored Meleager,
telling him the evils which can overtake
men whose town is violently seized—
how men are butchered and the city burned,
with women and children seized by strangers.
Once he'd heard of these disasters, his heart stirred.   750
He went outside, put his shining armour
around his body—and thus averted
a disastrous day for the Aetolians,
by following his heart. But the Aetolians
did not give him the many splendid gifts,
although he'd saved them from catastrophe.
My friend, don't think like Meleager.
Don't let some god make you choose that way.
Once the ships catch fire, it will be harder
to defend them. So accept the gifts.   760
Achaeans are honouring you like a god.
If you return to man-killing battle
without the gifts, you'll never get such honour,
even though you may push the conflict back."

Swift-footed Achilles then said in reply:

"Phoenix, dear old father, noble lord,
I don't need such honours, for I possess
honour in the will of Zeus. That will keep
me here beside my own hollow ships,
so long as there is breath within my body,   770
strength in my limbs. But I'll say this to you—
bear it in mind—do not confuse my heart
with these laments, these speeches of distress,
all serving that heroic son of Atreus.
You should not love him, in case I hate you,
who are now my friend. You would be noble
to join with me, and so injure the man
who injures me. Be equal king with me.
Take half my honours. These men report back.
You stay here. Sleep in your soft bed. At dawn,   780
we shall consider whether to go back

198

to our own land, or whether to remain."

Achilles spoke. His eyebrows gave a silent signal
to Patroclus to set a firm bed out for Phoenix,
so the others would quickly think of leaving.
But Ajax, godlike son of Telamon, spoke up:

"Noble son of Laertes, resourceful Odysseus,
let's be off. I don't think we'll bring this talk
to a successful end, not on this trip.
We must report this news, though it's not good,   790
to the Danaans waiting to receive it.
For Achilles has turned his great spirit
into something savage in his chest.
He's cruel and doesn't care for friendship
of his comrades, how we honoured him
above all others there beside the ships.
He has no pity. Any man accepts
reparations for a murdered son or brother.
The man who killed them pays a large amount
to stay there in his own community.   800
The other man's angry heart and spirit
are checked, once he takes the compensation.
But with you, gods have put inside your chest
unchanging evil passions, and all this
over a single girl. Now we are offering
seven of the best we have and much more.
You should turn your passion into kindness,
the hospitality of your own house.
For we are guests here under your own roof,
chosen from the Argive host. We believe   810
that we, of all Achaeans, are the ones
most dear to you, your closest friends,
far more so than all the others."

Swift-footed Achilles then said in reply:

"Ajax, noble son of Telamon, your people's leader,
everything you say matches what I feel.

But my heart chokes with rage when I recall
how that son of Atreus behaved towards me
with contempt, as if he were dishonoring
some vagrant. But you'd better go, take back   820
this message—I shall not concern myself
with bloody war until lord Hector,
murderous son of Priam, comes against
the huts and sea ships of the Myrmidons,
killing Achaean soldiers as he goes,
until he starts to burn our ships with fire.
I think that Hector will be held in check
around my hut, around my own black ship,
for all his eagerness to battle on."

So Achilles spoke. The men each took a goblet   830
with two handles, gave offerings, and went back to the ships,
with Odysseus in the lead. Patroclus ordered
his companions and the women servants to set up
a sturdy bed without delay for Phoenix.
They obeyed his orders and prepared a bed,
with sheepskin fleece and rug and fine linen sheets.
The old man lay down, to stay till morning.
Achilles slept in a corner of the well-built hut.
Beside him lay a woman he'd seized from Lesbos,
fair Diomede, one of Phorbas' daughters.   840
Patroclus slept opposite Achilles. Beside him
lay lovely Iphis, whom Achilles gave him
after capturing steep Scyros, Enyeus' city.

The others reached the huts of Atreus' son.
Achaea's sons stood up and welcomed them with toasts
in golden cups, one after another, asking questions.
The first to speak was Agamemnon, king of men:

"So come, tell me, famous Odysseus,
great glory of Achaeans, does he wish
to protect our ships from all-destroying fire,   850
or does he refuse, his mighty spirit
still gripped with anger."

Lord Odysseus,
who had endured much, replied:

"King of men,
mighty Agamemnon, son of Atreus,
that man's unwilling to let go his rage.
He's full of anger, more so now than ever.
He despises you, your gifts, and tells you
to think for yourself with the Argives
how you may save Achaean ships and men.
As for him, he made this threat—at first light   860
of dawn, he'll drag his trim balanced ships
down to the sea. He said he would encourage
others to sail home, for you'll not attain
your goal of lofty Ilion, since Zeus,
whose gaze ranges far and wide, holds his hand
over Troy, whose people now have confidence.
That's what he said. The others who went with me
will confirm this for you—Ajax and two heralds,
both prudent men. Old Phoenix stayed there,
to go to sleep, as Achilles told him,   870
so that he may go away with him
in his ships back to their dear native land,
if he wants, for he won't take him by force."

Odysseus spoke. They all were silent and disheartened,
especially by the force with which Achilles had refused.
Achaea's sons sat a long time speechless, troubled.
At last, Diomedes, skilled in war cries, spoke:

"Mighty Agamemnon, king of men,
you should not have begged noble Peleus' son,
offering countless gifts. At the best of times,   880
he's a proud man Now you've encouraged him
to be prouder still. Let's leave him alone,
whether he goes or stays. For he'll fight
when the spirit in his chest moves him,
or when god drives him to it. But come,
let's all follow what I now propose.

We've had our fill of food and wine. So now,
you should get some sleep, for strength and stamina.
When fair rosy-fingered Dawn appears,
you should range your army—men and horses—   890
before the ships, then rouse their spirits,
with you fighting at the front in person."

All the kings applauded horse-taming Diomedes.
They poured libations. Then each man went to his hut,
where he lay down and stretched out to take the gift of sleep.

Book Ten
A Night Raid

[Agamemnon's worries about the state of his army; he and Menelaus set
off to summon the chief leaders; at the meeting Nestor suggests someone
spy out the Trojan position; Diomedes volunteers but asks for a second
man; Diomedes selects Odysseus to go with him; Hector calls for a
volunteer to spy out the Achaean ships, promises Achilles' horses and
chariot; Dolon volunteers and set off; Odysseus and Diomedes catch and
interrogate Dolon; Diomedes kills Dolon; Odysseus and Diomedes attack
the Thracian camp, kill many men, and take the horses of king Rhesus;
Odysseus and Diomedes return in triumph to the ships]

By their ships, Achaea's most important leaders
slept through the night, overpowered by soft sleep,
all except Agamemnon, son of Atreus. Sweet slumber
did not enfold this shepherd of his people,
for his mind was disturbed with many worries.
Just as when Zeus, husband of fair-haired Hera,
flashes lightning to announce a massive rain storm,
an immense downpour of hail or snow, when fields
are sprinkled white, or to foretell some bitter warfare,
the gaping jaws of battle—in just that way then   10
the groans reverberated in Agamemnon's chest,
deep in his heart, making his whole body tremble.
Every time he looked out on the Trojan plain,
he was overcome at the sight of countless fires
burning in front of Ilion, at the sound of flutes,
pipes, the loud noise all those soldiers made. Looking back
at the Achaean army and the ships, he tugged
many tufts of hair out of his scalp, roots and all,
praying to high Zeus above, his brave heart groaning.
To him the best plan seemed to be to go to Nestor,   20
son of Neleus, before seeing anybody else,
to check if he could come up with some good advice,
some plan to save all the Danaans. So he got up,
slipped a tunic on over his chest, laced up
fine sandals over his sleek feet, and then put on

a tawny lion's skin, large and fiery red,
extending to his feet. Then he got his spear.

Menelaus, too, was troubled with anxieties.
No sleep sat on his eyelids either. He was afraid
Argives would be hurt, those who on his account   30
had crossed wide seas to Troy, planning to make war.
He covered his broad back with a spotted leopard skin,
picked up his bronze helmet, set it on his head,
then picked a spear up in his powerful fist.
Next he went to rouse his brother, commander
of the Argives, who worshiped him just like a god.
Menelaus found him putting his fine armour on
by his ship's stern. Agamemnon welcomed him,
as he approached. Menelaus, skilled in war cries,
spoke first:

> "Brother, you're arming yourself. Why?   40
> Are you going to encourage some companion
> to scout the Trojans out? I really doubt
> that anyone will do that for you,
> set off to spy against a hostile force
> under the cover of immortal night.
> Such work would require a courageous heart."

Mighty Agamemnon answered Menelaus:

> "You and I, lord Menelaus, need advice,
> some shrewd plan to protect or save the Argives,
> together with their ships. Zeus' mind has changed.   50
> His heart prefers Hector's sacrifices
> more than ours. For I've never witnessed yet,
> nor heard anyone report, how one man
> made so much havoc in a single day,
> as Hector, Zeus' friend, has brought upon us,
> Achaea's sons, all by himself. He's not a god,
> nor even a god's son. But he's damaged
> Argives in a major way, with actions
> they'll remember for many years to come.

That's how badly Hector's harmed Achaeans.
But, come, why don't you run quickly by the ships
to summon Ajax and Idomeneus.
I'll go for godlike Nestor, to rouse him,
see if he wants to check our watchmen
and tell that strong contingent what to do.
They'll attend to him ahead of anyone,
because his son is captain of the sentries,
along with Meriones, an officer
of Idomeneus. We entrusted them,
above all others, with this special work."

Menelaus, expert at war cries, then replied:

"How do you want me to carry out
your orders? Shall I stay there with them,
wait for you to come, or hurry back to you,
once I've told them your instructions?"

Agamemnon, king of men, answered Menelaus:

"Stay there, in case we somehow miss each other
as we go, for there are many pathways
through the camp. But make sure you call out
each place you pass, telling troops to stay awake.
Call each soldier by his father's name,
complimenting all of them. Don't make a show
of your own proud heart. We must work hard, too—
that's what Zeus charged us with when we were born,
a heavy burden of responsibility."

Agamemnon spoke, sending his brother off
with detailed orders. Then he set out to find Nestor,
shepherd of his people. He came across him
beside his hut and his black ship, on a soft bed.
His fine armour lay there with him—shield, two spears,
his glittering helmet, and that shining belt
which the old man strapped around him every time
he armed himself to lead his troops in battles

which destroy men's lives. Nestor made no concessions
to the infirmities of age. Sitting up there,
head resting on his arm, he spoke to Agamemnon,
questioning him:

        "Why are you alone like this,
wandering among the ships throughout the camp
in the pitch dark night, while others sleep?
What are you looking for? A mule? Some comrade?   100
Tell me. Don't approach in silence. What do you need?"

Agamemnon, king of men, replied:

        "O Nestor,
son of Neleus, great glory of Achaeans.
You should recognize me—Agamemnon,
son of Atreus, the one whom Zeus
always loads with miserable fortune,
more so than other men, so long as breath
stays in my chest and movement in my limbs.
I'm wandering like this because sweet sleep
won't sit upon my eyelids. Instead, this war,   110
this danger to Achaeans, has me worried.
I'm dreadfully afraid for the Danaans.
My spirit isn't resolute. It wavers.
My heart's about to burst outside my chest.
My fine limbs tremble. If you want some action,
since sleep hasn't come to you here either,
go with me. We'll walk down to the sentries
and check if they're exhausted and asleep,
worn out, forgetting to maintain a watch.
Hostile troops are camped close by. We don't know   120
if somehow they may be keen to fight at night."

Geranian horseman Nestor then said in reply:

        "Glorious son of Atreus, king of men,
Agamemnon—Counselor Zeus won't fulfill
all the things that Hector has in mind,

all his present hopes. In my opinion,
Hector will be struggling with more troubles
than you face, if Achilles changes his fond heart
from its hard anger. Yes, I'll come with you.
And let's get other leaders stirring also—   130
Tydeus' son, famous for his spear,
Odysseus, swift Ajax, and Phyleus' brave son.
Someone should go summon two more men,
godlike Ajax and lord Idomeneus.
Their ships aren't near here—they're a long way off.
But I have some harsh words for Menelaus,
although he's a friend and I respect him.
I won't hide that, even if I anger you.
For he's still sleeping, leaving you alone
to do the work. Right now he should be active,   140
working on all the finest men, begging them
to help us. The need confronting us is urgent."

Agamemnon, king of men, replied to Nestor:

"Old man, at other times I'd urge you on
to criticize him, for often he holds back,
reluctant to carry out the heavy tasks,
not because he's lazy or soft in the head,
but because he's looking for my signal,
waiting for me to make a move. But this time,
he was up and roaming well ahead of me.   150
He came to see me. I sent him off
to summon those very men you mention.
Let's go. We'll find them right before the gates,
where I ordered them to meet the sentries."

Geranian horseman Nestor then replied:

"If that's the case, none of the Argives
will say bad things of him or disobey,
when he stirs them on or issues orders."

With these words, Nestor put a tunic on his chest,

laced lovely sandals over his sleek feet. Around him 160
he buckled on a purple cloak in a double fold,
one thickly lined with wool. Selecting a strong spear
with a sharp bronze point, he set off on his way
down to the bronze-clad Achaeans' ships. The first person
Geranian horseman Nestor roused from sleep
was Odysseus, equal to the gods for wise advice.
Nestor called out to him. His voice entered
Odysseus' mind at once. He came out of his hut,
then questioned Nestor:

"What are you doing here,
going around alone like this among the ships, 170
in the immortal night? Is there something urgent?"

Geranian horseman Nestor answered Odysseus:

"Divinely bred son of Laertes,
resourceful Odysseus, don't be angry.
Achaeans are experiencing much suffering.
But come now, so we may rouse another man,
someone who should be there when we discuss
our plans, whether we should flee or battle on."

Nestor finished speaking. Resourceful Odysseus
went into his hut, then slung across his shoulder 180
his finely decorated shield and set off with them,
to find noble Diomedes, son of Tydeus.
They came across him with his weapons outside his hut.
His comrades were asleep around him, their shields
under their heads, spears driven upright in the ground
by the butt spike. Their bronze spear points glittered
like Father Zeus' lightning. Diomedes slept
with the hide of a field ox spread out under him
and a bright rug underneath his head. Approaching him,
Geranian horseman Nestor shoved him with his foot, 190
waking him up. Nestor then said teasingly:

"Wake up, son of Tydeus. Why sleep

all night long? Aren't you aware that Trojans
are encamped here on the edges of the plain,
near the ships, only a short distance off?"

Nestor spoke. Diomedes woke up quickly,
then answered him—his words had wings:

"Old man,

you're a hard one. You never stop working.
What about Achaea's other sons,
the younger ones? Can't each of them go round   200
waking up the kings? You old man,
we can't do anything to check you."

Geranian horseman Nestor answered Diomedes:

"My friend, everything you say is true enough.
I have excellent sons and many soldiers.
Any of them could go round with orders.
But Achaeans here are in their greatest need.
For now things stand upon a razor's edge—
miserable destruction for Achaeans
or their salvation. You're a younger man,   210
so if you feel compassion for me,
set off and wake up Meges and swift Ajax."

Nestor spoke. Diomedes threw a lion's skin
around his shoulders, a huge red pelt which reached his feet.
Then Diomedes grabbed a spear and went away.
He woke those warriors and brought them back with him.
When they joined up with the company of sentries,
they did not find the captains of the watchmen sleeping.
They were all sitting with their weapons, wide awake.
Just as dogs maintain a tired watch over their sheep   220
in some farm yard, when they hear a savage beast,
who's just moved down from wooded hills, men and dogs
raising a din around it, so those dogs get no rest,
that's how sweet sleep had left those sentries' eyelids,
as they kept guard that wretched night, always turning

towards the plain, in case they heard the Trojans coming.
Old man Nestor was pleased to see them. He called out,
speaking winged words of encouragement.

"That's the way, dear friends, to keep good watch.
Don't let sleep seize on any one of you, 230
so we don't bring pleasure to our enemies."

With these words, Nestor hurried through the ditch. Argive kings,
those who'd been called to council, accompanied him.
Meriones went, as did Thrasymedes, too,
Nestor's noble son, who'd been asked to join the group.
They went through the scooped-out ditch. Then in an open spot
they sat down where there seemed to be no corpses,
no bodies of the slain. It was where fearful Hector
turned back from killing Argives, once night hid everything.
Sitting down there, they talked to one another. 240
Then Geranian horseman Nestor began to speak.

"My friends, is there some man confident enough
of his own daring spirit to venture out
among stout-hearted Trojans, to see
if he can trap an enemy soldier,
some straggler, or catch wind of some report
of what the Trojans say among themselves,
whether they are keen to stay beside the ships,
away from home, or to go back to the city,
now that they have beaten the Achaeans? 250
A man who could find out these things,
return to us unharmed, would be famous
among all men living under heaven,
and get rich gifts, as well. For our best men,
those commanding every ship, will give him
a black sheep with suckling lamb. Compared to that,
there's no possession finer. At banquets
and our drinking parties, he'll be always there."

Nestor spoke. The others were quiet, saying nothing.
Then Diomedes, expert in war cries, spoke up: 260

210

"Nestor, my heart and my proud spirit prompt me
to infiltrate the hostile Trojans' camp,
which stands close by. But another man
should come with me. Things would go much better.
We'd have more confidence. When two set out,
one may see something good before the other.
A man alone might notice it, but his mind
is less perceptive, less resourceful, than two."

Diomedes spoke. Many men wished to volunteer.
The two Ajaxes, attendants of the war god Ares,   270
were willing, Meriones, too. And Nestor's son
was really eager. Famous spearman Menelaus,
son of Atreus, was ready, and brave Odysseus
was keen to steal into the Trojan army,
for the spirit in his chest was always daring.
Then, Agamemnon, king of men, spoke up:

                    "Diomedes, son of Tydeus,
    you delight my heart. But you must choose
    the other man. Take the one you want,
    the best of those in view. Many are keen.   280
    Don't reject the better man, following
    a sense of duty in your mind, taking
    someone less worthy as your comrade,
    thinking only of his birth. Don't do that,
    even if the second is the greater king."

Agamemnon spoke, afraid for fair-haired Menelaus.
Diomedes, skilled in war cries, spoke to them again:

    "If you bid me choose a companion for myself,
    how could I reject godlike Odysseus,
    with his heart and daring spirit always eager   290
    for every challenge? Pallas Athena loves him.
    With Odysseus at my side, we'd both return,
    even from blazing fire. For he knows,
    better than other men, how to use his mind."

211

Odysseus, that long-suffering, godlike man, replied:

"Son of Tydeus, don't over-praise me,
or censure me. You're speaking to the Argives,
who know everything about me. Let's go.
Night is passing quickly. Dawn approaches.
The stars have shifted forward. Most of the night   300
has passed, two thirds of it, with one third left."

This said, the two men pulled on fearful armour.
Warlike Thrasymedes gave a two-edged sword
to the son of Tydeus, for he'd left his own
beside the ships, and a shield as well. On his head he put
a helmet made of leather, without crest or plume,
what people call a skull-cap. It protected heads
of brave young men. Meriones gave Odysseus
bow, quiver, and a sword. On his head Odysseus set
a hide cap, on the inside skillfully reinforced   310
with leather thongs. Outside, wild boars' white teeth
were placed here and there, strategically and well.
In between these layers was a piece of felt.
This cap had once been stolen by Autolycus,
from Amyntor, Ormenus' son. He'd broken in
his well-built home in Eleon. Some time later,
Autolycus gave it to Amphidamas of Cythera,
to take back home to Scandeia. Amphidamas
then gave the cap to Molus, as a present
for his hospitality. Molus later gave it   320
to his son Meriones. And now it sat there,
covering Odysseus' head.[1]

                              The two men,
having put their fearful armour on, set off,
leaving behind there all the most important chiefs.
On their right, close to the path, Pallas Athena
sent them a heron. In the darkness of the night
they didn't see it with their eyes, but they heard its cry.

[1]Autocylus, the original one who stole the cap, is Odysseus' grandfather, well known
for his clever, thieving ways.

Odysseus was pleased with this omen of the bird.
He prayed then to Athena:

> "Child of aegis-bearing Zeus,
> untiring goddess, hear me. You've always stood   330
> beside me in all sorts of troubles.
> I don't move without your watching me.
> But now especially be my friend, Athena.
> Grant that we two come back to the ships
> covered in glory, after doing something great,
> something the Trojans will regret."

Then noble Diomedes, skilled in war cries, prayed:

> "Child of Zeus, invincible goddess, hear me.
> Stand by me as you did my father,
> lord Tydeus, at Thebes, that time he went   340
> as messenger, sent there by Achaeans.
> He'd left bronze-clad Achaeans at the Asopus,
> taking peace proposals to Cadmeans.
> On his way back, he did some fearful things,
> with keen support from you, divine goddess.
> Be willing now to stand by me like that,
> protect me, and I'll sacrifice to you
> an unbroken yearling ox with a broad head
> which no man yet has put beneath the yoke.
> I'll make that sacrifice to you, and more—   350
> on that beast I'll plate both horns with gold."

So they prayed, and Pallas Athena heard them.
Their prayers to the daughter of great Zeus complete,
they continued on their way, like two lions,
in the darkness of night, through the slaughter,
through corpses, armour, through black pools of blood.

                                        For his part,
Hector did not let his proud Trojans go to sleep.
He called their finest men together, all the ones
who commanded Trojans troops, with all their rulers.

213

To those assembled, he laid out a shrewd idea:

"Is there someone who'll undertake for me
an exploit, who'll do it for a worthy gift?
I guarantee he'll get a fine reward.
I'll give a chariot and two strong-necked horses,
the finest ones there are by those fast ships
of the Achaeans, to any man who dares,
who's fit to seize the glory for himself,
by approaching close to those swift ships,
to find out whether they're being guarded,
as before, or whether those men, beaten   370
at our hands, plan among themselves to flee,
and no longer wish to keep alert at night,
exhausted by their desperate efforts."

Hector finished. They all sat there in silence,
saying nothing. Now, among the Trojans
was a man called Dolon, son of Eumedes,
a sacred herald, a man rich in gold and bronze.
Dolon wasn't much to look at, but he ran fast.
He was the only male child, with five sisters.
At that point he spoke up to Hector and the Trojans: 380

"Hector, my heart and my proud spirit prompt me
to volunteer to sneak up to those fast ships
and find out what I can. Come, raise your sceptre,
swear to me that you'll give me those horses
and that chariot decorated all in bronze
which carry the fine son of Peleus.
I'll not be a useless scout or disappoint you.
I'll go straight through the army, till I reach
Agamemnon's ship, where their best men
must be in council talking of their plans,   390
whether to flee or to continue fighting."

Dolon spoke. Holding up his sceptre, Hector swore:

"Let Zeus himself, Hera's loud-thundering husband,

214

be my witness, that no other Trojan
will be carried by those horses. I affirm
that you will glory in them all your life."

Hector spoke. He'd sworn an empty oath, but Dolon
was encouraged. At once, he slung across his shoulder
his curved bow, then threw a gray wolf skin on it.
On his head he set a cap of marten skin,   400
grabbed a sharp spear, and set off, going from the camp
towards the ships. He would not be coming back,
bringing Hector information from the ships.
But when he left the crowd of men and horses,
he went eagerly along the path. As he moved,
noble Odysseus saw him and said to Diomedes:

"Diomedes, someone's coming from the camp.
I don't know if he's going to scout our ships
or strip some dead man's corpse. Let's let him
at first get past us on the plain, just a bit.   410
Then we can go after him and catch him fast.
If his feet outrun ours, we'll keep following him
and chase him from his camp towards our ships.
Keep brandishing your spear behind him,
so he doesn't make it to the city."

After these words, the two men lay down beside the road,
among the corpses. Dolon ran past them quickly,
quite unaware. When he'd gone about as far
as mules plough in a single day—and in deep fields
they outwork oxen pulling double-jointed ploughs—   420
the two men ran after him. When he heard their noise,
Dolon stopped, hoping in his heart they were comrades
coming from the Trojans to get him to turn back,
Hector having changed the orders. But when they came
within the distance of a spear throw or even less,
he saw that they were enemies and started running,
to get away as quickly as his legs could carry him.
They set off chasing him with speed. Just as when two dogs,
skilled hunting hounds with sharp fangs, harass some doe

215

or hare relentlessly across a wooded country,   430
the prey screaming as it runs, that's how Tydeus' son
and Odysseus, destroyer of cities, pursued him,
keeping Dolon from his people with their constant chase.
When Dolon was about to run into the sentries
in his flight towards the ships, at that point
Athena put fighting power into Tydeus' son,
so no bronze-clad Achaean could make the boast
that he'd hit Dolon first and that Diomedes
had come up later. Springing forward with his spear,
powerful Diomedes yelled:

                    "Stop!   440
Or I'll hit you with my spear. I don't think
you'll long escape complete destruction at my hands."

Diomedes shouted this, then threw the spear,
deliberately missing Dolon. The polished spear point
sailed over his right shoulder, then stuck in the ground.
Dolon just stood there terrified, stammering, pale with fear—
his teeth were chattering in his mouth. The two men ran up,
panting, and grabbed his hands. Dolon began to cry and beg:

        "Take me alive, and I'll ransom myself.
        At home there is bronze, gold, well-wrought iron.   450
        My father will give lots of it to you—
        an immense ransom—if he once finds out
        I'm at Achaean ships and still alive."

Crafty Odysseus smiled at him and said:

        "Don't worry. Don't let death weigh down your heart.
        Come now, tell me—and be sure to speak the truth.
        Why are you going like this to the ships alone,
        away from your army in the dead of night,
        when other warriors are fast asleep?
        Are you going to strip some dead man's body,   460
        or has Hector sent you as a spy,
        to learn something about the hollow ships?

Or did your own spirit prompt you to this?"

Dolon answered Odysseus, his limbs trembling.

"Hector led my mind astray with foolish hopes,
lots of them. He promised he'd give me
the sure-footed horses of Achilles,
Peleus' excellent son, and his chariot
with its bronze decoration. He told me
to venture out into the swift dark night,   470
get close to hostile troops, and then find out
if they were guarding their swift ships as before,
or whether, now we have defeated them,
they were planning flight among themselves,
unwilling to keep up watch at night,
exhausted by their desperate efforts."

Shrewd Odysseus, still smiling, then continued:

"Your heart has been ambitious for big gifts.
Those horses of warrior Achilles,
descendant of Aeacus, are hard to manage   480
or control for any mortal person,
except Achilles, son of an immortal mother.
Tell me, now, and be sure to speak the truth.
When you came here, where did you leave Hector,
shepherd to his people? Where's his armour?
Where are his horses? How are the sentries
of the other Trojans set? Where are they sleeping?
Tell me what they talk of amongst themselves,
whether they're keen to stay beside the ships,
quite far from home, or whether they'll return   490
to the city, with Achaeans beaten."

Dolon, son of Eumedes, answered Odysseus:

"I'll answer you in this quite truthfully.
Right now Hector is with his advisors,
holding a council meeting by the tomb

217

of godlike Ilus, some distance from the noise.[1]
As for the guards you asked about, noble sir,
there's nothing special to protect the troops,
or keep lookout. By all Trojan watch fires,
as necessity requires, there are men   500
who stay awake, calling to each other,
to keep up their guard. But the allied force,
which comes from many lands, is sleeping.
They leave it toTrojans to stay on watch,
for their wives and children aren't close by."

Crafty Odysseus, with a smile, then asked Dolon:

"Now, those allies—are they intermingled
with horse-taming Trojans where they sleep
or separate from them? Tell me. I need to know."

Dolon, son of Eumedes, answered Odysseus: 510

"I can reveal the truth of this as well.
By the sea lie Carians, Paeonians,
with their curved bows, Lelegians, Caucones,
god-like Pelasgians. Around Thymbre
are positioned Lycians, Mysians,
impetuous fighters, and Phrygians,
who fight on horseback, and from Maeonia
there are charioteers. But why ask me details
of these matters? If you're keen to infiltrate
the Trojan army, over there are Thracians,   520
fresh troops, new arrivals, furthest distant
from the rest, among them their king Rhesus,
son of Eioneus. His horses are the best,
the finest and largest ones I've ever seen,
whiter than snow, as fast as the winds.
His chariot is finely built—with gold
and silver. He came here with his armour—
an amazing sight—huge and made of gold.

[1]Ilus was a king of Troy in the distant past. His tomb is a prominent landmark
outside Troy, frequently mentioned in the poem.

It's not appropriate for mortal men
to wear such armour, only deathless gods.   530
But take me now to your fast ships, or else
tie me up, leave me here in painful fetters,
so you can go and check my story out,
see whether I have told the truth or not."

Mighty Diomedes scowled at Dolon and said:

"Don't fill your heart with thoughts you'll get away,
Dolon, even though your news is good.
You've fallen in our hands. Now, if we
released you or set you free for ransom,
you'd come back to the swift Achaean ships,   540
either to spy or fight us openly.
But if my hands subdue you and you die,
you'll pose no problems for the Argives later."

As Diomedes finished, Dolon was intending
to cup his chin with his strong hand in supplication.
But with his sword Diomedes jumped at him,
slashed him across the middle of his neck, slicing
through both tendons. Dolon's head rolled in the dust,
as he was speaking. They stripped the cap of marten skin,
then took the wolf hide, long spear, and his curved bow.   550
Lord Odysseus held these objects high above him
for Athena, goddess of battle spoils, and prayed:

"Goddess, these are for you, to bring you joy.
We invoke you first of all immortal gods
living on Olympus. Send us on again
to where Thracians sleep and to those horses."

So Odysseus prayed. He lifted the loot up high,
placed it on a tamarisk bush, then set there
a clear marker, grabbing up reeds and branches
of tamarisk in full bloom, so they wouldn't miss   560
finding the spoils in the dark night, when they returned.
The two proceeded on through weapons and black blood.

They quickly reached the camp of Thracian soldiers.
The men were sleeping, worn out by their hard work.
Their lovely armour lay on the ground beside them,
properly arranged in triple rows. Beside each man
stood his yoked horses. In the middle Rhesus slept,
close by him his swift horses, tethered with their straps
to the chariot's top rail. Odysseus saw him first.
He pointed him out to Diomedes.

                        "There's our man,   570
Diomedes. And these are the horses
which Dolon told us of, the man we killed.
Come, now, let's see that mighty strength of yours.
It's not right for you to stand there idly
with your weapons. So loose those horses.
Or else kill the men, while I take care of them."

Odysseus spoke. Athena with her glittering eyes
breathed fighting power into Diomedes.
Moving around everywhere, he began the killing.
Agonizing groans came from those his sword then butchered.   580
The earth grew soggy with their blood. Just as a lion
comes across an unguarded flock of sheep or goats
and leaps on them, heart thirsting for the kill,
so Tydeus' son went at those Thracian soldiers,
until he'd slaughtered twelve. Whenever Diomedes
stood over some man he'd just killed with his sword,
crafty Odysseus, from behind, would grab his feet
and drag the body clear. For his mind was planning
how he might steal the fine-maned horses easily,
if he didn't frighten them by forcing them to step   590
on dead men's bodies, for they were not used to that.
Tydeus' son came across the king, the thirteenth man
whose sweet life he had taken. Rhesus lay there,
in his last gasp. A bad dream had stood beside his head
that night, a device sent by Athena—and that dream
was the son of Tydeus. Meanwhile, bold Odysseus
untied the sure-footed horses, roped them together,
and drove them from the camp, prodding with his bow,

for he'd forgotten to pick up the shining whip
from the ornate chariot. Then he gave a whistle,   600
to signal noble Diomedes. But he just stayed there,
wondering how he could do something really bold.
Should he take away the chariot, which contained
the king's finely decorated armour, pull it
by the pole, or lift it up above his head
and carry it like that? Or should he take the lives
of still more Thracians? While Diomedes turned over
these matters in his mind, Athena came, stood by him,
then said to noble Diomedes:

                 "Think of going back,
to the hollow ships, son of great-hearted Tydeus,   610
in case you get driven there in quick retreat,
if some other god wakes up the Trojans."

She spoke. He recognized the goddess by her voice.
He quickly climbed up on one of the horses.
Odysseus smacked them with his bow. They raced ahead,
in a rush to reach the swift Achaean ships.

But Apollo of the silver bow had not been
unvigilant, once he'd perceived Athena
taking care of Tydeus' son. Angry with her,
he went down into that huge crowd of Trojans   620
and woke up Hippocoön, a Thracian counselor,
one of noble Rhesus' family. Roused from sleep,
he saw that where the horses stood was empty,
the fearful carnage with men gasping in their death throes.
He screamed in grief, crying out for his companion,
calling him by name. Trojans created a commotion,
totally confused, as they rushed in all at once,
to gaze astonished at the terrible destruction
those two men did before returning to the hollow ships.

When the pair came to where they'd slaughtered Hector's spy,   630
Odysseus, dear to Zeus, pulled their swift horses up.
The son of Tydeus jumped down onto the ground,

handed over to Odysseus their bloodstained spoils,
then got back on his horse. They whipped the horses on,
racing willingly towards the hollow ships
with eager hearts. Nestor was the first to hear them.
He spoke up:

"Friends, Argive leaders and counselors—
my spirit prompts me to speak. But will I say
something true or false? A sound beats in my ear,
fast-moving horses' hooves. Perhaps, as we speak,   640
Odysseus and mighty Diomedes are driving
sure-footed horses back from Trojans. But I fear,
in my anxious heart, that Achaea's best
are in trouble from pursing Trojan forces."

Before Nestor could finish, the two men arrived.
They dismounted and were welcomed joyfully.
Men shook their hands, with warm congratulations.
Geranian horseman Nestor was the first with questions:

"Renowned Odysseus, great glory of Achaeans,
tell me how you two obtained these horses.   650
Did you sneak into that crowd of Trojans?
Or did you meet some god who gave them to you?
They're astounding, like rays of the sun.
I'm always going in among the Trojans,
and I claim I don't malinger by the ships,
although I'm an old man for a warrior.
But I've never seen, never imagined
horses like these. I think some god met you
and gave them to you. For cloud-gathering Zeus
loves both of you, as does bright-eyed Athena,   660
daughter of aegis-bearing Zeus."

Odysseus grinned at Nestor and answered him:

"O Nestor, son of Neleus, great glory
of Achaeans, if a god wanted to,
he'd easily give even better horses,

222

for gods are much more powerful than us.
But these horses which you ask about,
old man, are from Thrace, new arrivals.
Brave Diomedes killed their master,
along with all twelve of his companions,   670
their finest men. There was a thirteenth killed,
a spy we captured near the ships, sent there
by Hector and the other haughty Trojans,
to scout around our camp."[1]

Odysseus finished. Then he laughed with triumph,
driving the sure-footed horses past the ditch.
Other Achaeans came after him, rejoicing.
When they reached Diomedes' well-constructed hut,
they tethered the horses with cut straps in the stall
where Diomedes' own swift horses stood, munching   680
their sweet grain. Odysseus put the bloodstained loot
from Dolon into his ship's stern, until they'd made
an offering to Athena. Then the two men waded
into the sea, washed off their legs and necks and thighs,
removing all the sweat. Once the surf had taken
layers of sweat from off their skin and their hearts
had been refreshed, they stepped in shining tubs and bathed.
They washed, rubbing lots of smooth oil on themselves,
then sat down to eat. From the brimming wine bowl
they drew off sweet wine and poured libations to Athena.

---

[1]The number in Odysseus' report doesn't quite tally with earlier details, which list
the number of dead as fourteen.

Book Eleven
The Achaeans Face Disaster

[The description of Agamemnon's armour as he prepares for battle; the battle resumes; Agamemnon's exploits on the battlefield; the Trojans are pushed back close to the city; Zeus sends Hector a message; Agamemnon is wounded, has to withdraw from the battle; Hector re-enters the battle, kills many Achaeans; Diomedes and Odysseus make a stand against the Trojans; Diomedes is wounded by Paris; Odysseus is left alone; Odysseus is wounded; Menelaus and Ajax come to help Odysseus; Machaon is wounded, taken from the battle by Nestor; Hector moves against Ajax; Ajax is forced to retreat; Eurypylus is wounded; Achilles sends Patroclus to find out news of the battle; Patroclus visits Nestor and Machaon; Nestor's long speech about his youthful fighting; Nestor questions Patroclus about Achilles; Patroclus meets Eurypylus, takes him to his hut, gives him medicines]

As Dawn rose from her bed beside lord Tithonus,
bringing light to immortal gods and men alike,
Zeus sent Strife down to the fast Achaean ships,
the savage goddess, carrying the sign of war.
She stood by Odysseus' broad-beamed black ship
in the middle of the line, so she could be heard
in both directions, from the huts of Ajax,
son of Telamon, to those of Achilles,
whose well-balanced ships were drawn up at the ends,
for these men trusted courage and their own strong hands.   10
Standing there, the goddess screamed out a piercing call,
a dreadful sound. In the heart of each Achaean,
she put strength for war, for unremitting combat.
To men war then became sweeter than sailing back,
going home in their hollow ships to their dear native land.
The son of Atreus shouted to his Argives
to get their armour on. He pulled on his shining bronze.
First on his legs he set his shin guards—beautifully made,
fitted with silver ankle clasps. Then he put
a breast plate round his chest, something he'd received   20
as a gift of hospitality from Cinyras,

who'd learned in Cyprus the great news that Achaeans
were intending to set sail in their ships for Troy.
So to please the king, Cinyras gave the breastplate
to Agamemnon. On it were ten metal strips,
each dark blue, twelve of gold, and twenty made of tin.
On each side, three enameled snakes coiled to the neck,
like rainbows which the son of Cronos sets in clouds,
prophetic omens for mortal men. On his shoulder,
he slung his sword studded with shining gold.   30
The scabbard was silver, fitted with golden straps.
Then he picked up his richly decorated shield,
which covered his whole body, a beautiful work,
with ten bronze circles, twenty bosses of white tin,
and in the centre a boss of blue enamel.
On that shield, as crowning symbol, stood the Gorgon,
a ferocious face with a horrific stare.
Terror and Panic were placed on either side.
On the shield's silver strap writhed an enamel snake,
its three heads intertwined, all growing from one neck.   40
On his head Agamemnon placed his helmet,
with four bosses, a double ridge, and horsehair plume,
which nodded menacingly on top. He took two strong spears,
sharp ones with bronze points, whose glitter shone from him
right up to heaven. Athena and Hera gave
peals of thunder overhead, paying tribute to him,
Agamemnon, king of Mycenae, rich in gold.

Then each man told his charioteer to curb his horses
and line up in good formation at the ditch's edge,
while they marched ahead on foot in all their armour,   50
moving fast, shouting bravely in the early dawn.
They arranged their ranks on the far side of the ditch,
well beyond the chariots following at some distance.
Then Cronos' son brought them confusing signs of trouble,
sending down from high in heaven a rain of blood
dripping from the sky, for his intention was
to hurl the heads of many brave men down to Hades.

On the opposite side, by the high ground on the plain,

Trojans gathered round Hector, fine Polydamas,
Aeneas, whom Trojan people honoured like a god,   60
and three sons of Antenor—Polybus, Agenor,
godlike man, and youthful Acamas, who seemed
like one of the immortals. In the front ranks,
Hector carried his shield, an even perfect circle.
As some ominous star now suddenly appears,
shining through the clouds, and then disappears again
into the cloud cover, that's how Hector looked,
as he showed up in front, then in the rear,
issuing orders. All in shining bronze, he flashed
like lightning from Father Zeus, who holds the aegis.   70

Then, just as reapers work in some rich man's fields,
arranged in rows facing each other, cutting the crop,
wheat or barley, scything handfuls thick and fast,
that's how Trojans and Achaeans went at each other,
slicing men down. No one thought of lethal flight.
The sides were matched in fury equally—they fought
like wolves ripping at each other. Looking on, Strife,
goddess who brings much sorrow, was delighted.
She was the only god present at this battle.
The others were far off, sitting at their ease,   80
in their own homes on many-ridged Olympus,
where a fine house had been built for each of them.
All blamed the son of Cronos, lord of the dark cloud,
because he planned to give glory to the Trojans.
But Father Zeus was not concerned on their account.
Withdrawing some distance from them, he sat apart,
exultant, glorious. He looked out at Troy,
at the Achaean ships, at the flashing bronze,
at warriors killing, and at warriors being killed.

Throughout the early morning, as that sacred day   90
grew stronger, weapons thrown by both sides
took their grim toll—men kept on falling.
But at the hour a woodcutter prepares his meal
in some mountain glade, when his arms are tired
cutting big trees, when weariness comes in his heart

and sweet appetite for food overtakes his mind,
that's when Danaans, calling to each other in the ranks,
courageously broke through. The first to kill a man
was Agamemnon. He slaughtered Bienor,
shepherd of his people, and his companion, too,   100
Oïleus, the charioteer, who'd jumped down
from the chariot to challenge Agamemnon.
He'd charged straight at him, but his forehead took a blow
from a sharp spear. The rimmed helmet made of heavy bronze
didn't stop the spear, which smashed through it, through the bone,
and splattered his brain inside the entire helmet.
That stopped his bloodthirsty charge. Agamemnon,
king of men, stripped off their tunics and left them there,
their white skin showing. Then he moved on to butcher
Isus and Antiphus, two of Priam's sons—   110
one was a bastard, the other one legitimate—
both traveling in a single chariot. The bastard,
Isus, held the reins, and renowned Antiphus
stood beside him as the fighting man. These two men
Achilles had once tied up with willow shoots,
when he'd captured them while they were herding sheep
along Mount Ida's lower slopes. He'd let them go
for ransom. But this time, wide-ruling Agamemnon,
son of Atreus, with his spear struck Isus in the chest,
above the nipple, and his sword sliced Antiphus   120
right by his ear, throwing him out of the chariot.
He quickly stripped off their fine armour. He knew them,
for he'd noticed them before by the fast ships,
when swift-footed Achilles led them in from Ida.
Just as a lion chews up with ease the tender offspring
of some nimble deer, when he comes in their den—
his strong teeth seize them and rip out their tender life—
and the mother, even close by, cannot help them,
for a fearful trembling panic seizes her, so she runs fast,
bolting in a lather through dense foliage and trees,   130
from that mighty beast's attack—in just that way,
no Trojan then could save these two from slaughter,
for they were running off in flight from Argives.

Next, Agamemnon battled brave Hippolochus
and Peisander, sons of fiery-hearted Antimachus,
a man who'd received much gold from Alexander,
a splendid gift, so he'd agree not to hand back
Helen to fair-haired Menelaus. This man had two sons.
Mighty Agamemnon now caught them, both riding
in one chariot, attempting to control their horses.   140
The shining reins had fallen from the driver's hands,
panicking the horses. The son of Atreus jumped out
and faced them like a lion. From the chariot
the two warriors appealed to Agamemnon:

> "Take us alive, son of Atreus. You'll get
> a worthy ransom. There are many treasures
> in Antimachus' homes—bronze and gold
> and well-worked iron. Our father will be glad
> to give a massive ransom from all that,
> if he learns we're at Achaean ships alive."   150

The men said this in tears, addressing the king
with tender words. But the reply they heard was harsh.

> "If you're the two sons of Antimachus,
> that hot-hearted man who, when Menelaus came
> as envoy once to the assembled Trojans
> with godlike Odysseus, urged the Trojans
> to kill Menelaus, to stop him going back
> to the Achaeans, now you'll pay the price
> for those shameful actions of your father."

Agamemnon spoke. Then he struck Peisander.   160
He knocked him from the chariot to the earth
with a spear thrust to his chest. He crashed on the ground
and lay there motionless. Hipplochus jumped out.
But Agamemnon killed him on the ground.
His sword sliced away his arms and slashed his head off.
Then he set the head rolling through the crowd,
like some round stone. Leaving the bodies there, he charged
into the line where soldiers' ranks were most confused,

leading other well-armed Achaeans with him.
Their infantry cut down soldiers compelled to flee. 170
Chariots went at chariots. On the plain, dust clouds arose
from underneath, kicked up by thundering horses' hooves.
Men butchered men with bronze. Mighty Agamemnon
surged on ahead, always killing as he moved,
shouting out instructions to the Argives.
Just as destructive fire strikes thick woodland scrub,
driven in all directions by the swirling wind,
burning thickets to their roots, so they disappear,
swallowed up in the inferno's fiery rush,
that's how the heads of Trojans fell, as they ran off, 180
brought down by Agamemnon, son of Atreus.
Many strong-necked horses in the battle lanes
rattled past with empty chariots, missing their drivers,
excellent charioteers now lying on the ground,
far more friendly to the vultures than their wives.

Zeus pulled Hector back from the flying weapons,
dust, slaughter, blood, and noise, but Agamemnon,
bellowing orders to his Danaans, still pursued.
Trojans rushed back across the middle of the plain,
past the tomb of ancient Ilus, son of Dardanus, 190
even past the fig tree, desperate to reach the city.
But with his invincible blood-spattered hands,
Agamemnon kept up his pursuit relentlessly.
When Trojans reached the Scaean Gates and oak tree,
they stopped there, to wait for their remaining men.
But they were still in flight across the middle of the plain,
like cows scattered by a lion coming at them
in the dead of night—a general stampede,
but clearly grim destruction for one of them,
whose neck the lion first seizes in strong teeth, 200
breaks it, then gorges on the blood and all the innards—
that's how mighty Agamemnon, son of Atreus,
harassed Trojans, always killing off the stragglers,
as they fled back. Many men collapsed face down,
or on their backs, at the hands of Atreus' son,
as with his spear he raged up and down the field.

But just as Agamemnon was about to reach
the steep walls of the city, the father of gods and men
came down from heaven, sat on the peaks of Ida,
with its many springs, holding a thunderbolt.   210
He sent off gold-winged Iris with a message:

> "Go, swift Iris, and tell Hector this—
> as long as he sees Agamemnon,
> that shepherd of his people, rampaging
> at the front, mowing down rows of men,
> he must restrain himself, tell other troops
> to fight the enemy in the killing zone.
> But when Agamemnon, hit by a spear
> or wounded with an arrow, mounts his chariot,
> then I'll give Hector power to kill and kill,   220
> until he moves up to the well-decked ships,
> at sunset, when sacred darkness comes."

Zeus finished. Wind-swift Iris obeyed, going down
from Ida to sacred Ilion. She found Hector,
wise Priam's noble son, standing with his horses,
in his well-made chariot. Coming close beside him,
swift-footed Iris spoke:

> "Hector, son of Priam,
> like the gods for your wise counsel, Father Zeus
> has sent me to give you these instructions—
> for as long as you see Agamemnon,   230
> that shepherd of his people, rampaging
> at the front, mowing down rows of men,
> you must restrain yourself. Tell other troops
> to fight the enemy in the killing zone.
> But when Agamemnon, hit by a spear
> or wounded with an arrow, mounts his chariot,
> then Zeus will give you power to kill and kill,
> until you move up to the well-decked ships,
> at sunset, when sacred darkness comes."

After saying this, swift-footed Iris sped away.   240

With his weapons Hector jumped out of his chariot
down to the ground. Brandishing his sharp spear, he moved
all through the army, urging men to battle on,
encouraging their spirits for the dreadful fight.
The troops rallied and stood up against Achaeans.
Opposing them, the Argives reinforced their ranks.
Agamemnon was among them, first to charge ahead,
eager to fight well out in front of everyone.

Tell me now, you Muses inhabiting Olympus,
who was the first to come against Agamemnon—   250
one of the Trojans or one of their famous allies?
It was Iphidamas, son of Antenor,
a fine large man, raised in the fertile land of Thrace,
which nurtures flocks. His mother was lovely Theano.
Cisseus, his mother's father, raised him in his house
when he was very young. Once Iphidamas had reached
the age when younger men seek glory, Cisseus tried
to keep him there, marrying him to his own daughter.
But he'd left his bridal chamber to chase after fame
against Achaeans, taking with him twelve beaked ships,   260
which followed him. He'd left these well-balanced ships
at Percote, then come on foot to Ilion.
Now he moved out to face Atreus' son Agamemnon.
When the two were close, within each other's range,
Agamemnon threw and missed—his spear turned aside.
But Iphidamas struck Agamemnon in his belt,
just below the breast plate, thrusting with all his force,
trusting his strong hands. But he didn't penetrate
the gleaming belt, for the spear hit the silver first,
then bent aside, like lead. Wide-ruling Agamemnon   270
grabbed the spear in his fists and yanked it towards him
with the fury of a lion, pulling it away,
right out of Iphidamas' hands. Then he hit him,
his sword slashing through his neck—his limbs collapsed,
and Iphidamas fell there into a bronze sleep,
unhappy man, far from the wife he'd married,
to help his fellow citizens, far from that lady
from whom he'd had no favours, though for bride price

he'd offered much. First, he'd given a hundred cattle
and promised a thousand goats and sheep combined,   280
taken from the immense numbers in his flocks.
But then Agamemnon, son of Atreus, killed him,
stripped him, and went off through the Achaean throng,
carrying his armour.

              When Coön noticed this,
an eminent man, Antenor's eldest son,
his eyes darkened with grief for his fallen brother.
He moved out of lord Agamemnon's line of sight,
to one side, then struck his forearm with his spear,
just below the elbow. Coön's shining spear point
sliced straight through. Agamemnon, king of men, shuddered,   290
but didn't stop the fight or pull back from battle.
He charged at Coön, holding up his battered spear.
Coön was feverishly dragging his blood brother,
Iphidamas, out by the feet, crying for help
to all the finest men. Agamemnon struck him
with his bronze-tipped spear shaft below his embossed shield,
as he was pulling Iphidamas out from the crowd.
Coön's limbs gave way. Agamemnon stood over him,
then hacked off his head, so it fell on Iphidamas.
Thus, Antenor's sons came to their fatal end   300
at king Agamemnon's hands and went down to Hades.

While the warm blood was still flowing from his wound,
Agamemnon strode around the other ranks,
with spear and sword and massive boulders. But once that wound
began to dry and blood stopped flowing, then sharp pain
started to curb Agamemnon's fighting spirit.
Just as a sharp spasm seizes women giving birth,
a piercing labour pain sent by the Eilithyiae,
Hera's daughters, who control keen pangs of childbirth,
that's how sharp pain sapped Agamemnon's fighting strength.   310
He climbed into his chariot and told his driver
to go back to the hollow ships. His heart was heavy.
He gave a piercing shout, calling his Danaans:

"Friends, leaders, rulers of Argives,
it's up to you now to guard our seagoing ships
in this dangerous war. For Counselor Zeus
won't let me fight these Trojans all day long."

Agamemnon spoke. His charioteer lashed the horses
with the lovely manes toward the hollow ships.
The horses flew on willingly, chests flecked with foam,   320
their underbellies caked with dust, as they took
the exhausted king away and left the battle.

When Hector saw Agamemnon going back,
he gave a loud shout to the Lycians and Trojans:

> "Trojans, Lycians, Dardan spearmen,
> be men, my friends, call on your fighting strength.
> Their best man is leaving. Zeus, son of Cronos,
> gives me glory. Drive your sure-footed horses
> straight at those strong Danaans, so you can seize
> an even greater glory.

Hector spoke.   330
In every man he stirred up the spirit of war.
Just as a hunter urges on his white-fanged hounds,
to chase a lion or wild boar, that's how Hector,
son of Priam, like that man-destroyer Ares,
urged his great-hearted Trojans on against Achaeans.
He himself moved with those in front, fully confident,
falling on the enemy like a furious storm
swooping down to lash the purple ocean.

Who were the first, who were the last men slaughtered
by Hector, son of Priam, once Zeus gave him glory?   340
First was Asaeus, then Autonous, Opites,
and Dolops, son of Clytius, then Opheltius,
Agelaus, Aesymnus, Orus, and Hipponous,
a strong fighter. Hector killed these Danaan leaders.
Then he went after common soldiers. Like West Wind,
when it demolishes white South Wind's clouds,

striking them with heavy squalls, while many waves roll on,
massive and swollen, scattering spray high in the air,
under the howling of the veering wind storm—
that's how thick and fast Hector destroyed those men.   350
At that very moment, disaster would have struck,
inflicting on Achaeans irreparable damage—
they'd have been routed and fallen on their ships,
if Odysseus had not called out to Diomedes:

> "Son of Tydeus, what's the matter with us?
> Have we no memory of our warlike courage?
> Come here, friend, stand by me. We'll be disgraced,
> if Hector of the gleaming helmet takes the ships."

Powerful Diomedes then answered Odysseus:

> "I'll stay and stand up to their attack.   360
> But we won't enjoy this fight for very long,
> since cloud-gatherer Zeus would sooner give
> the victory to Trojans rather than to us."

Diomedes spoke. With his spear, he hit Thymbraeus
in his left nipple, tossing him from his chariot to the ground.
Odysseus struck Molion, godlike attendant
to lord Thymbraeus. They left the two men there,
for their fighting days were done, and charged to battle,
creating havoc. Just as two furious wild boars
fall on the dogs chasing after them, that's how   370
Diomedes and Odysseus turned back again
to slaughter Trojans. So Achaeans got welcome relief
in their flight from godlike Hector.

                                    The two warriors
then seized a chariot with two men, their people's finest,
two sons of Merops from Percote, a man skilled,
above all others, in prophecy. He wouldn't let his sons
go off to war's destruction. But they did not obey.
For Fates lured them on to the darkness of their deaths.
That famous spearman Diomedes, son of Tydeus,

stole their living spirit and stripped their lovely armour.   380
Odysseus then killed Hippodamus and Hypeirochus.

Gazing down from Ida, the son of Cronos made the fight
an equal combat, so on both sides men killed each other.
With his spear, Tydeus' son wounded brave Agastrophus,
son of Paeon, on the hip. There were no horses ready,
close at hand for his escape, a fatal blunder.
His attendant was holding them some distance off,
while he went on foot through those fighting at the front,
until lord Diomedes robbed him of his life.

Hector kept a sharp watch on those men. With a shout,   390
he went after them, taking ranks of Trojans with him.
Brave Diomedes, skilled at war cries, noticed this.
He shuddered and said to Odysseus, who was close by:

      "Mighty Hector's lethal wave engulfs us.
      Let's make a stand, stay here, and beat him back."

Diomedes spoke. He drew back his long-shadowed spear,
then hurled it unerringly. The spear hit Hector,
on the head, catching his helmet at the very top.
Bronze deflected bronze—the spear missed his splendid skin,
prevented by the triple layers on the helmet,   400
which he'd been given by Apollo. Jumping back,
Hector quickly rejoined the massed ranks of his troops.
He fell on his knee and stayed there, holding himself up
with his strong hand on the ground. Black night hid his eyes.
But as the son of Tydeus rushed in to retrieve his spear
from where it hit the earth among the front-line fighters,
Hector revived. He leapt into his chariot once more,
drove back into the crowd, eluding his black fate.
Brandishing his spear, powerful Diomedes yelled:

      "You dog—once more you're evading death for now.   410
      But you've narrowly escaped disaster.
      Phoebus Apollo has saved you once again.
      No doubt you always pray to him, every time

you go into the sound of thudding spears.
Next time we meet, I'll surely finish you
if some god is there to help me out, as well.
But now I'll attack the rest, any man
I chance to meet."

                                    Diomedes spoke.
Then he stripped the armour off the son of Paeon,
a famous spearman. But fair-haired Helen's husband,   420
Alexander, now aimed his bow at Diomedes,
his people's shepherd, leaning against a gravestone,
part of the funeral mound men had built for Ilus,
son of Dardanus, an elder of the people long ago.
Diomedes was stripping the gleaming breast plate
off the chest of strong Agastrophus, taking, too,
the shield from off his shoulders and his heavy helmet.
Alexander drew back on the centre of the bow.
He shot. The arrow did not leave his hand and miss.
It hit Diomedes' foot, the right one, on the top—   430
it passed through and drove into the ground. Laughing aloud,
Paris jumped from his cover, shouting out this boast:

        "You're hit. My arrow wasn't wasted.
        I wish I'd got you low down in the gut,
        taken your life. That way, there'd be some relief
        for Trojans from the misery you bring.
        Right now they shake with fear in front of you,
        like bleating goats confronted by a lion."

Without a sign of fear, strong Diomedes then replied:

        "You useless archer, brave only with your bow,   440
        seducer, if you stepped out to face me
        with real weapons, that bow and clutch of arrows
        would be no use to you. So now you've grazed me
        on my foot, and you boast like this. It's nothing—
        like some blow from a woman or witless child.
        A weapon from a coward has no bite at all.
        But from me, it's different, even a slight hit.

236

My spear is sharp. The man it hits, it kills.
His wife tears at her cheeks, his children then
are orphans. Earth is blood-soaked where he rots,   450
with vultures instead of women round him."

Diomedes spoke. Famous spearman Odysseus
came up and made a stand before him. He sat down
behind Odysseus and pulled the arrow from his foot.
Sharp pain shot through his flesh. Then he got in his chariot,
took the reins, and with a heavy heart went to the hollow ships.

Now famous spearman Odysseus was left alone,
no Achaean there beside him, for fear gripped them all.
Greatly troubled, he spoke to his proud heart:

      "Here's trouble. What's going to happen to me?   460
If I run away from this crowd in fear,
I'll be badly shamed. But to be trapped here,
all alone, that could be worse. For Cronos' son
has made the rest of the Danaans flee.
But why's my fond heart arguing all this?
I know that those who leave the war are cowards.
The man who wants to fight courageously
must stand his ground with force, whether he's hit,
or whether his blows strike the other man."

While in his mind and heart he turned this over,   470
ranks of shield-bearing Trojans advanced against him,
encircling him. But this only brought them trouble.
As when young men and hunting dogs harass a boar,
the beast charges from dense foliage on every side,
whetting white teeth on its curving jaws, and they dodge
all round it, to the sound of champing tusks,
hunters and dogs standing firm, for all their fear—
that's how Trojans then kept going at Odysseus,
whom Zeus loved. First he wounded fine Deïopites
above his shoulder, lunging at him with his sharp spear.   480
Then he killed Thoön, Ennomus, and Chersidamas,
whom Odysseus speared as he jumped from his chariot.

He hit him in the groin below his shield. As he fell,
he clawed handfuls of dust. Odysseus left these men,
then with his spear struck Charops, son of Hippasus,
blood brother of rich Socus. That god-like man
came up, stood close to him, and cried:

"Renowned Odysseus,
your store of tricks, of suffering, is infinite.
Today you'll boast you killed both sons of Hippasus,
slaughtered two men and stripped away their armour,   490
or else you'll lose your life, hit by my spear."

Saying this, Socus struck the even circle of Odysseus' shield.
The strong spear punctured the bright shield, forcing its way
through the finely decorated breastplate, slicing off
the flesh along his ribs. But Pallas Athena
stopped it from sinking into any vital organ.
Odysseus knew the spear had not hit a fatal spot.
He drew back and spoke to Socus:

"You poor man,
now's the moment grim death surely takes you.
Yes, you've prevented me from fighting Trojans,   500
but I promise here this very day you'll meet
the fatal darkness of your death, killed on my spear.
I'll get the glory. You'll give your life to horseman Hades."

Odysseus spoke. Turning round, Socus began to run.
But Odysseus hit him as he was moving off,
spearing him in the back between the shoulder blades,
driving the spear clean through his chest. He fell with a thud.
Lord Odysseus cried out in triumph:

"Ah, Socus,
son of fierce horse-taming Hippasus,
Death's final end was quick—no escape for you.   510
Unhappy man, you'll not have your father
or your noble mother close your eyes in death.
Flesh-eating birds will now rip you apart,

238

spreading their thick wings all over you.
But if I die, god-like Achaeans will provide
a proper burial for me."

                             With these words,
Odysseus pulled Socus' strong spear out of his flesh
and removed it from his shield. But as he drew it out,
he began to bleed. Odysseus grew concerned.
When great-hearted Trojans saw blood on Odysseus,   520
they shouted through the ranks and rushed him all at once.
Odysseus stepped back, calling out to his companions.
Three times he yelled, as loud as any man can shout.
Three times warlike Menelaus heard him call.
He quickly spoke to Ajax, who stood close by.

      "Ajax, divinely born son of Telamon,
leader of your people, I've just heard
a voice call—it belonged to brave Odysseus.
It sounds as if Trojans have him cut off,
caught him on his own in the killing zone.   530
Let's go to that crowd. We'd better save him.
I'm afraid that he's in trouble. He's a fine man—
he'd be a great loss to the Danaans."

Saying this, Menelaus led on. Ajax, that godlike man,
went with him. They found Odysseus, whom Zeus loved,
encircled by Trojans, like red mountain jackals
surrounding a horned stag wounded by an arrow
from some man's bow—its legs enable it to flee,
for while its warm blood flows, its limbs have power—
but as soon as that sharp arrow's drained its strength,   540
in some forest shade, wild mountain carnivores attack,
but should some god then lead a hungry lion there,
the jackals scatter, and the lion eats the stag—
that's the way resourceful fierce Odysseus was attacked
by many daring Trojans. The single warrior,
wielding his spear, held at bay his pitiless fate.
Then Ajax approached, carrying his towering shield.
He made a stand beside Odysseus. Trojans scattered

in all directions. Taking Odysseus by the hand,
warlike Menelaus led him from the crowd,
until his attendant could bring up his chariot.
Ajax then charged the Trojans. He killed Doryclus,
one of Priam's bastard sons. Then he hit Pandocus,
Lysander, Pyrasus, and Pylantes. As some river,
a mountain torrent in full winter flood, crashes down
onto the plain, gaining its power from Zeus' storms,
sweeping up many withered oaks and pine trees,
throwing piles of mud into the sea—that how
glorious Ajax then charged out onto the plain,
creating havoc, slaughtering men and horses.

Hector did not notice Ajax, for he was fighting
on the far left of the battle, by Scamander's banks,
where the slaughter was most fierce. A constant din arose
around great Nestor and warlike Idomeneus.
Hector was in the crowd there with them, grimly killing
with chariot and spear, decimating young men's ranks.
But the brave Achaeans would not have given way,
if Alexander, fair-haired Helen's husband,
had not stopped Machaon, shepherd of his people,
as he was proving himself among the very best.
Alexander's arrow, with a triple barb,
hit Machaon's right shoulder. Then Achaeans,
who breathe fighting spirit, feared for Machaon—
they thought he might he captured, should the battle change.
At that point Idomeneus spoke to Nestor:

> "Nestor, son of Neleus, great glory
> of Achaeans, come, climb up into my chariot.
> Let Machaon get in there beside you.
> Drive those sure-footed horses to the ships,
> and quickly, too. Machaon's a healer
> and so worth more than other men, with skill
> to cut out arrows and use healing potions."

He finished. Geranian horseman Nestor heard him.
He climbed into the chariot. Machaon got in beside him,

son of that excellent healer Asclepius.
Nestor whipped the horses. They dashed off willingly,
their spirits happy to be heading for the hollow ships.

Then Cebriones noticed Trojans were being driven back.
Going up to Hector, he spoke to him:

> "Hector,
> here the two of us mingle with Danaans,   590
> but on the outskirts of this hard-fought battle.
> Other Trojans, both men and horses,
> are being driven back in great confusion,
> routed by Ajax, son of Telamon.
> I know him well. He carries a huge shield
> around his shoulders. Let's get our horses
> and drive there in our chariot—that's where
> most of those fighting with horses or on foot
> are slaughtering each other, where men fight
> with most intensity. The noise never stops."   600

Saying this, Cebriones urged on their horses
with the lovely manes, cracking his whip over them.
Obeying the lash, they took the fast chariot at top speed
in the direction of the Trojans and Achaeans,
trampling on shields and corpses as they galloped on.
The axle was completely spattered underneath,
as were the rails behind, with gobs of blood thrown up
from horses' hooves and chariot wheels. Hector pushed on,
eager to join the throngs of men, to jump into the fight,
to smash that group to pieces. He made Danaans   610
totally confused—his spear hardly seemed to pause.
He ranged up and down Achaean soldiers' ranks
with spear and sword and massive rocks. But he kept away
from any fight with Ajax, son of Telamon.

Then Father Zeus, enthroned on high, put fear in Ajax.
He stood bewildered, shifted his seven-layered shield
onto his back, turned, looked round at throngs of Trojans,
like some wild beast, then backed off step by step, retreating,

but often turning back. Just as a tawny lion
is driven from a farmyard holding cattle   620
by dogs and farmers, who keep watch all night long
to stop it tearing some well-fed cow to pieces,
but the beast, ravenous for meat, keeps charging in,
without success, for a storm of spears rains down on him,
thrown by eager hands, followed then by burning sticks,
which, for all his fierce desire, make him afraid,
so, at dawn, he slinks away in bitter disappointment—
that's how Ajax most unwillingly retreated then,
away from Trojans, his spirit in distress.
He was very much afraid for the Achaean ships.   630
Just as when some donkey taken past a cornfield—
a stubborn beast on whose sides many sticks are broken—
bolts from boys tending it and goes to munch deep corn,
while boys beat it with sticks—although their strength is small,
at last they drive it out, once it's had its fill—
that's how proud Trojans and allies from many lands
then pushed back great Ajax, son of Telamon,
their spears always prodding at the centre of his shield.
From time to time, remembering his warlike spirit,
Ajax would turn again, holding off the ranks   640
of horse-taming Trojans. Then he'd turn back to retreat.
But he blocked the way to the swift ships for all of them.
He stood alone between the Trojans and Achaeans,
fighting furiously. Some spears hurled by brave hands
flew swiftly forward, then stuck in his great shield,
and many stood upright in the space between them,
impaled in earth, still eager to devour his flesh.

When Eurypylus, fine son of Euaemon,
saw Ajax being attacked by this hail of spears,
he went and stood by him. He hurled his shining spear   650
and hit Apisaon, son of Phausius,
a shepherd to his people, below his diaphragm,
in the liver. His legs gave way. Eurypylus rushed up
to strip armour from his shoulders, but he was seen
by godlike Alexander, as he was pulling off
the armour from Apisaon. So Paris grabbed his bow,

aimed at Eurypylus, then shot an arrow in his leg,
his right thigh. The arrow shaft snapped off.
His thigh was crippled. So Eurypylus moved back
among his comrades and thus escaped destruction.   660
But he shouted far and wide, calling to Danaans:

> "Friends, leaders and rulers of the Argives,
> rally your ranks. Save Ajax from a brutal death.
> He's being attacked with spears, and I don't think
> he's able to get out of this grim fight.
> Come, stand by great Ajax, son of Telamon!"

Eurypylus yelled this out as he lay wounded.
Men closed their ranks around him, leaning their shields
against their shoulders with their spears extended.
Ajax came to meet them. When he reached his comrades,   670
he turned around and stood his ground once more.

Thus these soldiers went at the fight like a raging fire,
as Neleus' horses carried Nestor from the fight.
Swift-footed Achilles, looking on, noticed Nestor.
Achilles stood by the stern of his broad-beamed ship,
watching the harsh work of battle, the pitiful retreat.
At once he spoke out to Patroclus, his companion,
calling him beside the ship. From inside the hut
Patroclus heard him. He came out, looking like Ares.
This moment marked the start of his final rush to death.   680
Patroclus, Menoetius' fine son, was the first to speak:

> "Why did you summon me, Achilles?
> Is there something you need me to carry out?"

Swift-footed Achilles then said in reply:

> "Fine son of Menoetius, joy of my heart,
> I think the time has come for the Achaeans
> to stand around my knees in supplication,
> for their needs have now become unbearable.
> But Patroclus, dear to Zeus, go now—

ask Nestor who that wounded person is   690
he's taking from the battle. From the back,
he looked exactly like Machaon,
son of Asclepius. But I didn't see
his face, for the horses passed me quickly
in their haste to gallop on."

                    Achilles spoke.
Patroclus then obeyed his dear companion.
He went on the run through Achaean huts and ships.

When the others reached the huts of Nestor, Neleus' son,
they stepped out on the fertile earth. Then Eurymedon,
Nestor's aide, unharnessed horses from the chariot.   700
The two men let the sweat dry on their tunics,
standing in the seashore breeze. They went inside the hut
and sat down on some chairs. Fair-haired Hecamede
made them a soothing drink. Old Nestor had taken her
from Tenedos, when Achilles ransacked the place.
Daughter of great-hearted Arsinous, she'd been chosen
for him by Achaeans, because he excelled them all
in giving wise advice. First, she pushed out in front of them
a well-polished table with feet of blue enamel.
Then she set there a bronze basket holding onions,   710
to spice up their drink, with pale honey and bread
made of sacred barley. Beside these she set a cup,
a magnificent work Nestor had brought from home,
studded with gold. There were four handles on it,
around each one a pair of golden doves was feeding.
Below were two supports. When that cup was full,
another man could hardly lift it from the table,
but, old as he was, Nestor picked it up with ease.
In this cup Hecamede, looking like a goddess,
made a soothing drink for them from Pramnian wine.   720
In it she shredded goat's cheese with a grater made of bronze,
then shook white barley grain on top. When she'd prepared it,
she invited them to drink. The two men drank
and quenched their parching thirst. They started talking,
enjoying each other's pleasant conversation.

Then Patroclus stood in the doorway, like some god.
Seeing him, old Nestor leapt up from his shining chair,
took him by the hand and invited him to sit.
Patroclus declined, staying where he was. He said:

> "Old man, divinely bred, I can't sit down. 730
> You'll not talk me into it. The man who sent me
> is honourable but quick to take offence.
> I'm here to learn the name of that wounded man
> you drove in with. But I see him for myself.
> I know Machaon, his people's shepherd.
> Now I'll go back and tell this to Achilles.
> You know well enough, divinely bred old man,
> what he's like—not someone to take lightly.
> He'd be quick to blame an innocent man."

Geranian horseman Nestor then said to Patroclus: 740

> "Why is Achilles showing pity now
> for Achaea's sons, those men hurt with spears
> and arrows? He knows nothing of our trouble,
> the great suffering which afflicts the army.
> For our best men lie injured at the ships,
> crippled by arrows, spears, and swords.
> Strong Diomedes, son of Tydeus, is hurt,
> as is Odysseus, famous for his spear,
> Agamemnon and Eurypylus as well,
> with an arrow in his thigh. This man here, 750
> hurt with an arrow from some bowstring,
> I've just brought in from battle. Achilles is brave,
> but shows no pity, feels nothing for Danaans.
> Is he waiting until our fast ships by the sea
> are set on fire with all-consuming flames,
> and Achaeans, powerless to stop it,
> are slaughtered one by one? My strength now
> in my supple limbs is not what it used to be.
> I wish I were as young, my strength as firm,
> as when the Eleans and our people 760
> went to war over stolen cattle, when I killed

245

Itymoneus, brave son of Hypeirochus,
a man from Elis, as I was driving off
what we'd seized in reparation. He was fighting
for his cattle. In the foremost ranks,
a spear from my hand struck him. He collapsed.
His country people ran away, and so we seized
a huge amount of plunder from that plain—
fifty herds of cattle, as many flocks of sheep,
fifty droves of pigs, fifty herds of wandering goats,   770
one hundred fifty horses, all chestnut mares,
many with foals still standing under them.
At night we drove these to the citadel
of Neleus' city Pylos. Neleus rejoiced,
glad at heart, because I'd shared in so much loot,
though I was just a young man going to war.
Next day at dawn, heralds proclaimed out loud
that all those to whom Elis stood in debt
should meet together. The leading men of Pylos
thus gathered to appropriate the spoils,   780
for Epeians were in debt to many men.
Those of us in Pylos were few and weak.
Mighty Hercules had come some years before
and sapped our strength by killing our best men.
Neleus once had twelve worthy sons—
I'm the only one remaining. The others
were all wiped out. Bronze-armed Epeians
at that point took advantage of us,
committing evil and aggressive acts.
From that plunder old Neleus selected   790
a herd of cattle, a large flock of sheep,
taking three hundred of them with their shepherds.
Holy Elis owed him an enormous debt—
four prize-winning horses with their chariot,
which had come to Elis to compete, intent
on racing for a tripod. But Augeias,
king of men, kept the horses there in Elis.
He sent their diver back, grieving for his team.
Old Neleus was angry with Augeias
for what he'd said and done. That's why he took   800

246

so much booty for himself. The rest he gave
to be distributed among the people
in equal shares, so no one would object.
We allocated each and every bit
and sacrificed to all the city gods.
On the third day Epeians came in force,
all together, with their sure-footed horses,
at top speed, lots of them. Among them came
the two Moliones, fully armed, still young,
not knowing much of serious warfare.   810
Now, there's a certain city Thryoessa,
far off on a steep hill by the Alpheius,
at the very end of sandy Pylos.
Desperately eager to destroy this place,
they pitched their forces round it in a siege.
But once Epeians crossed the entire plain,
Athena came speeding from Olympus
down to us at night. She brought a message—
we should arm ourselves. She mustered a force
of volunteers in Pylos, all keen for war.   820
Neleus would not let me take up arms.
He hid my horses—he thought I was ignorant
of anything to do with war. But even so,
though I fought on foot, I made my mark
among our charioteers. For Athena
planned the battle out in just that way.
There is a river Minyeïus, which meets the sea
near Arene. The Pylian horsemen
waited there till dawn while squads of men on foot
came streaming in. We moved out quickly   830
with our weapons, all together. At noon
we reached the holy river Alpheius.
We sacrificed fine beasts to Zeus almighty,
a bull to Poseidon, and one to Alpheius.
To Athena with the glittering eyes we offered up
a cow from our own herd. Then we had dinner
at our positions there throughout the camp.
We went to sleep, each man with his weapons,
along the river bank. The brave Epeians

were encircling the city, hearts set on razing it.
Before they managed that, they saw a fight,
a major battle. For when the sun appeared
above the earth, we sacrificed to Zeus
and to Athena, then started our attack.
When Pylians and Epeians began the battle,
I was the first to kill a man and seize
his sure-footed horses. That man was Mulius,
a spear fighter, son-in-law to Augeias.
He'd taken as his wife fair-haired Agamede,
the eldest daughter, who knew all medicines
this wide earth provides. As he came against me,
I struck him with my bronze-tipped spear. He fell
into the dust. I jumped in his chariot,
taking my place among the foremost fighters.
Stout-hearted Epeians saw the man go down,
leader of their horsemen, their best fighting man.
They ran away in all directions. I pursued,
going after them like some black whirlwind.
I captured fifty chariots. In every one
two warriors bit the dust, slain by my spear.
And I'd have slaughtered both the Molines,
Actor's descendants, but their father,
the wide-ruling shaker of the earth, Poseidon,
with a thick concealing mist let them escape.
Then Zeus put great power into Pylians.
We pursued Epeians over that wide plain,
killing them and gathering their splendid weapons,
until we pushed our horses into Bouprasium,
a wheat-rich region, to the rock of Olene,
the place which people call Alesium hill.
There Athena turned our soldiers back.
I killed the final warrior and left him there.
Achaeans quickly led their fast horses back
from Bouprasium to Pylos, all of them
paying tribute among all the gods to Zeus,
and among all men to Nestor. That's how
I once used to be, when I was a man
among the men. But what of Achilles?

His courage will profit no one but himself.
I think he might bitterly regret all this,   880
once our army is destroyed. O my friend,
that day Menoetius sent you from Phthia
in Agamemnon's cause, he gave you orders.
Both lord Odysseus and myself were present.
We heard all he said to you there in his house.
We'd come to the well-built home of Peleus,
mustering men across fertile Achaea.
And we found warrior Menoetius and yourself,
together with Achilles. In the courtyard,
old horseman Peleus was burning thigh bones   890
rolled in fat to thunder-loving Zeus.
He held a golden cup, poured gleaming wine,
libations, on the flaming sacrifice.
The two of you were busy with the ox meat.
We two stood in the doorway. Achilles
jumped up in great surprise, took our hands,
brought us inside, inviting us to sit.
Then we received fine hospitality,
the sort appropriate for strangers. Later,
when we'd had our fill of food and drink,   900
I began to speak, asking you to come with us.
You were really eager. Both older men
gave you instructions about many things.
Old Peleus ordered his son Achilles
always to be the best, to stand pre-eminent,
above all other men. Menoetius, son of Actor,
told you: 'My son, Achilles is by birth
a finer man than you. But you are older.
In strength he is by far your better,
but it's up to you to give shrewd advice,   910
prudent counsel, and direction to him.
He'll comply, for that works to his benefit.'
That's what the old man said. But you forget.
Even now, if you'd speak to fierce Achilles,
you might persuade him. Who knows? Some god
might help you shift his spirit with your words.
A friend's persuasion is an excellent thing.

249

But if his heart knows of some prophecy
that he's avoiding, something from Zeus
his mother's mentioned to him, then at least   920
let him send you to war, in command
of other Myrmidons—it may be
you'll prove a saving light to the Danaans.
Let him also give you his fine armour
to carry into battle, so Trojans may confuse
the two of you and thus refrain from fighting.
Achaea's warrior sons are tired out.
They might gain a breathing space, something rare
in warfare. Your troops are fresh. They might drive
Trojans worn out with fighting to the city,   930
far from our ships and huts."

                    Nestor finished speaking.
His words stirred up the heart inside Patroclus' chest.
He went off on the run along the line of ships,
towards Achilles, descendant of Aeacus.
But as Patroclus ran by lord Odysseus' ships,
right where they held assemblies and judicial court,
where they'd built their altars to the gods as well,
he met Eurypylus, royal son of Euaemon,
limping from the battle, his thigh wounded by an arrow.
Down his head and shoulders ran rivulets of sweat.   940
Black blood seeped from his nasty wound. But his spirit
was still strong. Seeing him, Menoetius' worthy son
felt compassion. He spoke winged words of sympathy:

        "You leaders, rulers of Achaeans,
        it seems to be your destiny to feed the dogs
        with your white flesh at Troy, far from your friends,
        far from your native land. But come now,
        Eurypylus, you royal warrior, tell me
        whether Achaeans will manage to contain
        warlike Hector, or whether they'll all die,   950
        slaughtered here on Hector's spear."

Wise Eurypylus then said in answer to Patroclus:

"Lord Patroclus, there's no longer anything
can save Achaeans, who'll fall back to their black ships.
All those who were our finest fighters
are lying by the ships, hurt or wounded
at Trojan hands, whose strength keeps growing.
But take me safely back to my black ship,
cut the arrow from my thigh, and with warm water
wash away the black blood there, then rub on   960
fine soothing medication, whose use, they say,
Achilles taught you, an art he learned
from Cheiron, most righteous of the Centaurs.
Of our healers, Podalerius and Machaon,
one, I believe, lies wounded in our huts,
himself requiring some worthy healer,
the other's out there on the plains, holding off
the fighting spirit of the Trojans."

Menoetius' fine son then said to Eurypylus:

"How can you get this cure? What can we do,   970
noble Eurypylus? I'm on my way
to inform warlike Achilles of the news
which Geranian Nestor, Achaea's guardian,
asked me to report. But I won't leave you
in such suffering."

        When Patroclus had finished,
he put his arm around Eurypylus' chest, then took
that shepherd of his people to his hut. Seeing them,
an aide put down some ox hides. Settling him there,
with a knife Patroclus cut out the arrow, razor sharp,
from his thigh, then with warm water washed the black blood off. 980
He put some bitter root onto his hands and rubbed it in,
something to relieve the hurt, remove all pain.
The wound then dried, and blood stopped flowing.

Book Twelve
The Fight at the Barricade

[The battle continues at the wall, with Achaeans hemmed in; Polydamas advises Hector to leave the chariots behind; Trojans organize themselves into five companies for the assault; two Lapith spearmen guard the Achaean gate; Trojans receive a bad omen; Polydamas advises Hector not to attack the wall; Sarpedon's speech to Glaucus about their warrior code; Sarpedon assaults the wall; Menestheus asks for help from Ajax and Teucer; Ajax responds; Glaucus is wounded; Hector demolishes the doors in the gate; the Trojans breach the wall; Achaeans retreat to their ships.]

Thus, as Patroclus, Menoetius' fine son, looked after
wounded Eurypylus in his hut, Trojans and Achaeans
kept fighting on in clusters. The Danaan ditch
and the high broad wall weren't going to hold out long.
They'd built the wall, then dug the ditch around it,
to protect the ships and guard the ample plunder
stored inside. But they'd built it without sanction
from immortal gods—they'd made no splendid offering,
no sacrifices to the gods, asking them to keep
their swift ships safe, so the wall soon fell apart.   10
As long as Hector lived and Achilles' anger
did not relent and Priam's city wasn't captured,
the huge Achaean wall remained intact.
But after so many of the finest Trojans died,
many Achaeans, too, though many did survive,
in the war's tenth year, Priam's city was destroyed.
When Achaeans sailed back to their dear native land,
then Poseidon and Apollo planned to erase that wall,
by stirring up the raging power of all rivers
flowing from Mount Ida to the sea—Rhesus,   20
Heptaporus, Caresus, Rhodius, Granicus,
Aesepus, the sacred Scamander and Simoeis,
where many ox-hide shields and helmets had fallen
in the dust, along with a race of people half-divine.
Phoebus Apollo merged the mouths of all these rivers,
then for nine days drove the flood against the rampart.
Zeus brought constant rain to wash the wall away

into the sea more quickly. And Poseidon, too,
the Earthshaker himself, holding his trident,
led the work, his waves eroding all foundations,   30
wood and stone Achaeans had worked so hard to set there.
He smoothed the shores of the fast-flowing Hellespont,
covering huge beaches once again with sand. The wall gone,
he changed the rivers, so they flowed on as before,
their lovely waters in their customary channels.
All this Apollo and Poseidon would do later on.

But then the din of war raged round the sturdy wall.
The battered timbers on the tower rattled.
Argives, broken by Zeus' whip, were all hemmed in
beside their hollow ships, held back by fear of Hector,   40
whose powerful presence scared them, for, as before,
he battled like a whirlwind. Just as some wild boar
or lion faced with dogs and huntsmen keeps turning,
confident of his strength, and men form in a line,
preparing to go against the beast, hurling spears
in volleys from their hands—still it doesn't tremble,
show any fear in its brave heart, but its courage
kills the beast—repeatedly it whirls itself around,
threatening the ranks of men—that's how Hector then
moved through the troops, urging men to attack the ditch   50
and charge across it. But his swift-footed horses balked,
standing at the very edge, neighing loudly,
terrified because the trench was wide to cross.
They couldn't easily jump over it or get through.
On both sides there were steep banks along its length,
with many large sharp stakes driven in the upper edge,
set there by Achaea's sons as a protection
against their enemies. There was no easy way
horses pulling chariots with wheels could move across.
Even men on foot weren't confident about it.   60
Then Polydamas, coming up beside bold Hector, said:

> "Hector, you other leaders, you allies,
> it's foolish to think of driving our swift horses
> through this trench. It's difficult to get across,

with those sharpened stakes projecting from it,
right by the Achaean wall. There's no way
any charioteer could get down and fight.
There's not much room. I think we'd get badly hurt.
If high-thundering Zeus intends to help the Trojans
and harm Achaeans, wipe them out completely,   70
I'd prefer that happened right away,
so Achaeans all die here, far from Argos,
unremembered. But if they turn us back,
drive us from the ships, and trap us in the trench,
and if Achaeans then reorganize,
I don't think any of us will get back
to our city with the news. But come,
let's all agree to what I now propose—
attendants should hold the horses at the ditch.
We'll arm ourselves with heavy weapons,   80
then all follow Hector bunched up tightly.
Achaeans will not push us back, if it's true
they're already headed for destruction."

What Polydamas had just proposed pleased Hector.
With his weapons, he jumped from his chariot to the ground.
The other Trojans did not hesitate. Seeing him do that,
they leapt quickly from their chariots and left them there.
Each man told his charioteer to keep the horses
in good order by the ditch. The men broke up in groups
and organized themselves to form five companies,   90
with each one following its own leadership.
Some went with Hector and worthy Polydamas.
They were the best and most numerous, especially keen
to breach the wall and fight on at the hollow ships.
Cebriones went with them as third commander.
Paris led the second group, along with Agenor
and Alcathous. Helenus and godlike Deïphobus,
two sons of Priam, led the third contingent,
with a third commander, warlike Asius,
son of Hyrtacus, whose huge horses had carried him   100
all the way from Arisbe by the Selleïs river.
The fourth group of warriors was headed by Aeneas,

Anchises' brave son, with Archelochus
and Acamas, two sons of Antenor, well skilled
in all the elements of war. The famous allies
Sarpedon led. He'd chosen to command with him
Glaucus and warlike Asteropaeus, for they seemed
clearly the best of all the others, after himself,
for among them all he was pre-eminent.
These men linked themselves with sturdy bull's hide shields,   110
then in their eagerness made straight for the Danaans.
They thought no one could stop them, as they charged the ships.

Other Trojans and their famous allies followed
what excellent Polydamas had said to them,
but Asius, son of Hyrtacus, leader of men,
did not want to leave his horses or their driver,
the attendant charioteer. He brought them with him
as he went for the ships. The fool! He would not escape
his grim fate and come back from the ships to windy Troy,
proudly boasting of his chariot and horses.   120
Before that happened an unwelcome fate took him
on the spear of Deucalion's proud son, Idomeneus.
Asius moved off to the left of the line of ships,
where Achaeans used to pass with horse and chariot
when returning from the plain. That's where he drove
his chariot and team. He found the gates unbarred—
men had drawn the long bolt and were holding them ajar,
just in case they might save one of their companions
escaping from the battle to the ships. At those gates
Asius firmly aimed his horses. His men followed,   130
shouting loudly. They thought Achaeans could hold out
no longer, that they'd be assaulting the black ships.
How wrong they were! For at the gates they found two men,
two of the finest—proud-hearted sons of Lapith spearmen.[1]
One was powerful Polypoetes, son of Peirithous,
the other Leonteus, a warrior like man-killing Ares.
These two made their stand before the lofty gate,
like two high-topped mountain oak trees which defy
wind and rain each and every day, anchored there

---

[1]The Lapiths are a warlike tribe living near Mount Olympus.

by huge extensive roots—just like that, these two men,   140
trusting the power in their arms, held their position,
as great Asius approached. They did not run off.
Holding bull's hide shields up high, with loud shouts,
Asius' men came straight for the well-built wall,
behind lord Asius, Iamenus, Orestes,
Adamas, Asius' son, Thoön, and Oenomaus.

Up to now, the two Lapiths had been urging
well-armed Achaeans from inside the rampart
to defend their ships. But when they noticed Trojans
charging the wall and Danaans running off and shouting,   150
the two men hurried out to fight beyond the gates.
Like wild mountain boars taking on a confused mob
of men and dogs attacking them—the beasts charge sideways,
shattering trees around them, ripping out the roots,
gnashing their teeth noisily, till someone
hits them with his spear and takes away their lives—
that's how the shining bronze sounded on these two,
as they moved out against the flying weapons.
But they fought bravely, relying on their strength
and on those troops standing on the wall above them,   160
who kept throwing rocks down from the sturdy tower,
defending themselves, their huts, their well-built ships.
Stones fell to earth like snowflakes which some strong wind
pushing shadowy clouds drives downward in a storm,
so they strike the fertile earth, that's how thick and fast
flying weapons rained down then from Trojans and Achaeans.
Helmets and bossed shields rang out as they were hit
with rocks the size of millstones. Then Asius,
son of Hyrtacus, groaned in vexation, struck his thigh,
and cried out:

              "Father Zeus, how you love to lie!   170
I didn't think these warrior Achaeans
could withstand the force of our all-powerful hands.
But they're like yellow-banded wasps or bees
who've made their home by some rough road
and won't leave their hollow house, but stay there,

guarding their offspring from the hunting men.
That's how these men refuse to yield the gate,
though there's just two of them, until they kill us
or are killed themselves."

Asius complained,
but his words did not win over Zeus' mind,   180
for in his heart he wished to give Hector glory.

Other troops were battling on at other gates.
It would be hard for me to report all these events,
even if I were a god. For by that stone wall
blazing fires broke out everywhere. Though in distress,
Achaeans had no choice but to defend their ships—
gods helping Danaans in the fight were sad at heart.

The two Lapiths now began to kill in earnest.
Powerful Polypoetes, son of Peirithous,
with his spear struck Damasus through his cheek piece.   190
The bronze helmet didn't stop the spear—its bronze point
tore straight through his skull, splattering his brains
all through his helmet. That checked his fighting fury.
Then he slaughtered Pylon, as well as Ormenus.
With his spear, Leonteus, Ares' assistant, hit
Hippomachus, son of Antimachus, in his belt.
Then, pulling out his sharp sword from its scabbard,
he charged the Trojan mass, struck Antiphates,
hitting him at close range first. So he lay there,
on his back, motionless. Leonteus then struck down   200
in quick succession Menon, Iamenus, and Orestes—
all these lay prone there, on the all-nourishing earth.

While the two Lapiths were stripping shining armour
from the dead, young troops with Polydamas and Hector,
the most numerous and bravest of the men,
the ones most keen to breach the wall and burn the ships,
still stood along the ditch in some perplexity.
For as they'd assembled, eager to cross the trench,
a bird had gone above them, a high-flying eagle,

moving past the left flank of the troops, gripping
in its talons a huge blood-red snake, still alive,
still struggling. It hadn't lost its will to fight.
Doubling up, it struck the bird that clutched it
beside the neck. The eagle, stung with pain,
let the snake fall down onto the ground, dropping it
right in the middle of the crowd. Then with a cry,
it flew off downwind. Seeing that writhing snake,
lying there in their midst, Trojans shuddered. It was a sign,
a powerful omen, from aegis-bearing Zeus.
Polydamas then approached bold Hector and spoke out: 220

> "Hector, you're always taking me to task,
> though I give good advice in our assemblies.
> For you maintain it's not appropriate
> that someone else speak out against you,
> either in a council meeting or in war,
> for he should always back your leadership.
> But now I'm going to say what seems to me
> the best course we should take. Let's not advance
> to fight Danaans by their ships. In my view,
> this is how all this will end. If that omen   230
> was sent to Trojans keen to cross the ditch,
> a high-flying eagle on our army's left
> holding in its talons a blood-red snake,
> still living, which it let drop before it reached
> its nest, thus failing in its purpose,
> to bring that snake back for its offspring,
> then, like that bird, if we, with our great strength,
> breach the gates and the Achaean wall,
> and if Achaeans then retreat, we'll come back
> from the ships by this same route in disarray,   240
> leaving behind many Trojans slaughtered
> by Achaean bronze, as they defend their ships.
> That's how a prophet would interpret this,
> someone who in his heart knew the truth of signs
> and in whom the people placed their trust."

Hector with his gleaming helmet scowled and said:

"Polydamas, I don't like what you've just said.
You know how to offer better comments.
But if you're serious in what you say,
gods themselves must have destroyed your wits.   250
You're telling me to forget the plans
of thunder-loving Zeus, what he promised,
what he himself agreed to. You tell me
to put my faith in long-winged birds. I don't care,
or even notice, whether they fly off
to the right, towards Dawn's rising sun,
or to the left, towards the evening gloom.
Let's put our trust in great Zeus' counsel,
for he rules all mortals, all immortals.
One omen is best—fight for your country.   260
Why are you afraid of war, of battle?
Even if the others are all slaughtered
by Achaean ships, you need have no fear
that you'll be killed. Your heart is neither brave
nor warlike. But if you hold back from war,
or with your words convince some other man
to turn away from battle, you die right then,
struck by my spear."

                    Hector finished speaking.
Then he led his troops away. They followed him,
making a huge noise. Thunder-loving Zeus then sent   270
gusting storm winds down from Ida, driving dust
straight at the ships, to disorient Achaeans
and give glory to Hector and the Trojans.
Trusting Zeus' sign and their own power, they tried
to force the great Achaean wall, dragging down
the tower's supporting beams, smashing parapets,
prying up projecting columns Achaeans had first put
into the earth to shore up their wall's foundations.
They dragged these back, hoping to undermine the wall.
But even now Danaans did not back away.   280
They repaired the parapets with leather hides,
then hurled out weapons from there across the rampart
at the attacking Trojans.

moved back and forth along the wall, urging men on,
firing up the fighting spirit in Achaeans.
To some men they called out words of encouragement.
Others, the ones they saw clearly moving off,
back from the fight, they taunted with abuse.

"Friends, whether you're an Achaean leader,
or average, or one of the worst—for men   290
are not all equal when it comes to battle—
there's enough work here for everyone,
as you yourselves well know. So let no one here
turn back towards the ships, now you've heard
from your commander. Keep pushing forward,
keep shouting to each other, so that Zeus,
Olympian lord of lightning, may grant
we beat off this attack, repel the Trojans,
and drive them to their city."

Shouting words like these,
the Ajaxes incited the Achaeans to fight on.   300
As snowflakes on a winter's day fall thick and fast,
when Counselor Zeus begins to snow, to demonstrate
to men his weapons—first he calms the winds,
then snows steadily, till he's completely covered
high mountain peaks, jutting headlands, grassy meadows,
fertile farms of men, shedding snow on harbours,
inlets of the blue-gray sea, where waves roll in
to push back snow, while, from above, all the rest
is covered over, when Zeus storms with heavy snow—
that's how thick the stones fell then on both sides,   310
some thrown on Trojans, some from Trojans on Achaeans.
The noise reverberated all along the wall.

At that point, glorious Hector and the Trojans
would not have crashed the gates or long bolts in the wall,
if Counselor Zeus had not stirred his son Sarpedon
against Achaeans, like a lion going at short-horn cattle.
Sarpedon held his round shield in front of him,

260

forged by a smith of beautifully hammered bronze,
the inside formed of leather stitched in layers,
held in place with golden wires encircling the rim.   320
Holding this shield before him, brandishing two spears,
he hurried forward like a mountain lion
long ravenous for meat, whose bold spirit pushes him
to go even into the protected sheep fold
to attack the flock, and even if he comes across
herdsmen with dogs and spears guarding sheep inside,
he won't leave that fold without making an attempt,
so he springs on one, seizes it, or is hit himself
in the first rush, by a spear from some swift hand—
that's how godlike Sarpedon's spirit drove him then   330
to assault the wall, break down the parapets.
He called to Glaucus, Hippolochus' son:

> "Glaucus,
> why are we two awarded special honours,
> with pride of place, the finest cuts of meat,
> our wine cups always full in Lycia,
> where all our people look on us as gods?
> Why do we possess so much fine property,
> by the river Xanthus, beside its banks,
> rich vineyards and wheat-bearing ploughland?
> It's so we'll stand in the Lycian front ranks   340
> and meet head on the blazing fires of battle,
> so then some well-armed Lycian will say,
> 'They're not unworthy, those men who rule Lycia,
> those kings of ours. It's true they eat plump sheep
> and drink the best sweet wines—but they are strong,
> fine men, who fight in the Lycians' front ranks.'
> Ah my friend, if we could escape this war,
> and live forever, without growing old,
> if we were ageless, then I'd not fight on
> in the foremost ranks, nor would I send you   350
> to those wars where men win glory. But now,
> a thousand shapes of fatal death confront us,
> which no mortal man can flee from or avoid.
> So let's go forward, to give the glory

to another man or win it for ourselves."

Sarpedon spoke. Without making any move
Glaucus agreed. They marched on straight ahead,
leading their large company of Lycians.
Seeing their advance, Menestheus, son of Peteos,
shuddered, for they were aiming at his part of the wall,   360
bringing destruction with them. He looked around
at the Achaean tower, hoping he might see
some leader to protect his comrades from disaster.
He saw both Ajaxes, so keen for war, standing there.
Nearby was Teucer, who'd just come from his huts.
But there was no way they'd hear him if he shouted—
the noise was too intense. The din of smashed-in shields,
gates, and horsehair helmets—that sound reached heaven.
The doors were now all barred. Men stood outside them,
trying to knock them down by force to pass on through.   370
Menestheus quickly sent herald Thoötes to Ajax:

> "Noble Thoötes, run and call Ajax—
> or rather both of them, if that's possible—
> that would be the best solution. Here we face
> complete destruction any minute now.
> Lycian leaders are pressing us so hard,
> the ones who previously in bloody fights
> have demonstrated their ferocity.
> But if they're having trouble where they are,
> with fights breaking out, let mighty Ajax,   380
> son of Telamon, come by himself.
> And let that expert archer Teucer come with him."

Menestheus finished. Thoötes heard him and obeyed.
He ran along the bronze-clad Achaeans' barricade,
then came and, standing by both Ajaxes, spoke up at once:

> "You Ajaxes, leaders of bronze-armed Achaeans,
> the son of Peteos, raised by gods, is calling you
> to go to him and help relieve the battle strain,
> if only for a while. And he'd prefer

262

you both come. That would be the best solution.   390
There they face an imminent destruction.
Lycian leaders are pressing them so hard,
the ones who previously in bloody fights
have demonstrated their ferocity.
But if you're having trouble where you are,
with fights erupting, then let mighty Ajax,
son of Telamon, come by himself.
And let the expert archer Teucer come with him."

Thoötes finished. Great Telamonian Ajax then agreed.
At once he spoke winged words to Oïlean Ajax: 400

"Ajax, you and powerful Lycomedes,
you both stay here, stand firm. Rouse Danaans
to battle hard. I'll go over there,
deal with that fight, and come back quickly,
once I've helped them out as best I can."

That said, Telamonian Ajax left. With him
went Teucer, his brother, both from the same father.
Pandion also went, carrying Teucer's curving bow.
Moving along the wall the three men reached the place
where stout-hearted Menestheus stood. Here they found   410
soldiers hard pressed in the fight. The Lycians,
led by powerful commanders, their kings,
were climbing up the parapets like some black whirlwind.
Ajax and the others jumped right into the fight.
The noise grew more intense.

                         Ajax, son of Telamon,
was the first to kill a man, brave Epicles,
companion of Sarpedon. Ajax hit him
with a massive jagged rock lying inside the wall,
near the top. No man now alive could heft that stone
in his two hands, not even someone young and strong,   420
but Ajax raised it high, then hurled it, smashing
the man's four-ridged helmet and completely crushing
his entire skull. Epicles fell, like a diver,

from that high tower, and his spirit left his bones.
Teucer struck mighty Glaucus, son of Hippolochus,
with an arrow shot from high up on the wall,
as Glaucus was moving up. He hit him on the arm,
on a part he saw exposed. That stopped Glaucus' charge.
He climbed back down the wall, but stealthily,
so no Achaean man could see that he'd been hit   430
and boast aloud about it. Sarpedon was upset
at Glaucus' departure, when he noticed it,
but he did not neglect to keep up the attack.
He lunged at Alcmaon, Thestor's son, speared him well,
then yanked his spear back, which pulled Alcmaon with it.
He fell forward—his finely decorated armour,
all of bronze, echoed as he crashed onto the ground.
With his strong hands, Sarpedon grabbed the parapet and pulled.
The whole construction fell apart, breaching the wall,
creating a passage through for many men.   440

Ajax and Teucer now advanced together
to attack Sarpedon. Teucer hit him with an arrow
on the gleaming strap around his chest which held
his protective shield. But Zeus defended his own son
from deadly fates to make sure he'd not be destroyed
by the ships' sterns. Ajax then jumped in, striking his shield.
The point did not pass through, but its momentum
knocked Sarpedon back in the middle of his charge.
Sarpedon withdrew a little from the parapet,
but did not retreat completely, for his heart   450
was set on seizing glory. So he called out,
rallying his godlike Lycians:

                              "You Lycians,
        Why is your fighting spirit lessening?
        It's hard for me, although I'm powerful,
        to breach this wall alone and carve a pathway
        to the ships. So come, battle on with me.
        The more men there are, the better the work done."

Sarpedon called. Fearing the censure of their leader,

troops made a heavy push around their counselor king.
On the other side, the Argives reinforced their ranks   460
inside the wall. For both sides a major fight ensued.
Lycians, though strong, could not break the Danaan wall
and cut their way through to the ships. Danaan spearmen
could not push the Lycians back, repel them from the wall,
now they'd reached it. As two men with measuring rods
quarrel over survey markers in a common field,
striving for a fair division in some narrow place,
that's how the parapet kept these troops apart.
High on the wall they hacked each other's armour—
leather bucklers and large round shields across their chests,   470
quivering targets. Many men were wounded,
flesh slashed with pitiless bronze, those who turned aside
and left their backs exposed while fighting and those
hit right through their shields. Everywhere along the wall,
along the parapet, men's blood was spattered
from Trojans and Achaeans. But even so,
Trojans could not dislodge Achaeans from the wall.
Just as an industrious and honest woman
holds her scales, a weight on one side, wool on the other,
until they balance, so she can glean a pittance   480
for her children, that's how evenly the battle raged,
until Zeus gave glory above all other men
to Hector, son of Priam, who was the first man
to jump inside that wall of the Achaeans.
He raised a resounding yell, crying to his Trojans:

> "Drive forward, you horse-taming Trojans.
> Breach that Argive wall. Then burn the ships
> with a huge fire."

                    With these words, he drove them on.
Their ears all caught his call. Hurling themselves at the wall
in a dense mass, gripping sharp spears, they began to climb.   490
Hector picked up a rock lying before the gates,
thick at its base but tapering sharply on the top.
Two of the best working men now living
could not lever that stone out of the ground easily

into their cart, but Hector carried it with ease alone.
Crooked-minded Cronos' son made it light for him.
Just as a shepherd has no trouble carrying
a ram's fleece in one hand, hardly noticing the weight,
so Hector lifted up that rock, then carried it
straight to the doors guarding the strongly fitted gates,   500
high double doors with two cross pieces holding them inside
secured with a single bolt. Hector moved up closer,
planted himself before the doors, his legs wide apart
to throw with greater force, then hurled that rock
right at the centre of the doors. He smashed both hinges.
The stone's momentum took it clear through the doors.
The gates groaned loudly. The bolts were sheared right off.
The impact of that boulder shattered all the planks.
Glorious Hector, his face like night's swift darkness,
leapt inside. The bronze which covered his whole body   510
was a terrifying glitter. In his hand he held two spears.
Once he'd jumped inside the gates, no one moving out
to stop him could hold him back, except the gods.
From his eyes fire blazed. Wheeling through the throng,
he shouted to his Trojans to climb the wall.
His men responded to his call. Some scaled the wall,
others came pouring through the hole made in the gates.
Danaans were driven back among their hollow ships
in a rout, and the noisy tumult never stopped.

Book Thirteen
The Trojans Attack the Ships

[Zeus turns away from the battle; Poseidon secretly helps the Achaeans, talks to the two Ajaxes and other warriors; Hector keeps advancing until stopped by close-packed Achaeans; Poseidon talks with Idomeneus; Idomeneus and Meriones meet at the huts, then return to battle; Idomeneus' exploits in the fight; Aeneas moves against him; Menelaus on the battle field; Polydamas gives advice to Hector; Hector insults Paris; Ajax and Hector exchange boasts; the armies resume the fight.]

Thus Zeus brought Hector and the Trojans to the ships.
Then he left the soldiers there to carry on their strife,
their wretched endless war. He turned his shining gaze
away from them, looking far off into the distance,
at the land of Thracian horsemen, Mysians,
men who fight hand to hand, proud Hippemolgi,
who drink mare's milk, to the most righteous men of all,
the Abii. Zeus no longer turned his radiant eyes
toward Troy, for in his heart he did not believe
a single one of the immortal gods would move   10
to give assistance to the Trojans or Danaans.

But mighty Earthshaker Poseidon was keeping watch.
High on the tallest crest of wooded Samothrace
he sat looking down upon the war going on.
From that point, Mount Ida was clearly visible,
Priam's city, too, and the Achaean ships.
He'd come up from the sea and seated himself there,
pitying Achaeans, as Trojans beat them back,
and nursing a powerful anger against Zeus.
Poseidon came down quickly from that rocky peak,   20
moving swiftly on his feet. Mountain peaks and woods
trembled under Poseidon's immortal stride.
He took three paces—with the fourth he reached his goal,
Aegae, where his famous palace had been built
of eternal gold and marble deep within the sea.
Going inside, he harnessed to his chariot
swift bronze-hooved horses with flowing golden manes.

267

Dressed in gold, he took his well-made golden whip,
climbed in the chariot, then set off across the waves.
From the depths, sea creatures played around him everywhere,   30
acknowledging their king. The joyful ocean parted.
He sped on quickly, keeping the bronze axle dry.
The prancing horses carried him to the Achaean ships.

Half-way between Tenedos and rocky Imbros,
a wide cavern sits deep within the sea. In that spot,
Earthshaker Poseidon reined in his horses,
freed them from the chariot, and threw down ambrosia,
food for them to eat. Around their feet he placed
golden hobbles which they could not slip or break,
so they'd remain secure there till their lord's return.   40
Then Poseidon moved on to the Achaean camp.

At that point, Trojans, like some fire or windstorm,
marched behind Hector, son of Priam, in a mass,
shouting and screaming with excitement, hoping
to seize Achaean ships and kill the best men there.
But Poseidon, who encircles and shakes the earth,
roused the Argives, once he'd moved up from the sea.
Taking on the shape and tireless voice of Calchas,
he first spoke to the Ajaxes, both keen to fight.

"You Ajaxes, you must save Achaean troops.   50
Think of your fighting power, not cold flight.
In other places, I don't fear the Trojans,
whose powerful arms have brought hordes of them
across our wall. For well-armed Achaeans
will check them all. But I fear them here,
where we may experience disaster,
because of Hector, who leads their charge.
He's like a man possessed, a blazing fire,
as if he were a son of mighty Zeus.
But perhaps some god will inspire the hearts   60
in both your chests, so you two can stand firm.
You could get other men to do the same.
Hector may be keen, but you could push him

back from our swift ships, even if Zeus himself
is driving him ahead."

                   Poseidon finished speaking.
Then, the shaker and encircler of the earth
touched both men with his staff, infusing them
with power, strengthening their legs and upper arms.
Then Poseidon left. Just as a swift-winged hawk
takes off while hovering above some high sheer rock,   70
swooping down over the plain to hunt another bird—
that how Earthshaker Poseidon went off then.
Swift Ajax, son of Oïleus, was the first
to recognize the god. At once he spoke to Ajax,
son of Telamon:

                   "Ajax, one of the gods
dwelling on Olympus, in a prophet's shape,
tells us both to fight on by the ships.
For that man was no prophet Calchas,
who reads our omens. It was easy for me,
as he went away, to see that from the back   80
by the markings on his feet and legs.
Besides, it's easy to recognize the gods.
So now the spirit here in my own chest
is even keener than before to fight.
My upper arms have lots of energy.
I feel it also in my lower limbs."

Telamonian Ajax then answered Oïlean Ajax:

"I'm ready to wrap my conquering hands
around my spear. My fighting power grows.
My feet can now move fast. So I'm eager   90
to meet Hector, son of Priam, one on one—
the man whose fury so desires this fight."

As the two Ajaxes talked like this to one another,
relishing the warlike spirit the god had put
into their hearts, the Encircler of the Earth

was encouraging Achaeans at the rear,
those whose spirits were recovering by the swift ships,
their limbs exhausted from their anguishing ordeals,
their hearts weighed down with sorrow at the sight
of Trojan soldiers coming over their great wall.   100
When they saw that, their eyes shed tears—they thought
they'd not escape destruction. Earthshaker Poseidon
moved round with ease, bringing strength into the ranks.
He moved first to encourage Teucer and Leïtus,
then brave Peneleous, Thoas, Deïpyrus,
then Meriones and Antilochus, both skilled
in war shouts. He spoke to them—his words had wings:

> "Shame on you Argives, nothing but young boys!
> I'm counting on your strength to save our ships.
> If you're holding back in this grim fight,   110
> then now's the day the Trojans overcome us.
> Alas! What my eyes witness here astounds me,
> a dreadful thing I never thought would happen—
> Trojans moving up to our own ships,
> men who previously were shy, like deer,
> which in the woods are prey to jackals,
> wolves, and leopards, as they wander round,
> alone and frightened, with no will to fight.
> Before now, Trojans never wished to stand
> confronting the fierce fighting power   120
> of Achaean arms, not even for a moment.
> But now, far from their city, they fight here,
> right by our hollow ships. And the reason's this—
> our leadership's been bad, our army slack.
> For those who quarrel with our general
> won't protect our fast-moving ships from harm,
> and so are being cut down among them there.
> But even if wide-ruling Agamemnon,
> heroic son of Atreus, is to blame,
> if he really is the reason for all this,   130
> because he treated swift Achilles badly,
> in this battle we must hold back nothing.
> Let's fix all this—and quickly. In their hearts

fine men can change. It's bad if you restrain
your fighting spirit any longer,
especially you, the best of all our troops.
Myself, I wouldn't argue with a man
not keen to fight because he is a coward.
But in you my heart is disappointed.
Friends, by this hanging back you'll help to make   140
an even worse disaster. Let each of you
feel shame and indignation in his heart.
A great battle has just started. Hector,
skilled at war cries, is fighting by our ships.
His force has smashed our gates, our long bolts, too."

By rousing men this way, Earthshaker Poseidon
pushed Achaeans into action. Round both Ajaxes
soldiers made a stand and strongly held their ground.
If Ares had come there, he would have approved of them,
as would Athena, who inspires men in war.   150
Those known for their great bravery did not back off.
They fought lord Hector and the Trojans spear for spear,
shield with layered shield, in close-packed formation,
shields linked together and helmet touching helmet,
troops shoulder to shoulder. As men moved their heads,
horsehair crests on shining helmet ridges touched—
that's how densely packed they stood in that formation.
Their strong hands held the spears so that they overlapped.
Their minds were firm and fully ready for the fight.

The Trojans came on in a mass, led by Hector,   160
always charging forward, like a rolling boulder,
which some river in a winter flood dislodges
from a cliff beside its banks, its great flood eroding
what supports that lethal stone. In its fall, it bounces—
woods crash underneath it, as it accelerates
in a straight line, unimpeded—then it hits the plain,
where, for all its impetus, its motion stops.
That's how Hector threatened then to smash his way
with ease down to the sea, to Achaea's huts and ships.
But when he ran into the tight-packed lines of men,   170

271

he came close but was held in check. Achaea's sons
faced up to him with swords, with double-bladed spears,
and pushed him back. Shaken, Hector had to give ground.
He let out a piercing shout, calling to his Trojans:

"Trojans, Lycians, you Dardan spearmen,
hold your place. Achaeans won't keep me back,
not for long. Even though they've set themselves
in a defensive wall, I think they will retreat
before my spear, if the greatest of the gods,
Hera's loud-thundering mate, inspires me."   180

Saying this, Hector gave heart and spirit to each man.
Deïphobus, son of Priam, moved out before them,
full of ambitious hopes. Holding his round shield
in front of him, he stepped lightly forward,
under cover of that shield. Then Meriones
after taking aim, threw his shining spear at him.
He didn't miss. He struck that round leather shield.
But the spear did not break through. Before it could,
it snapped off at the socket. Then Deïphobus,
his heart afraid of warlike Meriones' spear,   190
held his leather shield at arm's length away from him.
But Meriones had withdrawn into the group
of his companions, upset at his double loss—
the victory and the spear which he'd just shattered.
He set off for the Achaean huts and ships,
to fetch another spear he'd left inside his hut.

The others kept on fighting. The din was constant.
The first to kill a man was Teucer, son of Telamon.
He slew Imbrius, a spearman, son of Mentor,
who owned many horses. He'd lived in Pedaeum   200
before Achaea's sons arrived. He married
one of Priam's bastard daughters, Medesicaste.
When the curved ships of the Danaans came to Troy,
he went back. The people there thought much of him.
He lived with Priam, who honoured him as well,
as if he were his child. But the son of Telamon

with a long spear thrust hit Imbrius below the ear.
Teucer pulled the weapon back. Imbrius collapsed.
Just as an ash tree growing on a mountain top,
visible from every side, is chopped down by bronze,   210
its foliage crashing to the ground—that's how he fell.
His armour, finely decorated bronze, rang out,
reverberating round him. Teucer then jumped out,
eager to strip away his armour, but as he charged,
Hector threw a shining spear at him. Teucer,
seeing it coming, safely dodged the bronze spear point.
But Hector's spear hit Amphimachus, son of Cteatus,
Actor's son, in the chest, as he was coming up,
about to join the battle. He fell with a crash,
his armour echoing around him. Hector ran up,   220
eager to tug away the helmet tightly bound
around the temples of brave Amphimachus.
But with his bright spear Ajax lunged at Hector,
as he came forward. He didn't touch his flesh,
for Hector was encased in terrifying bronze.
But Ajax struck the central boss on Hector's shield,
and his great power pushed him back. Hector withdrew
and left the corpses, so Achaeans dragged them off.
Amphimachus was carried back to the Achaean troops
by Stichius and noble Menestheus,   230
who led Athenian troops. The two Ajaxes,
still full of battle rage, hauled Imbrius away.
As two lions snatch a goat from sharp-toothed hounds,
then take it in their jaws off through thick underbrush,
holding it well off the ground, that's how both Ajaxes
held Imbrius up. They stripped off his armour.
In his anger at the killing of Amphimachus,
Oïlean Ajax hacked through the tender neck,
then, with a swing of his body, threw away the head,
like some ball, into the crowd. It fell into the dust,   240
right at Hector's feet.

                    At that point, Poseidon,
angry that his grandson Amphimachus had died
in that harsh fight, went through Achaea's huts and ships,

rousing Achaeans, planning trouble for the Trojans.
He met the famous spearman Idomeneus
coming from a comrade who'd just left the fight.
A sharp bronze blow had struck him in the knee.
His companions brought him in. Idomeneus,
having issued his instructions to the healers,
was going to his hut, still eager to fight on.   250
The mighty Earthshaker spoke to him, making his voice
sound like Thoas, son of Andraemon, who ruled
Aetolians all through Pleuron and steep Calydon,
honoured by his people as a god:

                                                 "Idomeneus,
    Cretan counselor, what's happened to those threats
    Achaea's sons once made against the Trojans?"

Idomeneus, Cretan leader, then said in reply:

    "As far as I know, Thoas, no one's to blame.
    For all of us are very skilled in fighting,
    and no one is timid here or frightened,   260
    or, gripped by doubts, holds back from evil war.
    Somehow it must please Cronos' mighty son
    that Achaeans perish now without a name,
    far from Argos. But Thoas, in times past,
    you were a man who always stood his ground
    and encouraged other men to do the same,
    if you saw someone shirking. Don't stop now.
    Issue your instructions to each man."

Earthshaker Poseidon then replied:

                                                 "Idomeneus,
    may the man who will not fight today,   270
    and willingly, never return from Troy.
    May he become a toy for dogs to play with.
    But get your armour and then come with me.
    If we're to work well, we must work together,
    although we're only two. For courage

of the highest sort comes when men combine,
even among men worth very little,
and we two know how to battle with the best."

Having said this, Poseidon went away, a god
among the toiling men, and Idomeneus   280
went into his well-made hut, strapped fine armour
round his body, took two spears and then strode out,
looking like a lightning bolt which Cronos' son
grips in his hand and hurls down from bright Olympus,
revealing in its dazzling flash a sign for mortal men,
that's how, as he moved, bronze glinted on his chest.

Meriones, his brave attendant, met him
close by the hut. He'd come in search of a bronze spear.
Strong Idomeneus said to him:

                              "Meriones,
     swift-footed son of Molus, the companion   290
     I cherish most, why have you come here,
     leaving the war and giving up the fight?
     Have you been hurt? Or wounded by a spear?
     Are you in pain? Or have you come with news?
     Me, I don't want to stay here in my hut.
     I want to fight."

                         Wise Meriones then replied:

     "Idomeneus, counselor of bronze-armed Cretans,
     I've come to get a spear, if by any chance
     there's one left in your huts. The one I had
     shattered in pieces when I hit the shield   300
     of that arrogant fighter Deïphobus."

To this, Idomeneus, Cretan leader, then replied:

     "Spears? As many as you want—in my hut
     twenty one stand against the sunny wall,
     Trojans spears I take from warriors I kill.

I never think of fighting hostile troops
from far away—that's why I've got there
brightly shining spears and embossed shields,
with helmets, too, and body armour."

Wise Meriones then answered Idomeneus: 310

"In my hut, too, and in my black ship,
there's lots of Trojan loot. But it's not close—
too inconvenient. For I can claim
I don't neglect my fighting prowess.
Whenever battles start, I stand and fight
with men in front, in those encounters
where men win glory. Other Achaeans
might not know my fighting quality, but you,
I think you've seen it for yourself."

Idomeneus, leader of the Cretans, answered Meriones: 320

"I know your courage. Why talk that way?
If by the ships right now we were naming
the best men for an ambush, where one sees
a warrior's courage most conspicuously,
where cowards and brave men truly show themselves—
for a coward's colour always changes,
the man's so nervous he just can't sit still,
shifting around, resting first on one foot,
then another, heart pounding in his chest,
his mind preoccupied with thoughts of death,   330
and his teeth keep chattering in his mouth,
while a brave man's colour never changes,
he feels no great fear as he takes his place
in the group selected for the ambush,
no—he prays the killing will soon start.
In such a scene no one could challenge you,
or fault your battle rage or your strong arms.
For if, in the middle of the fighting,
some flying weapon hit you, or you were stabbed,
that weapon wouldn't strike your neck or body   340
in the back. No, you'd be hit in front,

in chest or stomach, as you charged ahead,
getting your joy from fighting at the front.
But let's not chat about this any longer,
standing here as if we were young children.
That could make some people very angry.
Go in my hut. Get yourself a heavy spear."

Idomeneus finished. Then Meriones,
like swift Ares, quickly took a bronze spear from the hut.
Filled with an urge to fight, he went with Idomeneus.   350
Just as man-killing Ares sets off to battle
accompanied by his son Terror, just as strong,
as fearless, who makes any man afraid,
no matter how courageous he may be—the two of them
setting out from Thrace, having armed themselves to fight
Ephyreans or brave Phlegyans, giving glory
to one of them, without listening to either side—
that's how Meriones and Idomeneus,
leaders of men, set off to battle, fully armed
in glittering bronze. Meriones was the first to speak: 360

     "Son of Deucalion, where do you think
we should rejoin the fight? On the right side
of the whole army, the middle, or the left?
To my mind, this last place is the one
where long-haired Achaeans stand most in need."

Cretan leader Idomeneus answered Meriones:

     "In the middle there are other men
to shore up the troops—the two Ajaxes,
Teucer, too, the best Achaean archer,
good in hand-to-hand combat as well.   370
Those warriors will give Hector, Priam's son,
all he can handle, even if he's keen
to fight and really strong. He'll find it hard,
though in full battle frenzy, to overcome
their spirit, their all-powerful hands,
and then burn the fleet, unless Zeus himself,

son of Cronos, hurls a flaming firebrand
on our swift ships. That son of Telamon,
great Ajax, will not yield to any mortal man
who eats Demeter's grain, who can be smashed   380
by massive rocks or bronze. He'd not give way
in a stand-up fight, not even to Achilles,
who destroys ranks of men and is so fast—
in running no one can beat Achilles.
No, we should move toward the army's left,
as you say, find out as soon as possible
if we'll win glory or give it to another."

Idomeneus spoke. Like swift Ares, Meriones
led the way until they reached the army,
where Idomeneus had instructed him to go.   390
When Trojans saw mighty Idomeneus,
like some flame, and his attendant Meriones
in his richly shining armour, they called out
to each other in the crowd, then made a massive charge.

By the ships' sterns both sides met in frantic battle.
Just as keen winds sometimes whip up gusts of air,
when dirt lies heavy on the roads, and stir up
all the dust into huge clouds—that's how this fight
gathered momentum then. In that crowd, men's hearts
were set to slaughter one another with sharp bronze.   400
That man-destroying combat bristled with long spears
gripped by men to hack each other's flesh apart.
As troops moved up tightly bunched, men's eyes went blind
in the blaze of glittering bronze, glaring helmets,
finely polished body armour, gleaming shields.
It would take a hard man to find joy in the sight
of all that suffering and show no trace of sorrow.

Then two mighty sons of Cronos, at cross purposes,
made painful trouble for those mortal warriors.
Zeus wanted victory for Hector and his Trojans,   410
to give swift Achilles glory—not that he wished
Achaea's army to be totally destroyed

in front of Troy, but he did want to honour Thetis,
and her great-hearted son, as well, Achilles.
But Poseidon moved around among the Argives,
urging action, coming out in secret from the sea,
angry that Trojans were destroying Achaeans,
and incensed at Zeus. Both gods had a common father—
the same family, too—but Zeus was older and more wise.
So Poseidon avoided giving any overt help.   420
He did his work in secret through the army,
in human form, urging men to fight. So these two
looped the cords of powerful war and deadly strife
around both contending armies, then pulled them taut,
a knot no one could undo or slip away from,
a knot that broke the limbs of many fighting men.

Idomeneus, though old enough to have gray hair,
called out to the Danaans and then charged the Trojans,
driving them away. He killed Othryoneus,
a man from Cabesus, who now lived in Troy.   430
He'd come recently, responding to the news of war.
He'd asked to marry Cassandra, most beautiful
of Priam's daughters, without paying a bride price.
Instead he'd promised a great action, saying he'd drive
Achaea's sons from Troy. Old Priam had agreed,
promising he'd give her to him. Othryoneus,
trusting the king's promises, went off to fight.
Aiming his shining spear at him, Idomeneus threw.
The spear struck him as he was strutting forward.
The bronze breastplate he was wearing didn't help him—   440
the spear lodged in his gut. He fell down with a crash.
Then Idomeneus cried out in triumph:

                    "Othryoneus,
          of all mortal men I'd consider you
          the happiest, if you'd accomplished
          all those things you promised Dardan Priam,
          so he'd give you his daughter. But come,
          we'll make you the same proposition—
          and we'll deliver. We'll give you the loveliest

of Agamemnon's daughters, bring her here
from Argos, so you can wed her, if you,   450
for your part, will join us to destroy
the well-built city Ilion. So let's go.
We can arrange the marriage contract
by our seaworthy ships. We'll be generous
about your marriage price."

                              As he said this,
warrior Idomeneus dragged him by the feet
through lines of fighting men. But Asius then stepped up
to guard Othryoneus. He was on foot,
going before his horses, which his charioteer
kept so close they breathed on Asius' shoulders.   460
He'd set his heart on hitting Idomeneus.
But Idomeneus was too quick for him.
He hit Asius with a spear below his chin,
forcing the bronze straight through his neck. Asius fell.
Just as a mountain oak, poplar, or tall pine falls,
cut down by working men with freshly sharpened axes,
to make timbers for some ship, that how Asius lay,
stretched out there before his chariot and horses,
gagging, his fingers clawing at the bloody dust.
His charioteer, scared out of whatever wits he'd had,   470
didn't think of wheeling round his horses to escape
his enemies' hands. Taking aim, bold Antilochus
speared him in the stomach. The bronze breastplate he wore
was no protection. The spear struck in his stomach.
He fell out of the well-made chariot gasping.
Antilochus, brave Nestor's son, then drove the horses
from the Trojans over to well-armed Achaeans.

Grieving the loss of Asius, Deïphobus
came up to Idomeneus and hurled his polished spear.
Idomeneus, seeing him clearly, dodged the spear,   480
covering himself with the round shield he carried,
one made of bull's hide and shining bronze in rings,
with two cross braces fitted on. Idomeneus
crouched down underneath this shield. The flying bronze

grazed the metal with a rasping sound. But that throw
from the strong arm of Deïphobus wasn't wasted.
His spear hit Hypsenor, son of Hippasus,
his people's shepherd, low down in the liver.
His legs collapsed. Deïphobus gave a noisy shout,
boasting aloud about his triumph:

> "Now Asius   490
> is avenged! As he goes down to Hades,
> the mighty gatekeeper, his heart, I think,
> will be pleased I've given him an escort."

Deïphobus spoke. His boast depressed the Argives,
and gave special pain to warlike Antilochus.
Despite his sorrow, Antilochus did not forget
his comrade. He came running up and stood over him,
with his shield above his body. Two loyal companions,
Mecistus, son of Echius, and Alastor, bent down,
then carried Hypsenor groaning to the hollow ships.   500

Idomeneus did not relent his fighting frenzy.
He kept on trying to wrap some Trojan soldier
in death's dark night or to fall himself, defending
Achaeans from disaster. He killed Alcathous,
dear warrior son of divinely bred Aesyetes,
Anchises' son-in-law. He'd married Hippodamia,
eldest of the daughters. Her mother and father
had set their heart's love on her when she was at home.
She surpassed all girls her age in beauty, work,
good sense. That's why the very finest man in Troy   510
had married her. Now at Idomeneus' hands
Poseidon slaughtered Alcathous. The god cast a spell—
he covered his bright eyes and froze his glistening limbs,
so he couldn't flee or dodge the spear, but stood there,
motionless, like a pillar or some high leafy tree.
Warrior Idomeneus hit him with his spear
square in the chest, shattering the bronze breastplate,
which earlier had kept his skin untouched by death.
But now it cracked aloud as the spear ripped through.

281

He fell with a crash, the spear stuck in his chest.
The power of his heart beat made that spear shaft quiver,
right to the butt, until great Ares stilled its force.
Idomeneus then spoke out, boasting aloud
about his triumph:

>   "Deïphobus,
> since you like to brag this way, my friend,
> shall we now call it even, three men killed
> a fair exchange for one? Why don't you step out—
> face me here, so you can see for yourself
> what kind of child of Zeus confronts you.
> Zeus first fathered Minos to rule Crete.   530
> Minos then fathered worthy Deucalion.
> Deucalion fathered me, a king ruling
> many men in spacious Crete. Now my ships
> have brought me here as a destroying force,
> against you, your father, and other Trojans."

Idomeneus spoke. Deïphobus was of two minds—
should he step back and pick out a companion
from stout-hearted Trojans, or should he try to fight
all on his own? As he thought about his options,
he thought his best plan was to find Aeneas.   540
He met him standing at the back, among the crowd,
for Aeneas, who excelled among the warriors,
always resented Priam for not showing him
enough respect. Deïphobus approached Aeneas,
then spoke to him—his words had wings.

>   "Aeneas, Trojan counselor,
> now you must defend your brother-in-law,
> if you feel any grief. It's urgent.
> Come with me and fight for Alcathous,
> who was your sister's husband. He raised you
> as an infant in his home. Now Idomeneus,   550
> that celebrated spearman, has just killed him."

Deïphobus finished. His words stirred the heart

in Aeneas' chest. He strode off to face Idomeneus,
fiercely eager for this fight. But no fear gripped
Idomeneus, as if he were some pampered child.
He stood his ground. Just as a wild mountain boar,
trusting its own strength, stands firm against a mob,
a crowd of men who chase it in some lonely place,
with hair bristling along its back, its eyes lit up,
like fire, gnashing its teeth ferociously, eager   560
to toss dogs and men aside—that's just the way
the famous spearman Idomeneus stood,
without backing off, as swift Aeneas came at him.
He called out to the companions he could see,
Ascalaphus, Aphareus, Deïpyrus, Meriones,
Antilochus—all famous for their war shouts.
Idomeneus yelled, urging them to help him—
his words had wings:

                              "My friends—over here!
I'm alone, so bring some help. I'm worried.
Aeneas, who moves fast, is coming at me.   570
He's powerful at killing men in battle.
He's also in the flower of his youth,
when strength is at its peak. Were I his age
and both of us had equal courage,
he or I would soon win a huge victory."

Idomeneus finished. All his companions,
united by a common spirit, came at his call.
They stood beside him as a unit, sloping their shields
down from their shoulders. On his side, Aeneas
called out to those companions he'd caught sight of—   580
Deïphobus, Paris, and Agenor—leaders,
just as he was, of those Trojan warriors.
Men came up behind them. Just as a flock of sheep
follows the ram from pasture to their water,
filling the shepherd's heart with joy, so Aeneas
was happy in his chest to see that band of soldiers
standing there around him.

                              The men now battled on,
close combat with long spears, over Alcathous.
As they lunged at one another in the crowd of men,
their bronze chests echoed with the fearful noise.   590
Two men stood out above the rest for bravery—
Aeneas and Idomeneus, equals of Ares,
striving to slash each other's flesh with ruthless bronze.
First, Aeneas threw a spear at Idomeneus,
who, seeing it coming, eluded the bronze spear,
which then impaled itself in earth, still quivering—
it had flown from that strong hand but missed its target.
Then Idomeneus struck Oenomaus in the stomach,
smashing the front plate on his body armour.
His bowels spilled out, as he dropped in the dust   600
and clutched the dirt. Idomeneus yanked his long spear
out of the corpse. But he couldn't strip away
any of the lovely armour on its shoulders,
for he was being attacked with flying weapons.
His lower limbs were no longer fast enough
for him to charge in quickly after his own spear
or dodge aside. He could keep grim death at bay
in pitched battle, but that's all his legs could do—
they were too slow for him to run away from combat.
As Idomeneus retreated step by step,   610
Deïphobus tried to hit him with a shining spear—
he'd always hated Idomeneus—but he missed,
hitting Ascalaphus instead, a son of Ares.
The heavy spear passed straight through his shoulder.
He collapsed in the dust, hands clawing at the ground.

Loud-voiced mighty Ares was not yet aware
his own son had fallen in the killing zone.
He sat on the highest part of Mount Olympus,
under golden clouds, confined by Zeus' will,
along with the rest of the immortal gods,   620
forbidden to participate in warfare.

The close fighting over Ascalaphus continued.
Deïphobus stripped off the corpse's shining helmet.

But Meriones, like swift Ares, jumped out
and speared him in the arm. The plumed helmet,
with a clang, fell on the ground. Like a vulture,
Meriones leapt out again, pulled the heavy spear
out of his upper arm, then moved back to his group,
But Deïphobus' blood brother Polites,
with both arms round his waist, hauled him from the fight,   630
until he came to his swift horses in the rear.
They were standing there, waiting for him,
with charioteer and finely decorated chariot.
These took him away, back to the city, tired out,
moaning heavily, blood dripping from his wounded arm.
The rest kept fighting, with no let up in the noise.

Then Aeneas went at Aphareus, son of Caletor,
as he was facing him. His sharp spear hit his throat.
Aphareus' head snapped back—his shield and helmet
fell down on him, and Death, which takes the living spirit,   640
gathered him in.

                              Antilochus kept watching Thoön.
As he turned, he rushed up and stabbed him,
severing the vein which runs the full length of the back
up to the neck—Antilochus slashed through this vein.
Thoön fell, stretching his arms up from the dust,
reaching to his friends. Antilochus jumped on him
and began to strip the armour on his shoulders.
But he kept his eyes alert, for he was surrounded,
with Trojan men on every side, thrusting their spears
at his broad shining shield. But their ruthless bronze   650
could not scratch the tender skin behind that shield,
for Earthshaker Poseidon was guarding Nestor's son,
even in that hail of spears. So Antilochus
never moved far from his enemies. He kept going,
ranging around among them. His spear never stopped,
always in motion, quivering, his eager heart
keen to throw that spear at someone or attack him.

As Antilochus went through that crowd of men,

he was observed by Adamas, son of Asius,
who charged close in—his sharp bronze spear struck   660
the middle of his shield. But dark-haired Poseidon,
unwilling to concede Antilochus' life,
made the spear point fail—so part of it got stuck
in Antilochus' shield, like the charred end of a stick,
and half fell on the ground. Adamas then withdrew,
returning to the group of his companions,
avoiding death. But Meriones went after him,
as he moved back, and hit him underneath his navel,
in the scrotum, the most agonizing way
for men to perish miserably in battle.   670
When that spear struck Adamas, he doubled up,
bent down over the spear, writhing like a bull
which farmers in the mountains bind with willow shoots
and drag along by force, against the creature's will.
That's how Adamas, once hit, twitched there for a while,
but not for long. Warlike Meriones, running up,
yanked out his spear. Then darkness covered up his eyes.

At close quarters, Helenus then hit Deïpyrus,
striking his helmet with a massive Thracian sword,
knocking it off, so it fell to earth and rolled away   680
among the soldiers' feet. Some Achaean picked it up.
Deïpyrus' eyes grew cloudy, and darkness took him.

Atreus' son Menelaus, skilled at war shouts,
was overcome with grief. He stepped up, threatening
and waving a sharp spear at warrior Helenus.
Helenus pulled back on the centre of his bow.
They both let fly together—one with a sharp spear,
the other with an arrow from his bowstring.
Priam's son hit Menelaus with his arrow—
on the front plate of his armour, in the chest.   690
The keen arrow bounded off. Just as black beans or peas
fly off a broad shovel on large threshing floors,
driven by the sharp wind or winnower's strength—
that's how the arrow point glanced off the breast plate,
then flew aside, away from glorious Menelaus.

When Atreus' son Menelaus, skilled at war shouts,
threw his spear, he hit Helenus in the hand,
the one which held the finely polished bow.
The bronze sliced through his hand into the bow.
Helenus drew back into the group of his companions,   700
escaping death. He let his hand hang by his side,
dragging the ash spear behind him, till brave Agenor
pulled it out. Agenor then bound up his hand
in a strip of twisted sheep's wool and made a sling,
which his attendant carried for him, his people's shepherd.

Then Peisander made straight for glorious Menelaus.
But an evil fate was leading him towards his death,
destroyed at your hands, Menelaus, in lethal war.
When the two men had approached each other,
standing at close range, Menelaus threw but missed—   710
his spear point was deflected. Then Peisander struck,
hitting glorious Menelaus' shield, but his bronze
could not break through. The broad shield withstood the blow,
which snapped the spear off at its socket. But in his heart,
Peisander still felt a joyful hope of victory.
The son of Atreus pulled out his silver-studded sword,
then leapt at Peisander, who, from under his own shield,
produced a fine axe of well-cast bronze, with a long shaft
of finely-polished olive wood. The two men met.
Peisander struck Menelaus on his helmet ridge,   720
at the top, just underneath the horsehair crest.
But as Peisander charged, Menelaus hit him—
right on the forehead, just above his nose.
The bones cracked. Both his bloody eyes fell out
into the dirt beside his feet. Peisander doubled up
and then collapsed. Menelaus stepped on his chest,
stripped off his armour, crying out in triumph:

> "You arrogant Trojans, who can't get enough
> of war's destructive noise, this is the way
> you'll go back from these ships of the Danaans,   730
> who ride fast horses. You're not reluctant,
> where insults and dishonour are concerned,

to go after me, you worthless mongrel dogs,
without fearing in your hearts harsh anger
from thundering Zeus, god of hospitality,
who some day will destroy your lofty town.
For you carried off the wife I married,
lots of my property, and brought them here,
although she'd entertained you royally
in her own home. Now you're madly eager   740
to throw deadly fire on our sea-going ships,
to kill Achaean warriors. But you'll be stopped,
no matter how much you now want to fight.
Oh Father Zeus, people say for wisdom
you exceed all others, men and gods alike.
Yet all this comes from you, the way you show
favours to these insolent men, these Trojans,
whose aggressive spirit has no limit,
who can never get enough of battle,
though they're not winning in an equal fight.   750
To all things there is a limit set—to sleep,
to love, sweet songs, and gorgeous dancing.
A man would rather have his fill of these, not war.
But Trojans here are gluttons for a fight."

After Menelaus spoke, he stripped the body,
then gave its bloody armour to his comrades.
He went back and rejoined those fighting in the front.

The next man to charge against him was Harpalion,
son of king Pylamenes, who came to fight at Troy
following his dear father. But he never did return   760
to his own country. With his spear at close range,
he struck the centre of Menelaus' shield,
but the bronze could not penetrate completely.
So he drew back into the throng of his companions,
escaping death. He looked around him carefully,
as he moved, so no warrior's bronze would hit his flesh.
But on his way back, Meriones shot at him.
The bronze-tipped arrow hit his right buttock, pushing
underneath the bone, going right into the bladder.

He sat down there, in the arms of his dear comrades,   770
choking his life away, convulsing on the ground,
like some worm. His dark blood gushed out, soaking the earth.
Brave Paphlagonians came up to help Harpalion.
They set him in a chariot and took him away,
full of sorrow, to sacred Ilion. His father
went back with them, in tears, for he could find
no satisfaction for the slaughter of his son.

Harpalion's death made Paris really angry.
For with the Paphlagonians he'd welcomed Paris
as his guest. In a fit of anger, Paris shot off   780
a bronze-tipped arrow. Now, there was a certain man
called Euchenor, son of Polyidus the prophet,
a rich, brave man, who lived at home in Corinth.
He'd set sail knowing full well his deadly fate,
for many times his brave old father, Polyidus,
had told him—he would either die in his own home
from some foul disease or be destroyed by Trojans
among Achaean ships. Euchenor thus escaped
both the stiff penalty exacted by Achaeans
and deadly sickness—he felt worthy in his heart.   790
The arrow Paris shot hit this man by his jaw,
right on the ear. At once his spirit left his limbs,
and hateful darkness carried him away.

Thus the men keep fighting like a blazing fire.
But Hector, dear to Zeus, hadn't heard and didn't know
how the Achaeans were killing off his army
at the left end of the ships. Glory in this battle
would soon have been awarded to Achaeans—
that's how powerfully Earthshaker Poseidon,
who enfolds the earth, was driving Argives forward,   800
helping them with his own strength as well. But Hector
charged on from where he'd first breached the gates and wall,
smashing up the close-packed ranks of the Danaans,
right to the ships of Protesilaus and Ajax,
drawn up on the beach beside the blue-gray sea.
By these ships the wall was lowest. So there the fight

with men and horses was particularly fierce.
There Boeotians fought, Ionians in long tunics,
Locrians, Phthians, and glittering Epeians.
But they had trouble standing up to Hector's charge,   810
as he attacked the ships. They couldn't push him back,
away from them, as he came up, like an inferno,
not even the finest men of the Athenians,
with their leader Menestheus, son of Peteos,
alongside Pheidas, Stichius, and brave Bias,
with the Epeians led by Meges, son of Phyleus,
Amphion, Dracius, and the Phthians,
led by Medon and Podarces, both brave men.
Medon was a bastard son of noble Oïleus
and Ajax's brother. But he lived in Phylace,   820
far from his native land, for he'd killed a man,
one related to Eriopis, his stepmother,
wife of Oïleus. Podarcus was Iphicles' son,
child of Phylaces. These men in their armour
were fighting at the head of those brave Phthians,
standing with Boeotians to defend the ships.

Ajax, son of Oïleus, would not move away
from Ajax, son of Telamon—he fought beside him.
Just as in a meadow a pair of wine-dark oxen
strain with the same heart to pull a jointed plough,   830
beads of sweat running from the bottom of their horns,
with nothing but a well-polished yoke between them,
as they labour down the furrows, till the plough
slices through the edges of the field—that's the way
the two Ajaxes stood together then, side by side.
Telamonian Ajax had many comrades with him,
courageous soldiers, who'd relieve him of his shield
when his sweaty limbs grew tired. But the Locrians
had not come forward with brave Oïlean Ajax—
they lacked courage for fighting in the killing zone,   840
for they had no plumed bronze helmets, no round shields,
and no ash spears. They'd come to Troy with Ajax
trusting in their bows and slings of twisted sheep's wool.
Later they battled on with these, firing thick volleys,

breaking ranks of Trojans. So one group of men,
those with glittering weapons, fought at the front
against bronze-armed Hector and his Trojans,
while another shot from safe positions at the back.
The arrows drained the Trojans' fighting spirit.

The Trojans would then have been shamed into retreat,   850
moving back from the ships and huts to windy Troy,
if Polydamas hadn't approached bold Hector, saying:

> "You're a difficult man to deal with, Hector,
> for you don't take advice. God has made you
> more excellent in war than other men.
> Thus, in council you want us all to think
> you're better than the rest. But in yourself
> you can't be everything at once. The gods
> make one man superior in warfare,
> another in the dance, or singing,   860
> or playing the lyre. For some others,
> all-seeing Zeus puts wisdom in their hearts—
> and from these men many people benefit,
> many are saved, for such men know what's right.
> So I'll say what I think it's best to do.
> All around you war's fiery circle rages,
> but some brave Trojans, having breached the wall,
> are standing idle with their weapons.
> Others, scattered around the ships, fight on—
> but in small groups against a larger mass.   870
> You should fall back, then summon here to you
> all our finest men. Then we can weigh our options—
> whether we should assault the well-decked ships,
> in the hope god wants to give us victory,
> or whether, for safety's sake, we leave the ships.
> I'm afraid Achaeans may avenge the hurt
> we gave them yesterday, since by their ships
> there sits a man with appetite for war—
> I think he may change his decision not to fight."

Polydamas finished. His advice pleased Hector.   880

291

At once he jumped out of his chariot to the ground.
He took up his weapons and spoke—his words had wings:

> "Polydamas, keep all the best men here.
> I'll go back to battle over there,
> returning when I've told them what to do."

Saying that, Hector strode off, like a snowy mountain,
going by Trojans and allies, shouting instructions.
When these men heard what Hector wanted them to do,
they all came running over to Polydamas,
kind son of Panthous. Hector marched through the ranks   890
of their best warriors, looking for Deïphobus,
brave prince Helenus, Adamas, son of Asius,
and Asius, son of Hyrtacus. But these men
had not come through unscathed. Some were already dead,
killed at Argive hands by the sterns of Achaea's ships.
Others inside the wall had spear or arrow wounds.
On the left flank of that destructive battle,
Hector met Paris, husband of fair-haired Helen,
encouraging his comrades, urging them to fight.
Approaching him, Hector taunted Paris: 900

> "You may be the best-looking man around,
> but you're a useless woman-mad seducer.
> Where are Deïphobus, brave prince Helenus,
> Adamas, son of Asius, and Asius,
> son of Hyrtacus? Where's Othryoneus?
> Tell me that. All of high Ilion
> has been destroyed. Your own death is certain."

Then noble Alexander answered Hector:

> "Hector, you're now blaming someone innocent.
> At other times I have held back from war,   910
> but not this time. When my mother bore me,
> she did not produce a total coward.
> Since the moment you told your men to fight
> beside the ships, we've been in combat here,
> in a constant struggle with Danaans.

Those companions you just mentioned have been killed.
Only Deïphobus and brave Helenus
have gone back, both wounded in the arm—
hit by a long spear—but Zeus saved them from death.
But now, lead on where your spirit tells you,   920
we'll follow you quite willingly. I don't think
we'll show a lack of courage while our strength holds out.
Once that goes, no matter how keen a man may be,
he can no longer continue in the war."

Warrior Paris' words won his brother's heart.
They set off for the centre of that noisy battle,
with Cebriones, noble Polydamas,
Phalces, Orthaeus, godlike Polyphetes,
Palmys, Ascanius, Morus, son of Hippotion,
men who'd come from fertile Ascania the day before   930
as reinforcements. Now Zeus incited them to war.
The Trojans advanced. Just like blasts of storming winds
striking the earth under Father Zeus' thunder,
then with a roar slicing into the sea, whipping up
a crowd of surging waves across a booming ocean,
with lines of arching foam, one following another—
that how Trojans marched behind their leaders,
in a tight formation, one behind the other,
glittering in bronze. Like man-destroying Ares,
Hector, son of Priam, led them. He held his shield   940
in front of him, an even circle made of hide,
densely packed, then covered with a solid layer
of hammered bronze, helmet gleaming round his temples.
He moved out, testing all parts of the Achaean lines,
to see if they'd retreat from him as he came forward
covered by his shield. But Achaean hearts stood firm.
The first fighter to challenge Hector was great Ajax,
who marched out with long strides and shouted:

                              "Come closer,
         you poor man. Why try to scare the Argives?
         When it comes to fighting, we're not ignorant.   950
         Zeus' harsh whip has lashed Achaeans back,

293

and your heart now wants to break our ships.
But we've got hands to raise in their defense.
In fact, I think it's far more likely now
we'll take your well-built city—these hands of ours
will smash it long before you seize our ships.
I say the time has come when you'll run back,
praying to Father Zeus and other gods,
to make your horses with their lovely manes
fly as fast as hawks, when they speed through dust   960
to get you to your city on the plain."

As Ajax spoke, a bird flew out on the right,
a high-flying eagle. Encouraged by the omen,
the Achaean soldiers responded with a cheer.
Glorious Hector then said to Ajax in reply:

"What are you saying, you stupid boaster?
I wish it were as certain that I was
the son of aegis-bearing Zeus himself,
with Hera for my mother, and honoured
like Apollo or Athena, as I am that this day   970
brings disaster to the Argives—all of them.
You'll lie among the dead, if you dare
to stand up to my long spear. It will slice
your lily skin. Then once you fall down there,
beside Achaea's ships, Trojan dogs and birds
will feed upon your flesh and fat."

Hector spoke.
Then he advanced—the troops moved up behind him,
making a huge din, even from soldiers at the back.
On the other side, the Argives raised a shout.
They hadn't lost their courage. They'd held their line   980
against the finest Trojans launching their attack.
The noise from both sides went up into bright Zeus' sky

294

Book Fourteen
Zeus Deceived

*[Nestor leaves his hut to look around, sees the Achaeans in retreat; Nestor
meets the wounded kings inspecting the field; Agamemnon advises going
home; Odysseus responds harshly to the suggestion; Diomedes advises
them to visit the battle; Poseidon continues to encourage the Argives;
Hera thinks of a plan to deceive Zeus; she prepares herself to look
seductive; Hera gets a Aphrodite's love charms; Hera visits Sleep and gets
his cooperation; Hera visits Zeus on Ida, has sex with him, and Zeus goes
to sleep; Poseidon rallies the Argives and leads them into battle; Ajax
wounds Hector badly with a rock; Hector withdraws; the killings
continue on both sides, the Argives getting the better of the battle.]*

As Nestor sat drinking wine, listening to the noise of war,
he said to Asclepius' son:

> "Noble Machaon,
> think about how this battle will end up—
> the shouting from our young men by the ships
> is getting louder. You should sit here for now.
> Drink some sparkling wine, till Hecamede
> with the lovely hair draws you a warm bath
> and washes the dried blood off your body.
> I'll go to a lookout, see what's going on."

Nestor took the well-made shield belonging to his son,   10
horse-taming Thrasymedes. It lay there in the hut,
gleaming bronze. The son was fighting with his father's shield.
Nestor took a strong spear with a sharp bronze point,
then stood outside the hut. At once he saw a shameful sight—
Achaeans in retreat, pushed back by their enemies,
high-hearted Trojans. The Achaean wall was breached.
Just as the great sea heaves with a sullen purple swell,
anticipating the swift passage of sharp winds—
but uncertainly—so its waves have no direction,
until some steady storm blows down from Zeus—that's how   20
the old man was lost in thought, his heart divided

between two courses. Should he seek out the crowd
of swift-riding Danaans, or see if he could find
Agamemnon, son of Atreus, his people's shepherd?
As he thought it over, the best course seemed to be
to find the son of Atreus.

                      Meanwhile, the other men
kept up the fight, kept on butchering each other.
Around their bodies the unwearied bronze rang out,
as they thrust with swords and double-bladed spears.
Then Nestor came across the kings the gods sustain—   30
they were walking round among the ships—all the ones
whom bronze had wounded—Diomedes and Odysseus,
along with Agamemnon, son of Atreus.

They'd drawn their ships on shore beside the blue-gray sea,
far from battle, dragging up their own ships first,
hauled them inland, then built the wall along the sterns.
The beach was wide, but not long enough for all the fleet.
The army didn't have much space to hold the boats.
So they'd set the ships in rows, and thus filled up
the whole wide coastal bay between the headlands.   40

The kings had set out in one group together,
each one leaning on a spear, to see the fighting
and check the progress of the war. Deep in their chests
they were very troubled. When old Nestor met them,
the anxiety in their Achaean hearts
was even more acute. Mighty Agamemnon
spoke to him and said:

                     "Nestor, son of Neleus,
great glory of Achaeans, why are you here?
Why have you left the battle? I'm afraid
that mighty Hector will make good those words   50
he used to threaten us, in that speech
he gave his Trojans, saying he'd not return
from our ships to Troy until he'd burned them
and slaughtered all the men. That's what he said.

And now it's happening. What chaos!
Other well-armed Achaeans in their hearts
must be angry with me, like Achilles,
unwilling to continue fighting by our ships."

Geranian horseman Nestor answered Agamemnon:

"What's happened so far is over, done with—   60
not even high-thundering Zeus himself
could make that something else—our wall is down.
We put our faith in it as a firm defence
for ships and for ourselves. At this moment,
men are constantly in action by our ships,
with no relief. Whichever way you look,
even if you really try, you cannot tell
from what direction we are being attacked.
It's all confused. The killing is haphazard.
The battle shouts fill heaven. As for us,   70
if thinking is a help, we should consider
how these events will end. I'm not saying
we should rejoin the fight—that's not expected
from those who have been wounded."

Agamemnon, king of men, replied:

           "Nestor,
since the men now fight at our ships' sterns,
and since our strong wall and ditch are useless—
something crushing for Danaans, whose hearts
had trusted they'd provide a firm defence
and keep our soldiers and our ships secure—   80
from this I gather that almighty Zeus
must enjoy it when Achaeans perish
without a name, right here, far from Argos.
I felt when Zeus was giving the Danaans
his full assistance, and I know it now,
when he gives the glory to the Trojans,
like blessed gods, while draining all our strength,
our fighting spirit. But come now, let's agree

to what I propose. Let's drag down those ships
drawn up in line closest to the surf   90
and pull them all into the sacred sea,
moor them there with stones in deeper water,
until the coming of immortal night—
which may prevent the Trojans' fighting.
Then we can shift the other ships. To flee
from ruin, even at night, brings no shame.
It's better to escape one's own destruction—
to run off—than let it overtake you."

In response to this, Odysseus scowled and said:

    "Son of Atreus, how can such words as these   100
come from your mouth? I'm finished with you.
I wish you ruled some other army,
some useless men, and were not our leader.
Zeus sees to it that from our youthful days
to our old age we must grind away
at wretched war, till, one by one, we die.
Are you really willing to leave Troy,
city of wide streets, for whose sake we've borne
so many evils? You'd better keep that quiet—
another Achaean man may hear the news,   110
learn what you've proposed in words no man
should ever let pass through his mouth at all,
no man whose heart has any understanding
of what's appropriate to say, no one
who is a sceptred king whom men obey—
as many as those Argive troops you lead.
From what you've said, I think you've lost your mind.
In the middle of a fight, you tell us now
to drag our well-decked ships down to the sea,
so that, though Trojans may be winning now,   120
they'd get what they most pray for realized—
the complete annihilation of us all.
For once we drag our ships into the sea,
Achaeans then will never go on fighting—
the whole time they'll be looking over here

298

and pulling out from battle. Then your plan,
you leader of the army, will destroy it."

Agamemnon, king of men, replied:

                                    "Odysseus,
that harsh rebuke of yours has stung my heart.
But I'm not the man to tell Achaea's sons   130
to drag our well-decked ships into the sea
if they're not willing. So show me someone
with a better plan than mine—young or old—
I'll welcome it."

                            Then Diomedes,
skilled in battle shouts, spoke up:

                                    "That man's close by.
We've no need to search too long, if you'll listen,
without any one of you resenting me
because I'm younger than the rest of you.
I claim worthy descent through Tydeus,
who lies in Thebes hidden underground.   140
Portheus had three fine sons in Pleuron
and steep Calydon—Agrius, Melus,
and a third, Oeneus, my father's father.
He was the most courageous of them all.
He stayed there, but my father roamed around.
He came to Argos. That was what Zeus willed—
other gods, as well. He married a daughter
of Adrestus, lived in a prosperous home,
with many wheat-bearing fields and orchards
planted all through his estate—and many sheep.   150
He was the best of all the Argive spearman.
You must have heard all this and know it's true.
So you would never label me by birth a coward,
a weakling, and thus demean what I advise,
if what I say is good. We must go back there,
to the battle, though we're wounded. Once there,
we'll stand back from combat, beyond the range

of flying weapons, in case someone is hit
and gets more wounds. But we'll urge on the others,
even those who, wallowing in their feelings,   160
have stood aside, without fighting up to now."

They listened well to Diomedes and agreed.
So they set off, led by Agamemnon, king of men.

Famous Earthshaker Poseidon saw all this.
He walked among them in the shape of an old man.
Taking Atreus' son Agamemnon by his right hand,
Poseidon talked to him—his words had wings.

> "Son of Atreus, in Achilles' chest
> his destructive heart is really happy now,
> to see Achaeans slaughtered and in flight.   170
> He's not in his right mind, not in the least.
> Well, he may be killed anyway—some god
> may strike him. As for you, the blessed gods
> aren't angry with you over anything,
> so Troy's kings and leaders may yet make dust
> while scurrying over this wide plain,
> while you watch them running to their city,
> back from these huts."

                      Poseidon said these words,
then, as he raced off to the plain, let out a mighty roar—
as loud as the din from nine or ten thousand men   180
when on a battleground they first clash with Ares.
That's how loud the sound was which came out then
from powerful Earthshaker's chest, infusing
great strength in each man's heart to keep on going,
to fight on there and not to pause for rest.

As this was happening, on a peak of Mount Olympus
Hera of the golden throne was standing watching.
She recognized her brother-in-law at once,
as he kept busy in the war where men win glory,
for he was her brother and her husband's, too.   190

Hera's heart was pleased. She looked across at Zeus,
sitting on the highest peak on top of Ida,
with its many fountains. Hatred filled her heart.
So ox-eyed queen Hera then began considering
how she might deceive the mind of aegis-bearing Zeus.
In her heart the best course of action seemed to be
to make herself look most attractive, go to Ida,
then see if Zeus would want to lie down with her,
embrace her, and make love. Then she could pour out
on his eyelids and his crafty mind a deep warm sleep.   200
She went off to her bedroom, which Hephaestus,
her dear son, had made for her, with close-fitting doors
set against their posts, secured with a secret lock,
which no other god could open. She went in there,
then closed the shining doors. First, with ambrosia
she washed from her lovely body all the stains,
then rubbed her skin with fragrant oil, divinely sweet,
made specially for her. If this perfume were merely stirred
inside Zeus' bronze-floored house, its scent would then diffuse
throughout heaven and earth. She used this perfume   210
all over her fair body, then arranged her hair.
With her own hands she combed her shining locks in braids,
a stunning style for an immortal goddess.
Then she wrapped around herself a heavenly robe,
which Athena made for her from silky fabric,
adorning it with gorgeous embroidery.
She pinned the robe around her breast with golden brooches.
On her waist she put a belt with a hundred tassels.
Hera then fixed earrings in her pierced ear lobes,
each with three gemstones, an enchanting glitter.   220
Next the queen of goddesses placed on her head
a fine new dazzling shawl, white as the sun.
She then slipped lovely sandals over her sleek feet.

Once Hera had dressed her body in this finery,
she left the room and summoned Aphrodite.
Some distance from the other gods, she said to her:

> "My dear child, will you agree to do

what I ask of you, or will you refuse,
because you're angry with me in your heart,
since I help Danaans and you aid the Trojans?"   230

Zeus' daughter Aphrodite answered her:

                                                                "Hera,
honoured goddess, daughter of great Cronos,
say what's on your mind. My heart tells me
I should do what you ask, if I can,
if it's something that can be carried out."

Then queen Hera, with her devious mind, replied:

"Then give me Love and Sexual Desire,
which you use to master all immortals,
and mortal men as well. I'm going to visit
the limits of this all-nourishing earth,   240
to see Oceanus, from whom the gods arose,
and mother Tethys, the two who reared me,
taking good care of me inside their home,
once they got me from Rhea, that time Zeus,
who sees far and wide, forced Cronos
underground, under the restless seas.
I'm going to visit them. And I'll resolve
their endless quarrel. For a long time now,
they've stayed apart from one another,
not sharing love there in the marriage bed,   250
since anger fills their hearts. If my words
could reconcile the hearts in these two gods,
bring them to bed again, once more in love,
they'd think of me with loving reverence."

Laughter-loving Aphrodite answered Hera:

"It wouldn't be appropriate for me
to say no to your demand, since you sleep
in the arms of Zeus, the greatest of the gods."

Aphrodite spoke, then loosened from her breasts
the finely decorated, embroidered garment   260
in which all her magic charms were fixed—for love,
erotic lust, flirtation, and seduction,
which steals the wits even of clear-thinking men.
Aphrodite put this in Hera's hands, then said:

> "Take this garment. Tie it round your breasts.
> Everything is interwoven in the cloth.
> I don't think you'll come back unsuccessful
> in getting what it is your heart desires."

Aphrodite finished. Ox-eyed queen Hera smiled,
and, as she did so, put the garment round her breasts.   270
Then Aphrodite, Zeus' daughter, went back home.

Hera sped off, leaving the crest of Mount Olympus.
She touched down on Pieria, lovely Emathia,
rushed by the highest mountains of Thracian horsemen—
her feet did not touch ground on those snow-covered peaks.
From Athos she went across the heaving sea,
coming to Lemnos, city of godlike Thoas.
There she met Sleep, Death's brother. Clasping his hand,
she spoke to him:

> "Sleep, king of all men and gods,
> if you've ever listened to what I say,   280
> obey me now. I'll be grateful always.
> Lull Zeus' radiant eyes to sleep for me,
> when I'm stretched out for sex beside him.
> I'll give you as a gift a lovely throne,
> indestructible gold which my own son
> Hephaestus with his ambidextrous skills
> will make for you. Under it he'll set a stool,
> so you can rest your feet when drinking wine."

Sweet Sleep then said in reply:

> "Honoured goddess Hera,

daughter of mighty Cronos, I could with ease   290
bring some other immortal one to sleep,
even the streams of river Ocean,
the source of all of them. But I won't come
near Zeus, lull him to sleep, unless he bids me,
asks in person. Your request some time ago
taught me my lesson, on that very day
when Hercules, son of almighty Zeus,
set sail from Ilion, after he'd sacked
the Trojans' city. That's when I seduced
the mind of aegis-bearing Zeus, pouring   300
my sweetness over him. You then carried
evil in your heart for Hercules, driving
blasts of hostile winds across the sea,
taking him at last to well-settled Cos,
far from all his friends. When Zeus woke up,
he was incensed, throwing gods around his house,
looking, above all, for me. He'd have tossed me
from heaven into the sea, if Night,
who subdues gods and men, had not saved me.
I ran away to her, and Zeus held back,   310
though still enraged, not wishing to offend
swift Night. Now here you are again, asking me
to do something I simply must not do."

Ox-eyed queen Hera then answered him:

                                                  "Sleep,
why concern your heart about these matters?
Do you think all-seeing Zeus feels for Trojans
the same rage he felt then for Hercules,
his own son? But come, I'll give you as your wife
one of the younger Graces. You can marry
Pasithea, whom you long for every day."   320

Hera finished. Sleep was overjoyed and said:

"All right, then. Swear to me by waters
of the inviolable river Styx, setting
one hand on the all-nourishing earth,

the other on the shimmering sea,
so all may witness our agreement,
even those gods underground with Cronos,
that you will give me one of the Graces,
Pasithea, whom I long for every day."

White-armed goddess Hera agreed to Sleep's request.   330
She made the oath, as he had asked, invoking
all the gods under Tartarus, those called the Titans.[1]
Once she'd finished saying the oath, they both set off,
wrapping themselves in mist. They left behind them
the cities of Lemnos and Imbros, moving quickly,
then came to Mount Ida with its many springs,
mother of wild creatures, and arrived at Lectum,
where for the first time they left the sea. They walked
on dry land, shaking treetops underneath their feet.
Sleep then stopped, before Zeus' eyes could see him,   340
climbed a high pine tree, at that time the tallest one
growing on Ida. It stretched up through the lower air
right into the sky. Concealed in that tree's branches,
Sleep perched there, shaped like the clear-voiced mountain bird
which gods call Chalcis, but people name Cymindis.

Hera moved quickly on to Ida's peak, high Gargarus.
Cloud-gatherer Zeus caught sight of her. As he looked,
his wise heart became suffused with sexual desire,
as strong as when they'd first made love together,
lying on a couch without their parents' knowledge.   350
Zeus stood up in front of her, called her, and said:

> "Hera, what are you looking for, coming
> down here from Olympus? Your chariot
> and your horses are not here. You should use them."

Queen Hera with her crafty mind then answered Zeus:

---

[1]The Titans are the generation of gods before Zeus, the ones he overthrew when he rebelled against his father, Cronos. They are imprisoned deep under the earth in a place called Tartarus.

"I'm going to visit the outer limits
of this all-nourishing earth, to Oceanus,
from whom gods came, and mother Tethys,
who looked after me in their own home.
They raised me well. I'll try to mediate   360
their endless quarrel. For a long time now,
they've stayed apart from one another,
not sharing love there in the marriage bed,
since anger fills their hearts. As for my horses,
they're standing at the foot of Ida,
with its many springs, to carry me
across dry land and sea. I've come here now,
down from Mount Olympus, to stop you
from being angry with me afterwards,
if I say nothing about going to visit   370
deep-flowing Oceanus in his home."

Cloud-gatherer Zeus then answered:

                                        "Hera,
you can go there later. But why don't we
lie down and make joyful love together?
I've never felt such sexual desire before
for any goddess, for any mortal woman.
It's flooding through me, overpowering the heart
here in my chest—not even when I lusted for
Ixion's wife, who bore me Peirithous,
a man as wise as gods, or Danaë,   380
with her enchanting ankles, daughter
of Acrisius, who gave birth to Perseus,
most illustrious of men, nor the daughter
of famous Phoenix, who bore me Minos
and godlike Rhadamanthus, nor Alcmene,
who gave birth to Hercules in Thebes,
a mighty hearted son, nor Semele,
who bore that joy to mortals Dionysus,
nor fair-haired lady Demeter, nor Leto,
that glorious girl, not even for yourself—   390
I felt for none of these the love I feel

for you right now—such sweet desire grips me."

Queen Hera with her cunning mind then said in reply:

"Most fearsome son of Cronos, what are you saying?
If you now want us to make love lying here,
on Ida's peaks, where anyone can see,
what if one of the immortal gods observes us,
as we sleep, then goes and tells the other gods?
I could not get up from this bed and go
into your home. That would be scandalous.   400
But if that's your wish, if your heart's set on it,
you have that bedroom your own son Hephaestus
had built for you. It has close-fitting doors
fixed into posts. Let's go and lie down there,
since you're so keen for us to go to bed."

Cloud-gatherer Zeus then answered her:

                                              "Hera,
don't be afraid that any god or man
will glimpse a thing. I'll cover you up
in a golden cloud. Even sun god Helios
will not see the two of us, and his rays   410
are the most perceptive spies of all."

Zeus finished. Then Cronos' son took his wife in his arms.
Underneath them divine Earth made fresh flowers grow—
dew-covered clover, crocuses, and hyacinths,
lush and soft, to hold the lovers off the ground.
They lay together there covered with a cloud,
a lovely golden mist, from which fell glistening dew.
Then Zeus slumbered peacefully on Mount Gargarus,
overcome with love and sleep, his wife in his embrace.

Sweet Sleep rushed to the Achaean ships, to inform   420
Poseidon, the Encircler and Shaker of the Earth.
Coming up to him, Sleep spoke—his words had wings:

307

"Poseidon, you could now assist the Argives
quite readily and give them glory,
if only for a while—Zeus is fast asleep.
I've covered him with a delicious sleep.
Hera has seduced him on a bed of love."

Saying this, Sleep left there for some well-known tribes of men.
But he made Poseidon want to help Danaans,
even more so than before. He ran to those in front,   430
calling in a loud voice:

                              "You Argives,
are we really going to give the victory
to Hector, son of Priam—allow him
to take our ships and get the glory?
That's what he says. He even boasts about it—
since Achilles stays beside his hollow ships,
anger in his heart. But we won't miss him much
if the rest of us get fighting strength
and help each other. So come, let's all follow
what I suggest. Let's arm ourselves with shields,   440
the best and biggest in our whole army,
cover our heads with gleaming helmets,
take in our hands the longest spears, and go.
I'll lead us. I don't think Hector, Priam's son,
will hold, no matter how much he wants to fight."

Poseidon spoke. The soldiers heard him and obeyed.
The kings themselves, though wounded, organized the men—
Agamemnon, Diomedes, and Odysseus.
Moving among the warriors, they supervised
the exchange of weapons. The best men put on   450
the best equipment, the worst men got the worst.
Once their bodies were encased in gleaming bronze,
they marched out. Earthshaker Poseidon led them,
gripping in his powerful fist a fearful sword,
with a long edge, like a lightning bolt, which no man
in grim battle could withstand—his fear would hold him back.
On the other side, glorious Hector organized his men.

Then he and dark-haired Poseidon launched the fight,
the most destructive moments of that battle,
one commanding Trojans, the other leading Argives.   460
The sea surged up to the Achaean huts and ships,
as the two sides met with a tremendous noise,
louder than ocean surf booming on shore, driven there
from the depths by the harsh North Wind, louder, too,
than roaring fire as it jumps to burn the trees
in some mountain clearing, louder than the wind
which howls through the highest branches of some oak tree,
a wind which at its worst makes the most piercing noise—
that's how loud the shouting came from Trojans and Achaeans,
terrifying screams, as they went at each other.   470

Glorious Hector first threw his spear at Ajax,
as he'd just turned to face him. The spear hit Ajax,
right where two straps intersected on his chest,
one for his shield, one for his silver-studded sword.
These saved his tender flesh. Hector was annoyed—
his weapon had flown from his hand and missed its mark.
He drew back into the group of his companions,
evading death. But great Telamonian Ajax
hit Hector with a rock as he was moving back—
there were many of them there rolling underfoot,   480
right where they fought, rock wedges used to prop the ships.
Ajax picked up one of these and struck Hector's chest,
just above the shield rim, close to Hector's neck.
The impact spun Hector like a top, reeling
round and round. Just like those times Father Zeus
uproots some oak tree with a lightning bolt—it falls,
with an awful smell of sulphur spreading from it,
which no one close by can look at without fear,
for Zeus' lighting bolts fill men with terror—
that's how mighty Hector fell down in the dust.   490
His spear dropped from his hand. His shield fell on him,
his helmet, too. The finely worked bronze armour
round his body rattled. Raising a loud shout,
Achaeans ran up, hoping to drag Hector back.
Their spears flew thick and fast, but no one could wound him,

that shepherd of his people, with sword or spear.
Before that happened, the best men rallied by him,
Polydamas, Aeneas, lord Agenor,
Lycian leader Sarpedon, and noble Glaucus.
None of the others ignored Hector. In front of him,   500
they held round shields. His companions picked him up
and took him out of the fighting in their arms,
until they came to his swift horses waiting for him
with their charioteer and richly ornate chariot
behind the battle lines. With chariot and horses
they took Hector, groaning badly, towards the city.
But when they reached the ford on that lovely river,
the swirling Xanthus, whose father is immortal Zeus,
they lifted him out and set him on the ground.
They poured on water to revive him. His eyes opened.   510
He rose to his knees, but then vomited dark blood
and fell down on his back again, lying on the ground.
Black night was covering up his eyes, for his spirit
was still overpowered by that blow from Ajax.

When Argives saw Hector carried back, they charged in,
going at Trojans even more, their battle fury roused.
Far ahead of all the rest came Oïlean Ajax.
Jumping out with his sharp spear, he struck Satnius,
son of Enops, who'd conceived him with a Naiad nymph,
while he was tending cattle by the river banks   520
at the Satnioeis. Ajax, son of Oïleus,
famous spearman, came up and struck him in the side.
Satnius fell backwards. Trojans and Danaans
then fought on around him. Spearman Polydamas,
son of Panthous, came up to help. He threw and hit
Prothoënor, son of Areilycus, in his right shoulder.
The heavy spear tore through the shoulder. He fell down—
lying in the dust and clawing dirt. Polydamas,
with a great shout, exulted in his triumph:

          "I don't think that spear flew in vain   530
          from the strong hand of Panthous' valiant son.
          Some Argive has got it in his flesh.

310

I think as he goes down to Hades' house,
he'll use it as a walking staff."

Polydamas' loud boasting pained the Argives.
He especially roused the spirit in fierce Ajax,
son of Telamon. For Prothoënor fell
right next to him. So Ajax quickly moved ahead
and hurled his shining spear. But jumping to one side,
Polydamas nimbly avoided his dark fate.   540
The spear hit Archelochus, Antenor's son—
the gods had planned his death. It struck his spine up high,
where the head attaches to the neck, slicing through.
It cut both sinews. As he fell, his head, mouth, and nose
hit the earth well before his knees, and Ajax cried
to brave Polydamas:

                    "Consider this, Polydamas,
          and tell me the truth—is not this man here
          worth killing to avenge Prothoënor?
          He doesn't seem to be unworthy,
          or from inferior parents. He looks like   550
          a brother of horse-taming Antenor,
          perhaps his son—he looks a lot like him."

Ajax shouted this, knowing very well the man he'd killed.
Trojans hearts were seized with grief. Then Acamas,
standing above his brother's body, with his spear
struck Promachus, a Boeotian, as he was trying
to drag Archelochus by his feet. Over the body
Acamas shouted then in triumph:

                    "You Argive boasters,
          how you love to threaten! Misery like this,
          all this suffering, is not for us alone.   560
          You too some day will be killed like this.
          See how your Promachus now sleeps in death,
          thanks to my spear. Whatever's owed to me
          for my brother has not been unpaid long.
          That's why in time of war a soldier prays

he leaves at home a brother to avenge him."

Acamas shouted this, bringing grief to Argives.
He really stirred the heart of warlike Peneleus.
He charged at Acamas, who did not stay there
to confront the charge of noble Peneleus,   570
so he then struck Ilioneus, son of Phorbas,
who owned many flocks, a man whom Hermes loved
above all Trojans, and he'd made him wealthy.
Ilioneus was the only child his mother bore
to Phorbas. But then he was hit by Peneleus,
below his eyebrows, just underneath his eye.
The spear knocked out the eyeball, went in his eye,
drove through his neck, and sliced the tendons at the nape.
Ilioneus collapsed, stretching out his arms.
Peneleus drew his sharp sword and struck his neck,   580
chopping head and helmet, so they hit the ground,
the spear still sticking from the socket of his eye.
Holding it up high, like a flowering poppy,
Peneleus shouted a loud boast at the Trojans:

> "Trojans, you can now tell the dear father
> and mother of fine Ilioneus to lament
> all through their house. When we Achaean lads
> sail in our ships from Troy, then the wife
> of this Promachus, son of Alegenor,
> will not be celebrating the return   590
> of her beloved husband."

                              Peneleos finished.
The Trojans were shaken, limbs trembling. Every man
looked around to see how he could evade grim death.

Tell me now, you Muses living on Olympus,
which of the Achaeans was first to carry off
bloody trophies from the men who'd just been slaughtered,
when famous Earthshaker turned the tides of war.
The first for that was Ajax, son of Telamon.
He hit Hyrtius, the son of Gyrtius,

312

who led the courageous Mysians. Then Antilochus
stripped spoils from Mermerus and Phalces.
Meriones killed Morus and Hippotion,
while Teucer slaughtered Prothoön and Periphetes.
and Menelaus hit Hyperenor in the side,
a shepherd to his people. As it went through him,
the spear forced out his guts. His life-spirit left him
through the wound, and darkness veiled his eyes.
But Ajax, swift son of Oïleus, killed the most.
For none could match his speed on foot, as he ran,
chasing men in flight when Zeus forced them to flee.

Book Fifteen
The Battle at the Ships

[Trojans are driven in retreat; Zeus wakes up on Ida, turns on Hera; Zeus instructs Hera to send Iris and Apollo to him; Hera returns to Olympus, gets Ares angry at Zeus; Athena restrains Ares; Iris and Apollo go to Zeus on Ida; Iris goes to Poseidon with Zeus' orders; Poseidon's resentment of Zeus; Poseidon withdraws from battle; Zeus sends Apollo to Hector; Apollo helps Hector recover; the battle starts again with Apollo leading the Trojans and pushing the Achaeans back; Apollo knocks down the wall and fills in the ditch; the armies fight around the ships; Ajax plays a leading role in defending the Achaeans; Hector seizes the stern of a ship, but Ajax holds Achaeans off with a long pike]

Trojans, in full retreat, passed the wall and ditch,
with many slaughtered by Danaans. Then they stopped,
regrouping by their chariots, pale with fear, terrified.
At that point Zeus, lying on the peaks of Ida
alongside Hera of the golden throne, woke up.
He stood up quickly, looked at Trojans and Achaeans,
saw Trojans running off with Argives driving them
from the back, among them god Poseidon.
He saw Hector lying on the plain, his companions
sitting round him. Hector was gagging painfully,   10
dazed and vomiting blood. The warrior who'd struck him
was not the weakest of Achaeans. Watching him,
the father of gods and men pitied Hector.
Looking at Hera with a fearful scowl, Zeus said:

"You're impossible to deal with, Hera,
devising such deceitful tricks to get
lord Hector from the fight and make the army
run away. But I think you may be the first
to get rewarded for your wretched scheme,
when I flog you with my whip. Don't you recall   20
the time I strung you up on high, putting
two anvils on your feet, tying your wrists
with unbreakable gold rope? You hung there,

314

in the air among the clouds. Other gods,
all through Olympus, were very anxious,
but just stood there, unable to untie you.
If I'd caught one trying, I'd have grabbed him,
tossed him from the threshold so he hit ground,
his strength all gone. But even with all that,
I couldn't ease the constant pain I felt   30
for god-like Hercules. You and North Wind
drove him with storm blasts over restless seas.
Your evil scheming later carried him
to well-settled Cos. I rescued him from there
and brought him back to horse-breeding Argos,
but only after he'd endured too much.
I'll remind you of these things once more,
so you'll stop your malicious trickery,
so you'll see the advantages you get
from this seduction, this couch where you lay   40
to have sex with me, when you came from the gods
intending to deceive me."

                    Zeus spoke. Ox-eyed queen Hera
trembled as she answered—her words had wings:

"Let earth and wide heaven above be witnesses,
with the flowing waters of the river Styx,
on which the most binding, most fearful oaths
are made by blessed gods—let your sacred head,
our marriage bed as well, stand witnesses,
things on which I'd never swear untruthfully—
the harm that Earthshaker Poseidon did   50
to Hector and the Trojans, to help Argives—
in all that I had no part. His own heart
pushed and drove him on. He saw Achaeans
being beaten by their ships and pitied them.
I'd not advise him to go against you,
lord of the dark cloud, but to follow you,
wherever you might lead."

                    Hera finished.

The father of gods and men smiled and then replied—
his words had wings:

"Ox-eyed queen Hera,
if from now on you and I were of one mind,   60
as you took your seat among immortals,
then, no matter how much Poseidon's views
differed from our own, he'd quickly bring them
into line with yours and mine. If you're being frank,
speaking the truth, go now to that group of gods,
and order Iris to come here with Apollo,
the famous archer, so she may visit
bronze-armed Achaean soldiers and instruct
lord Poseidon to stop fighting and return
to his own house. And Phoebus Apollo,   70
after reviving Hector for the fight,
will breathe new strength into him. He'll forget
that pain which now weighs down his spirit.
He'll drive Achaeans back a second time,
once he's turned them into cowards. They'll run
back to Achilles' ships with many oars.
The son of Peleus will send out his companion,
Patroclus, whom glorious Hector will then kill
in a spear fight right in front of Ilion,
after many other young men have gone down,   80
killed by Patroclus, including my own son,
godlike Sarpedon. Then, in his anger
at Patroclus' death, godlike Achilles
will slaughter Hector. From that moment on,
I'll make the Trojans steadily fall back,
leaving the ships, until Achaeans take
steep Ilion, with Athena's guidance.
Until that time, I'll not restrain my anger,
nor let any other immortal god
assist Achaeans here, not before   90
Achilles' wishes have been carried out,
as I first promised, nodding my assent,
that day when goddess Thetis held my knee
and begged me to bring honour to Achilles,

destroyer of cities."

                    Zeus finished speaking.
White-armed goddess Hera obeyed him, leaving
Mount Ida for high Olympus. Just as the mind
races in a man who's voyaged to many lands,
when in his fertile head he recalls everything,
and thinks "I wish I were here! I wish I were there!"—   100
that's how fast queen Hera hurried in her eagerness.
Reaching steep Olympus, she found immortal gods
together at Zeus' palace in a meeting.
Seeing her, they all stood up and offered her
their cups in welcome. Ignoring all the others,
Hera took the cup of fair-cheeked Themis, the first
who came running up to meet her. Themis spoke to her—
her words had wings:

               "Hera, why have you come?
    You look upset. Perhaps your husband,
    the son of Cronos, has frightened you?"   110

Ox-eyed queen Hera then replied:

                  "Goddess Themis,
    don't question me like this. You know his moods,
    how he can be so harsh and overbearing.
    You should start the communal banquet now,
    here in the palace. You'll learn about these things
    when all the immortals do—the evil plans
    Zeus is proposing, something, in my view,
    which won't please all hearts alike, in gods or men,
    although some may still enjoy our feast."

Hera finished speaking. Then she sat down.   120
In Zeus' palace gods were angry. Hera's lips smiled,
but above her dark eyebrows her forehead frowned.
Irritated with them all, Hera then burst out:

    "What fools we are to get incensed at Zeus

317

so stupidly! We're still keen to get close to him,
so we can hold him back with words or force.
But he sits there, all by himself, without a care,
without a worry, claiming he's supreme
among immortal gods, manifestly so,
for strength and power. So you just accept   130
whatever trouble he sends each of you.
In fact, I think bad trouble has now come
to Ares—in that fight his son's been killed,
his favourite man, Ascalaphus, whom Ares,
mighty war god, acknowledges as his."

Once Hera finished, Ares struck his sturdy thighs
with the flat of his hands and, in his grief, burst out:

"Don't blame me, you dwellers on Olympus,
if I go down now to Achaean ships,
to avenge my son's slaughter, even if   140
it's my fate to be struck by Zeus' lighting,
to lie there with the dead in blood and dust."

Ares finished. Then he told Terror and Flight
to yoke up his horses, while he dressed himself
in his glittering armour. Now, at that moment,
feelings between Zeus and other immortal gods
could have become much harsher, more incensed,
if Athena, fearing what might happen to the gods,
hadn't jumped from the throne where she'd been sitting,
rushed out the door, seized Ares' helmet from his head,   150
grabbed the shield from off his shoulders and the spear
out of his mighty fist, and thrown them to one side.
Then with these words Athena went at raging Ares:

"You idiot! Have you lost your mind, gone mad?
Do those ears of yours hear anything at all?
Where's your common sense or your discretion?
Did not you get what Hera said just now,
the white-armed goddess who's come straight from Zeus?
Do you want a belly full of trouble,

318

forced to come back to Olympus, though in pain,   160
sowing seeds of danger for the rest of us?
For Zeus will abandon men immediately—
those proud Trojans and Achaeans—and come here,
to Olympus, then start to go at us.
He'll lay his hands on each one of us in turn,
guilty or innocent. So I'm telling you—
set aside that anger for your son.
Better men with stronger hands than his
have already been destroyed and will be.
It's hard to keep the families and children   170
safe for everyone."

                       Athena finished.
Then she made angry Ares sit down on his throne.
Hera called Apollo from the house with Iris,
messenger for the immortal deities.
Hera addressed them both—her words had wings:

    "Zeus is ordering you two to go to Ida,
    as fast as possible. Once you get there,
    look in Zeus' face, do what he commands."

Having said this, queen Hera went inside the house,
sat on her throne. Flying off in a rush, the two gods   180
reached Ida with its many springs, mother of wild beasts.
They found all-seeing Zeus sitting on Gargarus,
wrapped in a finely scented cloud. The two approached,
came up, and stood there before cloud-gatherer Zeus.
Seeing them, Zeus felt no anger in his heart. They'd been quick
obeying his dear wife. Zeus spoke first to Iris—
his words had wings:

                  "Go now, swift Iris,
    convey to lord Poseidon these instructions,
    report it all precisely—he's to stop,
    to leave the battle strife, and go away   190
    to the group of gods or to his sacred sea.
    If he won't obey my orders and ignores them,

he should consider in his mind and heart
this point—no matter how mighty he may be,
he can't stand up to me if I attack him.
For I can say I'm stronger than he is,
more powerful. And I'm the first born.
Yet his fond heart thinks it's all right to claim
equality with me, whom all others fear."

Zeus spoke. Swift Iris, with feet like wind, obeyed.   200
She set off from Mount Ida for sacred Ilion.
Just as snow or icy hail flies down from clouds, swept on
by gales from North Wind, child of the upper sky,
that's how quickly swift and eager Iris moved.
She stood close by the famous Earthshaker and said:

> "A message for you, Encircler of Earth,
> dark-haired god—I've brought it here from Zeus,
> who holds the aegis. He orders you to stop,
> to leave the battle strife. You're to go away,
> to the crowd of gods or to your sacred sea.   210
> If you ignore and disobey his orders,
> he threatens you he'll come in person,
> to stand in war against you. And Zeus says
> you should avoid his hands, asserting
> he's a stronger god than you, more powerful,
> and was born first. Yet your fond heart
> thinks nothing of claiming equality
> with him, whom other gods all fear."

The famous Earthshaker, enraged, replied:

>   "It's unjust!
> He may be best, but he speaks too proudly,   220
> if he restrains me by force against my will,
> for I'm as worthy of respect as he is.
> We are three brothers, sons of Cronos,
> born from Rhea—Zeus, myself, and Hades,
> third brother, ruler of the dead. The whole world
> was divided in three parts, and each of us

received one share. Once the lots were shaken,
I won the blue-gray sea as mine to live in
for ever. Hades got the gloomy darkness,
Zeus wide heaven, with the upper air and clouds.   230
But earth and high Olympus still remained
to all of us in common. So I won't go.
I won't follow Zeus' will. Let him stay,
for all his strength, happy with his third.
Let him not try to scare me with the power
of his hands, as if I were some coward.
It would be better if he'd use his threats,
his bluster, on those sons and daughters
which he himself produced. They, at least,
will have to listen to his orders."   240

Swift Iris, with feet like the wind, replied:

"Dark-haired Earthshaker, is that the message
I'm to take from you to Zeus, these harsh,
defiant words? Or will you change your mind?
For the finest hearts can change. The Furies,
as you know, always serve the elder one."

Earthshaker Poseidon then said:

                              "Goddess Iris,
what you say is right. It's commendable
when a messenger understands things well.
But this business brings harsh pain into my heart,   250
my spirit, when the deity whose share
is the same as mine and who's been given
a common destiny, wants to abuse me
with angry words. However, for now
I'll concede, for all my indignation.
But I'll tell you—this threat comes from my heart—
if, despite me, Athena, goddess of spoils,
Hera and Hermes and lord Hephaestus,
Zeus spares steep Ilion, if he's unwilling
to destroy it and to give great power   260

to the Argives, let him know that with us
an anger will arise that no one can appease."

With these words the Earthshaker left Achaean troops.
Going to the sea, he plunged in. Achaeans troops
missed his presence there among them.

Cloud-gatherer Zeus then spoke to Apollo:

"Dear Phoebus,
go down to bronze-armed Hector. Poseidon,
who encircles and shakes the earth, has gone
back to the sacred sea and thus avoided
my harsh anger. If he'd fought it out with me,   270
others would certainly have heard about it,
even gods below, down there with Cronos.
But for me this is much better, and for him, too,
that before we came to blows he backed off,
away from my hands, despite his anger.
We'd have had to sweat it out to end it.
But take this tasseled aegis in your hand
and shake it well to scare Achaean warriors.
And Apollo, far-shooting god, make Hector
your special care. Infuse him with great strength,   280
until Achaeans run back to their ships
and reach the Hellespont. From that point on,
I'll figure out how in word and deed
Achaeans may get new relief from war."

Zeus spoke. Apollo did not disobey his father.
Swooping down from Mount Ida like some swift hawk
killing pigeons, the fastest of all flying creatures,
he found lord Hector, wise Priam's son, sitting up,
no longer prone. He was just starting to recover,
to recognize his comrades round him. He'd stopped   290
gasping and sweating, for aegis-bearing Zeus
had revived his mind. Apollo, the far worker,
stood close to him and said:

                             "Hector, son of Priam,
why are you having fainting spells right here,
away from all the others? Are you in trouble?"

Hector of the shining helmet, still weak, replied:

"Which of the mighty gods are you, my lord,
questioning me face to face? Don't you know
that Ajax, skilled at war cries, hit me,
as I was slaughtering his companions   . 300
by the ships' sterns? He got me in the chest
with a rock and stopped my frenzied fighting.
I thought today my heart would breathe its last,
that I'd be seeing the dead in Hades' house."

Lord Apollo, son of Zeus, then answered Hector:

"Take courage now. Cronos' son has sent you
a powerful defender from Mount Ida,
to stand beside you as your protector,
Phoebus Apollo with his golden sword,
who's helped you before, you and your city.   310
But come now, tell your many charioteers
to charge the hollow ships with their swift horses.
I'll go ahead and smooth the horses' path.
I'll turn back these Achaean warriors."

With these words Apollo breathed power into Hector,
his people's shepherd. Just as some horse in a stall
who at the manger has eaten well, then breaks his halter
and runs off across the plain at a thundering gallop,
eager for its usual bath in the flowing river,
exulting as it goes, with head held high, its mane   320
flowing across its shoulders, fully confident
of its own splendour, limbs carrying it lightly
to places where the mares are in the pasture,
that's how quickly Hector moved his feet and limbs,
as he urged on his charioteers, once he'd heard
Apollo's voice.

Just as dogs and country farmers
chase a horned stag or wild goat, but the creature
saves itself in a sheer rock face or dark underbrush,
and men have no luck finding it, but their shouts
attract a bearded lion to their path, who scatters them,   330
despite their eagerness—that's how Danaans
for a while continued to press on in groups,
thrusting away with swords and double-bladed spears.
But when they saw Hector moving among the ranks,
they were afraid. Each man's heart sank to his feet.
Then Thoas, Andraemon's son, spoke out, the best man,
by far, among Aetolians, expert in the spear throw,
good at fighting hand to hand, and in assemblies
few Achaeans could beat him when young men argued.
Thinking of their situation, Thoas said:

                                          "Here's something—   340
My eyes are watching an amazing sight.
Hector's got up again, evading death.
In our hearts we all hoped that he'd been killed
at the hands of Ajax, son of Telamon.
But some god has once more rescued Hector,
saved the man who's drained strength from many limbs
among Danaans. That will continue now,
I think, for he's not standing there like that,
so keen to fight, against the will of Zeus,
the thunderer. But come, let's all follow   350
what I propose. Let's tell most of the men
to move back to the ships. Those among us
who claim to be the best men in the army
will make a stand. If we can reach him first
and hold him off with our extended spears,
for all his fury I think his heart will fear
to mingle with this Danaan company."

Thoas spoke. The others heard him and readily agreed.
Those with Ajax, lord Idomeneus, Teucer,
Meriones, and Meges, like the war god Ares,   360
summoning the best men, recommenced the battle,

confronting Hector and his Trojans. Behind them,
most of the troops went back to the Achaean ships.

Trojans charged in a mass assault, led by Hector,
moving with huge strides. Phoebus Apollo marched
in front of Hector, his shoulders covered up in clouds,
holding the fearful aegis, with its double fringe
glittering ominously. The smith Hephaestus
had given it to Zeus to make men run from war.
Apollo now held this aegis in his hands,   370
as he lead on the army. The Argives, closely packed,
stood their ground. Shrill war cries came from either side,
arrows flew from bowstrings, many spears were thrown.
Some impaled themselves in the flesh of quick young men.
Many fell halfway before they reached white skin,
skewered in the earth, still longing to taste flesh.
As long as Phoebus Apollo held the aegis steady
in his hands, on both sides weapons hit their mark—
men kept on dying. But when Apollo stared directly
at the swift Danaans and then shook the aegis,   380
howling a horrific roar, he bewitched them all—
the spirit in their chests then lost the will to fight.
Just as two wild beasts stampede a herd of cattle
or large flock of sheep, coming suddenly in dark night,
with no herdsman present, that's how Achaeans,
in their weakness, were then put to flight. Apollo
sent the panic, glorifying Hector and his Trojans.

Then, as men killed each other, the battle front collapsed.
Hector slew Stichius and Arcesilaus—
one a leader of bronze-armed Boeotians,   390
one a trusted comrade of brave Menestheus.
Aeneas slaughtered Medon and Iasus.
Medon was a bastard son of noble Oïleus,
thus brother to Ajax, but lived in Phylace,
far from his native land. For he'd killed someone,
a relative of his step-mother Eriopis,
wife to Oïleus. Iasus, a commander
of Athenians, was known as a son of Sphelus,

son of Bucolus. Polydamas killed Mecistus,
and Polites killed Echius fighting at the front.   400
Then lord Agenor slew Clonius, and from behind
Paris struck Deïochus just below the shoulder,
as the latter fled from soldiers fighting in the front.
He drove the bronze spear straight through the man.

While Trojans were stripping armour from the corpses,
Achaeans jumped in the ditch they'd dug, on the stakes,
running to and fro, forced to withdraw behind their wall.
Hector then gave a great shout to his Trojans:

> "Charge the ships. Leave the blood-stained spoils alone.
> Whoever I see not moving to the ships   410
> on the other side, I'll make sure he dies
> right there. His relatives, men and women,
> won't be burying him, once he's dead,
> with the proper rites of fire. Instead,
> the dogs will rip him up before our city."

Saying this, Hector swung his whip down from his shoulders,
lashing on his horses, calling Trojans in the ranks.
They all shouted with him, then drove the horses
pulling chariots. A tremendous noise arose.
In front, Phoebus Apollo easily knocked down   420
the banks of the steep trench—with his feet he pushed dirt
into the middle, making a long broad causeway,
as wide as the distance a man can throw his spear
when he's showing off his strength. Trojans poured through,
wave after wave of them, with Apollo leading on,
holding up the priceless aegis. The Achaean wall
he easily demolished, as a child will scatter sand—
in a childish game beside the sea he builds a sand wall,
then with his hands and feet flattens it for fun.
That's how you, archer Phoebus, at that time knocked down   430
what the Achaeans built with so much effort,
such hard work. You sent them flying back in panic.
The Danaans halted to regroup beside their ships,
shouting to each other, lifting up their hands

to all the gods, with each man praying fervently.
Geranian Nestor, Achaea's guardian,
prayed most of all, hands stretched to starry heaven:

> "Father Zeus, if, in wheat-yielding Argos,
> any man has ever burned fat thighs
> of bulls or sheep in sacrifice to you,   440
> praying for his return, and you answered him,
> nodding your head and promising assent,
> Olympian god, remember that. Protect us
> from a pitiful doom. Don't let Trojans
> destroy Achaeans in this way."

                                      Nestor prayed.
Counselor Zeus, hearing the prayers of that old man,
son of Neleus, gave a great clap of thunder.
When Trojans heard aegis-bearing Zeus' thunder,
they attacked the Argives all the more, drawing on
their battle fury. Just as a great wave crashes   450
from the wide sea onto the planking of a ship,
driven by forceful winds whipping up the waves—
that's how Trojans, with tremendous shouts, came down,
through the wall, driving their chariots to the fighting,
the hand-to-hand combat with double bladed spears
by the ships' sterns. Trojans battled from their chariots,
Achaeans from high up on the planks of their black ships.
They'd climbed up on the decks to fight there with long pikes
lying in place for battles out at sea, jointed weapons
with forged bronze at the tip.

                            As long as Trojans and Achaeans   460
were fighting by the wall away from the swift ships,
Patroclus stayed sitting in Eurypylus' hut,
cheering him up with pleasant conversation,
relieving his black pain by spreading ointments
on his painful wound. But when he realized
Trojans were capturing the wall, while Danaans
were crying out and in retreat, Patroclus groaned.
Striking his thighs with the flat of his hands, he spoke

in evident distress:

> "Eurypylus, I can't stay
> with you any longer here, though you need help.　　　470
> For a fierce battle has begun. Your companion
> must look after you. I'll run to Achilles
> to urge him on to fight. Who know? With god's help,
> I may rouse his spirit with my words.
> A friend's persuasion perhaps can do some good."

Patroclus finished speaking and went off on foot.
Achaeans, with fewer numbers, still held firm
against advancing Trojans, but couldn't push them back
or dislodge them from the ships. Trojans could not break through,
get past Danaan ranks to assault the ships and huts.　　　480
Just as a carpenter's line makes ship's timber straight,
when a craftsman's hand applies it, a skilled expert
in all facets of his craft, inspired by Athena—
that's how tensely poised the fighting in that battle stood.
Men fought in various groups from one ship to the next.

Hector went straight for glorious Ajax, both men
struggling over the same ship. Hector was unable
to push Ajax back and burn the ship, while Ajax
could not drive Hector off, now that Apollo
had brought him so far. Noble Ajax hurled his spear.　　　490
He hit Caletor, son of Clytius, in the chest,
as he was bringing fire to the ships. With a crash,
he collapsed, and the burning torch dropped from his hands.
When Hector saw his cousin fall there in the dirt
by the black ship, right before his eyes, he called out
to his Trojans and Lycians with a powerful shout:

> "Trojans, Lycians, Dardan spearmen,
> don't hold back from battle in this danger.
> Save the son of Clytius, just in case
> Achaeans strip his armour now he's fallen　　　500
> among this group of ships."

                                        Saying this,
Hector threw his bright spear at Ajax, but missed.
Instead he hit Lycophron, son of Mastor,
from Cythera, one those attending Ajax.
Since he'd killed someone in holy Cythera,
he lived with Ajax. Hector's sharp bronze struck him
on the head, above his ear, as he stood near Ajax.
He fell into the dust, tumbling from the stern
down to the ground. Then his limbs went slack.
Ajax shuddered and cried out to his brother:

                              "Teucer, my friend,   510
        Mastor's son, our worthy comrade, has been killed.
        He lived with us when he arrived from Cythera.
        In our house we honored him just as we did
        our parents. Proud Hector has now killed him.
        Where are your swift lethal arrows and the bow
        Phoebus Apollo gave you?"

                                    Ajax finished.
Teucer heard him and came up running to stand there,
beside Ajax, with his curved bow in his hand
and a quiver full of arrows. He began to shoot,
loosing arrows in quick succession at the Trojans.   520
He hit Cleitus, fine son of Peisenor, a companion
of Polydamas, noble son of Panthous,
who was holding chariot reins. He'd been busy
managing his horses, which he'd been driving
to where the ranks were most confused, as a favour
to Hector and his Trojans. But he was struck
by that evil no man can defend himself against,
no matter how much he desires. The painful arrow
lodged behind his neck. He tumbled from the chariot,
forcing his horses to swerve aside—that made   530
the empty chariot rattle. Polydamas
saw this right away and was the first to rush
into the horses' path. He then handed them
to Astynous, Protiaon's son, firmly telling him
to keep them close and watch. Then Polydamas

went back to join those fighting at the front.

Taking out another arrow, Teucer tried to hit
bronze-armed Hector. That would have stilled his heart
and stopped his fighting at Achaean ships, if Teucer
had hit him as he was showing off how brave he was.   540
But the perceptive mind of Zeus guarding Hector
was paying attention. He robbed Teucer of that triumph
by snapping the fine bow's tightly twisted string,
just as Teucer was lining up a shot at Hector.
The heavy bronze-pointed arrow flew awry.
The bow fell from his hands. Teucer, with a shudder,
spoke out to his brother Ajax:

                                        "Look at that!
          Some god is thwarting all our efforts in this fight.
          He's knocked the bow out of my hands and snapped
          my freshly twisted bowstring. I strung it   550
          just this morning so it would last a while
          and I could shoot scores of arrows with it."

Great Telamonian Ajax then answered Teucer:

          "My friend, leave your arrows and your bow—
          set them down, since some god has broken them
          to spite Danaans. Take hold of a long spear,
          set a shield against your shoulder—fight the Trojans.
          Encourage other troops to do the same.
          They won't take our well-decked ships without a fight,
          even though they're overpowering us,   560
          so let's concentrate our minds on battle."

Ajax spoke. Teucer took his bow into his hut,
then slung a four-layered shield against his shoulder.
On his strong head he set a well-made helmet,
with a horsehair crest which nodded menacingly.
He took a strong spear with a sharp point and set off,
running quickly to take his place by Ajax.

When Hector saw that Teucer's arrow shot had missed,
he called in a loud voice to Trojans and to Lycians:

> "Trojans, Lycians, Dardan spearmen, 570
> be men, my friends. Recall your warlike power
> among these hollow ships. For I've witnessed
> with my own eyes how Zeus has canceled out
> an arrow shot at us by their best man.
> It's easy to see how Zeus assists men,
> those to whom he grants great victories,
> or how he drains men's strength, refusing
> to protect them, as he now saps the power
> among the Argives and works to help us,
> while we fight by the ships. So stay together. 580
> Should one of you meet his fate and die,
> stabbed by a spear or cut down with a sword,
> let the man die. To be killed defending
> one's own native land is no ignoble act.
> The man's wife is safe, his children live,
> his house and land remain, if Achaeans leave,
> returning to their country in their ships."

With these words, Hector roused each man's fighting spirit.
On the other side, Ajax called out to his companions:

> "For shame, Argives. Now the issue's clear— 590
> either we'll be killed or we'll be saved,
> if we can push the danger from our ships.
> Are you expecting, if the ships are taken
> by Hector of the shining helmet,
> you'll all get to your native land on foot?
> Don't you hear frenzied Hector urging on
> his men. He's frantic now to burn the ships.
> He's inviting them to fight, not to a dance.
> For us there's no better choice or tactic
> than to bring our arms and warrior strength 600
> against them and keep fighting hand to hand.
> It's better to settle this once and for all—
> whether we live or die—than be hemmed in,

fighting a long grim battle, as we are now,
among our ships against inferior men."

Ajax's words rallied the fighting spirit in each man.

Hector then killed Schedius, son of Perimedes,
leader of Phocians. Ajax slew Laodamas,
noble Antenor's son, who led up troops on foot.
Polydamas slaughtered Otus of Cyllene,   610
comrade of Phyleus' son, who led brave Epeians.
Seeing this death, Meges then attacked Polydamas,
who slipped away from him, eluding Meges' charge.
Apollo would not let Panthous' son be killed
among those fighting in the front. But Meges
thrust his spear into Croesmus, right in his chest.
He fell with a crash. Meges started stripping armour
from his shoulders, but Dolops charged at him,
the bravest son of Lampus, son of Laomedon,
a skilled spear-fighter, who knew all there was to know   620
about fighting close in. Dolops moved up to Meges,
then with his spear struck the centre of his shield.
Meges' thick armour with fitted breastplates saved him.
Phyleus had brought this armour from Ephyre,
from the river Selleïs. A guest of his there,
Euphetes, ruler of men, had given it to him
to wear in war, protection from his enemies.
Now this armour saved his son's flesh from destruction.
Meges then thrust his sharp spear at Dolops' helmet,
striking it on top, on the bronze ridge, which held in place   630
the horsehair plume. He sheared it off. The whole plume,
a bright fresh purple, fell onto the dusty ground.
While Meges fought on, still expecting victory,
warlike Menelaus came to his assistance.
Standing to one side, out of Dolops' line of sight,
Menelaus speared his shoulder from behind.
The eager spear kept going, driving into Dolops' chest.
He fell on his face. The two men hurried forward
to strip bronze armour from his shoulders. But Hector
shouted to his kinsmen one and all. The first man   640

he yelled at was strong Melanippus, Hicetaon's son,
who used to graze his shambling herds in Percote,
when enemies were far away. Once Danaans
arrived in their curved ships, he'd gone back to Ilion,
where Trojans held him in respect. He lived with Priam,
who honoured him as if he were a child of his.
Hector called to him, speaking some angry words:

> "Melanippus, why are you so feeble?
> Is that fond heart in you not worried
> for your slain relative? Do you not see   650
> how they're busy stripping Dolops' armour?
> Come on, we can't fight Argives from a distance.
> We've got to stay with them until we kill them off,
> or they capture Ilion completely,
> butchering her people."

                    Hector finished,
then led on. Godlike Melanippus followed.

Then great Telamonian Ajax roused the Argives:

> "Friends, be men. In your hearts remember shame.
> In the killing zone let each man shame the rest.
> That sense of shame saves more men than it kills.   660
> Those who flee help no one, and they get no glory."

Ajax spoke. The men were already keen to fight,
but they took his words to heart and fenced in the ships
within a hedge of bronze. Zeus drove the Trojans at them.
Then Menelaus, skilled at war shouts, urged Antilochus:

> "Antilochus, no other Achaean warrior
> is as young as you or quicker on his feet,
> or as brave in battle. So jump out there—
> see if you can hit one of the Trojans."

Menelaus finished speaking and moved back again.   670
But his words aroused Antilochus. He stepped forward,

ahead of those fighting at the front, glanced around,
and threw his shining spear. Trojans moved back,
as he made his throw. The spear wasn't thrown in vain.
It hit proud Melanippus, Hicetaon's son,
in the chest, as he was moving up to fight,
right beside his nipple. He collapsed with a crash,
and darkness fell upon his eyes. Then Antilochus
pounced on him, like a dog leaping on a wounded fawn,
which some hunter hits as it rushes from its den,   680
loosening its limbs. That how bold Antilochus
went after you, Melanippus, to strip your armour.
But Hector noticed him. He came up on the run
to face Antilochus directly. But the latter,
though an impetuous warrior, did not stand his ground.
He ran back, like some wild beast intent on mischief,
one that's killed a dog or herder with the cattle,
and scampers off before a crowd of people gather.
That's how Nestor's son scurried back. Trojans and Hector,
shouting loudly, showered him with lethal weapons.   690
When he reached the crowd of his companions,
Antilochus turned round and made a stand there.

Trojans attacked the ships like ravenous lions,
fulfilling Zeus' will. He kept on giving them
great fighting strength, while he drained Achaean hearts,
denying them glory, as he drove the Trojans forward.
Zeus' heart was set on glorifying Hector,
son of Priam, so he might throw onto the ships
a blazing tireless fire and thus fulfill completely
that disastrous request from Thetis. Counselor Zeus   700
was waiting to glimpse with his own eyes the blaze
from a burning ship, for that would be the moment
he was going to push the Trojans from the ships
and give the glory to Danaans. With this in mind,
Zeus drove Hector, son of Priam, against those ships,
something Hector was furiously keen to do.
He raged like spear-fighting Ares or deadly fire
in the thickets of deep mountain forests.
He was foaming at the mouth, below his eyebrows

the eyes were raging fire—the helmet round his temples
shook with menace, as Hector battled on, for Zeus,
the god of heaven, was his protector, giving him
glory and honour, though he was but one man
among so many, for Hector's life would soon cease.
Already Pallas Athena was pushing forward
that fated day when he'd die at the mighty hand
of Achilles, son of Peleus.

                         But now Hector
was striving to break through the warriors' ranks,
probing them wherever he saw the largest groups,
the finest armour. But he could not break through,
for all his eagerness. In their defensive wall,
Achaeans held their ground. Just as a huge stone cliff
by the blue-gray sea stands firm against the wind
howling straight at it or the surging surf which pounds it—
that's how Danaans stood up to the Trojans then,
firmly with no falling back. But then Hector,
blazing all over like some fire, charged the throng,
falling on them as a fierce wave whipped up by a storm
crashes against a ship, which gets hidden in the foam,
blasts of wind shrieking past the sail, and sailors' hearts
tremble with fear as they are carried off from death
inch by inch—that's how hearts in those Achaean chests
were cracking. Hector charged them like a vicious lion
going at cattle grazing in huge numbers
in the bottom wetlands of a spacious meadow,
guarded by a herdsman who still lacks the skills
to fight a wild beast for the mangled carcass
of some short-horn heifer—with the herd he goes
always beside the first or last ones of the group,
but the lion leaps into the middle and devours a cow,
as all the others scatter—that's how Achaeans then
were all driven back in awe-struck terror by Hector
and Father Zeus.

                 But Hector killed only one man—
Periphetes of Mycenae, dear son of Copreus,

who used to take messages from king Eurystheus
to mighty Hercules. This dishonourable man
had a son with much more virtuous qualities—
he could run fast and was an excellent fighter,
and for his mind among the best in Mycenae.
But this man then gave Hector even greater glory.   750
For as he turned, he tripped against a shield rim,
the one he carried, which extended to his feet
and protected him from spears. He stumbled and fell.
The helmet round his temples gave a dreadful clang,
as he went down. Hector saw this at once, ran up,
stood by Periphetes, and struck him with his spear
in the chest, killing him beside his dear companions.
Those men were sorry for their comrade, but could not help—
they were too afraid of godlike Hector.

By now they were in among the ships, encircled   760
by the outer row of those they'd dragged up first.
But Trojans kept on pouring in. So Argives were forced
to move back from the ships' first row. But they stayed
in a single group beside the huts, not scattering
throughout the camp, held there by shame and fear.
They called out to one another continually,
especially Geranian Nestor, Achaea's guardian.
He kept appealing to each man's parents, saying:

> "Friends, be men. Let sense of shame from all men
> fill your hearts. Remember, each of you,   770
> your children, wives, possessions, and your parents—
> whether alive or dead. They're not here,
> but, on their behalf, I beg you to stand firm.
> Don't let yourselves turn round and run away."

With these words, Nestor boosted each man's spirit.
Then Athena removed the strange cloudy mist
and cleared their eyes, so on both sides light streamed in,
back to the ships and out towards the battle groups.
They saw Hector, skilled at war cries, his companions,
all the soldiers standing idle in the rear,   780

336

all those warriors battling on by their swift ships.

The spirit in great-hearted Ajax could not bear
to take up a position with Achaea's sons
where there was no fighting. So with his huge strides,
he kept moving up and down the decks along the ships.
In his fists he held a long pike used in sea fights,
one with fitted with sockets—thirty feet in length.
Just as a man well skilled in guiding horses
harnesses together four chosen out of many,
then drives them at a gallop from the plain   790
to some large city on a public highway,
while many men and women look at him amazed,
as he keeps leaping from one horse to another,
landing firmly, never slipping as they race ahead—
that's how Ajax, with huge strides, kept on moving
over many decks on those swift ships, shouting
so his voice reached heaven, telling Danaans
in fearsome yells to defend their ships and huts.

Hector did not stay in the well-armed Trojan group,
but, like an eagle swooping down upon some flock   800
of winged birds feeding by a river bank—
wild geese or cranes or long-necked swans—he rushed
straight at the dark-prowed ships to take on Ajax.
With his mighty hand Zeus pushed him from the back,
while urging other warriors to accompany him.

The brutal fight began again among the ships.
You'd think they weren't tired at all, but only starting—
they went at each other with such ferocity,
as they faced each other in that battle. Each side
fought for different reasons—Achaeans thought   810
they'd never escape that danger and would be destroyed—
for Trojans, the heart in each man's chest was hoping
they'd fire the ships and kill Achaean warriors.
That's what they thought as they fought one another.

Hector grabbed hold of a seaworthy ship, at the stern,

the fine fast boat which brought Protesilaus to Troy,
though it didn't take him back to his own native land.
In close combat by this ship, Achaeans and Trojans
were hacking at each other. By this point, the battle
was no more a matter of standing at some distance,   820
enduring showers of spears and arrows, but of fighting
at close quarters—united by a common spirit—
battling with sharp axes, hatchets, long swords,
and double-bladed spears. Many lovely swords,
with dark mountings, fell to earth, from hands and shoulders
of those fighting warriors. Earth flowed black with blood.
Hector seized hold of that ship and would not let go—
gripping the ornamental marker on the stern,
yelling to his Trojans:

                              "Bring fire. Raise a general shout.
Now Zeus has given us a day that makes up   830
for everything—to seize the ships that came here,
contravening the gods' will, creating
many troubles for us, because our elders
in their cowardice restrained me, held back
my troops, when I was keen to fight it out
at the ships' sterns. But if all-seeing Zeus
dulled our minds then, now he commands us,
now he drives us forward."

                                          Hector shouted.
Then Trojans attacked the Argives even more intensely.

Ajax could not hold his position any longer.   840
Assailed by flying spears, he backed off a little,
abandoning the deck on that well-balanced ship.
He moved to the raised platform, seven feet high,
and looked for Trojans, always jabbing with his pike,
pushing from the ship any Trojan bearing tireless fire,
always yelling fearful shouts at the Danaans:

                                          "Friends,
        Danaan warriors, companions of Ares,

338

be men, my friends. Recall your battle fury.
Do we think we've got people to help out
somewhere behind us or some stronger wall   850
which will hold off our men's destruction?
There's no nearby city fenced with walls,
where we can defend ourselves or with many men
turn the tide of battle. No, we're here,
on this plain crammed with well-armed Trojans,
our backs to the sea, far from our native land.
The light that'll save us lies in our hands,
not in holding back from battle."

Saying this, Ajax kept on jabbing ferociously
with his sharp pike. Any Trojan who charged the ships   860
with blazing fire, seeking to please Hector,
found Ajax waiting to slice him with his pike.
He wounded twelve men in close fighting by the ships.

Book Sixteen
Patroclus Fights and Dies

*[Patroclus begs Achilles to send him back to the war to help the
Achaeans; Achilles agrees but sets conditions; Hector breaks Ajax's
spear, sets fire to the ship; Achilles sends Patroclus to war with the
Myrmidons; Patroclus arms himslef; Achilles organizes the Myrmidons
in fighting groups; Achilles prays to Zeus; Patroclus goes into battle,
driving Trojans back from the ships; Trojans retreat; Sarpedon rallies
the Lycians, fights Patroclus; death of Sarpedon; Apollo cures Glaucus'
wound; the fight over Sarpedon's body; Trojans are driven back
towards Troy; Hector kills Patroclus]*

While the men kept on fighting at the well-decked ships,
Patroclus went to Achilles, his people's shepherd,
shedding warm tears, like a fountain of dark water
whose stream flows over the lip of a sheer rock face.
Looking at him, swift-footed, godlike Achilles
felt pity. So he spoke to him—his words had wings:

"Why are you crying, Patroclus, like some girl,
an infant walking beside her mother,
asking to be picked up. She pulls the robe
and stops her mother strolling on ahead,   10
looking up at her in tears, until the mother
lifts her up. You're crying just like that girl,
Patroclus. Is there something you need to say
to the Myrmidons or me? Some news
from Phthia that only you have heard?
People say Menoetius, Actor's son,
is still living, and Peleus is alive,
Aeacus' son, among his Myrmidons.
If these two had died, then we'd have something
real to grieve about. Or are you feeling sad   20
for Argives as they're being obliterated
among the hollow ships for all their pride?
Speak up. Don't conceal what's on your mind.
Then we'll both understand."

With a heavy sigh,
horseman Patroclus, you then replied:

"Achilles,
Peleus' son, by far the strongest of Achaeans,
don't be angry with me. Such great despair
has overcome the Argives. For all those
who used to be the bravest warriors
are lying at the ships with sword and spear wounds—   30
powerful Diomedes, son of Tydeus,
hit by a spear, famous spearman Odysseus
with a stab wound, and Agamemnon, too.
An arrow struck Eurypylus in the thigh.
Many healers, exceptionally skilled
in various medicines, are with them now,
tending their wounds. But it's impossible
to deal with you, Achilles. I hope anger
like this rage you're nursing never seizes me.
It's disastrous! How will you be of use   40
to anyone in later generations,
if you won't keep shameful ruin from the Argives?
You're pitiless. Perhaps horseman Peleus
was not your father, nor Thetis your mother—
the gray sea delivered you, some tall cliff,
for you've an unyielding heart. If your mind
shuns some prophecy, or your noble mother
has told you news from Zeus, at least send me,
and quickly, with the others in our troop
of Myrmidons. I could be a saving light   50
for the Danaans. Give me your armour
to buckle round my shoulders, so Trojans,
mistaking me for you, may stop the fight.
Then Achaea's warrior sons could get some rest.
They're worn out. War doesn't offer much relief.
We're fresh, so we should easily repulse
the Trojans tired of the battle noise
back from our ships and huts towards the city."

Patroclus finished his entreaty. How wrong he was!

He was praying for his own death, his dreadful fate.
Swift-footed Achilles, with some heat, replied:

"My dear divinely born Patroclus,
what are you saying? I'm not concerned
with any prophecy I know about,
nor has my noble mother said a thing
from Zeus. But dreadful pain came in my heart
and spirit when that man wished to cheat
someone his equal and steal away that prize,
and just because he's got more power.
That really hurt, given that I've suffered   70
in this war so many pains here in my chest.
Achaea's sons chose that girl as my prize.
I won her with my spear, once I'd destroyed
her strong-walled city. Lord Agamemnon
took her back, out of my hands, as if I were
some stranger without honour. But let that be—
it's over, done with. Besides, my spirit
didn't mean to stay enraged for ever,
although I thought I wouldn't end my anger
until the cries of warfare reached my ships.   80
Come, put my famous armour on your shoulders
and lead war-loving Myrmidons to battle,
since black clouds of Trojans now surround the ships,
expecting victory, and Argives stand
crammed in by the sea shore, with little space,
while a city full of Trojans comes at them
without fear, because they don't see near them
my helmet with its glittering front. Soon enough,
they'd be running back, filling the gullies
with their dead, if mighty Agamemnon   90
treated me with kindness—but now they fight
all through our camp. For there's no spear raging
in the fists of Diomedes, son of Tydeus,
to protect Danaans from disaster.
I've not heard the voice of Agamemnon
crying out in his vile head. As for Hector,
that man-killer's voice echoes everywhere,

shouting at Trojans, who fill all the plain
with their noise, as they defeat Achaeans
in this battle. Even so, Patroclus,   100
you must stave off disaster from the fleet.
Go after them in force—they may fire those ships
and rob us of the journey home we crave.
Now, pay attention to what I tell you
about the goal I have in mind for you,
so you'll win me great honour and rewards,
so all Danaans will send back to me
that lovely girl and give fine gifts as well.
Once you push Trojans from the ships, come back.
If Zeus, Hera's mate, who loves his thunder,   110
gives you the glory, don't keep on battling
those war-loving Trojans with me absent.
You would decrease my honours. Don't let
the joy of fighting and of killing Trojans
lead you on to Ilion, just in case
some deathless Olympian god attacks you.
Apollo, the far-worker, loves his Trojans.
So make sure you come back here again,
once your saving light has reached our ships.
Let others keep on fighting in the plain.   120
O Father Zeus, Athena, and Apollo—
if only no single Trojan or Achaean
could escape death, and just we two alone
were not destroyed, so that by ourselves
we could take Troy's sacred battlements!"

As these two were talking on like this together,
Ajax was losing ground, under attack from spears,
overcome by the will of Zeus and Trojans,
who kept throwing weapons. The bright helmet on his head
rattled dangerously as it was struck. Many hits   130
landed on the well-made armour on his cheeks.
His left shoulder was worn out from always holding up
his shining shield. But for all the onslaught with their spears,
the Trojans couldn't budge him. Still, he was in trouble,
breathing heavily, sweat pouring down in rivulets

343

from every limb. He'd had no time for any rest.
In every way, his desperate plight was getting worse.

Tell me now, you Muses living on Olympus,
how the fire first got tossed onto Achaean ships.
It was Hector. He came up close to Ajax,   140
then with his great sword hacked at Ajax's ash spear,
right behind the point. He cut straight through it.
Telamonian Ajax still gripped the spear,
but it was useless without its bronze spear head,
which fell some distance off, clanging on the ground.
The heart in mighty Ajax recognized gods' work.
He shuddered, for he perceived how high-thundering Zeus
was denying completely all his fighting skill,
wanting the Trojans to prevail. Ajax backed off,
out of range. Then onto that swift ship the Trojans threw   150
untiring fire, which spread itself immediately
in a fiery blaze that no one could extinguish.
The ship's stern started to catch fire.

                                    At that moment,
Achilles, slapping his thighs, said to Patroclus:

                              "Up now,
          divinely born Patroclus, master horseman.
          In the ships I see destructive flames going up.
          Trojans must not seize our ships and leave us
          with no way to escape. Put armour on,
          and quickly. I'll collect the soldiers."

Achilles spoke. Patroclus dressed in gleaming bronze.   160
First, he fixed on his shins the beautiful leg armour,
fitted with silver ankle clasps. Around his chest
he put on the body armour of Achilles,
swift-footed descendant of Aeacus—finely worked
and glittering like a star. On his shoulders he then slung
his bronze silver-studded sword and a large strong shield.
On his powerful head he set the famous helmet
with its horsehair crest. The plume on top nodded

full of menace. Then Patroclus took two strong spears
well fitted to his grip. He'd didn't choose Achilles' spear,   170
for no Achaean man could wield that weapon,
so heavy, huge, and strong, except for brave Achilles.
It was made of ash wood from the peak of Pelion.
Cheiron gave it to Achilles' father to kill warriors.[1]
Patroclus told Automedon to yoke the horses quickly,
the man he most esteemed after Achilles,
breaker of men, and the one he trusted most
to carry out his orders in a battle.
For Patroclus Automedon put swift horses
in the harnesses, Xanthus and Balius, who flew along   180
as swiftly as the wind. These horses Podarge,
the harpy, had conceived with West Wind, as she grazed
in a meadow beside the stream of Oceanus.[2]
In the side traces he set Pedasus in harness,
a fine horse Achilles had taken for himself,
when he'd captured the city of Eëtion.
Though mortal, it kept pace with his deathless horses.

Meanwhile Achilles went to and fro among the huts,
getting all his Myrmidons to arm themselves.
They rushed out, like flesh-eating wolves, hearts full   190
of unspeakable fury, beasts which in the mountains
have caught and ripped apart some huge antlered stag.
Then in a pack they charge off, jaws all dripping blood,
to lap black surface water with their slender tongues
in some dark spring, vomiting up clots of blood
from their crammed bellies, while in their chests their hearts
are resolute. That's how the leaders and commanders
of the Myrmidons rushed around brave Patroclus,
comrade of swift Achilles, Aeacus' descendant,
who stood among them there, urging on the horses   200
and the warriors carrying their shields.

Achilles had brought fifty ships to Troy—

[1]Cheiron is the most famous of the centaurs, creatures that are half man and half
horse. He helped to train many important heroes.
[2]The harpies are flying monsters with the faces of young women, long claws, and
pale, hungry expressions.

in each were fifty men, his own companions.
He'd picked five leaders whom he trusted to give orders.
His great power gave him overall command.
The first contingent was led by Menesthius,
with his flashing breastplate, son of Spercheius,
the river fed from heaven. Lovely Polydora,
Peleus' daughter, had conceived Menesthius
with timeless Spercheius, a woman copulating   210
with a god. But in name Borus was his father,
son of Perieres, who'd married her in public,
after paying out a huge price for the bride.
The second group was led by warrior Eudorus,
a bastard child of Polymele, Phylus' daughter,
a lovely dancer. The god who slaughtered Argus,
mighty Hermes, fell in love when he noticed her
among the singing maidens in the chorus
dancing for Artemis, the golden-arrowed goddess
in the echoing hunt. Hermes the helper,   220
going at once into her upper room in secret,
had sex with her. She bore him a fine son, Eudorus,
outstanding as a warrior and speedy runner.
But when Eileithyia, goddess of labour pains,
brought him into the light and he saw sunshine,
then strong Echecles, Actor's son, took Polymele
to his home, after giving an enormous bride price.
Old man Phylus was very kind to the young boy.
He looked after him, surrounding him with love,
as if he were his son. The third commander   230
was warlike Peisander, son of Maemalus,
a man pre-eminent among the Myrmidons
for spear fighting, second only to Patroclus.
Phoenix led the fourth contingent, and Alcimedon,
splendid son of Laerces, was leader of the fifth.

Once Achilles had set all the ranks in order
behind their leaders, he addressed them sternly:

> "My Myrmidons, let none of you forget
> those threats you spoke about by our swift ships,

while I was angry—you'd go on and on   240
against the Trojans. Each of you blamed me:
'Cruel son of Peleus, surely your mother
suckled you with bile, you pitiless man,
who keeps his comrades by their ships
against their will. Why don't we go home
in our seaworthy ships, since evil rage
has fallen on your heart?' That's what you men
complained about me in your meetings.
Now a great work of war awaits you,
the sort of enterprise you used to love.   250
So make sure each man's heart is resolute,
as you go to battle with these Trojans."

With these words, Achilles stirred the spirit in each man.
As they heard their king, the ranks bunched up more closely.
Just as a man constructs a wall for some high house,
using well-fitted stones to keep out forceful winds,
that's how close their helmets and bossed shields lined up,
shield pressing against shield, helmet against helmet,
man against man. On the bright ridges of the helmets,
horsehair plumes touched when warriors moved their heads.   260
That's how close they were to one another. In the front,
ahead of all of them, two men stood fully armed—
Automedon and Patroclus—sharing a single urge,
to fight in the forefront of their Myrmidons.
Achilles went into his hut and opened up the lid
on a beautifully decorated chest
placed on board his ship by silver-footed Thetis
for him to take. She'd packed it with cloaks and tunics,
and woollen blankets, too—protection from the wind.
There he kept an ornate goblet. Other than Achilles   270
no one used it to drink gleaming wine. With this cup
Achilles poured libations to no god but Father Zeus.
Taking this out of the chest, first he purified it
with sulphur, then rinsed it out in streams of water.
He washed his hands and drew some gleaming wine.
Standing in the middle of the yard, he poured it out,
gazing up at heaven. Thunder-loving Zeus looked on.

"Zeus, king, lord of Dodona, Pelasgian,
you who live far off, ruling cold Dodona,
around whom live the Selli, your prophets,   280
with unwashed feet, who sleep upon the ground,
you heard me when I prayed to you before.
You gave me honour then by striking hard
at the Achaean army. So grant me now
what I still desire. I intend to stay
beside this group of ships, but I'm sending out
my comrade and my many Myrmidons.
Send glory with him, all-seeing Zeus.
Strengthen the heart inside his chest, so Hector
sees if Patroclus can fight on alone   290
or if his hands are always conquering
only when I'm with him in the raging war,
in the centre of the havoc Ares brings.
But when he's pushed the fight and battle noise
back from the ships, let him return to me,
here at my hollow ships, without a scratch,
with all his weapons and companions,
men who battle in the killing zone."

                                            So Achilles prayed.
Counselor Zeus heard his prayer. He granted part of it,
part he denied. Father Zeus agreed that Patroclus   300
should drive the battle fighting from the ships,
but not that he'd return in safety from the war.
Once Achilles had made his libation and prayed
to Father Zeus, he went back into his hut,
put the goblet in the chest, came out, and stood there,
before his hut, still wishing in his heart
to see the fatal clash of Trojans and Achaeans.

The armed warriors who went with brave Patroclus
marched out in formation, until, with daring hearts,
they charged the Trojans, immediately swarming out,   310
like wasps beside a road, which young lads love to torment,
constantly disturbing them in their roadside nests—
those fools make mischief for all sorts of people.

If some man going past along the road upsets them
by accident, they all swarm out with fearless hearts
to guard their young—with that same heart and spirit
the Myrmidons then poured out from their ships
with a ceaseless roar. In a loud shout, Patroclus
called out to his companions:

> "You Myrmidons,
> companions of Achilles, son of Peleus,   320
> be men, my friends, recall your fighting strength,
> so we may honour the son of Peleus,
> by far the best Achaean at the ships,
> with the finest comrades in a close combat.
> Wide-ruling Agamemnon, Atreus' son, will see
> his folly in not honouring Achilles,
> the best of the Achaeans."

With these words,
Patroclus spurred the strength and heart in every soldier.
Then, in a massed group, they fell upon the Trojans.
Terrifying cries came from Achaeans by their ships.   330

When Trojans saw the brave son of Menoetius
with his attendant, both in glittering armour,
all their hearts were shaken and their ranks fell back.
They thought Peleus' swift-footed son by his ships
had set aside his anger and made friends again.
Each man glanced around, checking how he might escape
his own complete destruction.

Patroclus was the first
to throw his bright spear right at the central mass
where most troops clustered, by the stern part of the ship
of great-hearted Protesilaus. He hit a man,   340
Pyraechmes, who'd led Paeonian charioteers
from Amydon, by the broad flowing Axius.
Struck by that spear in his right shoulder, he fell down
screaming on his back there in the dust. Comrades round him,
his Paeonians, ran off—Patroclus terrified them,

349

now he'd killed their leader and best fighter.
He drove them from the ships and doused the blazing fire.
The half-burnt ship he left there. The Trojans scattered,
making a tremendous noise. Danaans poured out
from among the ships throughout the constant uproar.   350
Just as from a high peak of some massive mountain,
Zeus, who gathers lightning, shifts a bulky cloud,
once more revealing all the peaks, high headlands,
and mountain glades, while from heaven the huge bright sky
breaks open—that's how Danaans saved their ships
from fire and could rest, if only for a moment,
since the fighting was not over yet. At this point,
Achaean troops had not fully pushed the Trojans
from the ships. They'd been forced back from the sterns,
but they still stood there, facing the Achaeans.   360
The leaders then began to kill each other
in the scattered fighting. First, Menoetius' brave son
with his sharp spear struck Areilycus in the thigh,
as he was turning. He drove the bronze straight through,
breaking the bone. Areilycus fell face down in the dirt.
Then warlike Menelaus hit Thoas in the chest,
in a place where it was open right beside his shield.
The blow collapsed his limbs. Meges, Phyleus' son,
saw Amphiclus charging at him, but hit him first,
spearing the top of his leg, where a man's muscle   370
is the thickest. The spear point sliced his tendons,
and darkness closed his eyes. Then the sons of Nestor
went into action. Antilochus jabbed his sharp spear
at Atymnius, driving the bronze point in his side,
so he fell forward. Maris, who was close by,
angry about his brother, charged Antilochus
holding his spear, and then stood by his brother's body.
But godlike Thrasymedes moved too quickly for him.
Before Maris could thrust, he lunged out at his shoulder.
He didn't miss. The spear point sheared off muscle   380
at the bottom of his arm and broke the bone in two.
Maris fell with a crash, and darkness veiled his eyes.
Thus, these two, slaughtered by two brothers, went off
to Erebus. They'd been Sarpedon's brave companions,

spearmen sons of Amisodarus—he'd reared
the raging Chimera, who'd killed so many men.
Ajax, son of Oïleus, jumped out at Cleobulus,
captured him alive, stuck in that confusion. Even so,
Ajax struck him with his sword across the neck,
draining his fighting strength. The sword grew warm with blood.   390
Dark death closed up his eyes, and strong Fate embraced him.

Then Peneleus and Lycon charged each other.
Each had thrown his spear and missed, wasting the throw.
So they went at one another once again with swords.
Lycon struck the helmet ridge on its horse-hair crest,
but his sword shattered at the hilt. Then Peneleus
slashed Lycon's neck below the ear. The sword bit deep,
sinking the entire blade, so Lycon's head hung over,
held up on one side only by the uncut skin.
His limbs gave way.

                Meriones, with quick strides,   400
caught up with Acamas, then hit him with his spear
in his right shoulder, as he was climbing in his chariot.
He tumbled out. A mist descended on his eyes.

Idomeneus' pitiless bronze then struck Erymas
right in his mouth—the spear forced itself straight through,
below his brain, splitting his white skull apart,
smashing out his teeth. His eyes filled up with blood.
More blood spurted from his nose and open mouth.
Then death's black cloud enveloped Erymas.

Thus these Danaan leaders each killed his man.   410
Just as ravenous mountain wolves suddenly attack
young goats or lambs and seize them from the flock,
when in the mountains an inattentive shepherd
lets them wander off—once the wolves see them,
they attack at once, for those young lack the heart to fight—
that's how Danaans then went after Trojans,
whose minds now turned to shameful flight, for they'd lost
their will to battle on.

Great Ajax kept on trying
to throw his spear at bronze-armed Hector.
But Hector's battle skills kept his broad shoulders hidden
behind his bull's hide shield, as he watched arrows
and thudding spears flying past. Hector realized
the tide of victory in that fight was changing,
but he stood there, trying to save his loyal companions.
Just as those times a cloud comes from Olympus,
moving from the upper air across the sky,
when Zeus brings on a rain storm—that's how Trojans
fled yelling from the ships, crossing the ditch again
in complete disorder. Hector's swift-footed horses
carried him and his weapons back, leaving behind,
against their will, the Trojans held up at the trench
dug by Achaeans. In that ditch many swift horses
lost their master's chariots when poles snapped at the end.
In pursuit, Patroclus, intent on killing Trojans,
yelled fierce orders to Danaans. Meanwhile, the Trojans,
shouting and scattering in panic, were jammed up
in every pathway. Under the clouds a high dust storm rose,
as sure-footed horses strained to get away,
leaving the huts and ships and rushing for the city.

Wherever Patroclus saw the biggest crowd
of soldiers in retreat, with a yell he charged at them.
Bodies kept rolling underneath his axle,
as men fell out when chariot cars rolled over.
His swift horses, those immortal beasts the gods gave
as a priceless gift to Peleus, flew straight on
across the ditch, charging forward. Patroclus' heart
was set on finding Hector, eager to strike him down.
But Hector's own swift horses carried him away.
Just as in late summer rainstorms, the dark earth
is all beaten down, when Zeus pours out his waters
with utmost violence, when he's enraged with men
who have provoked him with their crooked judgments,
corrupting their assemblies and driving justice out,
not thinking of gods' vengeance, so all the rivers
crest in flood, their torrents carving many hillsides,

as they roar down from the mountains in a headlong rush
toward the purple sea, destroying the works of men—
that's how, as they sped on, the Trojan horses screamed.

When Patroclus had cut the Trojans' front ranks off,
he pushed them back again towards the ships,   460
keeping them from the city they were trying to reach.
Between the ships, the river, and the lofty wall,
in that middle ground, he kept charging at them,
killing them, avenging deaths of many comrades.
There he first struck Pronous with his shining spear,
where Pronous' shield had left his chest exposed.
His limbs gave way, and he fell down with a thud.
Patroclus next rushed at Thestor, son of Enops,
who just sat crouching in his polished chariot,
paralyzed with terror, reins slipping from his hands.   470
Coming up, Patroclus struck him with his spear
right on the jawbone, smashing through his teeth.
Patroclus pulled his spear back, dragging Thestor
out across the chariot rail. Just as a man
sitting on a rocky point hauls up a monstrous fish
out of the sea, using a line and bright bronze hook—
that's how Patroclus dragged Thestor from his chariot,
mouth skewered on the shining spear. He threw him down,
face first. As Thestor fell, his spirit abandoned him.
Then Erylaus rushed up, but Patroclus struck him   480
with a rock right on his head, smashing the entire skull
inside his heavy helmet. Erylaus collapsed
face down in the dirt.

                    Death, who destroys men's hearts,
flowed all around Patroclus, as he slaughtered
Erymas, Amphoterus, Epaltes,
Tlepolemus, son of Damastor, Echius,
Pyris, Ipheus, Euippus, and Polymelus,
son of Argeas—all these Patroclus laid out,
one by one, on the earth, which nourishes all men.

When Sarpedon observed his Lycian companions,   490

who wear no belt around their tunics, being cut down
by the hands of Menoetius' son Patroclus,
he called out to reprimand his godlike Lycians:

"Shame on you Lycians! Where are you running?
Now's the time for you to fight on bravely.
I'll stand up to this man, so I'll find out
who it is that fights so well, who brings with him
so much destruction for the Trojans,
breaking the limbs of many fearless soldiers."

Sarpedon finished. He jumped out of his chariot   500
down to the ground holding his weapons. On the other side,
when Patroclus saw him, he leapt from his chariot.
Then they rushed at each other, screaming like vultures
fighting with hooked talons and curved beaks, screeching
on some rocky height.

            Looking down on the two men,
the son of crooked-minded Cronos pitied them.
He spoke to Hera, his sister and his wife:

"Alas—Sarpedon, dearest of all men,
is fated now to die, killed by Patroclus,
son of Menoetius. My heart's divided,   510
as I think this over. Should I snatch him up
while still alive and place him somewhere else,
in his rich land of Lycia, far distant
from this wretched fighting, or have him killed
at the hands of Menoetius' son."

Ox-eyed queen Hera then replied to Zeus:

            "Dread son of Cronos,
how can you say this? The man is mortal,
doomed long ago by Fate. Now you desire
to rescue him from miserable death.
Do as you wish. But we other gods   520
will not all agree with you. And I'll tell you

354

something else—make sure you remember it.
If you send Sarpedon home alive,
take care some other god does not desire
to send his dear son from the killing zone.
Around Priam's great city, many men,
sons of the immortals, are now fighting.
You'll enrage those gods and make them bitter.
But if Sarpedon's dear to you, if your heart
feels pity for him, then let him be killed   530
in a fierce combat at Patroclus' hands,
son of Menoetius. Once his living spirit
has abandoned him, send Death and sweet Sleep
to carry him away, back to the spacious land
of Lycia, where his brother and his kinsmen
will bury him with a mound and headstone.
That's what appropriate for those who die."

Hera spoke. The father of gods and men agreed.
But he shed blood rain down upon the ground, tribute
to his dear son Patroclus was about to kill   540
in fertile Troy, far from his native land.

The two approached within range of each other.
Patroclus threw and struck renowned Thrasymelus,
lord Sarpedon's brave attendant, low in the gut.
His limbs gave way. Then Sarpedon charged Patroclus.
His bright spear missed him, but it struck a horse,
Pedasus, in its right shoulder. The horse screamed,
gasping for life, then fell down in the dust, moaning
as the spirit left him. The two other horses reared,
their yoke cracked, and their reins got intertwined   550
with the trace horse Pedasus lying in the dust.
But famous spearman Automedon cleared the tangle.
Pulling out the long sword on his powerful thigh,
he dashed in and, without a pause, cut the trace horse loose.
The two other horses straightened out, then pulled
together in their harness. The two men kept going,
taking up again their heart-destroying combat.
Once more Sarpedon failed with his bright spear. Its bronze point

sailed past Patroclus' left shoulder, missing him.
Then Patroclus, in his turn, threw his bronze spear,   560
which did not leave his hand in vain. It struck
right between Sarpedon's midriff and his beating heart.
Sarpedon toppled over, as an oak tree falls,
or poplar or tall mountain pine which craftsmen cut
with sharpened axes, to harvest timber for a ship—
that's how he lay there stretched out before his chariot
and horses, groaning and clawing at the bloody dust.
Just as a lion moves into a herd, then kills a bull,
a sleek great-hearted steer among the shambling cattle,
which bellows as it dies right in the lion's jaws—   570
that's how Sarpedon, leader of the Lycian spearmen,
struggled as he died, calling to his dear companion:

> "Glaucus, my friend, you warrior among men,
> now you must really show yourself a spearman,
> a true courageous fighter. You must now
> embrace this evil war, if you're brave enough.
> First, move around and urge the Lycian leaders
> to make a stand here by Sarpedon. And then,
> you fight over me in person with your bronze.
> I'll be a source of misery to you,   580
> and shame as well, for all your days to come,
> if Achaeans strip my armour now I'm down
> among the fleet of ships. So hold your ground
> with force. Spur on the army."

                                                As he said this,
death's final end covered Sarpedon's eyes and nostrils.
Then Patroclus set his foot upon Sarpedon's chest,
pulled his spear out of the body. The guts came with it.
So in the same moment he tugged out the spear point
and took Sarpedon's life. Myrmidons reined in the horses,
snorting in their eagerness to bolt, now they'd left   590
their master's chariot.

                        When Glaucus heard Sarpedon's voice,
he was overcome with savage grief, his heart dismayed

that he could not have come to his assistance.
With his hand he grabbed and squeezed his wounded arm,
still painful from being hit by Teucer's arrow,
as he'd attacked him on that high defensive wall.
Teucer had been defending his companions
from disaster. So Glaucus prayed then to Apollo:

"Hear me, my lord. You may be in Lycia,
somewhere in that rich land, or here in Troy.   600
But you can hear a man's distress from anywhere.
Bitter grief has now come in my heart.
For I have this cruel wound. Sharp pains
run up and down my arm, the flow of blood
won't stop. The wound wears out my shoulder,
so I can't grip my spear with any force,
or move to fight against our enemies.
And our finest man has perished—Sarpedon,
child of Zeus, who would not assist his son.
But, my lord, heal my savage wound at least,   610
and ease my pain. Give me strength, so I can call
my Lycian comrades, urge them on to war,
and I can fight in person by the corpse
of our Sarpedon now he's dead."

So Glaucus spoke in prayer.
Phoebus Apollo heard him. He eased the pains at once,
stopped the dark blood flowing from the cruel wound,
and filled his chest with fighting strength. In his heart
Glaucus recognized with joy that the great god
had quickly heard his prayer. First, he moved around
and spurred on Lycia's leading men in every spot   620
to rally round Sarpedon. Then, with long strides,
he went among the Trojans—to Polydamas,
son of Panthous, and brave Agenor. He searched out
Aeneas and Hector dressed in bronze. Approaching him,
he spoke—his words had wings:

"Hector,
now you're neglecting all your allies,

357

men who for your sake are far away from friends,
their native land, wasting their lives away.
You've no desire to bring assistance.
Sarpedon, leader of Lycian spearmen,   630
lies dead, the man who protected Lycia
with his judgment and his power—slaughtered
by Ares on the bronze spear of Patroclus.
My friends, stand by him, keep in your hearts
your sense of shame, in case the Myrmidons
strip off his armour and mutilate his corpse,
in their anger at the dead Danaans,
the ones killed by our spears at their fast ships."

Glaucus finished. Trojans were completely overwhelmed
with grief—unendurable and inconsolable.   640
For Sarpedon had always fought to guard their city,
although he was a distant stranger. Many soldiers
followed him, and he was pre-eminent in war.
Full of furious passion, they went at Danaans,
Hector in the lead, angry about Sarpedon.
But Patroclus, Menoetius' son, with his strong heart,
rallied the Achaeans. He spoke first to the Ajaxes,
both eager for the fight:

                                "You two Ajaxes,
now you must get your joy protecting us,
as you've done before, but even better.   650
The man who was the first to jump inside
Achaea's wall lies dead—Sarpedon.
We must try to mutilate the body,
to seize and strip armour off its shoulders,
slaughtering with our pitiless bronze
any of his comrades who defend him."

Patroclus spoke. The Ajaxes both were fiercely eager
to fight off the enemy in person. Then both sides
reinforced their ranks—Trojans and Lycians,
Achaeans and Myrmidons. These forces struggled,   660
with terrific shouts across the dead man's corpse.

The warriors' armour rang out harshly. Then Zeus,
to make the fight for his dear son more difficult,
spread ominous darkness over that fierce battle.

At first the Trojans pushed bright-eyed Achaeans back,
for they hit a man who was by no means the worst
among the Myrmidons—noble Epeigeus,
son of great-hearted Agacles. He'd once been king
of populous Boudeum, but he'd killed a man,
a noble relative. So he came a suppliant   670
to Peleus and silver-footed Thetis, who'd sent him
to follow man-destroying Achilles, to sail with him
to Troy and fight the Trojans. Glorious Hector
struck him as he grabbed the corpse—with a rock
he hit his head and split the skull completely open
inside his heavy helmet. Epeigeus collapsed,
face down on the corpse. Death, who destroys men's hearts,
flowed over him.

                              Grief for his dead companion
filled Patroclus. He moved through those fighting in the front,
like a swift hawk swooping down on daws or starlings.   680
That's how fast, Patroclus, master horseman, you charged
the Lycians and Trojans then, with anger in your heart
for your companion. With a rock he hit Sthenelaus,
dear son of Ithaemenes, squarely in the neck,
snapping the tendons. Those fighting in the ranks in front,
including glorious Hector, moved back somewhat,
as far as a long javelin flies when it's been thrown
by a man in competition showing off his strength,
or in a battle with a murderous enemy—
that's how far Achaeans forced the Trojans to move back.   690
Glaucus, leader of the Lycian spearmen, was the first
to turn around. He killed great-hearted Bathycles,
Chalcon's dear son, who lived at home in Hellas,
a man pre-eminent among the Myrmidons
for a wealthy and successful life. With his spear,
Glaucus turned suddenly, as Bathycles came up
in pursuit, then struck him in the middle of his chest.

He fell down with a crash. Achaeans felt keen sorrow
that such a worthy man had fallen. But Trojans,
elated, gathered in a crowd to make a stand   700
around him. Achaeans did not forget their courage—
they brought their fighting spirit to the Trojans.

Meriones killed a well-armed Trojan warrior,
Laogonus, daring son of Onetor, a priest
of Zeus at Ida, honoured by his people as a god.
Meriones threw and hit him underneath the jaw.
His spirit swiftly left his limbs, and he was carried off
by hateful darkness. Then Aeneas, hoping
to hit Meriones as he advanced under his shield,
threw his bronze spear at him. But Meriones,   710
looking right at Aeneas, evaded that bronze spear
by bending forward. The long spear impaled itself
behind him in the ground, its shaft still quivering,
until strong Ares took away its power.
With anger in his heart, Aeneas then called out:

> "Meriones, you're a lovely dancer,
> but if my spear had hit you, your dancing days
> would have ended for all time to come."

Famous spearman Meriones then replied:

> "Aeneas,
> you may be brave, but it's hard for you   720
> to crush the fighting strength of every man
> who stands to defend himself against you.
> For you, too, are made of mortal stuff.
> If I threw, if my bronze spear hit you
> in the middle of your body, then no matter
> what your courage, or how much trust you place
> in your strong hands, you'd quickly give me glory,
> and your life to famous horseman Hades."

Meriones spoke. But then Menoetius' noble son
reprimanded him:

"Meriones, why do you,
an honorable man, talk on like this?
My friend, Trojans won't move back from the corpse
because someone abuses them with words.
They won't budge until the earth holds many men.
Our task here is to battle with our hands.
The assembly is the place for speeches.
We don't need more talk. We need to fight."

Saying this, Patroclus led off, and Meriones,
that godlike man, went too. Then the turmoil started—
just like the din woodcutters make in mountain forests,   740
a noise heard far away—that's how it sounded then,
the clamour rising from the widely traveled earth,
a clash of bronze and leather, well-made ox-hide shields,
as they fought there with two-edged spears and swords.
Not even a man who knew Sarpedon very well
could recognize him then, covered with blood and dirt
and weapons, from the soles of his feet up to his head.
For men were swarming round the corpse like farmyard flies
clustering by buckets full of milk in springtime,
when milk overflows the pails—that how those warriors   750
buzzed around Sarpedon then.

                       Zeus' bright eyes never once
glanced from that brutal combat, gazing down
and thinking in his heart of many different things
about how lord Patroclus ought to meet his death,
wondering whether glorious Hector should cut him down
with his bronze in that bitter fighting there
over godlike Sarpedon and then strip the armour
from his shoulders, or whether he should multiply
grim misery for still more men. As Zeus pondered,
he thought the best plan would be to let Patroclus,   760
brave companion of Achilles, son of Peleus,
drive the Trojans and bronze-armed Hector back again
towards their city, destroying the lives of many men.
So Zeus first took the courage out of Hector's heart,
so that he jumped into his chariot and turned in flight,

calling to other Trojans to run back, for he knew
that Zeus' sacred scales were changing. The Lycians,
though brave, did not hold their ground. They all fled back,
once they'd seen their king struck through the heart, lying there
in the pile of bodies. Many men had fallen down   770
on top of him, when Cronos' son intensified
fierce conflict. So the Achaeans stripped Sarpedon,
pulling the gleaming bronze from off his shoulders.
Menoetius' brave son gave it to his companions
to carry to the hollow ships. At that moment,
cloud-gatherer Zeus spoke to Apollo:

                                        "Up now,
dear Phoebus, and move Sarpedon out of range.
When you've cleaned the dark blood off his body,
take him somewhere far away and wash him
in a flowing river. Next, anoint him   780
with ambrosia, and put immortal clothes
around him. Then you must hand him over
to those swift messengers Sleep and Death,
twin brothers, to carry off with them.
They'll quickly place him in his own rich land,
wide Lycia, where his brothers and kinsmen
will bury him with mound and headstone,
as is appropriate for those who've died."

Zeus finished. Apollo did not disobey his father.
Descending from Mount Ida to that lethal war,   790
he carried lord Sarpedon quickly out of range.
Once he'd taken him a long way off, he washed him
in a flowing river. Next, he anointed him
with ambrosia and put immortal clothing round him.
Then Apollo gave Sarpedon up to Sleep and Death,
swift messengers, twin brothers, to take with them.
They quickly set him down in spacious Lycia,
his own rich land.

                         Patroclus then called to his horses
and to Automedon to pursue the Trojans,

the Lycians, as well. How blind he was, poor fool!
If he'd done what the son of Peleus had told him,
he'd have missed his evil fate, his own dark death.
But Zeus' mind is always stronger than a man's.
He can make even a brave man fearful, rob him
of his victory with ease. And Zeus can rouse a man
for battle, as he did then, putting desire to fight
into Patroclus' chest.

              Who was the first warrior you killed,
Patroclus, and who the last, that time the gods
called you on to death? Adrestus was the first,
then Autonous, Echeclus, Perimus, son of Megas,   810
Epistor, and Melanippus. Then Patroclus killed
Elasus, Mulius, and Pylantes. The other Trojans,
each and every one of them, set their minds on flight.
At that point Achaea's sons would have captured Troy
and its high gates, at Patroclus' hands, as he raged
with his frenzied spear, but for Phoebus Apollo,
who stood there on the well-built wall, intending
to destroy Patroclus and assist the Trojans.
Three times Patroclus started to climb up a corner
on that high wall. Three times Apollo shoved him back,   820
his immortal hands repelling the bright shield.
But when Patroclus, for the fourth time, came on
like some god, Apollo, with a terrific cry,
shouted these winged words at him:

                  "Go back,
      divinely born Patroclus. This city
      of proud Trojans, according to its fate,
      will not be ravaged by your spear, nor even
      by Achilles, a far better man than you."

Apollo spoke. Patroclus drew back a little,
evading the anger of Apollo, the far shooter.   830

Meanwhile, Hector pulled his sure-footed horses up
beside the Scaean Gate, uncertain what to do—

drive back to the confusion and then battle on,
or tell his soldiers to gather there inside the walls.
As he was thinking, Phoebus Apollo approached
in the form of Asius, a strong young man,
horse-taming Hector's uncle, Hecuba's blood brother,
Dymas' son, who lived by the river Sangarius
in Phrygia. In that shape, Apollo, Zeus' son,
spoke out:

> "Hector, why withdraw from battle?   840
> That's not worthy of you. I wish I were
> more powerful than you, as much as you're
> superior to me. Then you'd quickly leave
> this battle in disgrace. But come on,
> drive your strong-footed horses at Patroclus,
> so you can kill him, and then Apollo
> can give you glory."

Saying these words, Apollo left,
a god among the toiling men. Glorious Hector
then told fiery Cebriones to lash the horses on,
drive them to battle. Apollo slipped into the throng   850
of fighting men. He totally confused the Argives,
conferring glory on Hector and his Trojans.
The rest of the Danaans Hector left alone,
not killing any of them. His sure-footed horses
were heading at Patroclus, who, for his part,
jumped from his chariot onto the ground, holding a spear
in his left hand. In his right hand, he gripped a stone,
a large jagged rock, his fingers wrapped around it.
Taking a firm stance, he went for Hector right away.
He threw the rock and didn't waste his throw—he hit   860
Cebriones, Hector's charioteer, a bastard son
of famous Priam, as he held onto the reins.
The sharp rock struck him on the forehead, bashing in
his eyebrows, breaking through the skull. His two eyes
dropped down onto the ground, in the dust right at his feet.
Like a diver, Cebriones toppled over,
out of the well-made chariot. His spirit left his bones.

Then, horseman Patroclus, you made fun of him:

                    "Well now,
there's an agile man! What a graceful diver!
If he were on the fish-filled seas somewhere,   870
he'd feed a lot of men by catching oysters,
jumping over in the roughest water,
judging from that easy dive he made
out of his chariot onto the plain. I suppose
these Trojans must have acrobats as well."

This said, Patroclus rushed at warrior Cebriones,
moving like a lion who, while savaging some farm,
is hit in the chest, so his own courage kills him.
That's how you, Patroclus, rushed at Cebriones,
in your killing frenzy. Opposing him, Hector   880
leapt from his chariot down to the ground. The two men
then battled over Cebriones, like two lions
struggling on a mountain peak over a slaughtered deer,
both ravenous, both filled with fighting fury—
that's how those two masters of the war shout fought,
Patroclus, Menoetius' son, and glorious Hector,
over Cebriones, both keen to slash each other's flesh
with pitiless bronze. Hector grabbed the corpse's head,
refusing to let go. At the other end, Patroclus
gripped the feet. A desperate struggle then ensued   890
among the Trojans and Danaans fighting there.
Just as East and South Winds challenge one another
in mountain forests, shaking up deep stands of oak,
ash, and tapering cornel trees, hurling slim branches
one against the other, with tremendous noise
as the branches snap—that's how Trojans and Achaeans
collided with each other in that conflict.
Neither side had any thought of ruinous flight.
Around Cebriones many spears were driven home,
many winged arrows flew from bowstrings, many boulders   900
crashed on shields, as men kept fighting round him.
But the great man Cebriones, proud of his glory,
just lay there in the swirling dust, his horsemanship

now quite forgotten.

As long as the sun kept moving through
the middle sky, weapons from both sides found their mark—
men kept on dying. But when the sun came to the point
which shows the time has come to unyoke oxen,
then Achaeans, contravening Fate, were stronger.
They dragged warrior Cebriones out of range,
away from shouting Trojans, and stripped the armour   910
off his shoulders. Then Patroclus charged the Trojans,
intent on slaughter. Three times he assaulted them,
like war god Ares, with terrific shouts. Three times
he killed nine men. But when he attacked a fourth time,
then, Patroclus, you saw your life end. For Phoebus,
a terrible god, in that grim fight came up against you.
Patroclus failed to see Apollo, as he moved
through the confusion, for he advanced towards him
hidden in thick mist. Apollo stood behind him.
Then with the flat of his hand, he struck Patroclus   920
on his back, on his broad shoulders—that made his eyes
lose focus. Next, Phoebus Apollo knocked the helmet
from his head. The horsehair crest rolled with a clatter
under horses' feet. The dust and blood then stained
the helmet's plumes. Up to that time, gods had not let
that helmet with its horsehair plume get smudged with dirt,
for it was always guarding godlike Achilles' head,
his noble forehead, too. Later Zeus awarded it
to Hector to carry on his head, as his death loomed.
In Patroclus' hands, his heavy long-shadowed spear,   930
thick and strong, with its bronze point, was completely smashed.
His tasseled shield and strap fell from his shoulders
down on the ground. Next, Apollo, Zeus' son, loosened
the body armour on Patroclus. His mind went blank,
his fine limbs grew limp—he stood there in a daze.
From close behind, Euphorbus, son of Panthous,
a Dardan warrior, hit him in the back,
with a sharp spear between the shoulder blades.
Euphorbus surpassed all men the same age as him
in spear throwing, horsemanship, and speed on foot.

He'd already knocked twenty men out of their chariots, 940
and that was the first time he'd come with his own chariot
to learn something of war. Euphorbus was the first
to strike you, horseman Patroclus, but he failed
to kill you. Pulling the spear out of Patroclus' flesh,
Euphorbus ran back again to blend in with the throng.
He didn't stand his ground, even though Patroclus
had no weapons for a fight. So Patroclus,
overwhelmed by the god's blow and spear, withdrew,
back to the group of his companions, avoiding death.

But when Hector noticed brave Patroclus going back, 950
wounded by sharp bronze, he moved up through the ranks,
stood close to Patroclus and struck him with his spear,
low in the stomach, driving the bronze straight through.
Patroclus fell with a crash, and Achaea's army
was filled with anguish. Just as a lion overcomes
a tireless wild boar in combat, when both beasts
fight bravely in the mountains over a small spring
where they both want to drink, and the lion's strength
brings down the panting boar—that's how Hector,
moving close in with his spear, destroyed the life 960
of Menoetius' noble son, who'd killed so many men.
Then Hector spoke winged words of triumph over him:

"Patroclus, you thought you'd raze our city,
robbing our women of their life of freedom,
taking them in ships to your dear native land.
You fool! In front of them, Hector's horses,
swift of foot, came out to fight. With the spear
I'm the very best war-loving Trojans,
and I've saved them from their fatal day.
Now vultures will eat you here. You poor wretch, 970
even Achilles, for all his courage,
was no use to you. Though he stayed behind,
he must have given you strict orders as you left,
'Don't return to me, horseman Patroclus,
at the hollow ships, until you've slashed blood
all over man-killing Hector's tunic

from his own chest.' That's what he must have said
to win you over to such foolishness."

Then you, horseman Patroclus, your strength all gone,
replied:

"Boast on, Hector, for the moment.   980
Zeus, son of Cronos, and Apollo
have given you victory. They overcame me
easily, for they personally removed
the armour from my shoulders. If twenty men
came to confront me, just like you,
all would have died, slaughtered by my spear.
But deadly Fate and Leto's son have slain me—
and Euphorbus. So you're the third in line
at my death. But I'll tell you something else—
bear this in mind—you'll not live long yourself.   990
Your death is already standing close at hand,
a fatal power. For you'll be destroyed
at brave Achilles' hands, descendant of Aeacus."

As Patroclus said these words to Hector,
the finality of death flowed over him.
His spirit fluttered from his limbs and went to Hades,
lamenting its own fate, the loss of youthful manhood.
As Patroclus died, splendid Hector spoke to him:

"Patroclus, why predict my own death for me?
Who knows? It may happen that Achilles,   1000
son of fair-haired Thetis, is hit first
by a spear of mine and gives up his life."

As he said this, Hector set his foot down on the corpse,
pulled the bronze spear from the wound, and pushed the body
backwards. Then with that spear he set off at once,
going after Automedon, godlike attendant
to the swift-footed kinsman of Aeacus,
eager to strike at him. But he'd been carried off
by those swift immortal horses, the priceless gift
presented by the gods to Peleus.

Book Seventeen
The Fight Over Patroclus

*[The men fight over the body of Patroclus; the exploits of Menelaus in
that fight; Apollo rouses Hector to attack, Menelaus retreats; Ajax and
Menelaus then move up over the body; Glaucus upbraids Hector;
Hector attacks again, with Zeus' support; the battle goes back and forth
over the body; Zeus spreads fog over the battle field; Apollo rouses
Aeneas to fight; the horses of Achilles mourn Patroclus, refusing to
move; Automedon takes them into battle with Zeus' help; Hector and
Aeneas go after Achilles' horses, but are pushed back; Athena rouses
Menelaus to fight on; Apollo does the same for Hector; Achaeans are
driven back; Zeus lifts the fog from the battle; Menelaus goes to
Antilochus, tells him to give Achilles the news of Patroclus' death; the
Achaeans move off with the body of Patroclus, back towards the ships]*

In that battle, warlike Menelaus, son of Atreus,
noticed that the Trojans had just killed Patroclus.
Dressed in gleaming armour, he strode through the ranks
of those fighting in the front, then made a stand
over the corpse, like a mother beside her calf,
lowing over her first born, with no experience
of giving birth till then. In just that way,
fair-haired Menelaus stood above Patroclus.
In front of him he held his spear and a round shield,
eager to kill anyone who might come at him.   10
But Euphorbus, son of Panthous, with his ash spear,
also knew that brave Patroclus had been killed.
Moving up close to the dead body, he spoke out,
addressing warlike Menelaus:

> "Divinely raised Menelaus, son of Atreus,
> leader of men—go back. Leave this corpse.
> Abandon these battle trophies. No Trojan
> and no famous ally hit Patroclus
> before I struck him with my spear
> in that murderous fight. So let the Trojans   20
> give me the honour and the fame. If not,
> I'll steal your sweet life with one spear throw."

With a great scowl, fair-haired Menelaus then replied:

"By Father Zeus, such arrogant boasting
has no great merit. The spirit in a leopard,
lion, or ferocious boar, whose chest
contains the fiercest and the strongest fury—
none of these, it seems, can match the arrogance
in sons of Panthous with their long ash spears.
But not even horse-taming Hyperenor,   30
strong as he was, got much enjoyment
from his youthful vigour, once he'd mocked me,
as he waited when I came against him,
calling me the most unworthy warrior
among Danaans. I don't think he went home
to cheer up his dear wife and worthy parents
on his own two feet. So if you stand here
against me, I'll drain your strength as well,
just as I did his. In fact, I'd advise you
to retreat, get back to your companions.   40
Don't oppose me, in case you run into
something unwelcome. From experience
there are lessons even fools can learn."

                                    Menelaus spoke,
but he failed to sway Euphorbus, who replied:

"Now, indeed, divinely raised Menelaus,
you'll surely make up for my brother's death,
Hyperenor, whom you killed. You speak
in triumph about widowing his wife
in her new bridal home, bringing sorrow,
grief beyond enduring, to his parents.   50
I may provide them with a way of easing
their sad misery, if I bring home your head
and armour and toss them in the hands
of Panthous and queen Phrontis. In any case,
we won't delay our struggle long. Let's start—
fight on, whether for victory or flight."

Saying this, Euphorbus struck Menelaus' round shield.
But the bronze did not break through. The powerful shield
bent back the point. Then Menelaus, Atreus' son,
praying to Father Zeus, charged in clutching his spear,   60
as Euphorbus was moving back. He struck him
at the bottom of his throat, putting his full weight
behind the blow, with confidence in his strong fists.
The spear point drove straight through Euphorbus' soft neck.
He fell with a thud, his armour clanging round him.
His hair, as lovely as the fine curls on the Graces,
with braids in gold and silver clips, was soaked in blood.
Just as a man tends a flourishing olive shoot,
in some lonely place with a rich source of water,
a lovely vigorous sapling stirred with the motion   70
of every breeze, so it bursts out in white blossoms—
but then a sudden stormy wind arising rips it
from its trench and lays it out prone on the earth—
that's how Menelaus, son of Atreus, cut down
Panthous' son, Euphorbus of the fine ash spear.
He then began to strip the armour off.

Just as a mountain lion, trusting its own strength,
snatches the finest heifer from a grazing herd,
seizing her first by the neck in its powerful jaws,
then breaks the neck and savagely rips that cow apart,   80
gorging itself on blood and all the entrails,
while around it dogs and herdsmen cry out in distress,
again and again, but at a distance, unwilling
to confront the beast, pale in the grip of fear—
in just that way, no Trojan's heart was brave enough
to move up and fight against splendid Menelaus.
Then Atreus' son would have easily carried off
the celebrated armour of the son of Panthous,
if Phoebus Apollo had not been offended.
He urged Hector, swift Ares' equal, to challenge   90
Menelaus. Taking on the likeness of a man,
Mentes, leader of the Cicones, Apollo
addressed Hector with these winged words:

　　　　　　　　　　　　　　　　"Hector,
now you're going after something you'll not catch,
chasing the horses of warrior Achilles,
descendant of Aeacus. No mortal man,
except Achilles, can control or drive them,
for an immortal mother gave him birth.
Meanwhile, warrior Menelaus, Atreus' son,
standing by Patroclus, has just killed   100
the best man of the Trojans, Euphorbus,
son of Panthous, ending his brave fight."

With these words, Apollo withdrew again, a god
among the toiling men. A bitter cloud of sorrow
darkened Hector's heart. Looking through the ranks of men,
he quickly noticed Menelaus stripping off
the famous armour, with Euphorbus on the ground,
lying there, blood flowing from his open wound.
Armed in his gleaming bronze, Hector marched ahead
through those fighting in the front, with a piercing shout,   110
like the inextinguishable fires of Hephaestus.
Hearing that penetrating yell, Atreus' son
grew worried. He spoke to his courageous heart:

　　　　"Here's trouble. If I leave this fine armour
　　　　and Patroclus, who lies here because he tried
　　　　to avenge my honour, some Danaan,
　　　　seeing this, will call me a disgrace.
　　　　But if I fight Hector and his Trojans
　　　　all by myself out of a sense of shame,
　　　　then they'll surround me—many warriors   120
　　　　against one man. Hector's gleaming helmet
　　　　is bringing all the Trojans straight at me.
　　　　But why's my fond heart debating about this?
　　　　When a man wants to cross what gods have willed,
　　　　fighting a man the gods are honouring,
　　　　then some disaster soon rolls over him.
　　　　So none of the Danaans seeing me here
　　　　moving back from Hector will find that shameful,
　　　　seeing that Hector fights with gods' assistance.

But if I could find Ajax, skilled in war shouts,   130
the two of us, drawing on our fighting strength,
might come back, even against god's will,
so we could find a way to save this corpse,
for Achilles' sake, the son of Peleus.
In this bad situation, that's what's best."

As Menelaus thought these matters over
in his mind and heart, the Trojan ranks moved forward,
with Hector in the lead. Menelaus then backed off,
leaving the corpse behind. He kept looking round,
like a bearded lion which dogs and men chase off—   140
with spears and shouts they drive it from the farm. The beast's heart,
though brave, grows cold, moving from that farmyard
against its will—that's how fair-haired Menelaus
backed off from Patroclus. He turned round, standing firm,
once he'd reached the company of his companions.
He looked for mighty Ajax, son of Telamon,
and soon observed him on the left flank of the army,
rallying his companions, urging them to fight.
For Phoebus Apollo had made them all fall back
in an amazing panic. Going off on the run,   150
Menelaus came up to Ajax, then spoke out:

"Ajax, my friend, come here. Let's hurry over
to defend the dead Patroclus. Let's see whether,
for Achilles' sake, we can at least retrieve
the naked corpse. Hector with his bright helmet
already has the armour."

Menelaus spoke,
rousing the heart in warlike Ajax, who moved up
among those fighting in the front. With him went
fair-haired Menelaus. Once Hector had stripped off
the famous armour from Patroclus, he then tried   160
to drag away the body, so with his sharp bronze
he could hack Patroclus' head from off its shoulders,
then pull back the corpse to give to Trojan dogs.
But Ajax moved in close with his shield up, like a wall.

So Hector gave ground, withdrawing to the company
of his companions, then jumped up in his chariot.
He gave the splendid armour to some Trojans
to carry to the city, something that would bring him
special glory. Ajax then covered Menoetius' son
with his broad shield and made his stand there, like a lion   170
over its cubs, a beast which hunters run across
in the forest as it leads its young along.
The lion shows off its power and contracts its brows
into fine slits which conceal its eyes—that's how Ajax
defended warrior Patroclus. With him there,
on the other side, stood war-loving Menelaus,
son of Atreus, heart filled with utmost sorrow.

Then Glaucus, son of Hippolochus, commander
of the Lycians, looking at Hector with a frown,
criticized him harshly:

                      "Hector, to look at you,   180
you're the finest man we've got, but in battle
you're sadly lacking. That fame you have
as a courageous warrior is misplaced.
You're a man who runs away. Consider now,
how are you going to save your city
only with those soldiers born in Ilion?
For no Lycian will set out to fight
against Danaans for your city's sake,
since there's apparently no gratitude
for taking on our enemies without a rest.   190
How can you rescue a lesser warrior
from the thick of battle, ungrateful man,
when Sarpedon, once your companion,
your guest, you abandon to the Argives,
to become their battle spoils, their trophy.
He often served you well—both your city
and you personally, while he was alive.
But now you lack the courage to protect him
from the dogs. So now, if any Lycian man
will listen to me, we'll go home, and Troy   200

will witness its utter devastation.
If Trojans now could fill themselves with courage,
a resolute and dauntless spirit, the sort
men have when they defend their native land,
struggling hard against a hostile army,
then we'd haul Patroclus back to Ilion
at once. If we pulled him from the battle
and brought the corpse to Priam's mighty city,
Argives would quickly trade the lovely armour
belonging to Sarpedon, and we could then   210
take his body back to Troy. Their dead man
attended on the greatest of the Argives,
who leads the best spear fighters by their ships.
But you don't dare stand up to Ajax
in the thick of battle, look that brave warrior
in the eye, or confront him one on one,
since he's a better man than you."

Hector of the gleaming helmet, looking angry, then replied:

"Glaucus, why would a man like you speak out
so arrogantly? My friend, I thought you had   220
a better mind than any other man
living in fertile Lycia. But now,
on the basis of what you've just said,
I find your thinking questionable.
You say I didn't stand to fight great Ajax.
I'm not afraid of war, the din of chariots,
but there's always something more powerful,
the mind of Zeus, who bears the aegis.
Zeus makes even brave men run away,
stealing their victory with ease, or in person   230
rouses men to fight. But come, my friend,
stand here beside me. Look at what I do,
whether I'm a coward all day long,
as you allege, or whether I'll prevent
Danaans, for all their fighting frenzy,
from defending dead Patroclus."

Hector spoke.
Then, with a great shout, he called out to his Trojans:

"Trojans, Lycians, Dardan spearmen,
be men, my friends. Recall your battle fury,
until I can put on the lovely armour   240
of great Achilles, which I stripped off
the great Patroclus, once I'd killed him."

With these words, Hector of the shining helmet
left that furious conflict and strode quickly off
with rapid strides, following his companions,
the men taking the famous armour of Achilles
towards the city. He caught them a short distance off.
Then, standing apart from that dreadful fight,
he changed his armour. He gave his own equipment
to war-loving Trojans to carry to the city,   250
sacred Ilion, then put on the immortal armour
of Achilles, son of Peleus, which heavenly gods
had given to Achilles' well-loved father.
Once he'd grown old, Peleus gave it to his son,
who, for all his father's armour, did not reach old age.

From far away, cloud-gatherer Zeus gazed down on Hector,
as he dressed himself in the battle armour
of Peleus' godlike son. Shaking his head, Zeus
then spoke to his own heart:

                                        "You poor wretch,
you're not considering your own death at all—   260
it's getting closer. So you're putting on
the immortal armour of the finest man,
who makes other men afraid. You've just killed
his comrade, a kind, courageous man,
and then vainly stripped the armour off
his head and shoulders. But for the moment,
I'll give you great power, to compensate you,
since you'll not be coming back from battle,
or handing over to Andromache

The son of Cronos spoke, then nodded his dark brow.
He changed the armour so it suited Hector's body.
Then the fearful war god Ares entered Hector,
filling his limbs with strength and courage. He set off,
to the tremendous shouts of all his famous allies,
as he paraded there in front of them, dazzling them all
with the armour of the great-hearted son of Peleus.
Hector moved around with words of encouragement
to everyone—Mesthles, Glaucus, Medon,
Thersilochus, Asteropaeus, Deisenor,   280
Hippothous, Phorcys, Chroraius, and Ennomus,
who read omens found in birds. Hector urged them on—
his words had wings:

                                    "Listen to me,
        you countless tribes of allies, you neighbours.
        I called you here, each from your own city,
        not because I wished a large display
        or needed it, but so you might help me
        rescue Trojan wives and little children
        from warrior Achaeans. With this in mind,
        I squander the resources of my people,   290
        with food supplies and presents, to strengthen
        hearts in each of you. So now let everyone
        turn round and face the enemy directly,
        whether to survive or die. For in that choice
        we find the joy which we derive from war.
        Patroclus is dead, but whoever pulls him
        to horse-taming Trojans here and makes Ajax
        move away—I'll give him half the spoils,
        keeping the other half myself, and he'll get
        a share of glory equal to my own."   300

Hector finished. Trojans then threw their full weight
straight at the Danaans, holding spears up high,
their hearts hoping they would drag that body
away from Ajax, son of Telamon. What fools!

By that corpse Ajax took many of their lives.

Then Ajax said to Menelaus, skilled at war shouts:

"Divinely reared Menelaus, my friend,
I don't expect we two will be returning
from this battle. I'm not concerned so much
about Patroclus' corpse, which soon enough   310
will be food for Trojan dogs and birds,
but I fear for my own head, and yours, as well,
which may be in danger. Hector's become
a war cloud which envelops everything.
And our complete destruction's plain to see.
So come, call out to Achaea's finest men.
One of them may hear."

                                                  Ajax finished.
Menelaus, skilled at war shouts, followed his advice.
He shouted to Danaans with a piercing yell:

"Friends, rulers and leaders of Achaeans,   320
all you who drink your wine at public cost
with Agamemnon and Menelaus,
sons of Atreus, all you who rule your people,
to whom Zeus has given honour and glory,
it's difficult for me to see precisely
what each of you is doing—this conflict
rages on so fiercely. But all of you
must come here, even if not called by name,
for you'll feel shame and anger in your hearts,
if Patroclus should become a toy   330
for Trojan dogs to play with."

                                          Menelaus stopped.
Swift Ajax, son of Oïleus, heard him clearly.
He was the first to come running through the battle
to meet Menelaus. After him came others—
Idomeneus and his companion Meriones,
the man-killing war god's equal, and others, too.

But what man has a mind which could name all those
who came up behind these warriors in that conflict
to reinforce Achaeans?

                    Trojans then drove forward
in a single group with Hector leading them.   340
Just as a huge wave roars into a flowing stream
at the mouth of a river fed from heaven,
with headlands on both sides of the shoreline
echoing the boom of salt water surf beyond—
that's how Trojans roared as they came on in attack.
Achaeans held firm around Menoetius' son,
united by a common spirit, behind a fence
of their bronze shields. The son of Cronos
cast a thick mist down on their glittering helmets,
for Zeus had not felt hostile to Patroclus   350
in earlier days, when he was alive and comrade
to Achilles. So Zeus did not want Patroclus
to become merely a plaything for the dogs
of his Trojan enemies. Thus, he encouraged
Patroclus' companions to defend him there.
At first the Trojans drove bright-eyed Achaeans back,
so they retreated from the body, leaving it behind.
But the Trojans, though confident with their long spears,
did not kill anyone, for all their eagerness.
Still, they did begin to drag away the body.   360
But the Achaean pull back was only temporary,
for Ajax quickly rallied them. Of all Danaans
he was the finest in his looks and actions
after the son of Peleus. Ajax strode around
through those fighting in the front, like a mountain boar
who scatters dogs and strong young men with ease,
as it wheels through forest clearings—that's how Ajax,
splendid son of noble Telamon, easily pushed back
the Trojan ranks, as he moved among them. They stood there,
over Patroclus, wanting desperately to haul him off,   370
back to their city, and win glory for themselves.

Then Hippothous, noble son of Pelasgian Lethous,

began to drag the body by the feet back through the crowd.
He'd tied his shield strap round both ankle tendons,
eager to please Hector and the Trojans. But right away
he faced a danger which no one could avert,
no matter how much he might want to. For Ajax,
moving quickly through the throng, struck him at close range
on the bronze cheek piece of his helmet. The spear point
smashed through the helmet with its horsehair crest, driven on   380
by the force of Ajax's mighty fists in that huge spear.
Blood and brains gushed from the wound and oozed together
along the socket of the spear. The strength drained out of him
where he was standing. Hippothous let go the feet
of brave Patroclus, allowing them to fall and lie there.
Then he collapsed, falling face down on the body,
far away from rich Larissa. He did not repay
his parents for the work they'd done to rear him—
he did not live long enough, slaughtered on the spear
of great-hearted Ajax.

                    Hector then threw his shining spear   390
at Ajax. But he was directly facing Hector,
so he saw it coming. Ajax dodged the weapon,
but only just. It hit Schedius, by far the best
of men from Phocis, son of great-hearted Iphitus,
who lived at home in celebrated Panopeus,
ruling many men. Hector's spear struck this man
right on the collar bone. The bonze point drove on through
and came out by his shoulder. He fell with a crash,
his armour rattling round him. Then Ajax struck,
hitting warlike Phorcys, Phaenops' son, in the gut,   400
as he stood over Hippothous. Breaking the plate
on body armour, the bronze sliced out his innards.
Phorcys fell in the dust, fingers clawing at the earth.
At that point glorious Hector and his foremost men
drew back. With a tremendous shout, Argives dragged off
the bodies of dead Hippothous and Phorcys.
They began to strip the armour from their shoulders.

Right then war-loving Achaeans would have driven Trojans

back to Ilion, conquered by their own cowardice,
with Argives winning glory beyond what Zeus decreed,   410
through their own strong power. But Apollo himself
stirred up Aeneas, taking on the form of Periphas,
the herald, son of Epytos, who'd grown old
serving as herald to Aeneas' old father.
He was wise and well-disposed towards Aeneas.
In this man's form, Apollo, son of Zeus, spoke up:

       "Aeneas, can you not defend steep Ilion
in defiance of some god? I've seen other men
who trusted their strong power and courage
and with their numbers held their country   420
against Zeus' will. But Zeus wants us to win
far more than the Danaans, and you all suffer
countless fears and won't keep battling on."

He finished. Aeneas recognized Apollo,
the far shooter, once he'd looked into his face.
Aeneas then shouted out, addressing Hector:

       "Hector and the rest of you commanders,
both Trojans and allies, it would be shameful
if war-loving Achaeans drive us back
all the way to Ilion, if we're beaten   430
by our cowardice. Some god's just told me—
he came and stood beside me—that even now
in this fight high counselor Zeus is helping us.
So let's go straight at these Danaans,
and not let them carry dead Patroclus
back to their ships without a battle."

                       Aeneas finished.
He strode far ahead of all the fighters at the front,
then stood there. Trojans rallied round and made a stand,
facing the Achaeans. With his spear, Aeneas
then struck down Leocritus, son of Arisbas,   440
the courageous companion of Lycomedes.
As he fell, war-loving Lycomedes pitied him.

He moved in close, stood there, and threw his shining spear.
It hit Apisaon, a son of Hippasus,
shepherd of his people, below his abdomen,
right in the liver. Apisaon's limbs collapsed.
He'd come from fertile Paeonia, their best man
in a fight after Asteropaeus, and his fall
filled warrior Asteropaeus with sorrow.
He charged ahead, ready to fight Danaans.   450
But that was now impossible. For they stood there,
in a group around Patroclus, holding up their shields
on every side, with their spears extending outward.
Ajax moved around among them all, giving orders,
telling them that no man should move back from the corpse
or stride out to fight in front of massed Achaeans.
They must all stand firm around the body, fighting
hand to hand. That's what mighty Ajax ordered.
Dark blood soaked the earth. The pile of dead bodies grew,
as they fell—Trojans, proud allies, Danaans, too,   460
all together. For as Danaans fought, they shed
their own blood also. But far fewer of them died,
for they were careful to protect each other
from complete destruction in that fighting crowd.

So they fought on, like blazing fire. You couldn't tell
whether sun and moon still shone, for in that fight
a mist surrounded all the best men standing there
beside Menoetius' dead son. Meanwhile, other Trojans
fought other well-armed Achaeans undisturbed,
under a clear sky, bright sunshine all around them,   470
no clouds above the entire earth or on the mountains.
So they fought more casually, keeping their distance,
staying out of range of each other's painful weapons.
But soldiers in the centre were suffering badly
in the fog and fighting. The pitiless bronze
was wearing down the finest men.

       But two warriors,
Thrasymedes and Antilochus, well-known men,
had not yet learned about the death of lord Patroclus.

They thought he was still alive, fighting the Trojans
in the front ranks of the throng. These two were fighting   480
some distance off, watching their companions, keeping track
of who was killed or fleeing back, as Nestor had instructed,
when he'd urged them into battle by their black ships.

Throughout that entire day the great combat raged,
a bitter conflict. The men kept toiling on without a pause,
sweat dripping on their knees and legs, under their feet,
and running down men's eyes and hands, as both sides
battled over swift-footed Achilles' brave companion.
Just as a man gives his people a huge bull's hide
to stretch, after soaking it in fat, and they stand,   490
once they've picked it up, in a circle pulling hard,
so the moisture quickly leaves the hide, as the fat
soaks in under the tension of so many hands
stretching the entire skin as far as it will go—
that's how those men on both sides pulled at the corpse,
back and forth in a narrow space, hearts full of hope—
Trojans seeking to drag it back to Ilion,
Achaeans to their hollow ships. Around Patroclus
the conflict grew intense. Neither Ares nor Athena,
who incite warriors to battle, if they'd seen that fight,   500
would have disparaged it, not even if they'd been
intensely angry. That's how destructive Zeus made
the conflict for men and horses that day men fought
over Patroclus.

                    Godlike Achilles, at this time,
knew nothing of Patroclus' death, for they were fighting
under the walls of Troy, away from the fast ships.
He'd never imagined in his heart that Patroclus
was dead. He thought he was alive and would return
once he'd reached the gates. He didn't think
he'd lay waste the city with him or without him,   510
for often Achilles had learned this from his mother,
listening to her in private, when she'd told him
what great Zeus had planned. But at that time, Thetis
said nothing of the evil which had taken place,

the death of his companion, his dearest friend by far.

But those beside the corpse kept holding their sharp spears,
with no pause in the fighting. The mutual slaughter
continued on. Bronze-armed Achaeans talked together,
using words like these:

> "My friends,
> there'd be no glory for us if we went back   520
> to the hollow ships. So let the black earth
> open here for each of us. That would be better
> for us all by far than if we leave this corpse
> for horse-taming Trojans to carry off,
> back to their city, winning glory."

Great-heated Trojans, too, spoke words like these:

> "Friends, if we're all fated to be killed together
> by this man, let no one leave the battle."

Men talked like this to strengthen their companions.
Then they fought on, the smash of iron rising up   530
through the bronze sky. But the horses of Achilles,
descendant of Aeacus, stood some distance from the fight,
weeping from the time they first learned their charioteer
had fallen in the dust at the hands of Hector,
killer of men. Automedon, brave son of Diores,
often lashed them with a stroke of his quick whip,
and often spoke to them with soothing words or threats,
but the two weren't willing to withdraw back to the ships
by the broad Hellespont, or go towards Achaeans
locked in battle. They stayed beside their ornate chariot,   540
immobile, like a pillar standing on the tomb
of some dead man or woman, heads bowed down to earth.
Warm tears flowed from their eyes onto the ground,
as they cried, longing for their driver. Their thick manes,
covered in dirt, trailed down below their harnesses
on both sides of the yoke. Looking at those horses,
as they mourned, the son of Cronos pitied them.

Shaking his head, Zeus spoke to his own heart:

                    "Poor horses!
Why did we give you to king Peleus,
a mortal man, for you're immortal, ageless?   550
Was it so you'd experience sorrow
among unhappy men? For the truth is this—
of all the things which breathe or move on earth,
nothing is more miserable than man.
But at least Hector, Priam's son, won't mount you
or drive your finely decorated chariot.
That I won't permit. Is it not enough
he wears his armour and then brags about it?
I'll put strength into your legs and hearts,
so you can carry Automedon safely   560
from this battle to the hollow ships.
For I'll still grant glory to the Trojans,
to keep on killing till they reach the ships,
at sunset, when sacred darkness comes."

Saying this, Zeus breathed great strength into those horses.
The two shook out their manes, so the dirt fell on the ground.
They then set off towards the Trojans and Achaeans,
quickly pulling the fast chariot along with them.
Behind them Automedon joined the fighting,
though still grieving for his comrade, swooping down   570
in that chariot like a vulture on a flock of geese.
He easily escaped the Trojan battle noise
and then with ease charged into the large crowd once more.
But in these attacks he didn't kill a man,
as he rushed to chase them down. It was impossible,
for in the sacred chariot he was by himself.
He couldn't wield a spear and manage those swift horses.
But at last one of his companions noticed him,
Alcimedon, son of Laerces, Haemon's son.
Standing behind the chariot, he cried to Automedon: 580

        "Automedon, what god put inside your chest
this useless plan, stealing your common sense?

You're fighting against the Trojans by yourself,
in the front ranks of the crowd. Your comrade
has been killed, and on his shoulders Hector
is now wearing the armour of Achilles—
he celebrates his glorious triumph."

Automedon, son of Diores, replied:

"Alcimedon, what Achaean warrior
is better able to control and guide   590
these strong immortal horses than yourself,
except Patroclus, a man as wise as gods,
while he was alive? Now he's met his death,
his fate. So take the shining reins and whip.
I'll get down from the chariot and fight."

Automedon spoke. Then Alcimedon, springing up
into that fast chariot, quickly grabbed the reins and whip.
Automedon jumped out. Seeing this, glorious Hector
at once spoke to Aeneas, who was close by:

"Aeneas, counselor to bronze-armed Trojans,   600
I see the two-horse team of swift Achilles
coming to this fighting with poor charioteers.
That pair I'd like to capture, if your heart
is willing, since those men lack the courage
to confront the two of us, if we attack,
or to stand and fight against us both."

Hector spoke. Anchises' strong son was not unwilling.
So the two moved straight ahead, guarding their shoulders
under bull's hide shields, tanned and tough, with thick bronze
hammered out on top. With them went Chromius,   610
and godlike Aretus, fully hoping in their hearts
they'd kill the men, then drive those strong-necked horses off.
What fools! They would not return from Automedon
without shedding their own blood. Then Automedon
prayed to Father Zeus, and his dark heart was filled
with strength and courage. Immediately he spoke out

to Alcimedon, his loyal companion:

"Alcimedon,
make sure you keep the horses close to me,
so they breathe right on my neck. I don't think
Hector, son of Priam, will check his fury,   620
until he's killed the pair of us and climbed
behind the fine manes of these horses
belonging to Achilles, then driven in flight
the Argive ranks, or himself been slaughtered
among the front-line fighters."

Automedon finished,
then shouted to both Ajaxes and Menelaus:

"You Ajaxes, both Argive leaders, Menelaus,
leave that corpse to the rest of our best men,
who'll stand firm around it. Protect the two of us
from ruthless fate while we're still living.   630
For Hector and Aeneas, Troy's best men
in this harsh fight, are coming hard against us.
But these things lie in the lap of the gods,
so I'll attempt a throw—whatever happens,
it's all up to Zeus."

Saying this, Automedon
hefted his long-shadowed spear and threw it, hitting
the round shield of Aretus, which didn't stop it.
The bronze went straight on through, severed his belt,
then drove low in his stomach. Just as a strong man
with a sharp axe strikes a farm ox right behind its horns,   640
slicing clean through sinews, so the ox stumbles forward
and falls down—that's how Aretus jerked forward and then fell
onto his back. Once that sharp spear impaled itself,
quivering in his organs, his limbs gave way.
Then Hector threw his bright spear at Automedon,
but since he was directly facing Hector,
he saw the bronze spear coming and evaded it
by leaning forward. The long spear stuck in the ground

387

behind him, its shaft trembling until great Ares
stilled its force. Now they would have charged each other   650
and fought hand to hand with swords, but the Ajaxes
made them move apart for all their battle fury.
They came up through the crowd answering their comrade's shout.
Hector, Aeneas, and godlike Chromius,
afraid of both Ajaxes, moved back once again,
leaving Aretus lying there with a mortal wound.
Automedon, swift Ares' equal, stripped the armour,
boasting in triumph:

> "I've managed here
> to ease somewhat my heart's grief for the death
> of Menoetius' son, though the man I've killed   660
> is a lesser man than he."

With these words,
he took the blood-stained spoils and put them in the chariot.
Then he got in, feet and upper arms all bloody,
like a lion that's just gorged itself on cattle.

Then once more over Patroclus the bitter fight
resumed—fierce and full of sorrow. Athena
stirred up the conflict, coming down from heaven,
sent by wide-seeing Zeus to urge on the Danaans.
For his mind had changed. Just as for mortal men
Zeus bends his coloured rainbow down from heaven,   670
an omen prophesying war or some harsh storm,
upsetting flocks and stopping men from work
upon the earth—that's how Athena then placed herself
in the Achaean throng, wrapped in a purple mist.
She stirred up all the men, giving encouragement
first to courageous Menelaus, son of Atreus,
who was close by her. Taking the form of Phoenix,
in his untiring voice she said:

> "Surely, Menelaus,
> you'll be disgraced, have to hang your head in shame,
> if Achilles' fine and loyal companion   680

is ravaged by swift dogs beneath Troy's walls.
So be brave. Stand firm. Encourage all your men."

Menelaus, expert in war shouts, answered her:

"Old Phoenix, you venerable old man,
if only Athena would give me strength,
defend me from this shower of weapons,
I'd be happy to stand above Patroclus,
protecting him. His death has touched my heart.
But Hector has the power of deadly fire.
He won't stop cutting men down with his bronze,   690
for Zeus is giving him the glory."

Menelaus' words pleased the bright-eyed goddess,
Athena, for he'd first prayed to her of all the gods.
She put strength into his shoulders and his knees.
Then in his chest she set the persistence of a gnat,
which, no matter how much one brushes it away
from someone's skin, keeps on biting—it finds human blood
so sweet—with that stamina she filled up his dark heart.
Standing over Patroclus, he hurled his shining spear.
Among the Trojans was a rich, brave man called Podes,   700
son of Eëtion, to whom Hector gave
a special honour among men as his companion,
his good friend at a feast. Fair-haired Menelaus
struck him with his spear, as he began to flee.
He hit him on the belt. The bronze drove straight on through.
Podes fell with a thud. Then Menelaus, Atreus' son,
dragged the corpse away from Trojans into the crowd
of his companions.

                        At that point, Apollo
came up close to Hector to reinforce his spirit.
He took the form of Phaenops, son of Asius,   710
of all Hector's guests the one he liked the most.
Phaenops lived at home in Abydos. In his shape,
Apollo, son of Zeus, spoke out:

"Hector,
which of the Achaeans will now fear you,
since you're afraid of Menelaus,
who so far has been a feeble spearman?
But all by himself he's snatched a body
from the Trojans and gone off with it.
He's killed your trusty comrade Podes,
Eëtion's son, a noble front-line warrior."   720

As he spoke, black clouds of grief enveloped Hector.
He strode by the foremost fighters, armed in gleaming bronze.
Then the son of Cronos took his tasseled aegis,
all glittering, hid Ida behind clouds, then flashed
his lightning, with a tremendous peal of thunder,
as he shook the aegis, awarding victory
to Trojans and making Achaeans run away.

The first to begin the rout was Peneleus,
a Boeotian. Standing there facing the enemy,
as usual, he was hit in the shoulder by a spear   730
from Polydamas, who'd come in close to throw.
It was a glancing blow, but the point of the spear
sliced quite near the bone. Then at close quarters, Hector
attacked Leitus, son of great-hearted Alectryon.
Hector sliced his wrist, and so his fighting ended.
Looking around him anxiously, Leitus drew back—
he knew that if he couldn't grip his spear, he had no hope
of fighting Trojans. As Hector went at Leitus,
Idomeneus threw and struck his body armour
on the chest, right beside the nipple. But the long spear   740
broke at the socket. The Trojans gave a shout.
Then Hector threw a spear at Idomeneus,
Deucalion's son. He missed him, but not by much.
He did hit Coeranus, Meriones' comrade,
his charioteer, who'd followed him from well-built Lyctus.
Idomeneus had come from the curving ships that day
on foot and would've given the Trojans a great triumph,
if Coeranus hadn't quickly driven up
with his swift-footed horses. For Idomeneus

he came as a saving light, protecting him   750
from ruthless fate. But the act cost him his life
at the hands of man-killing Hector, who struck him
underneath his jaw and ear. The spear smashed his teeth,
roots and all, splitting his tongue in half. Coeranus
tumbled from the chariot. The reins fell on the ground.
Meriones stooped down and scooped them from the plain
with his own hands, then spoke to Idomeneus:

> "Now lash these horses on until you reach
> our swift ships. For you recognize yourself
> that Achaeans will not win this victory."   760

Meriones finished. Then Idomeneus
whipped the fair-maned horses back to the hollow ships,
for by now a fear had fallen on his heart, as well.

Great-hearted Ajax and Menelaus also knew
that Zeus had turned the tide of battle now, giving
victory to the Trojans. The first one to speak
was Telamonian Ajax:

> "Here's a problem.
> Even a fool can see that Father Zeus
> is now personally helping Trojans.
> All their flying weapons hit a target,   770
> whether a brave man throws them or a coward—
> Zeus makes them all fly straight. In our case,
> all our throws fall wasted on the ground.
> But come, let's sort out the best course of action,
> so we both can drag the corpse and then get back
> in person to bring joy to our companions.
> They must be anxious as they watch us here,
> thinking we can't check the fighting frenzy
> of man-killing Hector, his all-conquering hands,
> and we'll withdraw to our black ships. I wish   780
> some comrade would report back quickly
> to Peleus' son, for I don't think he's learned
> the dreadful news of his dear comrade's death.
> But I can't see any Argive who could do that.

Men and horses are all shrouded in this mist.
Father Zeus, rescue these Achaean sons
from this fog, make the sky clear, let us see
with our own eyes. Since it gives you pleasure,
kill us, but do in the light of day."

As he finished, Ajax wept. Father Zeus pitied him.   790
At once he dispersed the mist, scattering the haze.
The sun shone down, and all the fight came into view.
Then Ajax spoke to Menelaus, skilled at war shouts:

"Look now, divinely raised Menelaus,
see if you can spot Antilochus alive,
son of great-hearted Nestor. Get him to go
with speed to rouse up fiery Achilles,
by telling him his companion, the man
he loves the most by far, has just been killed."

Ajax spoke. Menelaus, expert at war shouts, agreed.   800
He went off like some lion moving from a farm,
exhausted by his attacks on dogs and men,
who prevent it tearing flesh out of some cow,
keeping their watch all night—but ravenous for meat,
the beast keeps charging in without success, for spears
rain down, thrown by keen hands, then burning sticks,
which, for all his fierce desire, make him afraid,
so he slinks away at dawn in disappointment—
that's how Menelaus, skilled at war cries,
left Patroclus, much against his will—he feared   810
Achaeans might be pushed back in painful flight,
leaving the corpse a trophy for the enemy.
He issued many orders to Meriones
to the Ajaxes, as well:

"You two Ajaxes,
Argive leaders, and you, Meriones,
let each man bear in mind the kindnesses
of poor Patroclus, who, when he was alive,
knew how to treat every man with care.

Now fatal death has overtaken him."

With these words, fair-haired Menelaus went away,   820
glancing warily in all directions, like an eagle,
which, men say, has the sharpest sight of all the animals
flying in the sky—a bird which, while soaring high,
doesn't miss the swiftly running hare crouched down
under a leafy bush, and, swooping low, seizes it
at once, and then tears out its life—that's how, Menelaus,
raised by gods, your bright eyes kept searching all around
through groups of many comrades, seeking Nestor's son,
to see if he was still alive. Then Menelaus,
quickly seeing him on the left flank of the battle   830
encouraging his companions, urging them to fight,
came up to him. Then fair-haired Menelaus said:

          "Divinely raised Antilochus, come here,
          so you can learn the painful news, something
          I wish had never happened. You already know,
          I think, for your own eyes can see it,
          how some god is rolling this disaster
          over the Danaans, giving victory
          to the Trojans. The best Achaean,
          Patroclus, has been slaughtered, a huge loss   840
          for the Danaans, who miss him badly.
          You must run quickly to Achaean ships
          to tell Achilles, so he can bring the corpse
          in safety to his ship—the naked body,
          for now Hector of the gleaming helmet
          wears his armour."

                              Menelaus finished speaking.
Hearing that news, Antilochus was overwhelmed.
For a long time he stood in shock, speechless. His eyes
filled up with tears, his strong voice failed. But even so,
he did not neglect what Menelaus told him.   850
Giving his armour to his noble comrade
Laodocus, who drove the horses close beside him,
he set off on the run. As he wept, his swift feet

393

took him from the battle, bearing the bad news
to Achilles, son of Peleus. And then your heart,
divinely raised Menelaus, had no desire
to help defend the hard-pressed comrades left there
by Antilochus, men of Pylos, who felt his loss
severely. But to assist them, Menelaus
sent godlike Thrasymedes. Then he went in person   860
to stand by warrior Patroclus. Running over,
he took up a position by both Ajaxes and said:

> "I've sent Antilochus to our fast ships,
> to swift Achilles. Still, I don't expect
> he'll come out now, no matter how enraged
> he is with godlike Hector. He can't fight
> at all against the Trojans without armour.
> But now we should consider for ourselves
> the best thing we should do, so we'll be able
> to haul off the corpse and leave this Trojan tumult,   870
> escaping our own death and our destruction."

Great Telamonian Ajax then answered him:

> "Glorious Menelaus, everything you say
> is true enough. So you and Meriones
> stoop down and lift the body quickly,
> as fast possible. Take it from this fight.
> We'll hold off the Trojans and godlike Hector,
> standing behind you with a single heart,
> just as we share one name. We've stood firm before,
> holding our positions by each other,   880
> in the face of Ares, the fierce god of war."

Ajax spoke. Then they raised the body off the ground,
lifting it high with one great heave. Behind them,
Trojans soldiers gave a shout, as they saw Achaeans
hoisting up the corpse. They went after them like hounds
charging ahead of youthful hunters, as they chase
some wounded wild boar, keen to rip it into pieces,
but once it wheels around on them, sure of its strength,

they run back in fear, scattering in all directions—
that's how groups of Trojans kept following them a while,   890
thrusting at them with swords and double-bladed spears,
but when both Ajaxes turned round to stand against them,
their colour changed, and no one dared rush forward
to battle for the dead.

                          So these men worked hard
to bring that body from the battle to the hollow ships,
in the face of a fierce conflict, like some fire
suddenly rushing at a city full of people,
setting it alight, so houses fall among the flames,
as winds whip the inferno on. That's how the din
of chariots and spearmen coming up against them   900
kept resounding as they moved along. But like mules
throwing their great strength into their work, as they haul
a beam or huge ship timber on an uneven path
down from the mountains, hearts worn out with the strain,
as they work on covered in sweat—that's how these men
strove hard to carry off the corpse. Behind them,
both Ajaxes held off the enemy. Just as
a wooded ridge which cuts across a plain holds back
a flood, even the strong flow of some harsh rivers,
pushing their waters back to go across the plain,   910
for the strength of their current cannot rupture it—
that's how both Ajaxes held back the Trojans then
in that fight. But Trojans kept up their pursuit,
especially two of them—Aeneas, Anchises' son,
and glorious Hector. Just as a flock of daws or starlings
flies off in screaming fear, once they see a falcon
as it comes after them, bringing death to all small birds—
that's how the young Achaean soldiers ran off then,
away from Hector and Aeneas, screaming in panic,
forgetting all their fierce desire for battle.   920
As Danaans fled, plenty of fine weapons fell
around the ditch. But there was no let up in the war.

Book Eighteen
The Arms of Achilles

*[Antilochus brings the news to Achilles of Patroclus' death; Achilles
collapses in grief; Thetis hears his grief, talks to her sister Nereids, then
visits Achilles, promises to bring him new armour from Hephaestus; Iris
visits Achilles with a message from Hera; Achilles displays himself to the
Trojans by the ditch and wall; Trojans debate what to do; Polydamas
advises retreat; Hector opposes him; Achaeans take Patroclus' body back
to the ships, begin their laments over Patroclus; Thetis visits Hephaestus,
requests new armour for Achilles; Hephaestus makes new armour,
especially a new shield; Thetis leaves with the armour]*

As the men fought on like a blazing fire raging,
swift-footed Antilochus came to Achilles
with his news. He found Achilles by his beaked ship,
sensing in himself what had already happened,
speaking with a troubled mind to his own great heart:

> "Why are long-haired Achaeans once again
> retreating to their ships, being beaten back
> across the plain in terror? I hope the gods
> have not done something that will break my heart.
> My mother told me once they'd do that,   10
> when she told me that while I was alive
> the best man of the Myrmidons would leave
> the sun's light at the hands of Trojans.
> So it must be the case that the fine son
> of Menoetius is dead, that reckless man.
> I told him to return back to the ships,
> once he'd saved them from consuming fire,
> and not face up to Hector man to man."

As Achilles in his mind and heart was thinking this,
noble Nestor's son approached, shedding warm tears.   20
He told him the agonizing truth:

> "Son of warlike Peleus,
> you must hear this dreadful news—something

I wish weren't so—Patroclus lies dead.
Men are fighting now around the body.
He's stripped. Hector with his gleaming helmet
has the armour."

                    Antilochus finished speaking.
A black cloud of grief swallowed up Achilles.
With both hands he scooped up soot and dust and poured it
on his head, covering his handsome face with dirt,
covering his sweet-smelling tunic with black ash.   30
He lay sprawling—his mighty warrior's massive body
collapsed and stretched out in the dust. With his hands,
he tugged at his own hair, disfiguring himself.
The women slaves acquired as battle trophies
by Achilles and Patroclus, hearts overwhelmed
with anguish, began to scream aloud. They rushed outside
and beat their breasts around warlike Achilles.
Then all the women's legs gave way, and they fell down.
Across from them, Antilochus lamented,
eyes full of tears, as he held Achilles by the hand.   40
Achilles' noble heart moaned aloud. Antilochus
feared he might hurt himself or slit his throat
with his own sword. Achilles gave a huge cry of grief.
His noble mother heard it from the ocean depths
where she was sitting by her ancient father.
She began to wail. Then around her gathered
all the divine daughters of Nereus deep in the sea—
Glauce, Thaleia, Cymodoce, Nesaea,
Speio, Thoe, ox-eyed Halië, Cymothoë,
Actaia, Limnoreia, Melite, Iaera,   50
Amphithoe, Agave, Doto, Proto,
Pherousa, Dynamene, Dexamene,
Amphinome, Callianeira, Doris, Panope,
lovely Galatea, Nemertes, Apseudes,
Callianassa. Also there were Clymene,
Ianeira, Ianassa, Maera, Orithyia,
Amatheia with her lovely hair, and others,
Nereus' daughters living in the ocean depths.
They filled the glistening cave, beating their breasts.

Thetis led them all in their laments:

"Sister Nereids, listen,
so all of you, hearing what I say,
will understand my heart's enormous sorrow.
Alas, for my unhappy misery,
that to my grief I bore the best of men.
For when I gave birth to a fine strong boy
to be an excellent heroic warrior,
when he'd grown as tall as some young sapling,
for I'd raised him like a lovely orchard tree,
I sent him out in the beaked ships to Ilion,
to war against the Trojans. But now,   70
I'll never welcome him back home again,
returning to the house of Peleus.
While he's still alive and sees the sunlight,
he lives in sorrow. When I go to him,
I can provide no help. But I shall go
to look on my dear child, to hear what grief
has overtaken him while he remains
detached from all the fighting."

With these words,
Thetis left the cave. Her sisters went with her in tears.
Around them sea waves parted, until they came   80
to fertile Troy. They emerged, climbing up on shore,
one after another, right where the Myrmidons
had dragged up their ships in close-packed formation
near swift Achilles. Then his noble mother moved
beside him, as he was groaning bitterly.
With a sharp cry, she cradled her son's head, then spoke.
As she grieved, she talked to him—her words had wings:

"My child, why are you crying? What sorrow now
has come into your heart? Speak out. Hide nothing.
Zeus has given you what you begged him to   90
when you stretched your hands out to him—
all Achaea's sons by their ships' sterns
are hemmed in there, desperate for your help

398

and suffering a terrible ordeal."

With a heavy groan,
swift-footed Achilles then answered Thetis:

"Yes, Mother,
Olympian Zeus has indeed accomplished
what I asked. But what pleasure's there for me,
when Patroclus, my beloved companion,
has been destroyed, the man I honoured
as my equal, above all my comrades.   100
I've lost him and the armour, which Hector took,
once he'd killed him, that massive armour,
so wonderful to look at, which the gods
gave as a priceless gift to Peleus
on that day they placed you in the bed
of a mortal man. If only you had stayed
among the eternal maidens of the sea
and Peleus had married a mortal wife.
But now there'll be innumerable sorrows
waiting for your heart, once your child is killed.   110
You won't be welcoming him back home again.
My own heart has no desire to live on,
to continue living among men,
unless Hector is hit by my spear first,
losing his life and paying me compensation
for killing Menoetius' son, Patroclus."

Through her tears, Thetis then answered Achilles:

"My son, from what you've just been saying,
you're fated to an early death, for your doom
comes quickly as soon as Hector dies."   120

Swift-footed Achilles answered her with passion:

"Then let me die, since I could not prevent
the death of my companion. He's fallen
far from his homeland. He needed me there

to protect him from destruction. So now,
since I'm not returning to my own dear land,
and for Patroclus was no saving light
or for my many other comrades,
all those killed by godlike Hector while I sat
here by the ships, a useless burden   130
on the earth—and I'm unmatched in warfare
by any other Achaean armed in bronze,
although in council other men are better—
so let wars disappear from gods and men
and passionate anger, too, which incites
even the prudent man to that sweet rage,
sweeter than trickling honey in men's throats,
which builds up like smoke inside their chests,
as Agamemnon, king of men, just now,
made me enraged. But we'll let that pass.   140
For all the pain I feel, I'll suppress the heart
within my chest, as I must. So now I'll go
to meet Hector, killer of the man I loved.
As for my own fate, let it come to me
when Zeus and the other deathless gods
determine. For not even strong Hercules,
the man lord Zeus, son of Cronos, loved the most,
escaped his death. He was destroyed by Fate
and by malicious Hera's anger, too.
And so for me. If a like fate has been set,   150
then once I'm dead, I'll just lie there. But for now,
let me seize great glory—let me make
so many Trojan and Dardan matrons weep,
and with both hands wipe tears from their soft cheeks,
and set them on to constant lamentation,
so that they'll know I've long refrained from war.
Don't keep me from battle. Though you love me,
you'll not convince me."

                Silver-footed Thetis
then said to Achilles:

                "My child, what you say is true—

it's no bad thing to protect companions   160
when they're in trouble from complete disaster.
But now the Trojans have your lovely armour,
all your glittering bronze. It's on the shoulders
of Hector with the shining helmet—
he boasts about it. But I don't think
his triumph will last long, since his death
is coming closer. But you must not rejoin
Ares' conflict until with your own eyes
you see me in the morning here again.
I'll return at sunrise, and I'll bring you   170
lovely armour made by lord Hephaestus."

Saying this, Thetis turned away from her own son
to address her ocean sisters:

        "Now you must plunge
into the broad lap of Ocean and go find
the Old Man of the Sea in our father's house.
Tell him everything. I'll go to high Olympus,
to that famous artisan Hephaestus,
to see if he is willing to give my son
some splendid glittering armour."

Thetis spoke. Her sisters quickly plunged under the waves.   180
Then the silver-footed goddess Thetis went away
to fetch that lovely armour from Olympus
for her beloved son.

        As Thetis' feet carried her
towards Olympus, Achaeans were running back,
with a huge noise, fleeing man-killing Hector,
until they reached their ships beside the Hellespont.
But those well-armed Achaeans couldn't extricate
Achilles' comrade, dead Patroclus, from the spears,
for they'd been overtaken by Trojan warriors
and chariots once again, with Hector, Priam's son,   190
as furious as fire. Three times glorious Hector,
from behind, seized the corpse's feet, keen to drag it off,

shouting furiously to his Trojans. Three times,
the two Ajaxes, clothed in their full battle strength,
beat him from the corpse. But Hector kept on coming
without a pause, confident of his fighting power.
Sometimes he charged right at them in the frenzied crowd.
Sometimes he just stood there and gave a mighty yell,
but he never yielded any ground. Just as shepherds
are unable to drive off from their farmyard   200
a tawny ravenous lion by some carcass—
so the two warrior Ajaxes could not push Hector,
Priam's son, back from that body. And now Hector
would have seized that corpse, winning infinite glory,
if swift Iris with feet like wind had not come down,
speeding from Olympus to the son of Peleus,
with a message that he should arm himself for war.
Hera had sent her, unknown to Zeus and other gods.
Standing by Achilles, Iris spoke—her words had wings:

> "Rouse yourself, son of Peleus, most feared of men.   210
> Defend Patroclus. For on his behalf
> a deadly conflict rages by the ships—
> men are butchering each other, some trying
> to protect the dead man's corpse, while others,
> the Trojans, charge in to carry it away
> to windy Ilion. The one most eager
> to haul the body off is glorious Hector,
> whose heart is set on hacking off the head
> from its soft neck. He'll fix it on a stake
> set in the wall. So get up. No more lying here.   220
> Your heart will be disgraced if Patroclus
> becomes a plaything for the dogs of Troy—
> his mutilated corpse will be your shame."

Swift-footed godlike Achilles then asked her:

> "Goddess Iris, which of the gods sent you
> with this message to me?"

> > > Swift Iris,

with feet like wind, then said to Achilles:

"Hera sent me, Zeus' glorious wife.
Cronos' son, who sits on high, doesn't know,
nor do any other immortal gods   230
dwelling on snow-capped Olympus."

Swift-footed Achilles then questioned Iris:

"But how can I rejoin that conflict?
Those men have my armour. My dear mother
has told me not to arm myself for war,
not until my own eyes see that she's come back.
She promised to bring me splendid armour
from Hephaestus. I don't know anyone
whose glorious equipment I could use,
with the exception of the shield of Ajax,   240
son of Telamon. But I expect he's out there
with his spear among the front-line warriors
in that conflict over dead Patroclus."

Wind-swift Iris then answered Achilles:

"We know well enough your lovely armour
is in Trojan hands. But you should go now,
just as you are, to the ditch. Show yourself
to Trojans. It may happen that the Trojans,
afraid of you, will pull back from battle,
giving Achaea's exhausted warlike sons   250
a breathing space. For rests in war are rare."

With these words, swift-footed Iris went away.
Then Achilles, loved by Zeus, moved into action.
Around his powerful shoulders Athena set
her tasseled aegis. Then the lovely goddess
wrapped his head up in a golden cloud, so from him
a fiery light blazed out. Just like those times when smoke
from a city stretches all the way to heaven,
rising in the distance from an island under siege

by an enemy, where men fight all day long
in Ares' hateful war, struggling for their city—
then at sunset, they light fires one by one,
beacons flaming upwards to attract attention
from those on near-by islands, so their ships will come
to save them from destruction—that's how the light
blazed then from Achilles' head right up to heaven.
He strode from the wall, then stood there by the ditch.
But recalling what his mother said to him,
he didn't mingle with Achaeans. As he stood there,
he cried out. From far away, Pallas Athena   270
added her voice, too, causing great consternation
among the Trojans. As thrilling as a trumpet's note
when it rings clearly, when rapacious enemies
besiege a city—that's how sharp and piercing
Achilles' voice was then. When the Trojans heard it,
that brazen shout Achilles gave, all their hearts
were shaken. Their horses with the lovely manes
turned back the chariots, anticipating trouble
in their hearts. Charioteers were terrified, seeing
the fearful inextinguishable fire blazing   280
from the head of the great-hearted son of Peleus.
For Athena, goddess with the glittering eyes,
kept it burning. Three times godlike Achilles yelled
across that ditch. Three times Trojans and their allies
were thrown into confusion. At that moment,
twelve of their best men were killed by their own chariots
and their own spears. Achaeans then, with stronger hearts,
pulled Patroclus out of spear range and laid him on a cot.
His dear companions gathered mourning round him,
Achilles with them, shedding hot tears when he saw   290
his loyal companion lying on a death bed,
mutilated by sharp bronze. He'd sent him out to war
with chariot and horses, but never welcomed him
at his return.

                    Then ox-eyed queen Hera
made the unwearied sun, against his will, go down
into the stream of Ocean. So the sun set.

Godlike Achaeans now could pause for some relief
from the destructive killing of impartial war.

For their part, once Trojans drew back from that harsh fight,
they untied swift horses from their chariots and then,   300
before they thought of food, called for a meeting.
There everyone stayed standing. No one dared sit down,
all terrified because Achilles had appeared,
after his long absence from that savage conflict.
The first to speak was Polydamas, Panthous' son,
a prudent man, the only one who weighed with care
the past and future. He was Hector's comrade,
both born on the same night. As a public speaker,
he was the better of the two, but Hector
far surpassed him with a spear. Bearing in mind   310
their common good, Polydamas addressed them:

      "My friends, consider both sides of this issue.
For my part, I advise us to return
into the city—we should not stay here,
on the plain, waiting for dawn beside the ships.
Our walls are far away. While Achilles
kept up his anger at lord Agamemnon,
Achaeans were easier to fight against.
Personally, I was glad to spend the night
by their swift ships, hoping then we'd capture   320
those curved vessels. But now I really have
a dreadful fear of Peleus' swift-footed son.
He has a reckless heart—he's not a man
to rest content in the middle of the plain,
where Trojans and Achaeans have a share
of Ares' battle fury. No, he'll fight on
for our city and our women. So let's go back,
return into the city. Trust me when I say
that's how things will go. For now, sacred night
has stopped the swift-footed son of Peleus.   330
But if tomorrow he moves into action
fully armed and encounters us still here,
we'll recognize him well enough. Anyone

who gets away and makes it back to Ilion
will be a happy man. For dogs and vultures
will eat many Trojans. I don't want to hear
that such events have happened. If we all
follow my advice, although reluctantly,
tonight we'll collect our forces in one group.
Walls, high gates, and doors with fitted planks,   340
polished and bolted shut, will guard the city.
But in the morning early, we'll arm ourselves,
then take up our positions on the walls.
If Achilles comes from the ships keen to fight
for our walls, then he'll be disappointed.
He'll go back to his ships, once he's worn out
his strong-necked horses with too much running,
scampering around below our city wall.
His heart won't let him force his way inside,
and he'll not lay waste our city, not before   350
our swift dogs eat him up for dinner."

With a scowl, Hector of the flashing helmet then replied:

"Polydamas, what you say displeases me—
you tell us to run back into the city
and stay inside it. Haven't you already
been cooped up long enough within those walls?
In earlier days, all mortal men would claim
that Priam's city was rich in gold and bronze.
But now those splendid treasures are all gone.
Many goods from our own homes we've sold.   360
They went to Phrygia or fair Maeonia,
once great Zeus, in anger, turned against us.
But now, when crooked-minded Cronos' son
allows me to win glory by the ships,
hemming the Achaeans in beside the sea,
this is no time, you fool, to say such things
before the people. Not a single Trojan
will take your advice. I won't permit it.
But come, let's all follow now what I suggest.
You must take your dinner at your stations   370

all through the army, making sure you watch,
with every man awake. Any Trojan
too concerned about his property
should gather it up and give it to the men
for common use. Better that one of us
gets use from it than that Achaeans do.
Tomorrow morning early, right at dawn,
we'll fully arm ourselves with weapons,
then take keen battle to those hollow ships.
If indeed it's true that lord Achilles   380
is returning to that battle by the ships,
if he wants that, so much the worse for him.
I won't run from him in painful battle,
but stand against him, fighting face to face,
whether great victory goes to him or me.
In war the odds are equal, and the man
who seeks to kill may well be killed himself."

Hector spoke. The Trojans roared out in response.
The fools! Pallas Athena had robbed them of their wits.
They all applauded Hector's disastrous tactics.   390
No one praised Polydamas, who'd advised them well.
Then throughout the army they ate their dinner.

Meanwhile, Achaeans mourned Patroclus all night long
with their elegies. Among them, Peleus' son
began the urgent lamentations, placing
his murderous hands on the chest of his companion,
with frequent heavy groans, like a bearded lion,
when a deer hunter in dense forest steals its cubs—
the lion comes back later, then sick at heart
roams through the many clearings in the forest,   400
tracking the man's footprints, in hopes of finding him,
as bitter anger overwhelms the beast—just like that
Achilles, amid his groans, addressed his Myrmidons:

"Alas, what a useless promise I made then,
the day I tried to cheer Menoetius up
at home, telling him when I'd sacked Ilion,

I'd bring his splendid son back there to him,
in Opoeis, and with his share of trophies.
But Zeus does not bring to fulfillment
all things which men propose. Now both of us   410
share a common fate, to redden the same earth
right here in Troy. Old horseman Peleus
will not be welcoming me at my return
back to his home, nor will my mother Thetis.
For in this place the earth will cover me.
And now, Patroclus, since I'm journeying
under the earth after you, I'll postpone
your burial till I bring here Hector's head,
his armour, too, the man who slaughtered you,
you courageous man. I'll cut the throats   420
of twelve fine Trojan children on your pyre,
in my anger at your killing. Till that time,
you'll lie like this with me by my beaked ships,
and round you Trojan and Dardanian women
will keep lamenting night and day, shedding tears,
the very women we two worked hard to win
with our strength and our long spears, by looting
prosperous cities of mortal men."

After these words, godlike Achilles told his comrades
to place a large tripod on the fire, so they could wash   430
the blood clots from his comrade's corpse. On the blazing fire,
they set a cauldron with three legs, poured water in it,
then brought split wood to burn below the water.
Fire licked the cauldron's belly and made the water hot.
Once it had boiled inside the shining bronze,
they washed him, rubbed oil thickly over him,
and filled his wounds with ointment nine years old.
Then they placed Patroclus on a bed, covering him
with a fine woolen cloth from head to foot
and a white cloak on the cloth. Then all night long,   440
the Myrmidons around swift-footed Achilles
mourned Patroclus with their lamentations.

Then Zeus spoke to Hera, his sister and his wife:

"You've got what you wanted, ox-eyed queen Hera.
Swift-footed Achilles you've spurred into action.
From your own womb you must have given birth
to these long-haired Achaeans."

                              Ox-eyed queen Hera
then replied to Zeus:

                    "Most dread son of Cronos,
what are you saying? Even a human man,
though mortal and ignorant of what I know,   450
can achieve what he intends for someone else.
And men say I'm the finest of all goddesses
in a double sense—both by my lineage
and my marriage to the ruler of the gods.
So why should I not bring an evil fortune
on these Trojans when they've made me angry?"

Thus these two conversed with one another then.

Meanwhile, silver-footed Thetis reached Hephaestus' home.
Made of eternal bronze and gleaming like a star,
it stood out among the homes of the immortals.   460
The crippled god had constructed it himself.
She found him working with his bellows, moving round,
sweating in his eager haste. He was forging
twenty tripods in all, to stand along the walls
of his well-built house. Under the legs of each one
he had fitted golden wheels, so every tripod
might move all on its own into a gathering of the gods
at his command and then return to his own house.
They were wonderful to look at. His work on them
had reached the stage where finely crafted handles   470
had still not been attached. He was making these,
forging the rivets. As he was working on them
with his great skill, silver-footed goddess Thetis
approached more closely. Noticing her, Charis,
lovely goddess with the splendid veil, came forward—
she was wife to the celebrated crippled god.

Taking Thetis by the hand, she called her name, and said:

> "Long-robed Thetis, why visit our house now?
> You're a welcome and respected guest, but to this point
> you haven't come by very much. Do step inside.   480
> Let me show you our hospitality."

With these words, the goddess led her inside the house.
She asked Thetis to sit in a silver-studded chair,
beautifully finished, with a footstool under it.
Then she called the famous artisan Hephaestus:

> "Come here, Hephaestus. Thetis needs to see you."

The celebrated lame god then replied to Charis:

> "Here's a fearful honoured goddess in my home,
> the one who saved me when I was in pain,
> after my great fall, thanks to my mother,   490
> that shameless one, eager to conceal me,
> because I was a cripple. At that time,
> I would have suffered heartfelt agonies,
> if Thetis and Eurynome, daughter
> of circling Ocean stream, had not taken me
> into their hearts. With those two, for nine years
> I made many lovely things—brooches,
> spiral bracelets, earrings, necklaces—
> inside their hollow cave. The Ocean stream
> flowed round me, always with the roar of surf.   500
> No one else knew, neither god nor mortal man.
> But Thetis and Eurynome—the ones
> who rescued me—they knew. And now Thetis
> has come into my home. So I must give her
> full recompense—fair-haired Thetis saved my life.
> But Charis, show her now our hospitality.
> I'll put away my bellows and my tools."

Huge god Hephaestus got up from the anvil block
with laboured breathing. He was lame, but his thin legs   510

moved quickly under him. He placed his bellows
far from the fire and collected all his work tools,
then stored them in a silver chest. With a sponge,
he wiped his face, both hands, thick neck, and hairy chest.
Then he pulled on a tunic and came limping out,
gripping a sturdy staff. At once he was helped along
by female servants made of gold, who moved to him.
They look like living servant girls, possessing minds,
hearts with intelligence, vocal chords, and strength.
They learned to work from the immortal gods.   520
These women served to give their master detailed help.
Hephaestus come limping up to Thetis and sat down
in a shining chair. Then, clasping her hand, he spoke:

    "Long-robed Thetis, why have you come here,
to our house, an honoured welcome guest?
To this point, you haven't come here often.
But say what's on your mind. My heart tells me
I shall do it, if I can accomplish it,
if it's something that can be carried out."

Thetis answered him in tears:

               "Oh, Hephaestus,   530
is there any goddess on Olympus
who's suffered so much painful sorrow
in her heart to equal the unhappiness
that Zeus, son of Cronos, loads on me
more than any other god? Of all goddesses
living in the sea, he made me subject
to a mortal man, Peleus, son of Aeacus.
So I had to put up with a man in bed,
though much against my will. Now he lies there,
in his home, worn out by harsh old age.   540
And I have still more pain. He gave me a son
to bear and raise as an outstanding warrior.
The boy grew up as quickly as a sapling.
Then, when I had reared him like a tree
in an abundant garden, I sent him off

411

in the beaked ships to fight in Ilion
against the Trojans. I'll never welcome him
returning home to the house of Peleus.
And while he still lives to glimpse the sunlight,
he lives in sorrow. When I visit him, 550
I cannot help him. Achaea's sons chose for him
as his prize a girl, whom great Agamemnon
seized right out of his arms. In grief for her,
his heart has pined away. Then the Trojans
penned Achaeans in by their ships' sterns,
not letting them come out. The senior men
among the Argives pleaded with my son.
They promised splendid gifts. But he refused,
declining to protect them from disaster.
But then he sent Patroclus to the war, 560
dressing him in his own armour, providing
a force of many men. They fought all day
around the Scaean Gates, and that very day
would have utterly destroyed the city,
if Apollo had not killed Menoetius' son,
after he'd inflicted bloody carnage.
He killed him at the front, giving Hector
all the glory. That's why I've come here now,
asking at your knees if you'd be willing
to give my son, who is fated to die soon, 570
a shield, helmet, good leg armour fitted
with ankle clasps, and body armour, too.
His previous equipment was all taken
when Trojans killed his loyal companion.
Now my son lies in the dust, heart filled with pain."

The famous crippled god then answered Thetis:

"Cheer up. Don't let these things afflict your heart.
I wish I could hide him from distressful death,
when his cruel fate arrives, as surely
as I know there'll be fine armour for him— 580
such splendid armour that it will astound
all the many men who chance to see it."

412

With these words, Hephaestus left her there, going to start
his bellows. He directed them right at the fire,
then told them to start working. So the bellows,
twenty in all, started blowing on the crucibles,
each one emitting just the right amount of air,
sometimes blowing hard to help when he was busy,
sometimes gently, whatever way Hephaestus wished,
so his work could go ahead. He threw on the fire   590
enduring bronze and tin, precious gold and silver.
Next, he placed the great anvil on its block, took up
a massive hammer in one hand and in the other his tongs.

The first thing he created was a huge and sturdy shield,
all wonderfully crafted. Around its outer edge,
he fixed a triple rim, glittering in the light,
attaching to it a silver carrying strap.
The shield had five layers. On the outer one,
with his great skill he fashioned many rich designs.
There he hammered out the earth, the heavens, the sea,   600
the untiring sun, the moon at the full, along with
every constellation which crowns the heavens—
the Pleiades, the Hyades, mighty Orion,
and the Bear, which some people call the Wain,
always circling in the same position, watching Orion,
the only stars that never bathe in Ocean stream.

Then he created two splendid cities of mortal men.
In one, there were feasts and weddings. By the light
of blazing torches, people were leading the brides
out from their homes and through the town to loud music   610
of the bridal song. There were young lads dancing,
whirling to the constant tunes of flutes and lyres,
while all the women stood beside their doors, staring
in admiration.

                    Then the people gathered
in the assembly, for a dispute had taken place.
Two men were arguing about blood-money owed
for a murdered man. One claimed he'd paid in full,

413

setting out his case before the people, but the other
was refusing any compensation. Both were keen
to get the judgment from an arbitration.   620
The crowd there cheered them on, some supporting one,
some the other, while heralds kept the throng controlled.
Meanwhile, elders were sitting there on polished stones
in the sacred circle, holding in their hands
the staffs they'd taken from the clear-voiced heralds.
With those they'd stand up there and render judgment,
each in his turn. In the centre lay two golden talents,
to be awarded to the one among them all
who delivered the most righteous verdict.

The second city was surrounded by two armies,   630
soldiers with glittering weapons. They were discussing
two alternatives, each one pleasing some of them—
whether to attack that city and plunder it,
or to accept as payment half of all the goods
contained in that fair town. But those under siege
who disagreed were arming for a secret ambush.
Their dear wives and children stood up on the walls
as a defence, along with those too old to fight.
The rest were leaving, led on by Pallas Athena
and Ares, both made of gold, dressed in golden clothes,   640
large, beautiful, and armed—as is suitable for gods.
They stood out above the smaller people with them.
When the soldiers reached a spot which seemed all right
for ambush, a place beside a river where the cattle
came to drink, they stopped there, covered in shining bronze.
Two scouts were stationed some distance from that army,
waiting to catch sight of sheep and short-horned cattle.
These soon appeared, followed by two herdsmen
playing their flutes and not anticipating any danger.
But those lying in ambush saw them and rushed out,   650
quickly cutting off the herds of cattle and fine flocks
of white-fleeced sheep, killing the herdsmen with them.
When the besiegers sitting in their meeting place
heard the great commotion coming from the cattle,
they quickly climbed up behind their prancing horses

and set out. They soon caught up with those attackers.
Then they organized themselves for battle and fought
along the river banks, men hitting one another
with bronze-tipped spears. Strife and Confusion joined the fight,
along with cruel Death, who seized one wounded man   660
while still alive and then another man without a wound,
while pulling the feet of one more corpse out from the fight.
The clothes Death wore around her shoulders were dyed red
with human blood. They even joined the slaughter
as living mortals, fighting there and hauling off
the bodies of dead men which each of them had killed.

On that shield Hephaestus next set a soft and fallow field,
fertile spacious farmland, which had been ploughed three times.
Many labourers were wheeling ploughs across it,
moving back and forth. As they reached the field's edge,   670
they turned, and a man came up to offer them
a cup of wine as sweet as honey. Then they'd turn back,
down the furrow, eager to move through that deep soil
and reach the field's edge once again. The land behind them
was black, looking as though it had just been ploughed,
though it was made of gold—an amazing piece of work!

Then he pictured on the shield a king's landed estate,
where harvesters were reaping corn, using sharp sickles.
Armfuls of corn were falling on the ground in rows,
one after the other. Binders were tying them up   680
in sheaves with twisted straw. Three binders stood there.
Behind the reapers, boys were gathering the crop,
bringing it to sheaf-binders, keeping them occupied.
Among them stood the king, a sceptre in his hand,
there by the stubble, saying nothing, but with pleasure
in his heart. Some distance off, under an oak tree,
heralds were setting up a feast, dressing a huge ox
which they'd just killed. Women were sprinkling white barley
on the meat in large amounts for the workers' meal.
Next, Hephaestus placed on that shield a vineyard,   690
full of grapes made of splendid gold. The grapes were black,
the poles supporting vines throughout were silver.

Around it, he made a ditch of blue enamel,
around that, a fence of tin. A single path led in,
where the grape pickers came and went at harvest time.
Young girls and carefree lads with wicker baskets
were carrying off a crop as sweet as honey.
In the middle of them all, a boy with a clear-toned lyre
played pleasant music, singing the Song of Linos,
in his delicate fine voice.[1] His comrades kept time,   700
beating the ground behind him, singing and dancing.

Then he set on the shield a herd of straight-horned cattle,
with cows crafted out of gold and tin. They were lowing
as they hurried out from farm to pasture land,
beside a rippling river lined with waving reeds.
The herdsmen walking by the cattle, four of them,
were also made of gold. Nine swift-footed dogs
ran on behind. But there, at the front of the herd,
two fearful lions had seized a bellowing bull.
They were dragging him off, as he roared aloud.   710
The dogs and young men were chasing after them.
The lions, after ripping open the great ox's hide,
were gorging on its entrails, on its black blood,
as herdsmen kept trying in vain to chase them off,
setting their swift dogs on them. But, fearing the lions,
the dogs kept turning back before they nipped them,
and stood there barking, close by but out of reach.

Then the famous crippled god created there a pasture
in a lovely valley bottom, an open ground
for white-fleeced sheep, sheep folds, roofed huts, and pens.   720

Next on that shield, the celebrated lame god made
an elaborately crafted dancing floor, like the one
Daedalus created long ago in spacious Cnossus,
for Ariadne with the lovely hair. On that floor,
young men and women whose bride price would require
many cattle were dancing, holding onto one another
by the wrists. The girls wore fine linen dresses,

[1]The song of Linos is a traditional harvest song.

the men lightly rubbed with oil wore woven tunics.
On their heads the girls had lovely flower garlands.
The men were carrying gold daggers on silver straps.   730
They turned with such a graceful ease on skillful feet,
just as a potter sits with a wheel between his hands,
testing it, to make sure that it runs smoothly.
Then they would line up and run towards each other.
A large crowd stood around, enjoying the dancing magic,
as in the middle two acrobats led on the dance,
springing, and whirling, and tumbling.

On that shield, Hephaestus then depicted Ocean,
the mighty river, flowing all around the outer edge.

When he'd created that great and sturdy shield,   740
he fashioned body armour brighter than blazing fire,
a heavy helmet shaped to fit Achilles' temples,
beautiful and finely worked, with a gold crest on top.
Then he made him leg guards of finely hammered tin.

When the famous lame god had made all the armour,
he took it and set it there before Achilles' mother.
Then, like a hawk, she sped down from Olympus,
carrying the gleaming armour of Hephaestus.

Book Nineteen
Achilles and Agamemnon

[Thetis brings the divine armour to Achilles; Achilles summons an assembly of Achaeans; Achilles and Agamemnon are reconciled; Agamemnon explains the origin of his folly; Odysseus urges Achilles to eat, Achilles refuses; Agamemnon gets his gifts for Achilles brought to the assembly; Agamemnon swears he has not touched Briseis; Briseis laments over the corpse of Patroclus; the elders continue to mourn Patroclus; Zeus sends Athena to help Achilles deal with his hunger; the troops move out to battle again; Achilles speaks to his horses, who prophesy his death]

When Dawn in her yellow robe rose from Ocean's stream,
bringing her light to immortal gods and mortal men,
Thetis reached the ships bearing Hephaestus' gifts.
She found her dear son lying beside Patroclus,
crying bitterly. Many of his companions
mourned around him. The noble goddess went to them.
Standing by Achilles, she clasped his hand, then said:

> "My son, we must let this man lie here,
> for all our grief. He's dead once and for all.
> It's the gods' will. Now you must accept   10
> this splendid armour from Hephaestus—
> no man has ever had such gorgeous armour
> to wear around his shoulders."

> > > With these words,
the goddess set the armour down before Achilles.
The wonderfully crafted metal rang out loudly.
Fear gripped all the Myrmidons. Not one of them
dared look directly at those weapons. They shrank away.
But when Achilles saw them, his anger grew.
His eyes glared underneath his eyelids, like a fire—
a terrifying light. But as his hands went over   20
the god's priceless gifts, he felt great joy. He gazed at them,
filling his heart with pleasure at the rich designs.
Then he spoke to his mother—his words had wings:

"Mother, this armour the god has given me
is a work fit for the immortals, something
no living human could create. So now,
I'll arm myself for war. In the meantime,
I have a dreadful fear that flies may burrow
in those wounds carved by the slicing bronze
into the body of Menoetius' noble son.   30
They may breed worms in him, defile his corpse,
now that the life in him is gone. If so,
all his flesh will fester."

                              Then Thetis,
goddess with the silver feet, answered Achilles:

"My child, don't let such things distress your heart.
I'll make the effort to protect him here
from those cruel swarms of flies which feed
on warriors who've been killed in battle.
Even if he lies here an entire year,
his flesh will stay just as it is or better.   40
But you must summon the Achaean warriors
to assembly, to renounce your anger
with Agamemnon, his people's shepherd.
After that, arm yourself for battle quickly—
clothe yourself in all your fighting strength."

Saying this, Thetis filled him with fearless power.
Then she inserted ambrosia and red nectar
into Patroclus, through his nostrils, so his flesh
would stay uncorrupted.

                              But Achilles, like a god,
strode down along the seashore, raising fearful shouts,   50
stirring Achaean warriors into action.
So even those who up to now used to remain
with the assembled ships—helmsmen who worked
ships' steering oars and stewards who stayed with the ships
rationing provisions—these men all showed up
for the assembly, because Achilles had appeared

after his long absence from that painful war.
Two associates of the war god Ares came in limping,
the brave offspring of Tydeus and lord Odysseus,
leaning on their spears—their wounds still pained them. 60
They came and sat down at the front of the assembly.
Last to arrive was Agamemnon, king of men,
still suffering from the wound Coön had given him,
Antenor's son, who in deadly conflict stabbed him
with his bronze-tipped spear. Once all Achaeans
were assembled, swift-footed Achilles rose to speak:

"Son of Atreus, has it been good for us,
for you and me, to continue squabbling
in a heart-rending quarrel full of grief
for both of us, over some girl? I wish 70
she'd been killed by Artemis' arrow
right beside my ships, the day I got her
as my prize, after we destroyed Lyrnessus.
Fewer Achaeans would have sunk their teeth
into this wide earth at enemy hands,
if I'd not been so angry. That's really helped
lord Hector and his Trojans. But Achaeans,
will, I think, long recall this argument
you and I have had. Still, though it hurts,
we should let all this pass, repressing hearts 80
within our chests—we must do that. So now,
I end my anger. It's not appropriate
for me to remain enraged for ever.
But come, quickly urge long-haired Achaeans
on to battle, so I may go out once again
to face the Trojans and see if they still wish
to spend the night beside our ships. I think
many of them will be glad to get some rest,
the ones who escape this deadly war
and who evade my spear."

Achilles finished speaking. 90
The well-armed Achaeans then were full of joy
that Peleus' great-hearted son had set aside

420

his anger. Next, Agamemnon, king of men,
addressed them:

"My friends, Danaan warriors,
companions of the war god Ares, it's good
to listen to a man who's standing up
to speak and not to interrupt him.
That makes things difficult, even for a man
skilled in speaking. When men all shout at once,
how can any one speak up or listen?   100
Even a clear-voiced speaker gets upset.
I'm going to address the son of Peleus,
but you other Argives pay attention—
let every one of you mark my words well.
You Achaeans have often criticized
and spoken ill of me. But I'm not to blame.
It's Zeus' fault and Fate—those Furies, too,
who walk in darkness. In our assembly,
they cast a savage blindness on my heart,
that day when on my own I took away   110
Achilles' prize. But what was I to do?
It is a god who brought all this about.
Zeus' eldest daughter, Ate, blinds all men
with her destructive power. Her feet are soft,
she walks, not on the ground, but on men's heads,
and she brings folly onto humankind,
seducing them at random. Even Zeus,
who they say is the greatest of the gods
and men, was blinded by her, when Hera,
a mere female, with her cunning tactics,   120
deceived him that very day Alcmene
was to give birth to mighty Hercules,
in Thebes, city with the splendid walls.
Zeus then boasted openly to all the gods,
'Listen to me, you gods and goddesses,
so I can say what the heart inside me bids.
The goddess of childbirth, Eileithyia,
today brings into the sun's light a man
who will rule all those who live around him,

421

one of the race of men with my blood in them.'
But then that deceitful lady Hera said to Zeus,
'You're not being candid. You don't really mean
what you now say. So come, Olympian,
swear a binding oath for me that the man
who falls out today between a woman's feet
will, in fact, rule those who live around him,
one of the race of men with your blood in them.'
That's what she said. Zeus didn't see the trick.
He swore a binding oath in his great blindness.
Hera then left that peak on Mount Olympus. 140
Darting off, she quickly came to Argos,
in Achaea, where she knew the strong wife
of Sthenelus, Perseus' son, was pregnant
with a son, in her seventh month. This child
Hera induced into the light before its term.
She then delayed Alcmene's childbirth,
getting the Eileithyiae to hold it back.
Then she brought the news to Zeus, Cronos' son,
saying, 'Father Zeus, lord of bright lightning,
I'll tell you my heartfelt news. Just now, 150
a noble man was born who'll rule the Argives,
Eurystheus, son of Sthenelus, Perseus' son,
of your own lineage. So it's fitting
he should become king of all the Argives.'
When Hera said that, sharp pain seized Zeus
deep in his heart. He seized Ate at once
by the shining hair wound round her head.
His heart was furious. He swore a great oath
that Ate, who blinds everyone, would no more
come to Olympus or to starry heaven. 160
That said, in one hand he swung her round,
then flung her clear out of the star-filled skies.
She quickly landed among toiling men.
Whenever Zeus saw his dear son Hercules
carrying out menial work in all his labours
for Eurystheus, he'd always groan aloud,
thinking of Ate. That's how I was, too,
when great Hector of the shining helmet

was killing Argives off at the ships' sterns.
I could not forget Ate, who blinded me   170
when all this started. But since I was blind,
since Zeus robbed me of my wits, I will agree
to make amends, to give priceless gifts.
But prepare yourself for battle, rouse up
all your other men. As for me, I'm ready
to give every gift which lord Odysseus
promised you in your hut yesterday.
Or, if you prefer, don't turn right now to war.
Though you're keen to go, let my servants fetch
those presents from my ship and bring them here,   180
so you can see if you approve of them."

Swift-footed Achilles then answered Agamemnon:

"Most glorious son of Atreus, Agamemnon,
king of men, if you wish to give me presents,
as is appropriate, or to withhold them,
that's up to you. Now we must think of war,
and with all speed. We should not be wasting time
in conversation or with such delays.
We have great work to do, so once again
men see Achilles with the front-line warriors,   190
destroying the Trojans' ranks with his bronze spear.
Keep this in mind when you confront your man."

Resourceful Odysseus then addressed Achilles:

"Though you're a brave man, god-like Achilles,
don't encourage Achaea's sons to fight
against the Trojans on empty stomachs.
If so, the fight won't last for long if troops
engage right now, once some god infuses strength
into both sides. No. Instruct Achaeans
to have some food and wine by their swift ships.   200
For they give strength and courage. No soldier
can fight the enemy all day till sunset
without some food. However fierce his heart

may be for battle, his limbs grow heavy
without his knowledge. Once thirst and hunger
overtake him, his knees get tired as he moves.
But the man who's had sufficient food and wine
fights all day long against his enemies
with a courageous heart. His limbs don't tire
until all warriors have left the battle.   210
So dismiss your men. Tell them to make a meal.
Let Agamemnon, king of men, present his gifts,
so all Achaeans here in our assembly
can see them first hand and delight your heart.
Let him stand up there among the Argives,
swear an oath to you he's never climbed
in that girl's bed to have sex with her,
as is usual, my lord, with men and women.
Let the heart in your own chest be open
to reconciliation. Then, Agamemnon   220
should offer you a fine and pleasing dinner
in his hut, so there'll be nothing due to you
which remains unsatisfied. As for you,
son of Atreus, you should be more righteous
with others from now on. There's no shame
when a king pays someone compensation,
if the king was the first to lose his temper."

Agamemnon, king of men, answered Odysseus:

"Son of Laertes, I am glad to hear
what you've just said. You've explained this well,   230
exploring all these matters very fairly.
I'm prepared to swear the oath, as my heart bids,
and, before the gods, I'll not swear falsely.
But let Achilles stay here a little while,
though he desires to fight, and let others
stay gathered here, until the gifts are brought
out of my hut and we can sacrifice
to seal our oaths. To you I assign this task—
select from the entire Achaean force
the five best young men to carry from my ships   240

all those gifts we promised yesterday
to give Achilles—that includes the woman.
Let Talthybius at once prepare for me
in the middle of this wide Achaean camp
a sacrificial boar to offer up
to Zeus and Helios, god of the sun."

Swift-footed Achilles then replied to Agamemnon:

"Mighty son of Atreus, Agamemnon,
ruler of men, it would be far better
to worry about all this some other time,   250
when there's a let up in the fight, when the heart
here in my chest is less enraged. For now,
all those killed by Hector, son of Priam,
when Zeus gave him glory, are lying there,
all mangled, and you are urging us to eat!
For my part, I'd lead Achaea's sons to war
right now, unfed, with empty stomachs,
then at sunset make them a great dinner,
when we've avenged our shame. Until that time,
no drink or food will pass my throat, at least,   260
while my dead comrade lies inside my hut,
mutilated by sharp bronze, with his feet
still pointing at the door, while his companions
mourn there around him. That's why my heart
cannot concern itself with what you've said,
only with killing, blood, men's dying groans."

To this, resourceful Odysseus then replied:

"Achilles, Peleus' son, of all Achaeans
the mightiest by far. You're stronger than me,
more than a little better with your spear,   270
but I might say I'm far better with advice,
since I'm older and know more. So your heart
should listen now to what I have to say.
In battle men quickly have enough, for there
bronze slices piles of straw onto the ground,

425

but there's a slender harvest, once Zeus
lifts up his scales, establishing for men
the outcome of the battle. Achaeans
cannot mourn a corpse by eating nothing.
Too many men are dying every day,   280
one after another. When would anyone
get some relief from fasting? No, the dead
we must bury, then mourn a single day,
hardening our hearts. But those who do survive
grim battle must remember food and drink,
so we can fight our enemies once more,
on and on incessantly, covering our flesh
with bronze which never tires. So let no soldier
hang back, waiting for another call to war.
This is the call, and things will not go well   290
for anyone left at Achaean ships.
Let's all set off together as one army,
taking cruel war to those horse-taming Trojans."

Odysseus finished. Then he took along with him
splendid Nestor's sons, Meges, son of Phyleus,
Thoas, Meriones, and Lycomedes,
Creon's son, and Melanippus. They went off
to the huts of Agamemnon, Atreus' son.
As soon as they gave out the order, the task was done.
From the hut they took seven tripods, as he'd promised,   300
twenty gleaming cauldrons and twelve horses.
They quickly led out seven women, all well skilled
in lovely handiwork. Eighth came the fair Briseis.
Odysseus weighed out a sum of ten gold talents.
Then he led them back, with the young Achaean men
carrying the gifts. These they placed in the assembly,
in the middle of them all. Agamemnon stood up.
Talthybius, whose voice was like a god's, was there,
by Agamemnon's side, his hands gripping a boar.
Agamemnon drew out the knife he always wore   310
by his sword's scabbard. He cut hairs from the boar
to start the ritual. Lifting up his arms,
he prayed to Zeus. Argives all sat in silence,

426

listening to their king with suitable respect,
as he gazed up to spacious heaven, saying this prayer:

"Let Zeus, the loftiest and finest god,
first witness, then Sun and the Erinyes,
those Furies under the earth who punish
men who've made false oaths—I hereby swear
I've never laid a hand on that girl Briseis,   320
either for sex or any other reason.
In my huts she stayed untouched. If what I say
is not the truth, then let gods punish me
with many painful sorrows, the sort they give
to men who in their oaths blaspheme them."

This said, he cut the boar's throat with the ruthless bronze.
Talthybius swung the body round, then threw it
in the vast gray sea, food for fish. Then Achilles,
standing up, addressed war-loving Argives:

                                    "Father Zeus,
you keep afflicting humans with great blindness.   330
For Atreus' son would never make my heart
so totally enraged here in my chest,
nor would he take that girl away from me,
so arbitrarily against my will,
if Zeus did not somehow desire the deaths
of Argives in large numbers. But now,
you should all eat, so we can start the fight."

Saying this, Achilles quickly ended the assembly.
The men dispersed, each one going off to his own ship.
Great-hearted Myrmidons looked after all the gifts,   340
taking them to godlike Achilles' ship and storing them
inside his huts. They left the women there, as well.
His noble attendants drove the horses to his herd.

Briseis, looking like golden Aphrodite,
then saw Patroclus mutilated by sharp bronze.
With a cry, she threw herself on him, hands tearing

at her breast, her tender neck, her lovely face,
fair as a goddess, lamenting:

                                    "Patroclus,
        you who brought the utmost joy to my sad heart,
        I left you here alive, when I went off,   350
        taken from these huts. But now, at my return,
        I find you dead, you, the people's leader.
        Again for me, as always, evil follows evil.
        I saw the husband I was given to
        by my father and my noble mother killed
        by sharp bronze before our city. My brothers,
        three of them, whom my own mother bore,
        whom I loved, have all met their fatal day.
        But when swift Achilles killed my husband,
        you wouldn't let me weep. You told me then   360
        you'd make me lord Achilles' wedded wife,
        he'd take me in his ships to Phthia,
        for a marriage feast among the Myrmidons.
        You were always gentle. That's the reason
        I'll never stop this grieving for your death."

As Briseis said this, she wept. The women joined her
in wailing for Patroclus, though each of them
had her own private sorrows. The Achaean elders
gathered round Achilles, urging him to eat.
But he refused, continuing to mourn: 370

        "If any of my dear companions here
        wishes to obey me, then I beg you
        don't ask me to satisfy my heart
        with food or drink when painful sorrow
        grips me. I'll remain like this till sunset,
        enduring everything."

                              Achilles finished speaking.
Then he sent away the leaders. But some remained—
both sons of Atreus, lord Odysseus, Nestor,
Idomeneus, and old horseman Phoenix,
each trying to console him in his painful grieving.   380

But his heart would find no joy until he'd entered
the bloody mouth of war. Thinking of Patroclus,
he sighed repeatedly, then said:

> "Poor man,
> most loved of all my comrades, in the past
> you used to set out tasty meals right here,
> making them well and quickly in my hut,
> when we Achaeans were in such a rush
> to set out against horse-taming Trojans
> in wretched war. Now you lie disfigured,
> my heart refuses meat and drink, though both   390
> are in this hut, because I miss you so.
> I could suffer nothing worse than this,
> not even if I learned my father's died—
> he must be shedding gentle tears in Phthia,
> missing a son like me, while I stay here
> among strange people, fighting Trojans
> over Helen, whom I detest, or if I heard
> my dear son had died, who's being raised for me
> on Scyros, if, in fact, he's still alive,
> godlike Neoptolemus. Up to now,   400
> the heart here in my chest hoped I alone
> would perish here in Troy, so far from Argos,
> where horses breed. You'd return to Phthia,
> taking my child in your swift black ship
> away from Scyros, show him all my things,
> possessions, servants, my high-roofed palace.
> For by now Peleus is either dead and gone,
> I must assume, or just barely living,
> afflicted with hateful old age, waiting
> all the time for distressful news of me,   410
> when he finds out that I have died."

As he spoke, Achilles wept. The elders also mourned,
each one remembering what he had left at home.
As they lamented, the son of Cronos saw them.
Feeling pity for them, Zeus spoke to Athena—
his words had wings:

          "My child, here's a man
you seem to be neglecting totally,
a special favourite of yours—Achilles.
Does your heart no longer care for him at all?
There he sits in front of his beaked ships,   420
mourning his dear companion. Other men
have all gone off to dinner, but he's fasting
and won't eat. Go now. Put into his chest
some nectar and beautiful ambrosia,
so hunger won't consume him."

                         With these words,
Zeus spurred Athena, already eager, into action.
She swooped down through the air, screaming shrilly,
like a broad-winged hawk. Then as Achaeans, with all speed,
armed themselves throughout the camp, she inserted
nectar and beautiful ambrosia in Achilles' chest,   430
so his limbs would not suffer pangs of hunger.
Then she left for her mighty father's well-built home.

Achaeans then came swarming out from their fast ships.
Just as freezing snowflakes fall thick and fast from Zeus,
driven by the raging sky-born North Wind—that's how
crowds of them streamed out then, pouring from the ships—
brightly gleaming helmets, strong-plated body armour,
ash spears and embossed shields—the glitter of it all
flashed up to heaven. All around, earth chuckled
to see that gleaming bronze. A noise like thunder rose,   440
drummed by the soldiers' marching feet. Amid them all,
noble Achilles armed himself for battle,
his teeth clenched, eyes blazing with a fiery light,
his heart filled with a sorrow not to be endured.
As he pulled on the divine gifts which Hephaestus
had made for him, he raged against the Trojans.
First, he strapped on his leg armour, beautifully made,
fitted with silver ankle clasps. Then on his chest
he fixed the body armour. Around his shoulders,
he slung his bronze silver-studded sword, then picked up   450
his huge strong shield which, like the moon, shone everywhere.

Just like the blazing light that sailors glimpse at sea
from a fire burning in some isolated farm,
high in the mountains, as winds blow them further out,
taking them against their will over the fish-filled seas
away from loved ones—that's how Achilles' shield,
so finely crafted, burned out far into the sky.
Then raising the great helmet, he set it on his head.
It glittered like a star, that helmet with its horse-hair plumes,
adorned with the golden hairs Hephaestus placed   460
so thickly round the crest. Noble Achilles,
trying out the armour for himself, made sure
it fit him so his splendid limbs could move with ease.
It was like his own set of wings, lifting him up,
this shepherd of his people. Then from its case,
he took his father's spear, heavy, huge, and strong.
No other Achaean could control that spear.
He was the only one with skill enough to wield it.
Made of ash wood from the top of Pelion,
that spear had been given to own his dear father   470
by Cheiron, so he could kill heroic warriors.

Automedon and Alcinous kept themselves occupied
yoking the horses, tying fine chest straps round them,
setting bits inside their jaws, and aligning reins
back in the well-made chariot. Taking the shining whip
which fit his grip, Automedon jumped in the chariot.
Achilles, fully armed, climbed up beside him,
his armour gleaming like dazzling Hyperion.[1]
Then he called out to those horses of his father,
in a terrifying voice:

                              "Xanthus, Balius,   480
          you famous children of Podarge, this time
          make sure you bring your charioteer back safely
          to the Danaan army, once we've had enough
          of battle. Don't leave him out there slaughtered,
          as you did Patroclus."

[1]Hyperion (or Helios) is god of the sun.

431

From under the yoke,
his swift-footed horse called Xanthus spoke to him,
ducking his head down quickly, so all his mane
streamed down from underneath his shoulder harness
beside the yoke towards the ground. Goddess Hera
gave Xanthus power to speak:

"Mighty Achilles,   490
on this occasion we will bring you safely back.
But the day you'll die is fast approaching.
We won't be the cause, but some mighty god
and a strong fate. It was not our laziness
or lack of speed which helped the Trojans
strip that armour from Patroclus' shoulders.
A powerful god born to Leto killed him
among those fighting at the battle front,
then gave Hector glory. The two of us
could run as quickly as the West Wind's blasts—   500
men say they are the fastest thing there is—
your fate still stays the same, to die in war,
killed by a mortal and a god."

Once Xanthus had said this,
the Erinyes removed his voice. Then Achilles,
in a fury, said to his horse:

"Xanthus,
why do you prophesy my death? There is no need.
I know well enough I'm fated to die here,
far from my loving parents. No matter.
I will not stop till I have driven the Trojans
to the limit of what they can endure in war."   510

With these words, he drove his sure-footed horses off,
speeding forward to the front, screaming as he went.

Book Twenty
Achilles Returns to Battle

[As the armies ready for battle, Zeus summons an assembly of gods,
tells them they can join the fight on either side; the gods leave
Olympus for the battle; Apollo persuades Aeneas to fight Achilles;
Aeneas and Achilles confront each other; Aeneas explains his ancestry;
Aeneas and Achilles fight; Poseidon saves Aeneas; Achilles starts his
slaughter of Trojans; Hector confronts Achilles; Apollo saves Hector;
Achilles continues his slaughter]

Then, son of Peleus, Achaeans armed themselves
around you, feeding your boundless appetite for war.
On the other side, higher up the sloping plain,
the Trojans did the same. At that very moment,
from the summit of many-ridged Olympus,
Zeus told Themis to summon gods to an assembly.
She raced around, calling them to Zeus' home.
None of the rivers was left out, except Oceanus,
nor any nymph. All those who live in lovely woods,
river springs, and grassy meadows came together   10
at cloud-gatherer Zeus' home, seating themselves
on porticoes of polished stone, built there
by Hephaestus' cunning arts for his father Zeus.
The gods gathered there in Zeus' house. Poseidon
also answered Themis' summons, coming from the sea
to join them. He sat in the middle of them all,
asking about Zeus' purposes:

              "Lord of bright lightning,
why have you called gods to this assembly?
Are you concerned for Trojans and Achaeans?
Right now their fight is close to flaring up   20
into a total war."

              Cloud-gatherer Zeus
then said to Poseidon in reply:

              "You understand, Earthshaker,

the plans here in my chest, the reasons why
I've summoned you. Yes, I am concerned for them.
Though they are being destroyed, I'll stay here,
sitting on a ridge of Mount Olympus.
From here I'll look on to my heart's content.
But all the rest of you can go away
to join Trojans and Achaeans, helping
either side, as your spirits each dictate.   30
For if we leave Achilles there alone
to fight the Trojans, they'll not hold out
against the swift-footed son of Peleus,
not even briefly. In earlier days,
if they saw him, their fear would make them shake,
and now his heart's so terribly enraged
for his companion, I fear he may go
beyond what Fate ordains and storm the walls."

With these words, Cronos' son then launched relentless war.
The gods charged off to battle, their hearts divided   40
in two groups. Hera went to the assembled ships,
with Pallas Athena and Poseidon, who shakes the earth.
Helper Hermes accompanied them as well, the god
with the most cunning mind of all. Hephaestus
also went along with them, exulting in his power.
Though he was lame, his feet moved quickly under him.
Ares with the shining helmet joined the Trojans,
taking with him long-haired Phoebus, archer Artemis,
Leto, Xanthus, and laughter-loving Aphrodite.

As long as the gods were far away from mortal men,   50
Achaeans won the glory, since Achilles
had come back, after staying away from war so long.
For every Trojan's limbs were seized with trembling fear
when they observed him there, swift son of Peleus
in that blazing armour, like man-killing Ares.
But once Olympians mingled in the crowds of soldiers,
then mighty Strife, who stirs men up in battle,
went into action, while Athena kept on shouting,
sometimes standing by the ditch they'd dug beyond the wall,

sometimes yelling out beside the roaring sea shore.
On the other side, like a black whirlwind, Ares
kept shouting out his piercing orders to the Trojans,
sometimes from the city heights, sometimes as he raced
along the banks of Simois to Callicolone.[1]
Thus, sacred gods spurred both sides on, urging them
to war, inciting cruel conflict. From on high,
the father of gods and men thundered ominously,
while Poseidon shook the vast earth under them
and lofty mountain crests. All the lower slopes of Ida,
with its many springs, trembled, as did the peaks, 70
the Trojan city, and Achaean ships. Under the earth,
the king of the dead, Aidoneus, was terrified.[2]
He leapt up from his throne afraid and shouting,
frightened that Earthshaker Poseidon would split up
the earth above him and reveal to gods and men
the dark and dreadful habitations of the dead,
which even gods detest, so massive was the shock
when gods collided in that war, with Poseidon
matched against Apollo with his feathered arrows,
glittery eyed Athena going against a mighty god, 80
Ares Enyalius, and Hera against Artemis,
with her golden arrows, goddess of the noisy hunt,
sister of Apollo, god who shoots from far away.
Strong Helper Hermes was opposed by Leto,
and Hephaestus by that huge and swirling river
the gods call Xanthus, but all men name Scamander.
So the gods went out to battle other gods.

But of all warriors in that fighting crowd, Achilles
was most eager to meet Hector, son of Priam.
His spirit urged him to glut Ares, warrior god 90
with the bull's hide shield, on Hector's blood, more so
than on the blood of any other man. But Apollo,
who inspires men to fight, sent out Aeneas
to confront the son of Peleus directly.
The god placed great force within him. Making his voice

[1]Callicolone (literally "fair mountain") is a location near Troy.
[2]Aidoneus is another name for Hades, god of the dead.

435

like Lycaon's, a son of Priam, Apollo,
Zeus' son, taking on that man's shape, spoke out:

> "Aeneas, Trojan counselor, where are now
> those threats you used to make to Trojan princes,
> as you drank your wine and promised them   100
> you'd fight Peleus' son, Achilles, man to man?"

Aeneas then said to Apollo in reply:

> "Son of Priam, why are you telling me
> to fight the arrogant son of Peleus,
> when I don't wish to? This isn't the first time
> swift Achilles and I have come to blows.
> Once before he chased me away from Ida
> with his spear—he'd come for our cattle,
> when he destroyed Lyrnessus and Pedasus.
> But then Zeus saved me—he gave me strength   110
> and made my legs run faster. Otherwise,
> Athena and Achilles would have killed me.
> She went on ahead of him to make things safe.
> Then she told him to kill off the Leleges
> with his bronze spear, as well as Trojans.
> No man can face Achilles in a fight—
> some god is constantly beside him, saving him
> and making sure his spear flies always straight,
> not stopping till it's hit some human flesh.
> If some god made sure our fight was equal,   120
> he'd not easily defeat me, even though
> he boasted he's completely made of bronze."

Apollo, son of Zeus, then said to Aeneas:

> "But, as a warrior, you, too, should pray
> to the immortal gods. For people say
> that Aphrodite, Zeus' daughter, bore you,
> while he comes from a lesser goddess.
> Your mother is great Zeus' daughter, but his
> a daughter of the Old Man of the Sea.

So go straight at him with your tireless bronze.   130
Don't let him hold you back with words,
expressing his contempt or making threats."

With these words, Apollo breathed great power then
into that shepherd of his people. Through the front lines
Aeneas strode, armed in gleaming bronze. As he moved,
going after Peleus' son among those crowds of men,
he did not go unnoticed. Seeing Anchises' son,
Hera gathered her companion gods and said:

       "Poseidon, Athena, both your hearts
should think about what's going on. Aeneas,   140
armed in gleaming bronze, is going to meet
the son of Peleus, at Apollo's urging.
So let's work to turn him back at once,
or else one of us should help Achilles,
give him great strength, so that his heart won't flinch.
And then he'll know the gods who love him
are the best of the immortals and those gods
who up to now have guarded Trojans
in this war's battles have only little power,
as feeble as the wind. We've all come here,   150
down from Olympus, to join this conflict,
so Achilles will not come to any harm
from Trojans, at least not in the fight today.
Later, he'll suffer everything which Fate
spun with her thread for him that very day
his mother bore him. But if Achilles
doesn't learn this from a god who speaks to him,
then he may be fearful if some god appears
against him in the battle. For the gods
are terrifying when they reveal themselves."   160

Earthshaker Poseidon then answered her:

                     "Hera,
don't let your rage defeat your common sense.
There's no need. For I have no desire
that gods should fight each other in this battle.

We should move off to one side and sit down
where we can watch, leaving this war to men.
But if Phoebus Apollo or if Ares
begins to fight or holds Achilles back,
not allowing him to go on fighting,
then we'll get in the conflict right away,   170
join in the battle. Soon enough, I think,
those two will remove themselves from warfare,
returning to Olympus, to the company
of other gods whom our strong hands have conquered."

With these words, the dark-haired god Poseidon led the way
to the remnants of the wall of godlike Hercules,
the high rampart Pallas Athena and the Trojans
had built for him, so he could protect himself
and escape that monster from the sea, when it forced him
to move in from the shore. Poseidon sat there,   180
beside the other gods, wrapping a concealing cloud
around their shoulders. The other group of gods
sat on the crest of Callicolone, around you,
archer Phoebus, and Ares, who destroys whole cities.
So these gods sat there on either side, making plans,
both groups holding back from fighting painful war.
Sitting high above them, Zeus stayed in control.

The whole plain by now was filled with men and horses,
all in gleaming bronze. The ground shook underfoot,
as men charged each other. Two of the finest men   190
then came at one another in the middle ground
between the armies, both prepared for combat—
Aeneas, Anchises' son, and godlike Achilles.
Aeneas strode out first, making threatening taunts,
his heavy helmet nodding as he moved around.
Holding his strong shield across his chest, he brandished
his bronze spear. The son of Peleus, from the other side,
charged up against him like a murderous lion
which a whole community is keen to slaughter.
At first, the beast moves on and leaves the group alone,   200
but when some quick young hunter hits it with a spear,

the lion gathers itself, opens its jaws wide,
foaming at the mouth, as its brave heart roars inside.
Its tail twitches to and fro against its ribs and flanks.
Then it drives itself to fight, charging straight ahead
with furiously glaring eyes to kill someone
or die there in the first attack. That's how Achilles,
driven by his furious proud heart, came on then
against the brave Aeneas. As they approached each other,
coming to close quarters, swift-footed Achilles yelled: 210

"Aeneas, why have you stepped forward,
standing here so far in front of all your men?
Does your heart prompt you to fight against me
in the hope you'll win Priam's royal honours
among horse-taming Trojans? If you kill me,
that won't make Priam put his regal power
in your hands. For he has his own sons.
Besides, he's healthy, and he is no fool.
Or have the Trojans given you some land
better than all the rest—a fine orchard,   220
as well as land to plough—yours to keep,
if you kill me? You'll find that hard to do.
My spear has sent you running once before.
Don't you remember? You were alone.
I chased you away from your own cattle.
You scampered off, down Mount Ida's slopes,
and quickly, too. That time we met, you ran
and never once looked back, then hid yourself
inside Lyrnessus. But I destroyed that city—
I attacked it with help from Athena,   230
as well as Father Zeus, seized their women
and took away their freedom. You were saved,
thanks to Zeus and other gods. But today,
I don't think he'll save you, as your heart hopes.
So I'm telling you to move back now,
retreat into the crowd. Don't stand against me,
or you'll come up against an evil time.
A man who doesn't face the facts is stupid."

Aeneas then said in response:

"Son of Peleus,
don't try to scare me off with words, as if   240
I were a child. I, too, know well enough
how to hand out threats and insults. We both know
each other's parents and our ancestry.
We've heard the famous tales of mortal men,
told long ago, though your eyes have not seen
my parents, nor mine yours. People say
you're noble Peleus' son, your mother
fair-haired Thetis, daughter of the sea.
Well, I claim I'm great Anchises' son,
and Aphrodite is my mother. Today,   250
one of them will mourn a dear dead son.
For I don't think that you and I will leave
without a fight, once we've exchanged
some childish conversation. But if you wish,
then listen to me, so you'll understand
my lineage well. Many people know it.
First cloud-gatherer Zeus fathered Dardanus,
who built Dardania, for sacred Ilion,
city of mortal men, was not yet built
here in the plain. His people settled there,   260
by the slopes of Ida with its many springs.
Dardanus, in turn, was father to a son,
king Erichthonius, and he became
the richest of all mortals, possessing
three thousand horses grazing in the fens,
all mares happy with their foals. Then North Wind
fell in love with them as they pastured there.
Taking on the form of a dark stallion,
he copulated with them. They conceived,
delivering twelve foals. When these foals played,   270
running across the fertile farmland, they'd skim
the highest ears of corn and never break them,
or they'd race across the sea's broad back,
gliding the surface of the breaking waves.
This Erichthonius had a son Tros,

440

who ruled the Trojans, and Tros then fathered
three outstanding sons—Ilus, Assaracus,
and godlike Ganymede, the handsomest man
among all mortal men, so beautiful,
gods kidnapped him and made him cup bearer   280
to Zeus himself, so he'd live among immortals.
Ilus had a noble son, Laomedon,
who fathered Priam and Tithonus,
Clytius and warlike Hicataon.
Assaracus fathered his son Capys,
who had Anchises. He is my father.
Priam's son is godlike Hector. That, then,
is my ancestry, the blood I boast of.
But as for courage, well, that's up to Zeus,
who makes it less or greater as he wills,   290
for he's the mightiest one of all. But come,
let's no longer talk this way, like little boys
standing in the middle of a battle.
Both of us have insults we could utter,
lots of them, so many that a cargo ship
with a hundred oars could not take on the load.
Men's tongues are glib, with various languages—
words can go here and there in all directions,
and the sorts of words one speaks will be
the sorts of words one has to listen to.   300
But what's the point? Why should the two of us
be squabbling here and fight by trading insults
back and forth, like two irritated women,
who, in some heart-wrenching raging spat,
go out into the street to scream at one another
with facts and lies, each one gripped by anger.
I want to fight—your words won't send me off,
not before we've fought it out with bronze,
man to man. So come. Let's start this now
and test each other with our bronze-tipped spears."   310

Aeneas finished. Then he threw his heavy spear
at Achilles' wondrous, dreadful shield. As it hit,
the spear point made the shield ring out. Peleus' son
held the shield away from him in his big fist,

441

fearing the long-shadowed spear from brave Aeneas
would easily go through. That was a foolish thought!
His heart and mind were not aware that gifts like that,
splendid presents from the gods to mortal men,
are not so easily defeated, nor do they fail.
So the mighty spear of warrior Aeneas   320
did not break the shield, stopped by the golden armour,
a present from the god. It drove on through two layers,
but there were still three more, for crippled god Hephaestus
had hammered out five layers, two made of bronze,
two inner ones of tin, with a gold one in between.
The gold one stopped that ash spear from Aeneas.
Then Achilles, in his turn, hurled his long-shadowed spear,
hitting Aeneas' round shield right on the rim,
where bronze and leather backing were the thinnest.
The spear of Pelian ash drove straight through the shield,   330
which rattled from the blow. Aeneas cowered down,
holding the shield out away from him in terror.
The spear flew high, above his back, then drove itself
into the ground. But it ripped apart two layers
on that protective shield. Having escaped the spear,
Aeneas straightened up, eyes glazed with shock,
frightened that the spear had come so close to him.
Drawing his sword, Achilles launched a frenzied charge
with a blood-curdling scream. Aeneas picked up a rock,
a heavy lift, which no two men now alive could do,   340
although he managed it with ease all by himself.
With that rock Aeneas would have struck Achilles,
as he charged at him, on his helmet or the shield
which had rescued him from death, and then Achilles
in close combat with his sword would have taken
Aeneas' life, had not the Earthshaker Poseidon
been paying attention. He spoke up immediately,
addressing the immortal gods beside him.

     "Here's trouble. I feel sorry for Aeneas,
     who'll be going down to Hades quickly,   350
     slain by Peleus' son, because Apollo,
     the far shooter, talked him into it, the fool!

Apollo won't protect him from grim death.
But why should an innocent man like him
suffer such misfortune, without doing wrong,
just because of other people's troubles?
With all his gifts, he's bringing pleasure
to the gods who live in spacious heaven.
So come, let's carry him away from death,
in case the son of Cronos grows enraged,   360
if he's killed by Achilles. For Fate ordains
that he'll escape, so the Dardanian race
will not die out and leave no seed alive.
For the son of Cronos did love Dardanus
above all other children born to him
from mortal women, though he's come to hate
the family of Priam. So now Trojans
will be ruled by powerful Aeneas,
his children's children born in years to come."

Ox-eyed queen Hera then said to Poseidon: 370

"Earthshaker, in your own heart and mind
you must decide whether to save Aeneas,
or to leave him, for all his nobleness,
to be killed by Peleus' son, Achilles.
We two, Pallas Athena and myself,
have often sworn among immortals
not to rescue Trojans from wretched death,
not even when all Troy is being engulfed
in all-consuming, blazing fire, set off
by Achaea's warrior sons."

                    Hearing her words,   380
Earthshaker Poseidon went down into the battle,
among the flying spears and came right to the place
where Aeneas stood with glorious Achilles.
At once he cast a dense mist on Achilles' eyes,
pulled the ash spear of Peleus' son out of the shield
of brave Aeneas and set it at Achilles' feet.
Poseidon then raised Aeneas up, swinging him

far above the ground. Aeneas soared high up,
above the many ranks of warriors and chariots,
flying from Poseidon's hand, and then came down   390
on the fringes of that battle, where the Caucones
were arming for the fight. Then Earthshaker Poseidon,
coming up beside Aeneas, spoke to him—
his words had wings:

                                        "Aeneas,
        what god brought on such foolishness in you—
        fighting man to man with proud Achilles,
        a stronger man and more loved by the gods?
        When you run into him, you must move back,
        or you'll end up in Hades' house, contravening
        what destiny ordains. But when Achilles   400
        has met his fate and died, then you may fight
        in full confidence among those at the front,
        for of all Achaeans no one else will kill you."

With these words, Poseidon left, once he'd explained
these matters to Aeneas. Then he removed
the wondrous mist over Achilles' eyes. He looked out,
testing his eyesight, and spoke to his great heart,
passionately confused:

                                "What's happening?
        My eyes are playing amazing tricks on me.
        I see my spear lying here upon the ground,   410
        but I don't see the man I threw it at
        in my eagerness to kill him. Aeneas
        must be really dear to the immortal gods,
        though I thought those things he boasted of
        were merely idle talk. Well, let him go.
        He'll have no heart to try me once again.
        He'll be delighted to escape being killed.
        Come, I'll give a shout to these Danaans
        to fight more Trojans—put them to the test."

Achilles finished. Then he leapt in among the ranks,   420 calling each man:

"Don't just stand there any more,
you fine Achaeans—don't stay away from Trojans.
Let each of you go up against your man
in full warrior fury. It's hard for me,
though I'm a powerful man, to attack
so many men and battle with them all.
Even deathless gods like Ares and Athena
could not fight them in the jaws of war
in such a conflict and keep on going.
But what I can do with my hands and feet   430
and my own power, I'll do. I'll not hold back,
but go straight at their lines. I don't think
a Trojan who gets within my spear range
will have reason to feel happy."

With these words,
Achilles urged them on. Then splendid Hector,
calling with a shout, announced that he'd come forward
to confront Achilles.

"You proud-hearted Trojans,
don't be afraid of that son of Peleus.
I, too, can battle anyone with words,
even the immortals. But with a spear,   440
that's more difficult—they're so much stronger.
Achilles won't accomplish everything
he says he will. Some of it he'll manage,
some he'll leave undone. I'll go against him,
though his blazing hands are like a fire,
his strength like glittering iron."

With these words
he roused them into action. Trojans held their spears up high,
then turned to face Achaeans. Both sides joined battle
in a terrific frenzy. Then Phoebus Apollo,
moving close to Hector, spoke to him:

445

"Hector,   450
don't step out to face Achilles openly.
Wait for him in the noisy crowd of men.
Don't let him hit you with his spear or slash you
at close quarters with his sword."

                          Apollo spoke.
Hector pulled back into the crowd of soldiers,
seized with fear at hearing a god's voice talk to him.
Giving a blood-curdling scream, Achilles leapt
among the Trojans, his heart wrapped in battle fury.
First he killed Iphition, Otrynteus' brave son,
who commanded many men. A Naiad nymph bore him   460
to Otrynteus, sacker of cities, in Hyde,
a fertile land, below snow-covered Mount Tmolus.
As he charged right at him, godlike Achilles
struck Iphition with his spear squarely in the head,
splitting his skull apart. He fell with a crash.
Godlike Achilles then cried out in triumph:

          "Lie there, son of Otrynteus, of all men
          the one we fear the most. Here you die.
          You were born beside the Gygaean lake,
          on your father's land, by the fish-filled Hyllus   470
          and the swirling Hermus rivers."

Achilles triumphed. But down on Iphition's eyes
the darkness fell, and then, in the first attack,
Achaean wheel rims on the chariots ripped him up.
After him, Achilles went for Demoleon,
Antenor's son, a brave defensive fighter,
hitting the bronze cheek armour on his helmet.
But that didn't check the spear—it smashed through,
breaking his skull, splattering all his brains inside.
That stopped his fighting charge. Then Hippodamas   480
jumped down out of his chariot to flee Achilles.
But Achilles speared him in the back. As he died,
panting his life away, he screamed—just as a bull roars,
when it's pulled around the altar of Poseidon,

lord of Helice, the Earthshaker, who delights
in those young lads who drag the beast—in just that way
Hippodamas bellowed then, as his noble spirit
slipped out from his bones. Then Achilles with his spear
attacked noble Polydorus, son of Priam.
His father would not let Polydorus fight,   490
for of all his children he was the youngest born,
the one most loved. He was the fastest runner, too.
Now, like a fool, he was showing off his speed,
sprinting through front lines until he lost his life.
As he ran past, swift-footed godlike Achilles
threw his spear into the middle of his back,
where the golden belt clasps joined together
on the overlapping body armour. The spear point,
going straight through, came out his navel. With a scream,
he fell onto his knees. Then black cloud enveloped him.   500
As he collapsed, his guts spilled out into his hands.

When Hector saw his brother Polydorus there,
down on the ground, collapsed and holding his own entrails,
a mist flowed right across his eyes. He could no longer
bear to keep his distance. He moved against Achilles,
waving his sharp spear, just like a flame. Achilles,
when he saw him, jumped out and roared in triumph:

> "He's getting closer—the very man
> who scarred my heart more than all other men.
> We won't be evading one another   510
> in the battle lanes much longer."

As he said this, Achilles scowled at godlike Hector,
then yelled at him:

> "Come closer,
> so you can meet your fatal doom more quickly."

Hector of the shining helmet, quite unafraid,
then cried out to Achilles:

"Son of Peleus,
don't try to frighten me with words, as if
I were some child. I, too, know well enough
how to shout out taunting words and insults.
I know you're brave, stronger than me by far.   520
But these things are in the lap of the gods.
Though I'm the weaker man, I'll take your life,
with one throw of my spear, for in the past
it's proved it's sharp enough."

                              With these words,
Hector raised his spear and threw it. But Athena,
with the slightest puff of breath, blew it aside,
away from glorious Achilles, turning it back
to godlike Hector. It landed there beside his feet.
Then, with a terrifying shout, Achilles charged,
lusting to kill. But Apollo snatched up Hector,   530
something a god can do with ease, then hid him
in thick cloud. Swift-footed, godlike Achilles
charged that cloud three times, striking hard each time
with his bronze spear. When for the fourth time
he came on like a god with a terrific shout,
Achilles cried out these winged words to Hector:

          "You dog—once more you're evading death for now.
          But you've narrowly escaped disaster.
          Phoebus Apollo has saved you one more time.
          No doubt you always pray to him as you go   540
          out into the sound of thudding spears.
          Next time we meet, I'll surely finish you,
          if some god is there to assist me, too.
          For now I'll fight the others, any man
          I chance to meet."

                              Achilles finished shouting.
Then he struck Dryops with his spear right in the neck.
Dryops fell at Achilles' feet. But he left him there.
Next, Achilles stopped Demouchus, Philetor's son,
a big brave warrior, with a spear thrust in his knee.

Then he hit him with his massive sword, taking his life.   550
After that, he went at Dardanus and Laogonus,
both sons of Bias, throwing them out of their chariot
onto the ground. He hit one of them with his spear
and slashed the other at close quarters with his sword.

Then Tros, Alastor's son, fell at Achilles knees,
clutching them, begging him to spare his life,
to capture him alive, instead of killing him,
moved by pity for a man the same age as himself.
What a fool! He did not know there was no way
to change Achilles' mind—he was not a tender man   560
with a soft heart, but full of fighting rage. With his hands
Tros tried to clutch Achilles' knees, desperate
to plead for mercy, but Achilles' sword struck him
in his liver, which slid out from the wound.
Black blood, pouring from the gash, filled up his lap.
Then darkness veiled his eyes, and his spirit left him.

Next, Achilles moved up to Mulius and with his spear
struck him on the ear. The bronze point, driven in hard,
came out his other ear. Then he hit Echeclus,
Agenor's son, with his hilted sword right on his head.   570
The blood made the whole blade hot. Then dark death,
his powerful fate, came down across his eyes.
Next, Achilles hit Deucalion—his bronze spear point
struck him in the arm where tendons meet the elbow.
His arm now useless, Deucalion stood there waiting,
staring death right in the face. Achilles hit him
with his sword blade in the neck, slicing off his head.
He knocked the head and the helmet far away.
From Deucalion's spine the marrow spurted out,
as his body lay there, stretched out on the ground.   580
Next, Achilles, after chasing the noble son of Peires,
Rhigmus, who'd come from fertile Thrace, hit him
with a spear throw in the gut, fixing the bronze
firmly in his belly. Rhigmus fell from his chariot.
His attendant, Areithous, wheeled the horses round,
but Achilles' sharp spear struck him in the back

and threw him from the chariot. The horses bolted.

Just as a terrifying fire rages through deep woods
on a parched mountain, burning dense stands of trees,
as the driving wind blows flames to every spot,   590
that how Achilles, like a god, raged with his spear,
attacking and killing men all through the fight.
The dark earth ran with blood. Just as a man yokes oxen,
big bulls, wide in the shoulder, to grind barley
on a well-built threshing floor, and lowing oxen
quickly flatten all the grain, that how brave Achilles
drove his sure-footed horses to trample on the dead
and on their shields as well. The chariot axle underneath
got sprayed with blood. Blood soaked the chariot rails,
thrown up in gouts from horses' hooves and wheel rims.   600
But Peleus' son pushed on to win more glory,
blood spattered over his all-conquering hands.

Book Twenty-One
Achilles Fights the River

[Achilles attacks the Trojans hiding in the river Xanthus (also called
Scamander); takes twelve young men alive to sacrifice for Patroclus;
Achilles meets Lycaon, who begs for mercy; Achilles replies and then
kills Lycaon; Achilles fights and kills Asteropaeus, then slaughters many
Paeonian leaders; the river objects to the slaughter; the river rises against
Achilles, who appeals to the gods for help; Hera tells Hephaestus to fight
the river; Hephaestus launches his fire against the flooding river; the river
gives up, so Hephaestus withdraws his fire; the gods begin to war against
each other; Athena fights Ares and then Aphrodite; Poseidon offers to
fight Apollo, who declines; Hera and Artemis fight; Apollo moves into
Ilion; Apollo deceives Achilles, enabling many Trojans to reach the city]

When the Trojans reached the ford across the Xanthus,
lovely swirling river born of immortal Zeus,
Achilles split them in two groups, chasing one
across the plain towards the city, where the previous day
Achaeans had fled in terror, when glorious Hector
had prevailed. Some Trojans fled back there in panic.
Hera sent fog in front of them to slow them down.
But half the Trojans were crammed in along the river,
trapped by its deep currents and its silver eddies.
They fell in there, making a huge commotion.   10
The noise roared down along the rushing river banks
amplifying the din. Men thrashed around, back and forth,
as they were sucked down in the current screaming.
Just as fire drives flights of locusts to seek refuge
in some river, when the tireless flames attack them
in a sudden onrush and they sink below the water—
that's how, faced with Achilles' attacking charge,
a confused mass of chariots and men filled up
the deep and swirling waters of the river Xanthus.

Then divinely born Achilles left his spear   20
beside a tamarisk bush and jumped into the stream,
like an inhuman thing, armed only with his sword,
his heart intent on killing. Turning in all directions,

he kept on striking. The men his sword slaughtered
cried out in terror. The water turned blood red.
Just as other fish swim off from a huge dolphin
filling safe corners of some sheltered harbour,
fearful because the beast eats all it captures—
that's how Trojans huddled then, under hanging banks,
all along the stream edge of that murderous river.   30
When Achilles' arms grew weary from the killing,
he plucked out of the river twelve young men alive,
as blood payment for the killing of Patroclus,
Menoetius' son. He led them up onto dry land,
like stupefied fawns, tied their hands behind them,
using belts they wore around their woven tunics,
and gave them to his men to lead back to the ships.
Then he jumped in again, eager to keep killing.

But then Achilles met someone fleeing the river—
Lycaon, a son of Dardanian Priam,   40
whom he'd captured once before in a night attack,
taking him against his will from his father's orchard.
With his sharp bronze Lycaon had been cutting
young shoots from off a fig tree to make chariot rails.
He'd had the bad luck to meet godlike Achilles.
That time, Achilles took him in his ship and sold him
in well-built Lemnos, where the son of Jason
had paid the purchase price. From there, Eëtion,
a friend and guest from Imbros, had ransomed Lycaon,
paying a huge sum, then sent him on to Arisbe.   50
He'd escaped from there in secret and gone home,
back to his father's house. Once he returned from Lemnos,
for eleven days his heart enjoyed his friends.
On the twelfth, some god threw him back again
into Achilles' hands, who was about to ship him,
against Lycaon's wishes, down to dwell with Hades.
When swift-footed, godlike Achilles saw Lycaon
totally unarmed, without his helmet, shield, or spear—
for he'd thrown these on the ground, exhausted
after he'd escaped the river, worn out and sweating   60
in all his lower limbs—Achilles, much surprised,

452

spoke to his own courageous heart:

"What's this?
My eyes are witnessing something amazing.
Great-hearted Trojans I've just slaughtered
will rise again, up out of murky darkness,
if this man's avoided death, returned like this,
after I'd sold him off in sacred Lemnos.
The gray sea, which holds many people back
against their will, hasn't seemed to stop him.
But come, let him taste my spear point. I'll see—   70
and in my heart confirm—if he'll return,
as he's just done, or if life-giving earth,
which keeps even strong men down, will hold him."

That's what Achilles thought, as he stood there waiting.
Lycaon, dazed with fear, approached Achilles,
eager to clasp his knees in supplication,
heart desperate to escape dark fate and evil death.
Godlike Achilles raised his long spear, prepared to strike.
But Lycaon, stooping down, slipped underneath the spear,
then clasped Achilles' knees. Flying above his back,   80
the spear stuck in the ground, hungry for human flesh.
With one hand, Lycaon grabbed Achilles' knee.
His other clutched the spear, refusing to let go.
He begged for mercy, addressing Achilles
with these winged words:

"By your knees, Achilles,
I beg you to respect me as a suppliant.
Have pity on me. I claim that sacred right,
my lord, because it was at your table
I first ate Demeter's grain the very day
you seized me in that well-built orchard.   90
You led me far from father and my friends,
then sold me off in sacred Lemnos. For me
you got the value of a hundred oxen,
but I was ransomed for three times that price.
It's now twelve days since I reached Ilion,

after my ordeal. Once more, deadly Fate
has placed me in your hands. I do believe
Father Zeus must hate me, to give me to you
for a second time. My mother, Laothoë,
daughter of old Altes, gave birth to me   100
to live a shortened life. Altes rules over
war-loving Leleges, in steep Pedasus,
by the river Satnioeis. His daughter
married Priam, who has many other wives.
She had two sons. Now you'll have slaughtered both.
You killed fine Polydorus with those men
fighting at the front, when your sharp spear
sent him to die. Now death comes for me, as well.
I don't expect to escape your hands this time,
since some god has guided me right to them.   110
But I'll say one more thing—take it to heart—
don't kill me. I'm not from the same womb
as Hector, the man who killed your comrade,
that kind and powerful warrior."

So Lycaon begged for mercy from Achilles.
But the response he got was brutal:

                              "You fool,
don't offer me a ransom or some plea.
Before Patroclus met his deadly fate,
sparing Trojans pleased my heart much more.
I took many overseas and sold them.   120
But now not one of them escapes his death,
no one whom god delivers to my hands,
here in front of Ilion, not one—
not a single Trojan, especially none
of Priam's children. So now, my friend,
you too must die. Why be sad about it?
Patroclus died, a better man than you.
And look at me. You see how fine I am,
how tall, how handsome? My father's a fine man,
the mother who gave birth to me a goddess.   130
Yet over me, as well, hangs Fate—my death.

There'll come a dawn, or noon, or evening,
when some man will take my life in battle—
he'll strike me with his spear or with an arrow
shot from his bowstring."

                                    Achilles finished.
Then Lycaon's knees gave way, his heart collapsed.
He let go of the spear and crouched there, both his hands
stretched out. Achilles pulled out his sharp sword and struck,
hitting him on the collar bone, beside his neck.
The whole two-edged blade sliced into him. Lycaon fell,   140
lying face down on the earth. His dark blood flowed out
and soaked the ground. Achilles seized him by the foot,
then flung him in the river, shouting out in triumph—
his words had wings:

                                    "Lie there, among the fish.
They'll lick blood from your wound with no respect.
Your mother won't set you on your funeral bed,
lamenting over you. No, Scamander,
the swirling river, will carry you away
to the broad lap of the sea. Many fish
will swim up to the darkly rippled surface   150
to eat white fat from Lycaon. So die,
all you fleeing Trojans, until we reach
that sacred city Ilion, with me there,
right behind you, fighting and killing you.
Your flowing river with its silver eddies
won't help, for all those bulls you've sacrificed
all these years, all the sure-footed horses
you've thrown alive into its swirling pools.
No matter—you'll suffer an evil fate,
till every one of you has paid in full   160
for Patroclus' death, for Achaea's dead,
the men you slaughtered by our swift ships,
when I was not among them there."

Achilles' words enraged the heart in river Xanthus,
who wondered how he might stop godlike Achilles

from his slaughter and protect the Trojans from disaster.
Meanwhile, Peleus' son, gripping his long-shadowed spear,
still eager to kill more, charged Asteropaeus,
son of Pelegon, born to the broad river Axius
and Acessamenus' eldest daughter, Periboea. 170
The deep swirling river had had sex with her.
Achilles went at Asteropaeus, who stood there,
facing him, holding two spears. In his anger
at the slaughter of young soldiers in the battle,
whom Achilles kept butchering along the stream,
showing no pity, Xanthus then put fighting strength
into Asteropaeus. But when the two men
had approached each other, moving close together,
godlike Achilles was the first to speak:

> "Who are you that dares to come against me? 180
> Where are you from? Children who confront me
> leave their parents full of sorrow."

The glorious son of Pelegon then said in reply:

> "Great-hearted son of Peleus, why ask me
> my lineage? I come from Paeonia,
> a fertile country far from here, leading
> Paeonians, men carrying long spears.
> It's now eleven days since I came here,
> to Ilion. I'm born from Axius,
> the wide-streaming river, whose waters 190
> are the loveliest which flow upon this earth.
> Axius fathered a famous spear man,
> Pelegon, whose son they say I am.
> But now, splendid Achilles, let us fight."

In response to that speech from Asteropaeus,
godlike Achilles raised his Pelian ash spear.
But then Asteropaeus, an ambidextrous man,
threw two spears at once. One hit Achilles' shield,
but did not break through. The gold, gift of a god,
had checked it. The other hit Achilles a glancing blow 200

on his right arm at the elbow. Dark blood flowed out.
But the spear passed over him and struck the ground,
still eager to taste flesh. Then Achilles, in his turn,
threw a straight-flying spear at Asteropaeus,
hoping to kill him. But he missed the man, hitting
the high river bank, driving half that ash spear
deep in the ground. Drawing the sharp sword by his thigh,
Peleus' son, enraged, went after Asteropaeus,
who was trying to pull the spear Achilles threw
out of the river bank with his huge fist. He failed.   210
Three times he shifted it in his frantic haste to grab it,
but three times he had to abandon the attempt.
The fourth time his heart was keen to bend and break
the ash spear of Achilles, but before he could,
Achilles himself charged in and took his life
with a sword thrust in the belly by the navel.
His guts fell out onto the ground. As he lay gasping,
darkness veiled his eyes. Jumping on his chest,
Achilles stripped his armour off, boasting aloud:

> "Lie there. It's hard to compete with children   220
> of the mighty son of Cronos, even though
> you are descended from some river. You claim
> your family stems from a broad flowing stream,
> but I boast a family coming from great Zeus.
> The man who is my father, Peleus,
> son of Aeacus, rules many Myrmidons.
> Aeacus came from Zeus himself, and Zeus
> is stronger than rivers flowing to the sea,
> so Zeus' line is stronger than all those
> descended from a river. Look beside you—   230
> there's a great stream there, but he can't help you.
> For there's no way to battle against Zeus,
> son of Cronos. Even lord Achelous
> cannot equal him, nor the great power
> of deep flowing Oceanus, from whom
> all rivers, seas, fountains, and deep wells
> derive their water—even Oceanus
> is afraid of lighting from great Zeus

and his thunder when it crashes in the skies."

Saying this, he pulled his bronze spear from the river bank. 240
Achilles left the corpse of Asteropaeus
lying there in the sand, dark water lapping round him.
Fish and eels then went at him, nibbling and chewing off
the fat around his kidneys. Achilles moved away,
attacking the Paeonian charioteers still crouched
beside the flowing river, terrified once they'd seen
their best man butchered in that desperate conflict
on the powerful sword of the son of Peleus.
There Achilles killed Thersilochus, Mydon,
Astypylus, Mnesus, Thrasius, Aenius, 250
and Ophelestes. Swift Achilles would have killed
still more Paeonians, but the deep-flowing river,
in its anger, taking on a human form, called out,
speaking from a deep swirling pool:

                                        "Achilles,
            you may be the most powerful of men,
            but you're inflicting too much damage here.
            Yes, the gods are always there to help you.
            And if Cronos' son is now enabling you
            to kill all Trojans, at least drive them off
            far from my stream. Carry out your work— 260
            this butchery—out there on the plain.
            Now corpses fill my channels, I can't let
            my waters flow through anywhere to reach
            the glimmering sea. I'm choking on the dead,
            while you keep up these harsh atrocities.
            Come, you leader of your people, let me be.
            I find your actions here astounding."

                                    In reply,
swift-footed Achilles then addressed the river:

            "Divinely raised Scamander, it shall be
            as you request. But I'll not stop killing 270
            these proud Trojans till I have them cornered

458

in their city and have tested Hector
in a fight, and he kills me or I kill him."

Saying this, Achilles fell upon the Trojans,
like something superhuman. Then Scamander,
the deep-flowing river, cried out to Apollo:

"What's happening, lord of the silver bow,
child of Zeus? You're not following Zeus' plans.
He clearly told you to assist the Trojans,
to defend them until evening comes,   280
casting its shadows on the fertile farm land."

The river spoke. Then famous spearman Achilles
jumped from the bank into the middle of the stream.
The river attacked him with a rising flood,
stirring all his waters into seething turmoil,
sweeping up many corpses crowded in the shoals,
men slaughtered by Achilles. Roaring like a bull,
the river hurled these bodies up onto the shore,
preserving in its lovely stream those still alive
by hiding them in deep wide pools. Around Achilles,   290
huge waves towered threateningly, beating down
his shield. The breaking waters pushed him backwards.
Achilles lost his footing. His hand reached out to grab
a large elm tree, fully grown, but the tree came loose,
roots and all, tearing the whole river bank away.
As it fell in the river, its thick branches blocked
that lovely stream, damming its flow. In terror,
Achilles scrambled up out of the raging waters,
trying on his swift feet to run out to the plain.
But the great god wasn't done. With a dark wave,   300
he went after godlike Achilles, to prevent
the killing and to rescue Trojans from destruction.
Peleus' son ran off as far as one spear throw,
moving as fast as a black eagle plummets,
the hunting bird which is the strongest and the fastest
of all flying things—that's how Achilles ran.
The bronze armour on his chest was clanging fearfully

as he swerved out from underneath the flooding river,
desperate to escape. But with a tremendous roar,
Scamander's flood rushed on in pursuit behind him. 310
Just as a man laying out a ditch from a dark spring
to his plants and gardens digs a water channel,
mattock in hand, removing what obstructs the flow,
and the water, as it starts to run, pushes aside
the pebbles, and then, gaining momentum, flows down
and overtakes the man who's guiding it—
that's how the flooding wave kept clutching at Achilles
for all his speed, since gods have much more strength than men.
Every time swift-footed, godlike Achilles
tried stopping to fight back, to see if all the gods 320
who live in spacious heaven were forcing him to flee,
a tremendous wave from that heaven-fed river
would crash down around his shoulders. He'd jump clear,
heart panicking, but the river kept tugging at his legs
with a strong undertow, washing out the ground
beneath his feet. Then gazing up into the wide sky
the son of Peleus cried out:

                  "Father Zeus,
why is no god standing by me here,
in this pitiful state, rescuing me
from this river? After this, I can endure 330
everything. I don't blame any Olympian
as much as I blame my own dear mother,
who led me astray with lies, telling me
I'd die from the swift arrows of Apollo,
under Trojan walls and fully armed.
Now I wish that I'd been killed by Hector,
the best man of those native to this region.
Then a fine man would have done the killing,
another fine man would have been destroyed.
But now it's been ordained that I'm to suffer 340
an ignoble death, caught by this great river,
like some child in care of pigs, swept away
while trying to cross a torrent in a rain storm."

Achilles spoke. Then Poseidon and Pallas Athena,
coming up quickly, stood in human form beside him.
They joined their hands with his, and with their words
they pledged their help. Poseidon spoke out first:

                              "Son of Peleus,
don't be so afraid. You need have no fear.
We two come from the gods, here to help you—
me and Pallas Athena, and Zeus approves.   350
It's not ordained that you're to die here,
killed by some river, which will soon recede,
as you will see. We have advice for you,
if you'll listen. Don't hold back your hands
in murderous warfare till you've cornered
inside the famous walls of Troy those men
now in retreat before you. Once you've taken
Hector's life, return back to the ships.
We giving you a chance for glory."

With these words, the two gods went away. Achilles,   360
greatly moved by what the gods had said, set off,
running across the plain, now full of flooding water,
with many lovely weapons of the slaughtered men
floating there among their corpses. As he went,
he raised his legs high, striving against the current.
The broad flowing river couldn't slow him down,
once Athena had put great power in Achilles.

But Scamander did not hold his fury back,
growing even more enraged at Peleus' son.
He raised himself up in a high-crested wave   370
and called out with a shout to Simoeis:

                              "Dear brother,
let's both together counter this man's power,
since he'll soon demolish Priam's city.
Trojans will not stand up to him and fight.
Come quickly. Help me. Fill your streams
with water from your springs. Whip up your torrents.

Then stand in a huge wave, raising a din
with rocks and tree trunks, so we can stop
this violent man, now in a conquering rage,
like some god. I don't think his strength will help him,   380
or his beauty, or that lovely armour—
that will lie somewhere underneath the flood,
buried in slime. I'll cover him in sand,
with an massive layer of silt on top,
beyond all measurement. I'll hide him there
with so much mud, Achaeans will not know
how to collect his bones. There where he'll lie,
I'll make him a tomb—he won't need a mound
when Achaeans organize his funeral."

Saying this, Scamander crested high against Achilles,   390
then charged, seething with foam and blood and corpses.
The dark wave of the heaven-fed river rose, towering
above Achilles, about to overwhelm him.
But Hera, afraid for Achilles, cried out, fearing
the great, deep, swirling river would sweep him off.
She called out to Hephaestus, her dear son:

                                  "Rouse yourself,
        my crippled child. We think that you're a match
        for swirling Xanthus in a fight. Come quickly.
        Help Achilles with a giant outburst
        of your flames. I'll stir up some winds—   400
        West Wind's harsh sea blasts and white South Wind—
        to whip on your destructive fires, so they may burn
        dead Trojans and their weapons. You must go
        along the river banks, burning trees,
        attacking river Xanthus with your flames.
        Don't let him slow you down in any way,
        not with gentle words or making threats.
        Don't check your fury till I tell you to.
        I'll give you a shout. Then you can pull back
        your inexhaustible fire."

                        Hera spoke.   410

462

Hephaestus then prepared a prodigious blaze.
First it burned up all the plain, incinerating corpses,
the many bodies of men slaughtered by Achilles
scattered everywhere. The entire plain dried up.
The shimmering river waters were held back.
Just as at harvest time North Wind quickly dries
well-watered orchards, to the farmer's great delight,
that's how the whole plain then grew dry, as Hephaestus
burned up the dead. Then he turned his blazing flames
against the river, burning elms, willows, tamarisks,   420
clover, rushes, sedge, all growing in abundance
along that lovely stream. In the river pools,
eels and fish were much distressed—they jumped everywhere
in that fine river, suffering the fiery blasts
prepared by that resourceful god Hephaestus.
The river, too, was burned. So Xanthus cried out,
calling to the god:

                         "No god, Hephaestus,
          can stand against you. I can't fight you
          when you burn with flames like this. So stop.
          End this strife. Godlike Achilles can continue.   430
          Let him drive the Trojans from their city.
          What do I care about assisting in this war?"

The river spoke, still burning from the fire,
his lovely waters seething. Just as a cauldron
with hot flames heating it boils inside and melts
the fat from off a well-fed hog, bubbling over,
once dry split wood is set down under it—that's how
the fire burned that lovely stream. Its seething waters
would no longer flow down river, held up there,
defeated by the power of that fiery blast   440
made by the skill of god Hephaestus. Then the river,
with a strong appeal to Hera, spoke these winged words:

          "Hera, why's your son burning up my stream,
          doing it more injury than any other?
          I'm not as much to blame as all the rest,

the ones who help the Trojans. If you say so,
I'll stop, if Hephaestus stops as well.
And I'll swear this oath—never again will I
protect a Trojan from his evil death,
not even when all Troy itself is burning,   450
ablaze with all-consuming fire, started
by Achaea's warlike sons."

     White-armed goddess Hera,
as soon as she'd heard this, spoke to Hephaestus,
her dear son:

    "Hold off, Hephaestus, splendid child.
It's not right to hurt a deathless god like this,
just for the sake of mortal men."

       When Hera spoke,
Hephaestus extinguished his stupendous fire at once.
The river's stream flowed once more in its channel.
When the fighting spirit in Xanthus had been broken,
the two gods fought no longer. Hera had stopped them,   460
though she was still enraged. But now the other gods
began a heavy conflict and a cruel fight
among themselves. The spirits in their hearts
pushed them in various directions. As they clashed,
with a tremendous din, the wide earth cried out,
and mighty heaven pealed, just like a trumpet.
Sitting on Olympus, Zeus heard the sound—his heart
laughed with delight to see these gods go at it
in mutual conflict. They no longer stood aloof.
Shield-breaker Ares started it, attacking   470
Athena first with his bronze spear, taunting her:

    "You dog fly, why is it you're once again
inciting gods to fight each other,
heart prompted by your own foolhardiness?
Don't you recall the moment you provoked
Diomedes, Tydeus' son, to wound me?
We all saw it—you grabbed his spear yourself

and drove it at me, scratching my fair skin.
Well, now I think you'll pay for all you've done."

Saying this, Ares struck Athena's tasseled aegis, 480
that fearful aegis which not even Zeus' lightning
can overcome. Bloodstained Ares' long spear struck it.
Drawing back, Athena picked up in her strong hand
a large, black, jagged rock, lying there on the plain.
In earlier ages men had set it there to indicate
the boundary of a field. With this rock Athena
struck raging Ares in the neck. His legs collapsed.
Ares fell. Stretched out he covered seven hundred feet.
His hair was dirtied with the dust. His armour rang.
Pallas Athena laughed, then cried in boastful triumph— 490
her words had wings:

> "You fool, still so ignorant
> of how much stronger I can claim to be
> than you, when you seek to match my power.
> This is the way you'll answer now in full
> your mother's vengeful rage. She's angry,
> planning nasty things for you, since you left
> Achaeans to support the arrogant Trojans."

With these words, she turned her glittering eyes away.
Zeus' daughter Aphrodite then took Ares
and led him off by hand, as he kept groaning— 500
he found it difficult to get his spirit back.
When white-armed goddess Hera saw Athena,
she spoke, addressing her with these winged words:

> "Look there, child of aegis-bearing Zeus,
> you tireless one, that dog fly once again
> is leading man-killing Ares through the crowd,
> away from battle. Go after her."

Once Hera spoke, Athena dashed off in pursuit,
delighted in her heart. Charging Aphrodite,
she struck her in the chest with her powerful fist. 510

465

Aphrodite's knees gave way, her heart collapsed.
So both gods lay there, on the all-nourishing earth.
Athena then spoke out winged words of triumph:

>"Let all those who assist the Trojans
>end up like this in warfare with Achaeans,
>with all the fortitude and boldness
>Aphrodite showed in helping Ares,
>standing up against my fighting power.
>We'll then soon end these hostile fights,
>once we've destroyed well-peopled Ilion."   520

As Athena spoke, white-armed goddess Hera smiled.
Then the mighty Earthshaker spoke to Apollo:

>"Phoebus, why do we two stand aloof?
>That's not right, now that others have begun.
>It would be shameful if we both went back
>to Olympus, to Zeus' bronze-floored home,
>without a fight. Since you're the younger one,
>you must begin. It's not fair play if I do,
>since I'm your elder and I thus know more.
>How foolish you are with your thoughtless heart!   530
>Don't you recall the trouble we two had
>around Troy, just the pair of us alone,
>with no other gods, that time when Zeus
>made us come here to work for a whole year
>at a fixed wage for proud king Laomedon?
>He was our master and told us what to do.
>I built the Trojans a wide and splendid wall
>around their city, to make it impregnable.
>You, Phoebus, worked with his cattle herds,
>taking his shambling bent-horned livestock   540
>through Ida's wooded spurs and valleys.
>When the joyful seasons stopped our working there,
>that despicable Laomedon robbed us.
>He kept our wages and sent us off with threats.
>He promised he'd tie up your hands and feet,
>then in some distant island sell you as a slave.

He said he'd slice off both our ears with bronze.
We came back really angry in our hearts,
enraged about those promised wages
he'd withheld. That's the man whose people   550
you're now keen to favour. You don't join us,
so we destroy these arrogant Trojans
once and for all, along with all their children
and their honourable wives as well."

Lord Apollo, who shoots from far, answered Poseidon:

"Earthshaker, you'd never call me prudent,
if I fought with you over human beings—
those pitiful creatures are like the leaves,
now full of blazing life, eating nourishment
the earth provides, then fading into death.   560
No, let's quickly end our quarrel, leaving
these mortal men to fight amongst themselves."

Saying this, he turned away, thinking it shameful
to fight in battle against his father's brother.
But his sister, forest goddess Artemis,
queen of all wild beasts, was furious with him.
She spoke to him with scorn:

                              "So, far worker,
you're running off, ceding total victory
to Poseidon, giving him an easy glory.
You fool! Why do you carry such a bow,   570
as useless as the wind? From now on,
I never want to hear you boasting,
as you used to among the deathless gods,
how you could fight Poseidon face to face."

Artemis spoke. Far-shooting Apollo did not answer.
But Hera, Zeus' honoured wife, was angry.
She went at the archer goddess, insulting her:

"You shameless bitch, you dare stand against me?

You'll find it hard to match my power,
even if you have your bow and Zeus made you   580
a lion among women, allowing you
to kill whichever one of them you please.
I say it's better to be slaughtering wild beasts,
deer in the mountains, than to fight all out
with those more powerful. Still, if you're keen
to learn about this war, to understand
how much more powerful I am, let's fight,
since you are challenging my strength."

With these words, Hera caught both arms of Artemis
in her left hand. With her right she grabbed the bow,   590
snatching it and its quiver off her shoulders.
Then she slapped her with those weapons. As she did so,
Hera smiled to see Artemis twist away and squirm.
The swift arrows tumbled out. Artemis ran off,
crying like a pigeon speeding from a hawk,
flying to some hollow cleft among the rocks,
for she's not fated to be caught—that's how Artemis
escaped, in tears, leaving her bow lying there.
Then Hermes, the guide, killer of Argus, spoke out,
addressing Leto:

                    "I'll not fight you, Leto.   600
It's dangerous to come to blows with those
married to cloud-gatherer Zeus. So you can tell
immortal gods your great strength conquered me—
and you can even boast about it."

                                   Hermes finished.
Leto then collected the curved bow and arrows,
which had fallen here and there down in the swirling dust.
Then she left, taking her daughter's weapons with her.

Artemis returned then to Olympus, to Zeus' home,
with its bronze floor. The girl sat on her father's lap,
her immortal garments shaking as she wept.   610
Her father, Cronos' son, holding her to him,

asked her with a gentle laugh:

> "My dear child,
> which of the heavenly gods has treated you
> so nastily, as if you were committing
> some evil act in public?"

> Then Artemis,
with her beautiful headband, answered Zeus:

> "It was your wife who hit me, father,
> white-armed Hera. Now, thanks to her,
> immortal gods engage in fights and quarrels."

As these two talked together in this fashion,   620
Phoebus Apollo went to sacred Ilion.
He was concerned about that well-built city wall,
afraid Danaans might breach it that very day,
contravening what Fate ordained. The other gods,
who live forever, went back to Olympus,
some incensed and others relishing their triumph.
They sat down by Zeus, lord of the dark cloud.

Meanwhile, Achilles still kept on killing Trojans,
both soldiers and their sure-footed horses, too.
Just as smoke rises up, reaching spacious heaven,   630
when a city burns from fires set by wrathful gods—
that's how Achilles brought the Trojans death and danger.

Then old Priam stood on that wall built by gods,
observing huge Achilles as he drove the Trojans
ahead of him in total panic, their spirit broken.
With a groan, he left the wall, came down to the ground,
and summoned the well-known sentries at the gates.

> "Hold the doors wide open with your hands,
> until the fleeing troops come to the city.
> For Achilles is coming closer, driving   640
> them in panic. I think disaster looms.

When the men have gathered here inside the wall,
able to get relief, then close the gates,
these tight-fitting doors, once more. I'm afraid
this murderer may jump inside our walls."

Then the men pushed back the bars, opening the gates,
and gave a saving light for those men on the run.

Then Apollo charged out to meet Achilles,
seeking to protect the Trojans from destruction,
as they fled straight for the high-walled city,   650
suffering from thirst and dusty from the plain.
Still in a rage, Achilles chased them with his spear,
his heart filled with strong and unremitting fury,
still eager to win glory. At that moment,
Achaea's sons would have captured Troy's high gates,
if Phoebus Apollo had not intervened,
by stirring up noble, godlike Agenor,
Antenor's son, a powerful warrior. In his heart
Apollo instilled courage and then stood by him,
leaning against the oak tree, covered in thick mist,
so he might ward off the heavy hand of death.   660
When Agenor saw Achilles, sacker of cities,
he made a stand, his heart pondering many things,
as he stood there. In his agitation, he spoke out,
addressing his proud heart:

                    "Here's trouble.
If I rush away before Achilles
where other men are running in their panic,
he'll catch me, then kill me as a coward.
But what if I let Achilles, son of Peleus,
drive them on, then dash away myself   670
to some other place, far from the wall,
out in the Trojan plain, until I reach
Ida's spurs, where there's a bush to hide in?
When evening comes, I could wash in the river,
get rid of all the sweat and then go back,
return to Ilion. But why's my fond heart

debating all these options? He might see me,
as I moved off from the city for the plain,
and catch me with a sprint of his swift feet.
I'd no longer have a chance to get away   680
from death, my fate. The man is really strong,
much more powerful than other men.
What if I go out to stand against him
before the city? My sharp bronze, I think,
can slice up his flesh, too. He's got one life,
no more. And men say that he's a mortal,
although Zeus, Cronos' son, gives him glory."

Saying this, Agenor stood up straight and waited,
the heart within him prepared for war and keen to fight.
Just as a leopard emerges from thick undergrowth,   690
to face a hunter, with no fear in its heart,
no hint of flight when it hears the baying hounds—
even if the hunter first hits it with his spear,
the wounded beast won't lose its fighting spirit,
until it closes with him or is killed itself—
that's how godlike Agenor, noble Antenor's son,
refused to run before fighting Achilles.
Holding his round shield in front of him, he aimed his spear
directly at Achilles, then shouted out:

        "Glorious Achilles, I'm sure you've set your heart   700
on destroying the city which proud Trojans hold
this very day. What foolishness! Much pain
must still be suffered in that enterprise.
We who live in Troy are men with courage,
and there are lots of us. We'll guard Ilion,
in front of our dear parents, wives, and sons.
Here you'll meet your doom, though as a fighter,
you are so formidable and brave."

                                   Agenor spoke.
Then he threw his sharp spear from his massive hand.
He hit Achilles on the shin, below the knee.   710
The spear did not miss its man. The armour on his leg,
newly hammered tin, gave out a fearful clang.

471

But the spear just struck the metal and bounced off,
without going through. The god's gift had protected him.
Then Peleus' son, in turn, went for godlike Agenor.
But Apollo didn't let him win the glory there.
He snatched Agenor up, hid him in dense mist,
then sent him quietly away from battle.
After that, he led the son of Peleus astray,
far from Trojan soldiers. The far shooter tricked him,   720
by standing right before Achilles' feet, looking
exactly like Agenor. Achilles charged off
in pursuit, chasing Apollo out across the plain,
past wheat fields, turning him towards the river,
the deep, swirling Scamander. Apollo raced on,
only a little bit ahead, using his cunning
to trick Achilles with his pace, so he'd think
he could catch up. Meanwhile, the other Trojans
fleeing in confusion, came crowding in the city,
throngs of them, cramming the gates, happy to be there.   730
They didn't dare to wait outside the wall, to check
who made it back and who had perished in the fight.
They streamed into the city in an eager rush,
all whose legs and knees had brought them safely in.

Book Twenty-Two
The Death of Hector

[The Trojans retreat into the city; Apollo reveals his deception to Achilles;
Hector remains outside the gates; Priam and Hecuba appeal to Hector to
come inside the walls; Hector debates what to do, then panics and runs
away; Achilles chases Hector around Troy; the gods look on; Zeus holds up
his golden scales; Athena intervenes to advise Achilles; Athena takes on
the form of Deiphobus to get Hector to fight Achilles; Hector and Achilles
fight; Hector is killed; the Achaeans mutilate Hector, and Achilles
dishonors the corpse; Priam and Hecuba see the corpse of Hector being
dragged past the city; Andromache reacts to the sight of her dead husband]

At this point, the Trojans, having fled like deer,
spread out through the city, resting by its sturdy walls,
drying their sweat and taking drink to slake their thirst.
Meanwhile, Achaeans were moving to the walls,
their shields held up against their shoulders. But Hector
was forced by deadly Fate to stay right where he stood
in front of Ilion, outside the Scaean Gate.

Then Phoebus Apollo spoke out to Achilles:

> "Son of Peleus, why are you, a mere human,
> running so hard in an attempt to catch me,   10
> an immortal god? You're still ignorant,
> it seems, of the fact that I'm a god.
> You keep coming at me with such anger.
> But what about your battle with those Trojans
> you put to flight? They're crowding in the city,
> while you chase off on a diversion here.
> But you will never kill me. I'm not someone
> whose fate it is to die."

Swift-footed Achilles,
in a towering fury, then answered Apollo:

"You've tricked me,
god who shoots from far away, deadliest   20

of all the gods. You've turned me from the wall.
Otherwise, before reaching Ilion,
many men would have sunk their teeth in earth.
You've robbed me of great glory, saving them
with ease, since you don't have to be afraid
of future retribution. I'd make you pay,
if only I were powerful enough."

With these words, Achilles set off towards the city,
his heart full, charging on like a prize-winning horse
pulling a chariot at full speed across the plain   30
with little effort—that's how fast Achilles ran,
sprinting with his legs and feet.

                                Meanwhile, old Priam
was the first to catch sight of Achilles, as he dashed
across the plain, blazing like that star which comes
at harvest time—its light shines out more brightly
than any of the countless lights in night's dark sky.
People call this star by the name Orion's Dog.
It's the brightest of the stars, but an unwelcome sign,
for it brings wretched mortals many fevers.
The bronze on Achilles' chest glittered like that star,   40
as he ran forward. With a cry, old Priam
struck his head with his hand, then, reaching up,
with many groans, he called out, pleading with his son,
who was still standing there before the gates,
firmly resolved to fight Achilles. The old man,
hands outstretched, appealed to Hector's sense of pity:

        "Hector, my dear son, don't stand out there alone,
facing that man with no one else to help you,
or you will quickly meet your death, slaughtered
by Peleus' son, who's much more powerful.   50
Don't be obstinate. If only the gods
would love Achilles just as much as I do,
then dogs and vultures would soon gnaw at him
as he lay there. And then my heart might shed
its dreadful sorrow, for he's taken from me

many valiant sons. Some he's butchered.
Others he's sold in islands far away.
Right now, I can't see two of my young sons,
Polydorus and Lycaon, among those
who've gathered with the Trojans in the city,   60
both delivered to me from Laothoe,
queen among women. If they're still alive
in the Achaean camp, we'll ransom them,
with bronze and gold we have stored at home.
For famous ancient Altes gave many gifts
when he gave me his daughter. But if they're dead
and already in that dwelling place of Hades,
that's a sorrow to my heart, their mother's, too,
their parents. But that's a briefer sorrow
for other people, unless you die as well,   70
killed by Achilles. Come here, my child,
inside the walls, so you can help to save
Trojan men and women. Don't give that man,
that son of Peleus, great glory. He'll take
your own dear life. Have pity on me, too.
Though full of misery, I still can feel.
Father Zeus will kill me with a cruel fate
on the threshold of old age, once I've seen
so many dreadful things—my sons slaughtered,
my daughters hauled away, their houses ransacked,   80
their little children tossed down on the ground
in this murderous war, my daughters-in-law
led off captive in hard Achaean hands.
In the end, I'll be ripped by ravenous dogs,
in front of my own doors when some man strikes me
with his sharp bronze or throws his spear in me,
robbing my limbs of life—the same dogs I raised
at home beside my table to guard the doors.
They'll drink my blood, then lie there at the gates,
their hearts gone mad. When a young man dies in war,   90
lying there murdered by sharp bronze, that's all right.
Though dead, he shows us his nobility.
But when the dogs disfigure shamefully
an old man, chewing his gray head, his beard,

his sexual organs, that's the saddest thing
we wretched mortals see."

As the old man spoke,
his hands tugged his gray hair and pulled it from his head.
But he could not sway Hector's heart. Beside Priam,
Hector's mother wept. Then she undid her robe,
and with her hands pushed out her breasts, shedding tears.   100
She cried out, calling him—her words had wings:

"Hector, my child, respect and pity me.
If I ever gave these breasts to soothe you,
remember that, dear child. Protect yourself
against your enemy inside these walls.
Don't stand out there to face him. Stubborn man,
if he kills you, I'll never lay you out
on your death bed or mourn for you, my child,
my dearest offspring—nor will your fair wife.
Far away from us, beside Achaean ships,   110
their swift dogs will eat you."

So these two, both crying, spoke to their dear son,
pleading with him incessantly. But Hector's heart
would not budge. He stood awaiting huge Achilles,
who was getting closer. Just as a mountain snake
waits for some man right by its lair, after eating
poison herbs so that a savage anger grips him,
as he coils beside his den with a fearful glare—
that's how Hector's dauntless heart would not retreat.
But then he leaned his bright shield up against the wall   120
where it jutted out, and, with a groan, spoke up,
addressing his courageous heart:

"What do I do?
If I go through the gates, inside that wall,
Polydamas will be the first to blame me,
for he told me last night to lead the Trojans
back into the city, when many died,
once godlike Achilles rejoined the fight.

But I didn't listen. If I'd done so,
things would have been much better. As it is,
my own foolishness has wiped out our army.   130
Trojan men will make me feel ashamed—
so will Trojan women in their trailing gowns.
I'm afraid someone inferior to me
may say, 'Hector, trusting his own power,
destroyed his people.' That's what they'll say.
For me it would be a great deal better
to meet Achilles man to man, kill him,
and go home, or get killed before the city,
dying in glory. But what would happen,
if I set my bossed shield and heavy helmet   140
to one side, leaning my spear against the wall,
and went out to meet noble Achilles,
just as I am, promising that Helen,
along with all the goods shipped here to Troy
by Alexander in his hollow ships,
the origin of our hostilities,
would be given to the sons of Atreus,
to take away with them—in addition,
to give the Achaeans an equal share
of all this city holds. Then later on,   150
I'd get Trojan elders to swear on oath
that not a single thing would be concealed,
that all would be divided equally,
every treasure our lovely city owns.
But why's my dear heart having this debate?
If I went out to meet him in that way,
he'd show me no respect. He wouldn't pity me.
Once I'd set aside my armour, he'd kill me
on the spot, unarmed, like some woman.
There's no way I can bargain with him now,   160
like a boy and girl chatting by some rock
or oak tree, as they flirt with one another.
No, it's better to clash in battle right away.
We'll see which one wins victory from Zeus."

That's what Hector thought as he stood there waiting.

But Achilles was coming closer, like Enyalius,
the warrior god of battle with the shining helmet.
On his right shoulder he waved his dreadful spear
made of Pelian ash. The bronze around him glittered
like a blazing fire or rising sun. At that moment,   170
as he watched, Hector began to shake in fear.
His courage gone, he could no longer stand there.
Terrified, he started running, leaving the gate.
Peleus' son went after him, sure of his speed on foot.
Just as a mountain falcon, the fastest creature
of all the ones which fly, swoops down easily
on a trembling pigeon as it darts off in fear,
the hawk speeding after it with piercing cries,
heart driving it to seize the prey—in just that way
Achilles in his fury raced ahead. Hector ran   180
under the walls of Troy, limbs working feverishly.
They ran on past the lookout and the wind-swept fig tree,
some distance from the wall, along the wagon track.
They reached the two fair-flowing well springs
which feed swirling Scamander's stream. From one of them
hot water flows, and out of it steam rises up,
as if there were a fire burning. From the other,
cold water comes, as cold as hail or freezing snow
or melting ice, even in summer. By these springs
stood wide tubs for washing, made of beautiful stone,   190
where, in peace time, before Achaea's sons arrived,
Trojan wives and lovely daughters used to wash
their brightly coloured clothing. The men raced past there,
one in full flight, the other one pursuing him.
The man running off in front was a brave warrior,
but the man going after him was greater. They ran fast,
for this was no contest over sacrificial beasts,
the usual prizes for a race. They were competing
for horse-taming Hector's life. Just as some horses,
sure-footed, prize-winning creatures, make the turn   200
around the post and race quickly as they strive to win
some splendid prize—a tripod or a woman
honouring a man that's died—that's how these two men raced,
going three times round Priam's city on their sprinting feet.

All the gods looked on. Among them the first one to speak
was Zeus, father of the gods and men:

"What a sight!
My eyes can see a fine man being pursued
around the walls. How my heart pities Hector,
who's often sacrificed to me, burning
many thighs of oxen on the crests   210
of Ida with its many spurs and valleys,
on the city heights, as well. And now,
godlike Achilles is pursuing him
on his quick feet round Priam's city. Come,
you gods, think hard and offer your advice—
do we wish to rescue him from death,
or kill him now, for all his bravery,
at the hands of Peleus' son, Achilles?"

Then Athena,
goddess with the glittering eyes, replied to Zeus:

"Father, lord of lightning and dark clouds,   220
what are you saying? How can you want
to snatch the man back from his wretched death.
He's mortal—his fate doomed him long ago.
Well, do as you wish, but we other gods
will not all approve your actions."

Cloud-gatherer Zeus then answered Athena:

"Cheer up, Tritogeneia, my dear child,
I'm not saying how my heart intends to act.
I want to please you. So you can do
whatever your mind tells you. Don't hold back."   230

Athena, who was already eager, was spurred on
by Zeus' words. She rushed down from Olympus' peak.

Swift Achilles was still pressing Hector hard
in that relentless chase. Just as in the mountains

479

a hound startles from its cover some young deer,
then goes after it through glens and valley gorges—
and even if the fawn evades it for a while,
cowering in some thicket, the dog tracks it down,
always running till he finds it—that's how Hector
could not shake off the swift-footed son of Peleus. 240
Every time he tried to dash for the Dardanian gates
to get underneath the walls, so men on top
could come to his assistance by hurling spears,
Achilles would intercept him and turn him back
towards the plain, always making sure he kept
running a line between Hector and the city.
Like a dream in which a man cannot catch someone
who's running off and the other can't escape,
just as the first man can't catch up—that's how
Achilles, for all his speed, could not reach Hector, 250
while Hector was unable to evade Achilles.
But how could Hector have escaped death's fatal blow,
if Apollo had not for one last time approached,
to give him strength and make his legs run faster?
Godlike Achilles, with a shake of his head,
prevented his own troops from shooting Hector
with their lethal weapons, in case some other man
hit Hector, robbed him of the glory, and left him
to come too late. But when they ran past those springs
the fourth time, Father Zeus raised his golden scales, 260
setting there two fatal lots for death's long sorrow,
one for Achilles, one for horse-taming Hector.
Seizing it in the middle, Zeus raised his balance.
Hector's fatal day sank, moving down to Hades.
At once Phoebus Apollo abandoned him.
Then Athena, goddess with the glittering eyes,
came to Peleus' son. Standing close to him, she spoke—
her words had wings:

> "Glorious Achilles,
> beloved of Zeus, now I hope the two of us
> will take great glory to Achaean ships, 270
> by killing Hector, for all his love of war.

480

Now he can't escape us any longer,
even though Apollo, the far shooter,
suffers every torment, as he grovels
before Father Zeus, who bears the aegis.
Stay still now. Catch your breath. I'll go to Hector
and convince him to turn and stand against you."

Once Athena had said this, Achilles obeyed,
rejoicing in his heart, as he stood there, leaning
on his bronze-tipped ash spear. Athena left him.   280
She came to Hector in the form of Deïphobus,
with his tireless voice and shape. Standing beside him,
she spoke—her words had wings:

                              "My brother,
swift Achilles is really harassing you,
with his fast running around Priam's city
in this pursuit. Come, we'll both stand here,
stay put, and beat off his attack."

Then Hector of the shining helmet answered her:

"Deïphobus, in the past you've always been
the brother I loved the most by far   290
of children born to Hecuba and Priam.
I think I now respect you even more,
since you have dared to come outside the wall,
to help me, when you saw me in distress,
while others all remained inside."

Goddess Athena with her glittering eyes replied:

"Dear brother, my father, my noble mother,
and my comrades begged me repeatedly
to stay there. They all so fear Achilles.
But here inside me my heart felt the pain   300
of bitter anguish. Now, let's go straight for him.
Let's fight and not hold back our spears,
so we can see if Achilles kills us both,

481

then takes the bloodstained trophies to the ships,
or whether you'll destroy him on your spear."

With these words, Athena seduced him forward.
When they'd approached each other, at close quarters,
great Hector of the shining helmet spoke out first:

> "I'll no longer try to run away from you,
> son of Peleus, as I did before, going   310
> three times in flight around Priam's great city.
> I lacked the courage then to fight with you,
> as you attacked. But my heart prompts me now
> to stand against you face to face once more,
> whether I kill you, or you kill me.
> So come here. Let's call on gods to witness,
> for they're the best ones to observe our pact,
> to supervise what we two agree on.
> If Zeus grants me the strength to take your life,
> I'll not abuse your corpse in any way.   320
> I'll strip your celebrated armour off,
> Achilles, then give the body back again
> to the Achaeans. And you'll do the same."

Swift-footed Achilles, with a scowl, replied:

> "Hector, don't talk to me of our agreements.
> That's idiotic, like a faithful promise
> between men and lions. Wolves and lambs
> don't share a common heart—they always sense
> a mutual hatred for each other.
> In just that way, it's not possible for us,   330
> for you and me, to be friends, or, indeed,
> for there to be sworn oaths between us,
> till one or other of us falls, glutting Ares,
> warrior with the bull's hide shield, on blood.
> You'd best remember all your fighting skills.
> Now you must declare yourself a spearman,
> a fearless warrior. You've got no escape.
> Soon Pallas Athena will destroy you

on my spear. Right now you'll pay me back,
the full price of those sorrows I went through   340
when you slaughtered my companions."

With these words, he hefted his long-shadowed spear,
then hurled it. However, anticipating the throw,
splendid Hector saw it coming and evaded it
by crouching down, so the bronze spear flew over him,
then struck the ground. But Pallas Athena grabbed it
and returned it to Achilles, without Hector,
that shepherd of his people, seeing what she'd done.
Hector then called out to Peleus' noble son:

   "You missed, godlike Achilles. So it seems   350
you learned nothing from Zeus about my death,
although you said you had. That was just talk.
You were telling lies to make me fear you,
so I might forget my strength and courage.
Well, with your spear you won't be striking me
in my back as I run away in fear.
You'll have to drive it through my charging chest,
as I come right at you, if a god permits.
Now, see if you can cope with my bronze point.
I hope you get this whole spear in your flesh.   360
This war would then be easier on Trojans
with you dead, for you're their greatest danger."

With these words, Hector balanced his long-shadowed spear,
then threw it. It struck the shield of Peleus' son,
right in the centre. That spear didn't miss its mark.
But it bounced some distance off the shield. Hector,
angry that the spear had flown from his hand and missed,
stood dismayed, for he had no substitute ash spear.
So he shouted out, calling to Deïphobus,
who carried a white shield, asking him with a yell   370
to pass him his long spear. But Deïphobus
was nowhere to be seen. Then Hector in his heart
saw everything so clearly—he said:

> "This is it, then.
> The gods are summoning me to my death.
> I thought warrior Deïphobus was close by.
> But he's inside the walls, and Athena
> has deceived me. Now evil death is here,
> right beside me, not somewhere far away.
> There's no escape. For a long time now,
> this must have been what Zeus desired,   380
> and Zeus' son, the god who shoots from far,
> and all those who willingly gave me help
> in earlier days. So now I meet my fate.
> Even so, let me not die ingloriously
> without a fight, but in some great action
> which those men yet to come will hear about."

Hector finished speaking. He pulled out his sharp sword,
that strong and massive weapon hanging on his thigh,
gathered himself, then swooped like some high-flying eagle
plummeting to the plains down through the murky clouds   390
to seize a tender lamb or cowering rabbit—
that's how Hector charged, brandishing his sharp sword.
Achilles attacked, as well, heart full of savage anger,
covering his chest with that richly decorated shield,
his shining four-ridged helmet nodding on his head,
the golden plumes Hephaestus had set there
shimmering around the crest. Just like that star
which stands out the loveliest among all those
in the heavenly night sky—the star of evening—
that's how the sharp point then glittered on the spear   400
Achilles hefted in his right hand, intent on
killing noble Hector. He inspected his fine skin,
to see where it was vulnerable to a blow.
But Hector's entire body was protected
by that beautiful armour he'd stripped off
powerful Patroclus, once he'd killed him,
except for that opening where the collar bones
separate the neck and shoulders, at the gullet,
where a man's life is most effectively destroyed.
As Hector charged, noble Achilles struck him there,   410

driving the spear point through his tender neck.
But the heavy bronze on that ash spear did not cut
his windpipe, so he could still address Achilles
and reply to him. Hector fell down in the dust.
Lord Achilles then cried out in triumph:

> "Hector,
> I suppose you thought you could safely strip
> Patroclus, without giving me a thought,
> since I was far away. That was foolish!
> By our hollow ships he'd left me behind,
> a much greater man, to take out my revenge.   420
> I've drained strength from your limbs—now dogs and birds
> will tear you into miserable pieces,
> while Achaeans are burying Patroclus."

His strength fading, Hector of the shining helmet
answered Achilles:

> "By your life, I beg you,
> by your knees, your parents—don't let dogs eat me
> by Achaean ships. No, you should accept
> all the bronze and gold you want,
> gifts my father and lady mother give you,
> if you'll send my body home again,   430
> so Trojans and Trojans' wives can bury me,
> with all the necessary funeral rites."

Scowling at Hector, swift-footed Achilles then replied:

> "Don't whine to me, you dog, about my knees
> or parents. I wish I had the heart and strength
> to carve you up and eat you raw myself
> for what you've done to me. So there's no one
> who'll keep the dogs from going at your head,
> not even if they bring here and weigh out
> a ransom ten or twenty times as much,   440
> with promises of more, or if Priam,
> son of Dardanus, says he'll pay your weight

485

in gold. Not even then will your mother
set you on a funeral bed and there lament
the son she bore. Instead, the dogs and birds
will eat you up completely."

Then, as he died,
Hector of the shining helmet said to Achilles:

"I know you well. I recognize in you
what I expected— you'd not be convinced.
For your heart and mind are truly iron.   450
But think of this—I may bring down on you
the anger of the gods that very day
when Paris and Phoebus Apollo,
in spite of all your courage, slaughter you
at the Scaean Gate."

As Hector spoke,
death's final end slid over him. His life slipped out,
flying off to Hades, mourning his fate to have to leave
such youthful manliness. Over dead Hector,
godlike Achilles then cried out:

"Die there.
As for my own death, I accept it   460
whenever Zeus and the immortal gods
see fit to bring it to me."

Saying this,
He pulled his bronze spear from the corpse, set it aside,
and stripped the blood-stained armour from the shoulders.
Then the rest of Achaea's sons came running up.
They gazed at Hector's stature, his handsome body.
All the men who came up to the corpse stabbed it,
looking at each other, saying:

"Look here,
it's easier for us to deal with Hector now
than when his fire burned our ships."   470

With words like this, they came up close and wounded Hector.
When swift-footed godlike Achilles had stripped the corpse,
standing among Achaeans, he spoke these winged words:

"My friends, leaders and rulers of the Argives,
since gods have granted that this man be killed,
who's done much damage, more than all the rest,
let's test these Trojan by attacking them
with armed excursions round their city,
to see what they intend—whether they'll leave
their lofty city now that Hector's dead,   480
or stay there, still keen to fight without him.
But why's my fond heart discussing this?
By our ships lies a dead man—unwept,
unburied—Patroclus. I'll not forget him,
as long as I remain among the living,
as long as my dear limbs have motion.
If down in Hades men forget their dead,
even there I will remember my companion.
Come, young Achaeans, sing a victory song,
as we're returning to our hollow ships.   490
We'll take the body. We've won great glory,
killing noble Hector—Trojans prayed to him
in their own city, as if he were a god."

Achilles finished. Then on noble Hector's corpse
he carried out a monstrous act. He cut through
the tendons behind both feet, from heel to ankle,
threaded them with ox-hide thongs, and then tied these
onto his chariot, leaving the head to drag behind.
He climbed up in his chariot, brought on the splendid armour,
then lashed his horses. They sped off eagerly,   500
dragging Hector. A dust cloud rose above him,
his dark hair spread out round him, and Hector's head,
once so handsome, was covered by the dust, for Zeus
had given him to his enemies to dishonour
in his own native land. So all his head grew dirty.

When she saw her son, his mother pulled her hair,

487

threw off her shining veil, and began to shriek.
His dear father gave a pitiful groan. Around them,
people were overwhelmed with wailing and laments
throughout the city. It was as if all Ilion
were engulfed in flames, all over the summit
of that towering rock. The people then had trouble
restraining the old man in his frantic grief,
his desperate wish to go through the Dardanian gate.
He begged them all, groveling in the dirt, calling out,
naming each of them:

> "My dear friends,
> leave me alone. I know you care for me,
> but let me leave the city by myself,
> go to the Achaean ships, then beg him,
> that ruthless man, that violent monster.
> He may feel shame in front of comrades.
> He may pity my old age. For he, too,
> has a father, one just like me, Peleus,
> who sired and raised him to butcher Trojans.
> On me especially he's loaded sorrow,
> more than on any other man. He's killed
> so many of my sons, all in their prime.
> But, despite that sorrow, I don't grieve
> for all of them as much as I do for one,
> for Hector. The sharp pain I feel for him
> will bring me down to the house of Hades.
> If only he had died here in my arms,
> we could have had our fill of weeping,
> of lamentation—me and his mother,
> who gave birth to him, to her own sorrow."

As he said this, Priam wept. The townsfolk mourned.
Hecuba led Trojan women in their loud laments:

> "My child, how can I live with this misery,
> such wretched sorrow, now that you are dead?
> You were my pride and joy, night and day,
> and in the city, a blessing to us all,

to Trojan men and women in the state,
who received you like a god. To them
you were great glory when you were alive.
Now Death and Fate have overtaken you."

Hecuba spoke through her tears. But so far Hector's wife
knew nothing of all this, for no messenger
had come to tell her clearly that her husband
had remained outside the gates. She was in a room
inside their lofty home, weaving purple fabric   550
for a double cloak, embroidering flowers on it.
She'd told her well-groomed servants in the house
to place a large tripod on the fire, so Hector
could have a hot bath when he came home from battle.
Poor fool! She'd no idea that a long way from that bath,
Athena with the glittering eyes had killed Hector
at Achilles' hands. Then she heard the wailing,
laments coming from the walls. Her limbs began to shake.
The shuttle fell out of her hands onto the floor.
She spoke out once more to her well-groomed housemaids: 560

    "Come here you two and follow me. Let's see
what's happened. For I've just caught the sound
of my husband's noble mother's voice. In my chest,
my heart leapt in my mouth, my lower limbs
are numb. Something disastrous has taken place
to Priam's children. I hope reports like these
never reach my ears, but I'm dreadfully afraid
that godlike Achilles may have cut off
my bold Hector from the city, driving him
into the plain all by himself, then ended   570
that fearful courage which possessed him.
He's never one to hold back or remain
within the crowd of men—he always moves ahead,
well in front, second to none in fury."

Saying this, she hurried through the house, heart pounding,
like some mad woman, accompanied by servants.
Once she reached the wall crowded with men, she stopped,

489

stood there, and looked out from the wall. She saw Hector
as he was being dragged past before the city,
with swift horses pulling him ruthlessly away   580
to the Achaeans' hollow ships. At the sight,
black night eclipsed her eyes. She fell back in a faint,
gasping her life away. From her head she threw off
her shining headdress—frontlet, cap, woven headband,
the veil that golden Aphrodite gave her
when Hector of the shining helmet led her
from Eëtion's house as his wife, once he'd paid
an immense price for his bride. Around her
stood her husband's sisters and his brother's wives.
They all helped pick her up, almost dead from shock.   590
When she'd recovered and her spirit had returned,
she started her lament. In a sobbing voice,
she cried out to the Trojan women:

                             "Ah, Hector,
how miserable I am. We both seem born
to a single fate, you in Priam's house
in Troy, and I in Eëtion's home
in wooded Thebe. He raised me from childhood,
an ill-fated father and a child who's doomed.
How I wish he'd never fathered me.
Now you go to Hades' house deep underground,   600
abandoning me to bitter sorrow,
widowed in our home. Our son's an infant,
born to wretched parents, you and me.
No good will come to him from you, Hector,
now that you're dead, nor will he help you.
Even if he gets through this dreadful war
with the Achaeans, his life will always be
a constant pain and sorrow. For other men
will take away his lands. The day a child
becomes an orphan all his friends are gone.   610
He cannot hold up his head for anyone,
his cheeks are wet from crying. In his need,
the child goes to his father's comrades,
plucking one man's cloak, another's tunic.

Some pity him and then hold out a cup,
letting him for a moment wet his lips,
without moistening his palate. Another man
whose parents are still living pushes him
out of the feast, hitting him with his fist,
insulting him: 'Go away, just as you are.   620
You've no father at our feast.' So, in tears,
the child returns to his widowed mother.
That child is our son Astyanax, who,
in earlier days on his father's knees,
ate only marrow and rich fat from sheep.
When sleep overpowered him and he'd stopped
his childish play, he'd lie in his own bed,
in his nurse's arms—on a soft couch,
his heart full of happy dreams. But now,
now that he's missing his dear father,   630
he'll suffer much, our dear son Astyanax,
Lord of the City. Trojans called him this,
because you alone kept their gates safe from harm,
their towering walls. But now by the beaked ships,
far from your parents, wriggling worms will eat you,
once dogs have had their fill of your bare corpse.
In your home are lovely well-made clothes,
produced by women's hands. In a blazing fire
I'll burn them all. They're no use to you,
since you can't wear them. So I'll honour you,
on behalf of Trojan men and women."

Saying this, she wept. The women added their laments.

Book Twenty-Three

The Funeral Games for Patroclus

[Achilles keeps his troops together to mourn Patroclus; Patroclus' ghost visits Achilles, requesting a burial; Achaeans gather wood and prepare Patroclus' funeral pyre; Achilles cuts the hair dedicated to the river Spercheus; Achilles sacrifices animals and humans on Patroclus' pyre; Achilles gets the help of the winds to get the fire to light under Patroclus; Achilles brings out prizes for the Funeral Games, which then take place in series: the chariot race, boxing, wrestling, foot-racing, armed combat, throwing a weight, archery, and spear throwing; Achilles awards Agamemnon the prize for the last event without any contest]

Meanwhile, as Trojans were lamenting in the city,
Achaeans reached their ships beside the Hellespont.
There they scattered, each man going to his own ship.
But Achilles didn't let his Myrmidons disband.
He spoke out to his warrior companions:

> "Fast-riding Myrmidons, trusty comrades,
> let's not loose our sure-footed horses yet,
> untying them from their chariots. We must go
> with horse and chariot up to Patroclus,
> to mourn for him. For that's a dead man's right.   10
> Once we've had our fill of sorrowful tears,
> we'll unyoke our horses, then all eat here."

At these words, they all began their group lament,
led by Achilles. Three times around the body
they drove their well-groomed horses, mourning as they went.
Thetis stirred up in them a strong desire to weep.
Their tears made the sands wet, men's armour, too,
for they were mourning the loss of a great warrior,
who'd made men flee. Peleus' son led their loud lament,
placing his man-killing hands on his comrade's chest: 20

> "Rest in peace, Patroclus, even though
> you're in Hades house, for I'm completing here
> all I promised you before—to drag in Hector,

then give him to the dogs to eat up raw,
and cut the throats of twelve young Trojans,
splendid children, on your funeral pyre,
in my rage that you've been slaughtered."

He finished. Then he continued to dishonour
noble Hector, stretching his body out face down
in the dirt, beside the bier of Menoetius' son.   30
Then each man took off his glittering bronze armour.
They untied their loud-neighing horses, then sat down,
thousands of them, by swift-footed Achilles' ship.
He prepared a funeral feast to ease their spirits.
Many sleek oxen bellowed underneath the knife,
as they were butchered. Many sheep, bleating goats,
and white-tusked pigs rich in fat were laid out
to roast over Hephaestus' fires. All around the corpse,
blood ran so thick men scooped it up in cupfuls.

Then Achaean leaders led the swift-footed prince,   40
son of Peleus, to lord Agamemnon.
They had trouble convincing him to go there—
his heart was still so angry for his comrade.
Reaching Agamemnon's hut, they issued orders
for clear-voiced heralds to heat up a large cauldron,
to see if they could persuade Peleus' son to wash,
to rinse off the spattered blood. In his stubbornness,
he refused to do that, swearing this oath:

                                        "By Zeus,
        highest and most excellent of all gods,
        it's not right that water touch my head,   50
        until I've laid Patroclus on his fire,
        piled up a burial mound, and shaved my hair,
        since such grief will never reach my heart
        a second time, not while I still remain
        among the living. But for the moment,
        let's agree to dine, though I hate to eat.
        In the morning, Agamemnon, king of men,
        you must urge men to gather wood, arrange

all things required for a man who's died,
as he goes below to murky darkness,   60
so tireless fires can cremate him quickly
and remove him from our sight. Then soldiers
can resume their duties."

                              Achilles spoke.
They all listened to him and readily agreed.
Men all rushed out, prepared a meal, and dined,
eating to their heart's content and sharing equally.
Once they'd satisfied their need for food and drink,
each man returned to his own hut to get some rest.
But Peleus' son lay moaning loudly on the shore,
beside the crashing sea, with many Myrmidons,   70
in an open spot, where waves washed up on shore.
When sleep took hold of him and eased his aching heart
by sweetly flowing round him—for his splendid limbs
were tired out from chasing after Hector
by wind-swept Ilion—then poor Patroclus
came to him as a ghost, looking exactly like him
in all respects—in stature, handsome eyes, and voice.
He stood there, above Achilles' head, body covered
with the same clothes he used to wear over his skin.
The ghost spoke to Achilles, saying:

                              "You're asleep, Achilles.   80
You've forgotten me. While I was alive,
you never did neglect me. But now I'm dead.
So bury me as quickly as you can.
Then I can pass through the gates of Hades.
The spirits, ghosts of the dead, keep me away.
They don't let me join them past the river.
So I wander aimlessly round Hades' home
by its wide gates. Give me your hand, I beg you,
for I'll never come again from Hades,
once you've given me what's due, my funeral fire.   90
We'll no more sit together making plans,
separated from our dear companions.
The jaws of dreadful Fate are gaping for me,

ready to consume me—my destiny
from the day that I was born. You, too,
godlike Achilles, you have your own fate,
to die under the walls of wealthy Troy.
I'll say one more thing, one last request,
if you will listen. Achilles, don't lay your bones
apart from mine. Let them remain together,   100
just as they were when we grew up in your home,
once Menoetius brought me as a youngster
into your land from Opoeis, for I'd done
a dreadful murder on that day I slaughtered
Amphidamas' son, in my foolishness.
I didn't mean to, but I was enraged
over some game of dice. Horseman Peleus
welcomed me into his home, raised me
with love, then made me your attendant.
So let the same container hold our bones,   110
that gold two-handled jar your mother gave you."

Swift-footed Achilles then said in reply:

"Dear friend, why have you come to me here,
telling me everything I need to do?
I'll carry out all these things for you,
attend to your request. But come closer.
Let's hold each other one short moment more,
enjoying a shared lament together."

Saying this, Achilles reached out with his arms,
but he grasped nothing. The spirit had departed,   120
going underground like vapour, muttering faintly.
Achilles jumped up in amazement, clapped his hands,
and then spoke out in sorrow:

"How sad!
It seems that even in Hades' house,
some spirit or ghost remains, but our being
is not there at all. For this entire night
the ghost of poor Patroclus stood beside me,

weeping, lamenting, asking me to do things,
in every detail amazingly like him."

Achilles' words stirred the desire to keep mourning   130
in all of them. When rose-fingered Dawn appeared,
they were still lamenting by that cheerless corpse.

Then mighty Agamemnon sent out men and mules,
from huts in every quarter, to gather wood.
The man who supervised was Meriones,
brave attendant to kind Idomeneus. They set off,
grasping axes to chop wood and well-woven rope.
The mules went on ahead. The men kept going,
up and down the slopes, sometimes tracking sideways,
sometimes doubling back, till they reached Ida's foothills   140
with their many springs. At once they started working—
cutting high-branched oak trees with their long-edged bronze.
Men worked hard, falling each tree with a mighty crash.
Achaeans then split the trees into convenient lengths,
tied logs behind the mules, whose feet ploughed up the ground
as they strained through thick underbrush towards the plain.
Woodsmen all carried logs as well, under orders
from Meriones, attendant to kind Idomeneus.
Men threw these logs down in a line along the shore,
where Achilles planned a massive burial mound   150
for Patroclus and himself. When they'd piled up
immense amounts of wood on every side, they sat
all together there and waited. Then Achilles
quickly told war-loving Myrmidons to dress in bronze,
ordering each man to get his horses harnessed
in their chariots. They leapt up to get armour on.
The warriors and charioteers climbed in their chariots
and moved out first. Then came the men on foot
in their thousands. In the middle, his companions
bore Patroclus, whose corpse they covered with the hair   160
they'd cut from their own heads and thrown onto the body.
Godlike Achilles came behind them, cradling
Patroclus' head and grieving. For he was sending
down to Hades' home a comrade without equal.

When they reached the spot Achilles chose for them,
they set the body down and quickly piled up wood
as he directed. Then swift-footed lord Achilles
thought of something. Standing some distance from the pyre,
he cut a lock of his own fair hair, one he'd grown
as a rich offering to the river Spercheus.   170
Looking out over the wine-dark sea, he spoke out
in passionate distress:

> "Spercheus, my father Peleus
> promised you that, once I came back home
> to my dear native land, I'd cut my hair
> for you, then make a holy sacrifice,
> offering up fifty uncastrated rams
> to your waters, where you have your own estate
> and fragrant altars. That oath was useless.
> It's what the old man swore, but you failed
> to bring about what he desired. So now,   180
> since I'll not be returning home again,
> let me give this lock to warrior Patroclus
> to carry with him."

Having said these words,
Achilles placed his hair in the hands of his dear comrade,
stirring up in each of them desire to lament.
Now they would have mourned till sunset, but Achilles
soon got up and said to Agamemnon:

> "Son of Atreus,
> Achaean troops will listen to your words
> more than to anyone. Men can grieve too much.
> So dismiss them from the pyre for now.   190
> Tell them to prepare a meal. Those of us
> with special cause to mourn will take care of this.
> But let the leaders remain here with us."

When Agamemnon, king of men, heard these words,
he quickly sent the troops off to their balanced ships.
The chief mourners stayed behind. They piled up wood,

497

making a square pyre, each side one hundred feet in length.
On that pyre's highest point they laid out the corpse,
hearts full of sorrow. Then, in front of the pyre,
they flayed and made ready many sturdy sheep   200
and shambling cattle with twisting horns. From all these,
great-hearted Achilles took the fat, using it
to cover up the corpse from head to foot, piling
skinned carcasses around it. Next, he placed on top
two-handled jars of oil and honey, leaning them
against the bier. Then, crying with grief, Achilles
threw four strong-necked horses quickly on the pyre.
Patroclus had owned nine dogs who ate beside his table.
Slitting the throats of two of them, Achilles
tossed them on the pyre. Then, with his bronze, he butchered   210
those twelve noble sons of the courageous Trojans,
his feelings grimly set on this atrocity.
After that, he lit the fire to work its iron force
and burn up everything. With a groan he called out,
addressing his companion:

                              "Rest in peace,
          Patroclus, though you're in Hades' house.
          For I'm now completing everything
          I promised you before. Flames will burn
          twelve noble sons of great-hearted Trojans,
          all cremated with you. But as for Hector,   220
          Priam's son, I'll not feed him to the fire,
          but to the dogs."

                              Achilles made this threat,
but dogs would not touch Hector. For Aphrodite,
Zeus' daughter, kept them away, day and night.
She covered him with immortal oil of roses,
so Achilles would not wear away his body
by dragging him around. Phoebus Apollo
brought a dark cloud from the sky across the plain,
shadowing the entire place where Hector lay,
to stop Sun's power from shriveling up the flesh   230
on limbs and sinews.

But now the pyre of dead Patroclus
would not catch fire. So swift-footed Achilles
thought of something else. Standing away from the pyre,
he prayed to the two winds—Boreas of the north,
Zephyrus of the west—promising fine offerings.
Pouring frequent libations from a golden cup,
he begged them to come quickly to ignite the wood,
so flames might incinerate the corpses quickly.
Hearing his prayer, Iris at once took his message
to the winds, who were feasting all together   240
in blustery West Wind's home. Iris sped up,
then stood on the stone threshold. Their eyes soon saw her.
They all jumped up, each one inviting her to sit
beside him. Iris declined their invitation,
saying to them:

           "I can't sit down. I must return
    to Oceanus' stream, back in the land
    of Ethiopians, where there's a sacrifice
    to the immortals. I'd like to be there
    for that sacred feast. But now Achilles
    prays that North Wind and loud West Wind will come.   250
    He's promising you splendid offerings
    to stir the flames, so they burn up the pyre
    where Patroclus lies, whom all Achaea mourns."

After saying this, Iris left. The two winds rose up.
With an astounding roar, driving clouds before them,
they quickly stormed across the sea, whipping up waves
with their howling breath. They came to fertile Troy,
then fell upon that pyre. The fire crackled up
into a prodigious blaze. All night long they howled,
blowing their shrill blasts together on the flames.   260
And all night long with a two-handled cup in hand
swift Achilles kept drawing wine from a golden bowl
and pouring it upon the earth, soaking the ground
and calling on the spirit of poor Patroclus.
Just as a father mourns his son, when he burns his bones,
his newly married son, whose death brings parents

dreadful sorrow—that's how Achilles kept crying then,
as he burned his companion's bones, dragging himself
round and round the pyre, lamenting endlessly.

But at that hour when the Morning Star appears,   270
announcing that light is coming to the earth,
the star after which Dawn in her yellow robe
moves out across the sea, by then the fire was dying.
The flames went out. So the winds returned once more,
back to their homes, going across the Thracian Sea,
where a seething storm roared out. Then Peleus' son,
moving away from the smouldering pyre, lay down
exhausted. Sweet Sleep quickly slipped around him.
But then the troops came up with Agamemnon,
all together. The noise they made, as they marched in,   280
woke up Achilles. Sitting bolt upright, he said:

> "Sons of Atreus and you other leaders
> of Achaean forces, you must first douse
> the smouldering pyre with gleaming wine—
> everything the powerful flames have touched.
> Then we'll collect bones from Patroclus,
> Menoetius' son, separating them with care
> from all the rest. They're easy to distinguish,
> for he lay in the centre of the pyre—
> the others burned some distance from him   290
> on the edges, the humans and the horses.
> Let's place his bones inside a golden urn,
> in a double layer of fat, until the time
> I myself am hiding there in Hades.
> I'm asking you to build a burial mound,
> nothing excessive—what seems appropriate.
> You Achaeans must build it high and wide,
> but later, once I'm gone, those who still remain
> beside our ships with many oars."

                    Once Achilles spoke,
they did as the swift-footed son of Peleus wished.   300
First, they doused the smoking pyre with gleaming wine,

wherever flames had reached or ash was deep.
Weeping, they picked the white bones of their comrade out
and put them in a double layer of fat inside a golden urn.
They placed the urn under soft linen in a hut.
Then they traced out the dimensions of a mound,
using stones to mark its base around the pyre,
and then piled earth on top.

               When they'd made the mound,
they started to return. But Achilles checked them,
keeping soldiers there. He asked them to sit down   310
in a wide group. Then he brought prizes from his ship—
cauldrons, tripods, horses, mules, powerful oxen,
as well as fine-dressed women and gray iron.

First, he set out prizes for swift charioteers—
for the winner, a woman skilled in fine handicrafts
and a tripod with handles holding twenty measures.
For second place he led out a mare six years old,
unbroken and with a mule foal in her womb.
For the man who came in third, he set out a cauldron
untouched by fire, a fine piece which held four measures.   320
For fourth place he set a prize of two gold talents,
while the fifth-place prize was a two-handled bowl,
not yet put on the fire. Then Achilles stood up
and spoke directly to the Argives:

                   "Sons of Atreus,
you other well-armed Achaean warriors,
these prizes lie set out here for a contest
among the charioteers. If Achaeans
were now hosting these games for someone else,
then I myself would surely win first prize
and take it to my hut, since, as you know,   330
my horses are far better than the rest,
for they're immortal, Poseidon's gift
to Peleus, my father, who gave them to me.
But I and my sure-footed horses now
will stand down, for they've lost their charioteer,

a strong, brave man, so kind he'd often pour
soft oil all through their manes, while washing them
in clean water. They stand there mourning him,
manes trailing on the ground. So they won't race.
Their hearts feel too much grief. But you others,   340
get yourselves prepared all through the camp,
any Achaean who has faith in his own horses
and his well-made chariot."

                    Once Achilles finished speaking,
swift charioteers rushed into action. First to move,
well before the rest, was Eumelus, king of men,
dear son of Admetus and excellent with horses.
After him came forward mighty Diomedes,
son of Tydeus, driving those yoked horses
from Tros' herd, which he'd just taken from Aeneas,
though Apollo had snatched away their owner.   350
After Diomedes came fair-haired Menelaus,
royal son of Atreus, driving a yoked team,
two fast creatures—his own horse Podargus
and Agamemnon's mare Aethe, which Echepolus,
Anchises' son, had given to Agamemnon
as a gift, so he wouldn't have to go with him
to wind-swept Ilion, but could remain at home,
enjoying himself, for Zeus had given him great wealth.
He lived in spacious Sicyon. This was the mare
Menelaus now led up in harness, a racehorse   360
filled with a desire to run. The fourth contestant,
Antilochus, got his fair-maned horses ready.
He was a noble son of proud king Nestor,
son of Neleus. Swift-footed horses bred at Pylos
pulled his chariot. His father came up to him
to give him practical advice, a wise man speaking
to one who could appreciate another's skill:

        "Antilochus, you may still be quite young,
        but Zeus and Poseidon have been fond of you.
        They've taught you all sorts of things with horses,   370
        so there's no need to issue you instructions.

You understand well how to wheel around
beside the turning post. But your horses
are the slowest in the race, and so I think
you've got some problems here to deal with.
The others' horses may be faster runners,
but the drivers are no better skilled than you.
So, dear boy, fix your mind on all that skill,
so those prizes don't elude you. You know,
skill in a woodsman matters more than strength.   380
It's skill that lets a helmsman steer his course,
guiding his swift ship straight on wine-dark seas.
And it's skill, too, that makes one charioteer
go faster than another. Some racing drivers,
trusting their chariot and horses, drive them
carelessly, moving back and forth, weaving
on the course. They don't control their horses.
But a cunning man, though he's got worse horses,
keeps his eye on that turning point, cutting
the pillar close. Such a man also understands   390
how to urge his horses on, right at the start,
using leather reins. But he keeps control.
His mind doesn't wander, always watching
the man in front. Now I'll tell you something—
there's a marker, so clear you cannot miss it.
It's a dry stump of oak or pine standing
about six feet high. Rain hasn't rotted it.
On both sides of that stump, two white stones
are firmly fixed against it. At that spot
the race course narrows, but the ground is smooth,   400
so a team can wheel around that stump.
It may be a memorial to some man
long dead, or perhaps men placed it there
to serve as a racing post in earlier times.
Swift-footed lord Achilles has made that stump
his turning point. You need to shave that post,
drive in really close as you wheel around
your chariot and horses. You should lean out
from that well-sprung platform, to your horses' left,
giving the right-hand horse the lash, calling   410

to him with a shout, while with your hands
you let him take the reins. The inside horse
must graze the post, so the well-built wheel hub
seems to scrape the pillar. But be careful—
don't touch the stone, because if you do,
you'll hurt the horses, you'll smash the chariot,
which will delight the others but shame you.
So, dear boy, take care and pay attention.
If you can pass them by as you catch up
right by the turning post, then none of them   420
will reach you with a sudden burst of speed,
much less overtake you, no, not even
if he were driving godlike Arion
behind you, that swift horse of Adrestus,
from heavenly stock, or the very horses
of king Laomedon, the finest ones bred here."

Nestor, Neleus' son, spoke and sat down in his place,
once he'd gone over all the details with his son.
Then Meriones, the fifth contestant in the race,
harnessed his fine-maned horses, and all the racers   430
climbed in their chariots. They gathered up the lots,
which Achilles shook. The first to tumble out
was for Antilochus, Nestor's son. Mighty Eumelus
was next, then came spearman Menelaus,
son of Atreus. After him, Meriones
drew his place. Last of all, and by far the best,
Tydeus' son drew for his horses' lane.
They took their places in a line. Then Achilles
showed them the turning point far out on the plain.
Beside it he'd placed an umpire, godlike Phoenix,   440
his father's follower, to observe the racing
and report back truthfully. Then all together,
they raised their whips above their horses, lashed them
with the reins, and shouted words of encouragement
to urge them forward. The horses raced off quickly,
galloping swiftly from the ships. Under their chests
dust came up, hanging there like storm clouds in a whirlwind.
In the rushing air their manes streamed back. The chariots,

at one moment, would skim across the nourishing earth,
then, in another, would bounce high in the air.   450
Their drivers stood up in the chariots, hearts pounding,
as they strove for victory. Each man shouted out,
calling his horses, as they flew along that dusty plain.
When the swift horses were starting the last stretch,
racing back to the gray sea, their pace grew strained.
Then the drivers each revealed his quality.
The swift-footed horses of Eumelus raced ahead,
followed by Diomedes' team from Tros' breed
not far behind—really close, almost as if they'd charge
right up the back of Eumelus' chariot.   460
Their breath felt hot on his broad shoulders and his back,
for, as they ran ahead, they leaned right into him.
Now Tydeus' son would have passed Eumelus,
or made the issue doubtful, if Phoebus Apollo,
angry at him, hadn't struck the shining whip
out of his hand. Then from Diomedes' eyes
tears of rage streamed out, once he saw Eumelus' team
running even faster than before, while his own
were at a disadvantage, running with no whip.
But Athena had observed Apollo as he fouled   470
the son of Tydeus. She came running at top speed
after that shepherd of his people, then gave back
his whip, putting strength into his horses.
Then, in anger, she went after the son of Admetus.
The goddess snapped his chariot yoke. The horses swerved,
running all around the course. The shaft dropped down
and hit the ground—this threw Eumelus from the chariot
beside the wheel. On his elbows, mouth, and nose
the skin was badly scraped. Above his eyebrows,
his forehead had a bruise. His two eyes filled with tears,   480
his strong voice failed him. Tydeus' son swerved aside,
then drove his sure-footed horses far ahead,
outdistancing the rest, for Athena had put strength
into his team, to give Diomedes glory.
Behind him came Atreus' son, fair-haired Menelaus.
But then Antilochus called to his father's horses:

"Get going, you two. Push yourselves. Move up now,
as fast as you can go. I'm not asking you
to try to beat those horses up ahead,
the team of that warlike son of Tydeus,   490
whom Athena has just helped run faster
to give their driver glory. But overtake
those horses of the son of Atreus—
quick now—don't let them get too far ahead.
You don't want to suffer shame from Aethe,
who's just a mare. Why are you falling back,
you strong horses? Let me tell you something
which is sure to happen—if you slack off now
and I win some inferior prize, then Nestor,
his people's shepherd, will stop feeding you.   500
He'll take out his sharp bronze and kill you both,
here and now. So keep on after them.
Pick up the pace—as fast as you can run!
My task will be to think of something,
devise a way of getting past them there,
where the road narrows. I won't miss my chance."

Antilochus finished. His horses, frightened
by their master's threat, ran faster for a stretch.
Suddenly brave Antilochus saw up ahead
a place where the road was hollowed out and narrow,   510
with a channel in the ground where winter rains
had backed the water up, washing out some of the road
and making all the ground subside. Menelaus
was coming to this spot, leaving no space at all
for a second chariot to move along beside him.
But Antilochus guided his sure-footed horses
off the track, charging up a little to one side.
Atreus' son, alarmed, shouted at Antilochus:

"Antilochus, you're driving like an idiot!
Pull your horses back! The road's too narrow.   520
It gets wider soon—you can pass me there!
Watch you don't hit me. You'll make us crash!"

Menelaus shouted, but Antilochus kept going,
moving even faster and laying on the whip,
as if he hadn't heard. They raced on like this
about as far as a discus flies when tossed
with a shoulder swing by a powerful young man
testing his strength. But then the son of Atreus' team
slowed down and fell behind, reined in deliberately,
in case the sure-footed teams somehow collided   530
and overturned their well-sprung chariots in the road,
leaving their drivers, for all their eagerness to win,
sprawling in the dust. Then fair-haired Menelaus,
in anger at Antilochus, yelled out:

                              "Antilochus,
        you're more reckless than any man alive!
        Damn you! Achaeans were all wrong to think
        you were a man with some intelligence.
        But even so, you still may not win the prize,
        without the need to swear you won it fairly."

Menelaus yelled this, then called out to his horses: 540

        "Don't slow down or stand there sad at heart.
        Their feet and limbs will tire before yours do,
        for those two horses are no longer young."

Menelaus spoke. Excited by their master's shout,
his horses ran on even faster.

                        Meanwhile, the Argives,
sitting all together, kept watching for the horses
racing on the dusty plain. The first to spot them
was Idomeneus, leader of the Cretans.
He sat some distance from the crowd, in a higher spot,
a fine lookout. The man in front was still far off,   550
but when he called his horses, Idomeneus
recognized his voice and could see quite clearly
the horse in front—it was all brown, with a mark
on his forehead as round and white as a full moon.

Idomeneus stood up and called out to the Argives:

"My friends, leaders and rulers of Argives,
am I the only one to see those horses,
or can you glimpse them, too? It seems to me
that another team is now in front,
with another charioteer approaching.   560
Going out, Eumelus' mares were in the lead,
but they must have run into some trouble
out there, somewhere on the plain. I saw them
wheeling round the turning post in front.
Now I can't see them anywhere, though my eyes
keep searching the entire Trojan plain.
Perhaps the charioteer let go the reins
and couldn't guide his chariot round the post
and failed to make the turn. I think he fell
out there somewhere and smashed his chariot.   570
His horses must have panicked in their hearts
and run away. But stand up. Look for yourselves.
I can't see all that clearly, but the man
seems to be of Aetolian descent,
an Argive king, mighty Diomedes,
son of horse-taming Tydeus."

                              At that point,
swift Ajax, son of Oïleus, mocked Idomeneus
with these insulting words:

                                        "Idomeneus,
why are you always nattering? Those prancing mares
are still far distant, with a lot more ground   580
to race across. And of all the Argives here
you're not the youngest—those eyes in your head
don't have the keenest vision. But for all that,
you still chatter on. You don't need to babble,
when there are better men than you around.
Those same mares as before are out in front,
Eumelus' team, and he's standing there, as well,
holding the reins."

The leader of the Cretans,
furious with Ajax, then replied:

"You're great at insults,
Ajax, but really stupid. In everything,   590
you're the most useless Argive of them all,
because your mind is dull. Come on then,
let's bet a tripod or a cauldron on it—
which horses are in front—so you'll learn
by having to pay up. As our umpire,
let's have Agamemnon, son of Atreus."

At Idomeneus' words, swift Ajax, son of Oïleus,
jumped up at once, in a rage, ready to answer
with more angry words. At that point, their quarrel
might have got much worse, but Achilles himself   600
stood up and said:

"No more of this,
Idomeneus and Ajax, no more angry words,
no more insults—that's not appropriate.
You'd both feel angry if another man
behaved this way. So sit down with the group
and watch for horses. It won't be long
before their eagerness to win brings them here.
Then you can both see the Argive horses,
who's in the lead and who's behind."

As Achilles spoke, Tydeus' son came charging in   610
really close to them. He kept swinging his whip
down from the shoulder, so his horses raced ahead,
raising their hooves up high as they ran the course.
Clouds of dust kept falling on the charioteer,
as his chariot made of gold and tin raced on,
drawn by swift-running horses, who left behind
only a slight trace of wheel rims in the dust,
as the team flew speeding by. Diomedes pulled up
right in the middle of the crowd. Streams of sweat
dripped from the horses' necks and chests onto the ground.   620

He jumped down from his gleaming chariot, leaning the whip
against the yoke. Strong Sthenelus didn't wait for long
to get the prizes—he retrieved them right away,
giving the woman to his proud comrades to lead off
and the two-handled tripod to carry with them.
Then he untied the horses from their harnesses.

Next in came the horses driven by Antilochus,
grandson of Neleus, who just beat Menelaus—
he won by cunning, not by his horses' speed.
But Menelaus was bringing his swift horses in   630
very close behind. The space between the two
was as far as a horse is from the chariot wheel,
when it strains to pull its master fast across the plain—
its tail ends touch the spinning wheels behind it—
there's not much space between them, as they move
at top speed on the plain—that's about how far
Menelaus lagged behind noble Antilochus.
At first, he'd been about a discus throw behind,
but he was quickly catching up, for the spirit
in Agamemnon's mare, the fair-maned Aethe,   640
kept getting stronger. Had the course been longer
for both contestants, he'd have surely passed him,
without leaving the result in doubt. The next one in
was Meriones, Idomeneus' brave attendant,
a spear-throw length behind splendid Menelaus.
His horses were the slowest, and he himself
had the least skill at driving in a chariot race.
Last one in was Admetus' son, well behind the rest,
driving his horses in front of him and pulling
his chariot behind. Seeing Eumelus coming in,   650
swift-footed lord Achilles felt sorry for him.
Standing among Argives, he spoke—his words had wings:

> "The best man brings up his sure-footed horses
> in last place. Come, let's give him a prize,
> as seems fitting—the award for second place.
> Let Diomedes take the first-place prize."

Achilles spoke. They all agreed with his suggestion.
So now he would have given Eumelus the mare,
as Achaeans had agreed, but Antilochus,
great-hearted Nestor's son, stood up to claim his right.   660
Addressing Achilles, son of Peleus, he said:

> "Achilles, I'll be angry with you,
> if you carry out what you've proposed.
> For you want to rob me of my prize,
> claiming that his chariot and swift horses
> ran into trouble—as he did himself,
> though he's an excellent charioteer.
> But he should have prayed to the immortals—
> in the race he would not have finished last.
> If you're feeling sorry for Eumelus,   670
> if he's someone your heart is fond of,
> in your hut there's lots of gold. You've got bronze,
> sheep, women slaves, and sure-footed horses.
> Why not take some of that and then give him
> an even greater prize sometime later on?
> Or do it now. Achaeans will applaud you.
> But I won't give up the mare. If someone
> wants her, let him try doing battle with me,
> hand to hand."

>   Antilochus finished speaking.
Swift-footed, god-like Achilles smiled, delighted   680
with Antilochus, who was a close companion.
In reply, he spoke these winged words:

>   "Antilochus,
> if you're telling me to give Eumelus
> some other prize inside my huts, I'll do it.
> I'll give him the breastplate I took away
> from Asteropaeus. It's made of bronze,
> with a casting of bright tin around it.
> For Eumelus it will have great value."

After saying this, Achilles ordered Automedon,

his close companion, to fetch the breastplate from the hut.   690
He went and brought it back and gave it to Eumelus,
who was delighted to receive the armour.
But then Menelaus stood up before them all.
His heart was bitter with unremitting anger
against Antilochus. A herald put the sceptre
in Menelaus' hand, then shouted out for silence
among the Argives. God-like Menelaus spoke:

> "Antilochus, you used to have good sense,
> before all this. Now look at what you've done.
> You've brought my skills here into disrepute,   700
> fouling my horses when you hurled your team
> in front of me out there, that team of yours
> which is far inferior to mine. Come now,
> you leaders and rulers of the Argives,
> judge between the two of us—and fairly,
> so Achaeans armed in bronze will never say,
> 'Menelaus beat Antilochus with lies,
> when he received that mare. Though his horses
> were much slower, he used his influence,
> his rank and power.' In fact, I myself   710
> will judge the case, and no Danaan,
> I claim, will find fault with me in any way,
> for justice will be done. Antilochus,
> come here, my lord, and, as our customs state,
> stand there before your chariot and horses,
> holding that thin whip you used before.
> With your hand on your horses, swear an oath,
> by the god who surrounds and shakes the earth,
> that you didn't mean to block my chariot
> with some trick."

           Antilochus, a prudent man, replied: 720

> "Don't let me offend you, king Menelaus.
> I'm a younger man than you—you're my senior
> and my better. You know how a young man
> can do foolish things. His mind works quickly,

512

but his judgment's suspect. So be patient
in your heart. That mare I was awarded
I freely give you. And if you requested
something greater from my own possessions,
I'd want to give it to you right away,
rather than lose your good will, my lord,   730
for ever and offend against the gods."

The son of great-hearted Nestor finished speaking.
He led out the horse, then placed it in the hands
of Menelaus, whose heart melted like the dew
on ripening ears of corn, when fields are bristling
with the crop—that's how, Menelaus, your heart
softened in your chest. He spoke to Antilochus—
his words had wings:

                "Now, indeed, Antilochus,
I'll give up my anger with you. Before now,
you haven't been too reckless or a fool.   740
This time your youth overcame your judgement.
In future, you shouldn't try to do such tricks
against your betters. Another Achaean
would not have won me over quite so fast.
But you've worked very hard, endured a lot—
you, your noble father, and your brother—
in my cause. So I'll agree to your request.
What's more, though she's mine, I'll give you the mare,
so all these people here will recognize
my heart's not arrogant or unyielding."   750

Saying this, Menelaus gave the mare to Noëmon,
a comrade of Antilochus, to lead away.
Menelaus carried off the shining cauldron.
Meriones then collected the two talents
for his fourth-place finish. But the prize for fifth place,
the two-handled jar, went unclaimed. So Achilles
awarded it to Nestor. Carrying the prize
into the crowd of Argives, he stood beside him.

Then Achilles said:

> "Take this now, old man.
> Let it be your treasure, in memory   760
> of Patroclus' burial. For you'll see him
> no more among the Argives. This prize
> I'm giving you without a contest.
> For you won't be competing as a boxer,
> or in wrestling, or the spear throw.
> Nor will you be running in the foot race.
> For old age now has you in its cruel grip."

With these words, Achilles placed the jar in Nestor's hands.
He was happy to accept it. Then Nestor spoke,
saying these winged words to Achilles: 770

> "Indeed, my son, you've made a valid point.
> For my limbs and feet are no longer firm,
> my friend. Nor do I find it as easy
> to extend my arms out from my shoulders,
> as I did before. Would that I were young,
> my strength as firm, as it was that day
> Epeians buried lord Amarynceus
> at Bouprasium. His sons awarded prizes
> in honour of their king. No man could match me,
> none of the Epeians, my own Pylians,   780
> nor any of the brave Aetolians.
> In boxing I defeated Clytomedes,
> Enops' son, in wrestling Ancaeus,
> from Pleuron, who fought against me.
> In the footrace, I outran Iphicles,
> who was outstanding, and in the spear throw,
> I beat Phyleus and Polydorus.
> I was beaten only in the chariot race
> by the two sons of Actor. They pushed ahead,
> for there were two of them, both really keen   790
> to win, because they'd set the greatest prize
> for that particular race. They were two twins.
> One always held the reins—he was the driver.
> The other used the whip. That's the man I was,

back then, but now let younger men compete
in events like these. For I must follow
the dictates of a cruel old age these days,
though as a warrior I once excelled.
But come, you must continue with these games
to honour your companion. As for this gift,   800
I accept it gladly. It delights my heart
that you think of me always as your friend.
You don't forget the honours due to me
among Achaeans. May the gods grant you,
as a reward for that your heart's desires."

Nestor finished. Once he'd heard all of Nestor's story,
Peleus' son moved through the large Achaean crowd.
Then he set out prizes for the painful contest—
the boxing. To the group he led out a sturdy mule,
an unbroken female, six years old, the hardest   810
to break in. For the loser, he put out a cup,
one with two handles. Then Achilles, standing up,
addressed the Argives:

                          "Son of Atreus,
          all you other well-armed Achaeans,
          for these prizes here we need two good men,
          the best there are, to put up their fists and box.
          The one to whom Apollo gives endurance
          and Achaeans all acknowledge winner,
          let him then take this mule back to his hut.
          The beaten man gets this two-handled cup."   820

Achilles' words at once stirred into action
a strong, brave man, well skilled in boxing—Epeius,
son of Panopeus. Putting his hand on the mule,
Epeius said:

                          "Let whoever's going to get
          the two-handled cup step forward. For I say this—
          no Achaean will beat me with his fists
          and take this mule. I claim I'm the winner.

515

I may not be the best in battle. So what?
A man can't be well skilled in everything.
But I'll say this—and what I say will happen—   830
I'll break apart the skin and crush the bones
of the man who fights me. Those close to him
had better stay here in a single group
to help him off, once my fists have thrashed him."

Epeius' words reduced them all to silence.
The only one to stand up to oppose him
was godlike Euryalus, son of Mecisteus,
son of Talaus. He'd once come to Thebes,
for the funeral games of fallen Oedipus.
There he'd triumphed against all the sons of Cadmus.   840
Famous spearman Diomedes helped him prepare,
encouraging Euryalus with his words—
he really wanted him to win the contest.
First, he set the loin cloth on him, then gave him
leather thongs, fine-cut hide from a farmyard ox.
When the two men had laced up their hands, they strode
into the middle of the group. Raising their arms,
their powerful fists, they went at each other.
Their hands exchanged some heavy punches, landing
with painful crunches on their jaws. From their limbs   850
sweat ran down everywhere. Then Euryalus feinted,
but godlike Epeius moved and punched his cheek bone.
Euryalus could not keep his feet for long.
His splendid limbs collapsed there on the spot—
as a fish jumps through the rippling surface water
in a forceful North Wind breeze near a weed-filled shore,
before a black wave hides it—that how Euryalus
jerked up as he was hit. But great-hearted Epeius
grabbed him and set him on his feet. Around him,
his close comrades gathered. They led him through the crowd   860
spitting gobs of blood, dragging his feet behind him,
with his head down on one side. They took him off,
set him down with them, still semi-conscious,
then went themselves to collect the two-handled cup.

For the Danaans, Peleus' son then set out
a display of prizes for the third contest,
the hard-fought wrestling match. The winning prize
was a huge tripod to place above a fire,
whose value among themselves Achaeans set
at twelve oxen. Into the middle of the crowd   870
he then brought out the loser's prize, a woman
skilled in every kind of work, worth four oxen.
Standing up among the Argives, Achilles said:

    "Step up now the two who'll try this contest."

At these words, great Telamonian Ajax got up,
as did Odysseus, the crafty master of deceit.
They strapped on their belts and strode out to the crowd,
then, with their powerful hands gripped each other's elbows—
locked together like rafters on some lofty house,
fitted by skilled craftsmen to keep out blasts of wind.   880
Their backs cracked as their strong hands applied the pressure.
Streams of sweat poured down, and red blood welts appeared
across their ribs and shoulders, as both contestants
kept up their struggle to prevail and get the prize,
that well-made tripod. But it was impossible
for Odysseus to trip up Ajax or throw him down,
or for Ajax to do the same thing to Odysseus,
for Odysseus' strength prevented him from that.
But when well-armed Achaeans started to get bored,
great Telamonian Ajax said to Odysseus: 890

    "Divinely born son of Laertes,
    resourceful Odysseus—try lifting me,
    or I'll try lifting you. And we'll let Zeus
    decide the outcome."

              Saying this, Ajax tried a lift.
But Odysseus did not forget his various tricks.
He kicked Ajax behind the knee, taking out his leg.
Ajax toppled backward, with Odysseus falling
on his chest. The spectators got excited then.

Next resilient, godlike Odysseus tried a lift.
He managed to move Ajax off the ground a bit,   900
but couldn't lift him. Then Ajax hooked him
with his leg around the knee, so the two men fell
close together on the ground, covered both in dust.
Now they would have jumped up to wrestle a third fall,
but Achilles himself came up and held them back.

      "You two need not continue wrestling.
      Don't let the pain exhaust you. For both of you
      are winners. You must take equal prizes.
      Once you leave, other Achaeans can compete."

Hearing these words, both men agreed. The two of them   910
cleaned their bodies of the dust and put on tunics.

After that, Peleus' son quickly set out other prizes
for the footrace—a finely crafted silver mixing bowl,
holding six measures. It was very beautiful,
the loveliest object in the world by far.
Sidonian experts in skilled handicrafts who made it
had shaped it well. Then Phoenician men had brought it
over the dark sea, unpacked it in the harbour,
and given it as a gift to Thoas, ransom
for Lycaon, Priam's son, paid by Euneus,   920
son of Jason, to warrior Patroclus. This bowl
Achilles set out as a prize to honour his companion,
a trophy for the man who in the footrace
proved he was the fastest. As prize for second place,
he led out a huge ox, rich in fat. For third place,
he offered half a talent. Then Achilles stood up
and announced to the Achaeans:

                "Up all those of you
      who want to make the effort for this prize."

At that, swift Oïlean Ajax jumped up at once.
Next came resourceful Odysseus and Nestor's son   930
Antilochus, who, of all the young men there,

could run the fastest. These men stood in line,
as Achilles pointed out the turning post—
the race course was the distance there and back.
The son of Oïleus quickly raced in front,
with godlike Odysseus really close behind,
as close as the weaving bar comes to the breast
of a well-dressed woman when she deftly pulls it
in her hands to pass the weaving spool through thread,
keeping the rod against her chest—that's how close   940
Odysseus ran behind, his feet hitting Ajax's footprints
before the dust could settle there. Godlike Odysseus
ran so close, his breath touched the back of Ajax's head.
All the Achaeans were cheering on Odysseus,
as he strove to win the race, yelling at him
to push his energy right to the limit.
While they were running the last section of the course,
Odysseus in his heart prayed to Athena,
goddess with the glittering eyes:

> "Hear me, goddess.
> Be good to me. Help me. Speed up my feet."   950

Odysseus prayed, and Pallas Athena heard him.
She made his legs, feet, and upper arms feel lighter.
Then, as they were about to sprint in for the prize,
Ajax slipped in mid stride—for Athena fouled him—
right where the bellowing cattle had dropped their dung
as they were slaughtered, the ones which swift Achilles
had killed in honour of Patroclus. So Ajax
finished with his mouth and nostrils full of dung,
as resilient Odysseus raced on ahead,
came in first, and won the prize. Ajax got the ox.   960
He stood there, hands on the horn of that farmyard beast,
spitting out cow dung, and then said to the Argives:

> "So the goddess played tricks with my feet—
> the one that always helps Odysseus out,
> taking care of him, just like a mother."

Ajax spoke.
They all had a good laugh at him. Antilochus
took the prize for coming last. He smiled, then said,
as he spoke to the Argives:

"Friends, I'll tell you this,
something you already know—immortal gods
still honour older men, even today.   970
Ajax is just a little older than myself,
but Odysseus comes from another time,
an older generation. But his greater age,
so people say, is green. So it's difficult
for Achaeans to beat him in a race—
all except Achilles."

Antilochus finished speaking.
He'd acknowledged the swift-footed son of Peleus,
so Achilles answered him and said:

"Antilochus,
you've not paid that tribute here for nothing.
I'll add a gold half-talent to your prize."   980

With these words, Achilles handed him the gold.
Antilochus was very pleased to get it.

Next, the son of Peleus brought to the gathering
a long-shadowed spear. He set it down, and with it
a shield and helmet. It was Sarpedon's armour,
which Patroclus had taken from him. Standing there,
Achilles then said to the Argives:

"We're calling for two men,
two of the best, to battle for these prizes,
clothed in armour, wielding their sharp bronze,
testing each other here before this crowd.   990
Whichever man hits the other's fair skin first,
under the armour, drawing his dark blood,
will get from me this silver-studded sword,

a lovely one from Thrace, which I seized
from Asteropaeus. Both men will take
this armour here, sharing it in common.
And in my hut we'll get a banquet ready
for both of them."

                              Achilles finished.
Then great Telamonian Ajax moved out front,
and strong Diomedes, son of Tydeus, got up.   1000
On each side of the crowd they armed themselves,
then both strode to the middle, prepared to fight,
both glaring fearfully. All Achaeans were then gripped
with anxious expectation. Once the two men
approached each other at close quarters, they attacked,
charging three times, three times going at it hand to hand.
Ajax struck through the even circle of the shield
of his opponent, but did not touch his flesh.
The breastplate kept his body guarded from the spear.
Tydeus' son was trying to aim his gleaming spear point   1010
over the huge shield, to get Ajax in the neck.
But then Achaeans, in their fear for Ajax,
called for a halt and an award of equal prizes.
So Achilles gave the great sword to Diomedes—
the scabbard and the well-cut strap as well.

Then Peleus' son put out a lump of rough-cast iron,
which, in earlier days, Eëtion had used for throwing.
Godlike, swift-footed Achilles had slaughtered him,
then taken his iron and all his other goods
away in his swift ship. Achilles then stood up,   1020
and addressed the Argives:

                    "Step up all those
who want to try this competition.
Whoever wins this iron can use it
to serve his needs for five successive years,
even though his rich fields are far away.
His herders and his ploughman will not need
to travel to the town through lack of iron.

This will give them all that they require."

Achilles spoke. Then up came Polypoetes,
a strong fighter, and godlike Leonteus,   1030
a powerful man, then Telamonian Ajax,
and godlike Epeius. They stood there in a line.
Godlike Epeius gripped the weight, swung it round,
then threw. The Achaeans all laughed at the result.
The second one to throw was Leonteus,
offshoot of Ares. Great Ajax, son of Telamon,
was third to throw. His strong hand tossed the weight,
hurling it beyond the marks of all the others.
But then that strong warrior Polypoetes
picked up the weight and threw it even further   1040
than all those in the contest, by the same distance
a herdsman throws his staff, so it flies spinning
in among his cattle herd. The crowd all shouted.
Then the comrades of strong Polypoetes stood up
and carried off their king's prize to the hollow ships.

Next, Achilles set out the prizes for the archers,
things made of blackened iron—ten double axes
and ten with single blades. Then he set up,
far off in the sands, the mast of a dark-prowed ship.
Attached to it with a slender cord, he placed   1050
a quivering dove with the cord tied to its foot.
He then told competitors to shoot the dove.

                    "The man who hits it,
            that quivering dove, can carry off
            all these double axes. He can take them home.
            If he misses the bird and hits the cord,
            he'll be less successful, but he'll take as prize
            these single-bladed axes."

                              Achilles finished speaking.
Powerful lord Teucer then got up, and Meriones,
courageous attendant to lord Idomeneus.
They took lots and shook them in a helmet made of bronze.   1060

Teucer's lot gave him first attempt. He loosed an arrow,
a powerful shot, but he'd made no promise
to Apollo that he'd give a splendid offering
of new born lambs. So he failed to hit the bird—
Apollo wouldn't give him that. But he hit the cord
tethering the bird near its foot and cut it.
The keen arrow sliced right through. The dove escaped,
flying up into the sky, chord dangling down
towards the ground. Achaeans then all cheered the shot.
But Meriones quickly snatched the bow from Teucer.   1070
He'd been holding an arrow ready for some time,
as Teucer aimed. He offered up a rapid prayer
to Apollo, the far shooter, promising
he'd make a splendid sacrifice of new-born lambs.
He saw the trembling dove high up, under the clouds.
As she circled there, he shot her through the middle,
under the wing. The arrow passed straight through, falling
back to earth again. It struck by Meriones' foot.
The dove fluttered to the mast of the dark-prowed ship,
her head hung down, her wings drooped, as life   1080
fled quickly from her limbs. She fell from the mast
a long way to the ground. The crowd looked on amazed.
So Meriones carried off ten double axes,
while Teucer took back to his hollow ships
the single-bladed ones.

                    Then Peleus' son
brought out a long-shadowed spear and set it down
before the gathering and a brand new cauldron,
not yet touched by fire, with a floral pattern on it.
Its value was one ox. Then warriors got up
for the spear-throw competition—the son of Atreus,   1090
wide-ruling Agamemnon, and Meriones,
courageous attendant to lord Idomeneus.
But then swift-footed, godlike Achilles spoke:

                    "Son of Atreus,
        we know how you surpass all others,
        how in the spear throw you're much stronger,

better than anyone. So take this prize,
as you go to your hollow ships. Let's give
the spear to warrior Meriones, if your heart
is pleased with that. It's what I'd like to do."

Achilles spoke. Agamemnon, king of men, agreed.   1100
The warrior king gave the spear to Meriones,
then handed his own prize, the lovely cauldron,
over to Talthybius, his herald.

Book Twenty-Four
Achilles and Priam

*[Achilles continues to mourn and to dishonour Hector's corpse; the gods
debate his action; Zeus resolves to deal with the problem; Iris goes off to
fetch Thetis; Zeus instructs Thetis to visit Achilles; Thetis tells Achilles
Zeus' instructions; Achilles agrees to give up Hector's body for ransom;
Iris visits Priam, telling him to go to the Achaean ships; Hecuba objects
to the trip; Priam insults his sons, then collects the ransom and leaves
with Idaios, the herald; Zeus sends Priam an omen and tells Hermes to
guide Priam to Achilles; Hermes meets Priam on the road; Hermes takes
Priam to the Achaean camp; Priam meets Achilles; Achilles agrees to
give back Hector; Achilles and Priam have dinner; Priam sleeps
overnight outside Achilles' hut; Priam and Idaios return to Troy with
Hector's body; the women lament over Hector; the Trojans bury Hector]*

Once the funeral gathering broke up, the men dispersed,
each one going to his own ship, concerned to eat
and then enjoy sweet sleep. But Achilles kept on weeping,
remembering his dear companion. All-conquering Sleep
could not overcome him, as he tossed and turned,
longing for manly, courageous, strong Patroclus,
thinking of all he'd done with him, all the pain
they'd suffered, as they'd gone through wars with other men
and with the perilous sea. As he kept remembering,
he cried heavy tears, sometimes lying on his side,   10
sometimes on his back or on his face. Then he'd get up,
to wander in distress, back and forth along the shore.
He'd see Dawn's approach across the sea and beaches,
then he'd harness his fast horses to their chariot,
tie on Hector and drag him behind, driving
three times around the tomb of Menoetius' dead son.
Then in his hut he'd rest again, leaving Hector
stretched out, face down in the dust. But Apollo,
feeling pity for Hector, though he was dead,
guarded his skin from any lacerations,   20
covering his whole body with the golden aegis,
so as Achilles dragged him, he did not tear his skin.

Still Achilles kept dishonouring godlike Hector.

Then the blessed gods, looking on, pitied Hector.
So they urged keen-eyed Hermes, killer of Argus,
to steal the corpse, an idea that pleased them all,
except for Hera, Poseidon, and Athena,
the girl with glittering eyes, who kept up the hatred
they'd felt when they first started to loathe Ilion,
Priam and his people, for Alexander's folly—   30
he'd been contemptuous of those goddesses,
when they were visiting his sheep-fold, choosing
the one who volunteered to serve his dangerous lust.[1]
But after the twelfth dawn had come since Hector's death,
Phoebus Apollo spoke out to the immortals:

> "You gods are cruel and vindictive.
> Did Hector never sacrifice to you,
> burning thighs of perfect bulls and goats?
> And can't you now rouse yourself to save him,
> though he's a corpse, for his wife, his mother,   40
> and his child to look at, and for Priam, too,
> his father, and the people, who'd burn him
> with all speed and give him burial rites?
> No, you want to help ruthless Achilles,
> whose heart has no restraint. In that chest
> his mind cannot be changed. Like some lion,
> he thinks savage thoughts, a beast which follows
> only its own power, its own proud heart,
> as it goes out against men's flocks, seeking
> a feast of cattle—that's how Achilles   50
> destroys compassion. And in his heart
> there's no sense of shame, which can help a man
> or harm him. No doubt, a man can suffer loss
> of someone even closer than a friend—
> a brother born from the same mother
> or even a son. He pays his tribute

[1]This is a reference to the famous Judgment of Paris, when Paris awarded the apple "for the fairest" to Aphrodite, rather than to Hera or Athena, because Aphrodite had offered him the most beautiful woman in the world if he gave her the prize. This event is the origin of the war and helps to explain how the gods align themselves.

with his tears and his laments—then stops.
For Fates have put in men resilient hearts.
But this man here, once he took Hector's life,
ties him behind his chariot, then drags him   60
around his dear companion's burial mound.
He's done nothing to help or honour him.
He should take care he doesn't anger us.
Though he's a fine man, in this rage of his
he's harming senseless dust."

                       Then Hera,
angry at Apollo, spoke up in reply:

                "Lord of the silver bow,
yes, indeed, what you say may well be true,
if you gods give Hector and Achilles
equal worth. But Hector is a mortal man,
suckled at a woman's breast, while Achilles   70
is the child of a goddess I raised myself.
I brought her up and gave her to Peleus
to be his wife, a man dear to the hearts
of the immortal gods. All of you were there,
when they got married. You, too, were with us
at the banquet, you friend of evil men,
clutching your lyre, as slippery as ever."

Cloud gatherer Zeus then answered Hera, saying:

            "Hera, don't get so angry with the gods.
These two will not both share equal honours.   80
Still, of all mortal men in Ilion,
Hector was the favourite of the gods.
At least that's what he was to me.
He never failed to offer me fine gifts.
At their communal feasts, my own altar
never went without the proper offerings,
libations and sacrificial smoke,
as is our right. But we'll not let this corpse,
brave Hector's body, be taken secretly.

Achilles would for certain learn of it,   90
since his mother sees him all the time,
both day and night. But one of the gods
should tell Thetis to come here before me,
so I can put a useful plan to her,
how Achilles can get gifts from Priam
and then give Hector back to him."

Once Zeus had spoken, storm-swift Iris rushed away,
bearing Zeus' message. Half way between Samos
and rocky Imbros she plunged into the sea.
As waters roared above her, she sank way down,   100
just as a plummet sinks when fastened to a lure,
one fashioned out of horn from some farmyard ox
to bring death to hungry fish. She met Thetis
sitting in a hollow cave with other sea gods
thronging there around her. In the middle of them all,
Thetis was lamenting the fate of her fine son,
who would die in fertile Troy, far from his home.
Standing right beside her, swift-footed Iris spoke:

          "Rouse yourself, Thetis. Zeus, whose thoughts
          endure forever, is calling for you."   110

Silver-footed Thetis then said in reply:

          "Why is that mighty god now summoning me?
          I'm ashamed to associate with immortals,
          my heart holds such immeasurable grief.
          But I'll go. And no matter what he says,
          his words will not be wasted."

                              Saying this,
Thetis, queen of goddesses, took a dark veil,
the blackest of her garments, then set off on her way.
Swift Iris, with feet like wind, went on ahead.
The surging sea parted round the two of them.   120
When they emerged on shore, they raced on up to heaven.
They found the wide-seeing son of Cronos in the midst
of all the other blessed gods, who live forever.

Once Athena had made room for her, Thetis sat
with Father Zeus. Hera placed a gold cup in her hand,
with words of welcome. She drank, then handed back the cup.
The father of the gods and men spoke first:

> "You've come here to Olympus, goddess Thetis,
> though you're grieving, with endless sorrows
> in your heart. I know that. But even so,   130
> I'll tell you the reason why I've called you here.
> For nine days immortals have been quarreling
> about Achilles, sacker of cities,
> and Hector's corpse. They keep urging Hermes,
> keen-eyed killer of Argus, to steal the body.
> But I want to give honour to Achilles,
> maintain my respect for you in future,
> and keep our friendship. So you must leave quickly.
> Go to the army. Tell your son what I say.
> Tell him the gods are annoyed at him,   140
> that of all immortals I'm especially angry,
> because, in his heartfelt fury, he keeps
> Hector at his beaked ships, won't give him back.
> Through fear of me, he may hand Hector over.
> I'll also send Iris to great-hearted Priam,
> telling him to go to the Achaean ships,
> to beg for his dear son, bearing presents
> for Achilles to delight his heart."

Silver-footed Thetis did not disagree with Zeus.
She went speeding from Olympus' peak to her son's hut.   150
She found him there, still mourning endlessly.
Around him, his close companions were all busy,
in a hurry to get their morning meal prepared.
Inside the hut they'd butchered a large woolly sheep.
His noble mother sat close by him, caressed him
with her hand, then spoke to him, saying:

>   "My son,
> how long will you consume your heart with tears,
> with this grieving, not thinking about food

or going to bed. To have sex with a woman
would do you good. I won't see you still alive   160
much longer—for at this moment, Death,
your powerful fate, is standing close at hand.
But quickly, listen to me. For I'm here
as messenger from Zeus. He told me this—
the gods are angry with you. Zeus himself
is the angriest of all immortals,
because, in your heartfelt fury, you keep
Hector by your beaked ships, won't return him.
So come, now. Give him back, and for that corpse
accept a ransom."

                    Swift-footed Achilles   170
then replied to Thetis, saying:

                         "So be it.
Whoever brings the ransom, let that man
have the corpse, if that's what the Olympian
in his own heart truly desires."

Thus, among the assembled ships, mother and son
spoke to each other many winged words.

Meanwhile, Cronos' son urged Iris to be off
to sacred Ilion:

                   "You must go right away,
swift Iris. Leave your home here on Olympus.
Take this message to great-hearted Priam,   180
inside Ilion—tell him he must visit
Achaean ships to ransom his dear son,
taking gifts to please Achilles' heart.
He must go alone. No other Trojan man
is to accompany him. One herald,
an older man, can make the journey with him,
to drive the mules and sturdy wagon
and bring back to the city the body
of the godlike man Achilles killed.

He mustn't think of death or be afraid.   190
A fitting escort will accompany him—
Hermes, killer of Argus—as a guide,
until he brings him to Achilles.
Once he's led him to Achilles' hut,
that man will not kill him—he'll restrain
all other men. For he's not stupid,
blind, or disrespectful of the gods.
He'll spare a suppliant, treat him kindly."

Zeus spoke. Storm-footed Iris rushed off with the message.
Reaching Priam's house, she found him weeping there   200
and mourning. His sons were sitting with their father
inside the courtyard, wetting garments with their tears.
The old man sat with them, cloak tightly wrapped around him.
Both his head and neck were covered with the dung
he'd groveled in and grabbed up by the handful.
His daughters and sons' wives were crying through the house,
thinking of many noble warriors who'd been killed
at Achaean hands. Zeus' messenger approached.
Standing beside Priam, she spoke in a soft voice,
but nonetheless his limbs began to tremble.   210

> "Let your heart be brave, Priam, son of Dardanus.
> Don't be afraid. I've not come with news
> of any harm to you, but to do good.
> I am a messenger to you from Zeus—
> he may be far off, but he looks out for you,
> cares very much, and feels pity for you.
> The Olympian is telling you to ransom
> godlike Hector. Take presents to Achilles,
> fine things his heart will find delightful.
> You must go alone. No other Trojan man   220
> is to go along with you. A herald,
> an older man, may make the journey with you,
> to drive the mules and sturdy wagon
> and bring back to the city the body
> of the godlike man Achilles killed.
> You mustn't think of death or be afraid.

531

A proper escort will accompany you—
Hermes, killer of Argus—to guide you,
until he brings you to Achilles.
Once he's led you to Achilles' hut,   230
that man will not kill you—he'll restrain
all other men. For he's not stupid,
blind, or disrespectful of the gods.
He'll spare a suppliant, treat him kindly."

With these words, swift-footed Iris went away.
Priam told his sons to prepare a sturdy mule cart
and lash on a wicker box. Then he went in person
down to the sweet-smelling vaulted storage chamber
lined with cedar, which held many of his treasures.
He summoned Hecuba, his wife, then said: 240

                                        "My lady,
a messenger has come to me from Zeus,
instructing me to ransom our dear son.
I'm to go to the Achaean ships, taking
gifts for Achilles to delight his heart.
So come, tell me what you feel about this.
My own heart and spirit are urging me,
in a strange and fearful way, to go there,
to the ships and wide Achaean camp."

At Priam's words, his wife cried out. Then she replied:

        "Where's your mind gone, that wisdom you once had,   250
for which in earlier days you were well known
among your subjects and with strangers, too?
How can you want to visit the Achaean ships,
to go alone, before the eyes of the very man
who's killed so many of your noble sons?
You've an iron heart. If he captures you,
once he sees you, that man's so savage,
so unreliable, he'll show no pity.
He'll not respect you. No, let's mourn here,
in our home, sitting far away from Hector.   260

That's what mighty Fate spun out for him
when he was born, when I gave birth to him—
that swift-running dogs would devour him
far from his parents beside that powerful man.
How I wish I could rip out that man's heart,
then eat it. That would be some satisfaction
for my son, who wasn't playing the coward
when he killed him. No, he was standing there,
defending deep-breasted Trojan women
and Trojan men, not thinking of his safety   270
or running off in flight."

                              The old man,
godlike Priam, then said in response to Hecuba:

"I want to go. Don't try to stop me.
Don't be a bird of ill omen in our house.
You won't convince me. If some other man,
some earthly mortal, had told me this,
a prophet who interprets sacrifices
or some priest, we'd think it false, reject it.
But this time I heard the goddess for myself.
I stared her in the face. So I will go.   280
Her message won't be wasted. If I'm fated
to die by the bronze-clad Achaeans' ships,
that's what I wish. Let Achilles kill me,
once I've embraced my son and satisfied
my desire to mourn."

                          Priam finished speaking.
Then he threw open fine lids on the storage chests.
From there he took twelve lovely robes, twelve single cloaks,
as many blankets, white coverlets, and tunics.
He brought gold, weighing out a total of ten talents,
then two gleaming tripods, four cauldrons, and a cup,   290
a splendid one given to him by men of Thrace,
when he'd gone there as an envoy, a fine treasure.
Even this cup the old man didn't leave at home—
he was so eager to pay ransom for his son.

Then Priam chased the Trojans from his courtyard,
shaming them with angry words:

> "Go away,
> you wretches! You ought to be ashamed.
> Have you nothing to cry about back home,
> so you come here tormenting me like this?
> Isn't it enough that Zeus, Cronos' son,   300
> gives me this grief, that I must lose my son,
> the best one of them all? Well, you'll soon find out.
> Now he's been killed, it will be easier
> for Achaeans to kill you, too. As for me,
> may I go down to Hades' home, before I see
> this city plundered and destroyed."

With these words, Priam went at the people with his staff,
lashing out. They moved off, beyond the old man's rage.
Then he began shouting at his sons, cursing them—
Helenus, Paris, noble Agathon, Pammon,   310
Antiphonus, Polites, skilled in war shouts,
Deïphobus, Hippothous, and proud Dios.
To these nine, the old man yelled his orders.

> "Hurry up, you useless children, my shame.
> I wish you'd all been killed instead of Hector
> by those swift ships—the entire bunch of you!
> My life's so miserable and empty.
> I fathered sons, the best in spacious Troy.
> I don't think a single one of them is left—
> not Mestor, or horseman Troilus, or Hector,   320
> that god among men. He didn't seem to be
> the child of any mortal man, but of a god.
> Ares destroyed all those sons of mine.
> The ones still left here are disgraceful—
> liars, prancing masters of the dance floor,
> who steal lambs and goats from their own people.
> Will you not prepare a wagon for me—
> and quickly? Put all those items in it,
> so we can start out on our way."

                                        Priam finished.
The sons, shaken by their father's torrent of abuse,   330
brought out the sturdy, well-made wagon, a new one.
They lashed the wicker basket on it, then took down
from its peg a box-wood yoke to fit a team of mules,
furnished with guiding rings and with a knob on top.
They brought out with the yoke the lashing for it,
a strap five metres long. They placed the yoke with care
across the polished pole at its front end, then set
the rope's eye on the peg and bound it up securely
with three twists round the knob. They lashed it to the pole,
twisting the end below the hook. Next, they brought out   340
from the storeroom and stowed in the well-polished cart
the huge ransom to be paid for Hector's head. The mules
they then put into harness, underneath the yoke,
strong-footed beasts, a splendid gift which Mysians
once gave Priam. Then to Priam's chariot they yoked up
the team the old man kept for his own personal use,
taking care of them in his own gleaming stables.

While harnessing these animals went on this way
in the lofty courtyard for Priam and his herald,
two men with wisdom in their hearts, Hecuba approached.   350
She came up to them with her heart in great distress.
In her right hand she held out in a golden cup
some honey wine, so the men could pour libations
before setting out. Standing there beside their horses,
she addressed them, saying:

                              "Take this wine.
        Pour a libation out to Father Zeus,
        and pray that you'll come home again,
        back from your enemies, since your heart
        urges you against my will to those swift ships.
        So pray to Cronos' son, lord of dark clouds   360
        and god of Ida, who sees the land of Troy,
        and ask him to send a bird of omen,
        that fast messenger which is to him
        the favourite of all birds, the mightiest.

                              535

Let that bird appear over to your right,
so, once you witness it with your own eyes,
you can have faith, as you go to the ships
of those fast-riding Argives. But should Zeus,
who sees far and wide, not send that messenger,
I'd not urge you or advise you go there,   370
to Achaean ships, for all your eagerness."

Godlike Priam then said in reply to Hecuba:

"Wife, I'll not disregard what you advise.
It's good to extend one's hand to Zeus,
if he's inclined to pity."

                        Priam spoke.
Then the old man ordered his servant woman
to pour pure water on his hands. She came out,
bringing with her a basin and a water jug.
Priam washed his hands. Taking the cup from his wife,
he prayed, standing in the middle of the courtyard.   380
Gazing up to heaven, he poured out some wine,
then spoke aloud, saying:

                       "Father Zeus,
lord of Ida, most glorious and great,
grant that when I come to Achilles' hut,
I'll be welcomed kindly and with pity.
Send me a bird as omen, a swift messenger,
the one that is your favourite, the strongest.
Let it appear to my right overhead,
so, once I witness it with my own eyes,
I can have faith as I go to those ships   390
of the fast-riding Danaans."

                     So Priam prayed.
Counselor Zeus heard him. At once he sent an eagle,
of all flying things the surest omen, a dark one,
which people call black eagle, with wings as wide
as doors on some rich man's vaulted store house,

one fitted well with bolts—that's how wide this eagle
spread its wings on either side, appearing on the right,
speeding across the city. When they saw that bird,
they all rejoiced. Hearts in their chests felt great relief.
The old man, in a hurry, climbed in his chariot,   400
then drove out through the gate and echoing courtyard.
In front the mules drew on the four-wheeled wagon,
led by wise Idaios. The horses came behind.
The old man kept laying on the whip, urging them
swiftly through the city. All his family followed him
in tears, as if Priam were going off to his death.
When they'd passed the gate and reached the plain,
his sons and sons-in-law turned back to Ilion.
But as those two men came out into the plain,
they did not go unobserved by wide-seeing Zeus.   410
Looking down on that old man, Zeus pitied him.
At once he spoke to Hermes, his dear son:

> "Hermes, since your favourite task by far
> is acting in a friendly way to men
> and listening to any man you like,
> go down there. Guide Priam to Achaeans,
> to their hollow ships, so no one sees him,
> so no Danaan even is aware of him,
> until he comes to the son of Peleus."

Hermes the Guide, killer of Argus, hearing Zeus,   420
did not disobey. At once he laced up on his feet
his lovely sandals, immortal golden shoes
which carry him across the seas and boundless earth
as fast as winds can blow. With him he took the rod
which puts to sleep the eyes of any man he wishes
or wakes up others who are slumbering.
With this rod in hand, mighty Hermes flew away.
He quickly came to Troy and to the Hellespont.
There he walked on in the form of a young prince
with his first hair on his lip, looking that age   430
when charms of youth are at their loveliest.

When the two men had passed the burial mound of Ilus,
they reined in the mules and horses, stopping there
beside the river for a drink. For by this time
darkness had come down over the earth. Looking round,
the herald saw Hermes approaching. He said to Priam:

> "Be careful, son of Dardanus. At this point,
> we need to think with prudence. I see a man,
> and it seems we may be cut to pieces soon.
> Come, let's go in your chariot, or at least   440
> clasp him by the knees and beg for mercy.
> He may feel pity for us."

Idaios spoke.
The old man's mind was very troubled.
He was dreadfully afraid. On his bent limbs,
the hairs stood out, and he stayed there in a daze.
But Hermes the Helper came up by himself,
took the old man's hand, then asked him questions:

> "Father, where are you going with these horses
> and these mules through this immortal night,
> when other living men are fast asleep?   450
> Aren't you afraid of those Achaeans,
> hostile, fury-breathing, ruthless soldiers—
> they're not far off. If one of them should see you
> bearing all this treasure in the swift black night,
> what would you do then? You're not that young.
> Your escort here is elderly, too old
> to defend himself against someone
> who wants to start a fight. But as for me,
> I'll not harm you. In fact, I will protect you
> from other men, because in you I see   460
> my own dear father."

Old godlike Priam
then said to Hermes in reply:

> "My dear child,

Things are indeed just as you say. But some god
holds his hand over me, to send me here
a traveler like you who comes to meet us,
an auspicious sign, with your handsome shape
and your fine common sense. Those parents of yours
who gave birth to you are surely fortunate."

Messenger Hermes, killer of Argus, then said:

"Old man, what you say is very true.   470
But come now, tell me—and tell me truly—
are you sending so much treasure out
for foreign people to keep safe for you,
or are you leaving sacred Ilion
in fear, now that the finest man's been killed,
your own son, who never was reluctant
in any battles with Achaeans."

Old godlike Priam spoke again to Hermes:

"Who are you, good sir? Who are your parents?
You speak so fairly of my doomed son's fate."   480

Hermes the Guide, killer of Argus, then replied:

"You want to test me, old man, by asking me
of godlike Hector. My eyes have seen him
many times in fights where men win glory.
And when he drove the Argives to their ships,
killing and butchering them with his sharp bronze,
we stood there astonished. For Achilles,
still in a furious rage with Agamemnon,
would not let us fight. I attend on him.
The same ship brought us here. I'm a soldier,   490
one of the Myrmidons. My father's Polyctor,
a man of substance, about as old as you.
He has six other sons—I'm the seventh.
By casting lots with them I was selected
to sail here. I've come now from our ships
here to the plain. At dawn bright-eyed Achaeans

539

will organize for battle round the city.
They're restless, just sitting idly there.
And it's impossible for Achaea's kings
to keep in check their eagerness for war."   500

Old godlike Priam then said to Hermes:

"If you, indeed, do serve with Achilles,
son of Peleus, then tell me the whole truth—
is my son still beside the ships, or has Achilles
already carved his body limb from limb
and thrown him to the dogs to eat?"

Hermes the Guide, killer of Argus, answered:

"Old man, birds and dogs have not yet fed on him.
He's lying still beside Achilles' ship,
among the huts, the same as when he died.   510
For twelve days he's lain there, but his flesh
has not decayed. Worms are not eating him,
as they do with men who die in battle.
Each dawn, Achilles drags him ruthlessly
around his dear companion's burial mound,
but that does not lacerate the corpse.
It would amaze you, if you went in person,
to see how he lies there as fresh as dew,
with all blood washed away, no stain on him.
All the wounds he got have closed completely,   520
and many people stuck their bronze in him.
But that's how blessed gods care for your son,
though he's a corpse. For their hearts loved him."

At these words, the old man felt joy. He replied:

"My son, it's good to pay immortal gods
what's due to them. It's certainly the case,
as true as that my son was once alive,
he never once neglected in our home
the gods who hold Olympus. That's the reason

they now remember him for what he did,   530
even his dead body after death. Come now,
take this lovely goblet as my gift to you.
Protect me. Be my guide with the gods' help,
until I reach the hut of Peleus' son."

Messenger Hermes, killer of Argus, answered Priam:

"You're testing me, old man, because I'm younger.
You won't convince me when you ask me
to take your gift without Achilles' knowledge.
My heart fears that man, but I respect him
too much to rob him, in case something bad   540
comes to me later. But I'll be your guide—
even all the way to famous Argos—
attending to your every need on a swift ship
or else on foot. No man will fight against you
because he's thinks too little of your guide."

With these words, Hermes jumped up in the chariot
behind the horses, quickly grabbing reins and whip.
He breathed great strength into those mules and horses.

When they reached the ditch and towers round the ships,
the sentries there were starting to prepare their meal.   550
Hermes, killer of Argus, poured sleep on all of them,
then opened up the gates at once, pulling back the bars.
He led in Priam with the wagon load of priceless gifts.
They then reached the lofty hut of Peleus' son,
which Myrmidons had built there for their king, cutting
pine beams for it, then roofing it with downy reeds
gathered from the meadows. They'd built around it
a large courtyard for their king, strongly fenced with stakes.
A single beam of pine kept the gate securely closed.
It needed three Achaeans to push it into place,   560
and three to draw that great bolt from the door,
three of the rest of the Achaeans, for Achilles
could push it into place alone. Helper Hermes
opened the gate himself for old man Priam,

then brought in those splendid gifts for swift Achilles.
He climbed down from the chariot and said:

                                 "Old man,
I am Hermes, an immortal god. I've come,
because my father sent me as your guide.
But I'll go back now. I won't approach
within sight of Achilles. There'd be anger   570
if an immortal god greeted mortal men
face to face. But you should go inside,
appeal to him in his father's name,
his mother with her lovely hair, his child,
so you may stir his heart."

                              With these words,
Hermes went on his way, back to high Olympus.
Priam then climbed from his chariot to the ground.
He left Idaios there to tend the mules and horses.
The old man went directly in the hut
where Achilles, dear to Zeus, usually sat.   580
He found Achilles there, with only two companions,
sitting some distance from him—warrior Automedon
and Alcimus, offshoot of the war god Ares—
busy attending him. He'd just completed dinner.
He'd had food and drink, but the table was still there.
The men did not see great Priam as he entered.
He came up to Achilles, then with his fingers
clasped his knees and kissed his hands, those dreadful hands,
man-killers, which had slain so many of his sons.
Just as sheer folly grips a man who in his own land   590
kills someone, then runs off to a land of strangers,
to the home of some rich man, so those who see him
are seized with wonder—that's how Achilles then
looked on godlike Priam in astonishment.
The others were amazed. They gazed at one another.
Then Priam made his plea, entreating:

                              "Godlike Achilles,
remember your own father, who's as old as me,

on the painful threshold of old age.
It may well be that those who live around him
are harassing him, and no one's there   600
to save him from ruin and destruction.
But when he hears you're still alive,
his heart feels joy, for every day he hopes
he'll see his dear son come back home from Troy.
But I'm completely doomed to misery,
for I fathered the best sons in spacious Troy,
yet I say now not one of them remains.
I had fifty when Achaea's sons arrived—
nineteen born from the same mother's womb,
others the women of the palace bore me.   610
Angry Ares drained the life of most of them.
But I had one left, guardian of our city,
protector of its people. You've just killed him,
as he was fighting for his native country.
I mean Hector. For his sake I've come here,
to Achaea's ships, to win him back from you.
And I've brought a ransom beyond counting.
So Achilles, show deference to the gods
and pity for myself, remembering
your own father. Of the two old men,   620
I'm more pitiful, because I have endured
what no living mortal on this earth has borne—
I've lifted up to my own lips and kissed
the hands of the man who killed my son."

Priam finished. His words roused in Achilles
a desire to weep for his own father. Taking Priam's hand,
he gently moved him back. So the two men there
both remembered warriors who'd been slaughtered.
Priam, lying at Achilles' feet, wept aloud
for man-killing Hector, and Achilles also wept   630
for his own father and once more for Patroclus.
The sound of their lamenting filled the house.

When godlike Achilles had had enough of weeping,
when the need to mourn had left his heart and limbs,

he stood up quickly from his seat, then with his hand
helped the old man to his feet, feeling pity
for that gray head and beard. Then Achilles spoke—
his words had wings:

"You unhappy man,
your heart's had to endure so many evils.
How could you dare come to Achaea's ships,   640
and come alone, to rest your eyes on me,
when I've killed so many noble sons of yours?
You must have a heart of iron. But come now,
sit on this chair. Though we're both feeling pain,
we'll let our grief lie quiet on our hearts.
For there's no benefit in frigid tears.
That's the way the gods have spun the threads
for wretched mortal men, so they live in pain,
though gods themselves live on without a care.
On Zeus' floor stand two jars which hold his gifts—   650
one has disastrous things, the other blessings.
When thunder-loving Zeus hands out a mixture,
that man will, at some point, meet with evil,
then, some other time, with good. When Zeus' gift
comes only from the jar containing evil,
he makes the man despised. A wicked frenzy
drives him all over sacred earth—he wanders
without honour from the gods or mortal men.
Consider Peleus. The gods gave him gifts,
splendid presents, right from birth. In wealth,   660
in his possessions, he surpassed all men.
And he was king over the Myrmidons.
Though he was mortal, the gods gave him
a goddess for a wife. But even to him
the gods gave evil, too, for in his palace
there sprang up no line of princely children.
He had one son, doomed to an early death.
I'll not look after him as he grows old,
since I'm a long way from my native land,
sitting here in Troy, bringing pain to you   670
and to your children. Think of yourself, old man.

544

We hear that you were fortunate in former times.
In all the lands from Lesbos to the south,
where Macar ruled, and east to Phrygia,
to the boundless Hellespont, in all these lands,
old man, they say that you surpassed all men
for wealth and children. But from the time
you got disaster from the heavenly gods,
man-killing battles round your city
have never ceased. You must endure it all,   680
without a constant weeping in your heart.
You achieve nothing by grieving for your son.
You won't bring him to life again, not before
you'll have to suffer yet another evil."

Old godlike Priam then answered Achilles:

"Don't make me sit down on a chair, my lord,
while Hector lies uncared for in your huts.
But quickly give him back, so my own eyes
can see him. And take the enormous ransom
we've brought here for you. May it give you joy.   690
And may you get back to your native land,
since you've now let me live to see the sunlight."

With an angry look, swift-footed Achilles snapped at Priam:

"Old man, don't provoke me. I myself intend
to give you Hector. Zeus sent me here
a messenger, the mother who bore me,
daughter of the Old Man of the Sea.
And in my heart, Priam, I recognize—
it's no secret to me—that some god
led you here to the swift Achaean ships.   700
No matter how young and strong, no living man
would dare to make the trip to our encampment.
He could not evade the sentries or push back
our door bolts—that would not be easy.
So don't agitate my grieving heart still more,
or I might not spare even you, old man,

though you're a suppliant here in my hut.
I could transgress what Zeus has ordered."

Achilles spoke. The old man, afraid, obeyed him.
Then Peleus' son sprang to the door, like a lion.   710
Not alone—his two attendants went out with him,
warrior Automedon and Alcimus, whom he honoured
the most of his companions after dead Patroclus.
They freed the mules and horses from their harnesses,
led in the herald, the old man's crier, sat him on a stool.
Then from the polished wagon they brought in
that priceless ransom for Hector's head, leaving there
two cloaks and a thickly woven tunic, so Achilles
could wrap up the corpse before he gave it back
for Priam to take home. Achilles then called out,   720
ordering his servant women to wash the body,
and then anoint it, after moving it away,
so Priam wouldn't see his son, then, heart-stricken,
be unable to contain his anger at the sight.
Achilles' own spirit might then get so aroused
he could kill Priam, disobeying Zeus' orders.
Servants washed the corpse, anointed it with oil,
and put a lovely cloak and tunic round it.
Achilles himself lifted it and placed it on a bier.
Then together he and his companions set it   730
on the polished wagon. Achilles, with a groan,
called to his dear companion:

                              "O Patroclus,
        don't be angry with me, if you learn,
        even in Hades' house, that I gave back
        godlike Hector to his dear father.
        He's brought to me a fitting ransom.
        I'll be giving you your full share of it,
        as is appropriate."

                    Godlike Achilles spoke,
then went back once more into the hut and sat
on the richly decorated chair he'd left   740

by the opposite wall. Then he spoke to Priam:

"Old man, your son has been given back,
as you requested. He's lying on a bier.
You'll see him for yourself at day break,
when you take him. We should think of eating.
Even fair-haired Niobe remembered food,
with twelve of her own children murdered in her home,
her six young daughters and her six strong sons.
Apollo was so enraged at Niobe,
with his silver bow he killed the sons. The daughters   750
Artemis the Archer slaughtered, for Niobe
had compared herself to lovely Leto,
saying the goddess only had two children,
while she had given birth to many. Even so,
though only two, those gods killed all her children.
For nine days they lay in their own blood,
for there was no one there to give them burial.
Cronos' son had turned the people all to stone.
The tenth day, the gods in heaven buried them.
That's when, worn out with weeping, Niobe   760
had thoughts of food. And now, somewhere in the rocks
in Sipylus, among the lonely mountains,
where, men say, goddess nymphs lie down to sleep,
the ones that dance beside the Achelous,
there Niobe, though turned to stone, still broods,
thinking of the pain the gods have given her.
But come, royal old man, let's think of food.
Later you can lament for your dear son,
when you have taken him to Ilion,
where you'll shed many tears for him."   770

Swift Achilles finished. Then, jumping up, he killed
a white-fleeced sheep. His companions skinned it,
then prepared the meat, slicing it skillfully
and putting it on spits. They cooked it carefully,
then pulled spits from the pieces. Taking bread,
Automedon set it in fine baskets on the table.
Achilles served the meat. Then their hands went to it,

taking the food prepared and set beside them.
When they'd satisfied their need for food and drink,
then Priam, son of Dardanus, looked at Achilles,   780
wondering at his size and beauty, like gazing
face to face upon a god. Achilles looked at Priam,
marveling at his royal appearance and the words he heard.
Once they'd had their fill of looking at each other,
the first to speak was the old man, godlike Priam:

> "My lord, show me my bed now with all speed,
> so we may lie down and enjoy sweet sleep.
> For since your hands took my son's life away,
> my eyelids have not closed my eyes, not once.
> I always weep, brooding on my sorrows,   790
> my endless grief. I grovel in the dung
> inside my closed-in courtyard. Now I've eaten,
> tasted meat, and let myself drink gleaming wine.
> Before this, I'd eat nothing."

                                    Priam spoke.
Achilles told his comrades and the servants
to set beds out on his portico, laying on them
fine purple rugs with blankets spread on top,
placing above them wool-lined cloaks for clothing.
Women slaves went from the hall with torches.
Right away they spread out two beds, working quickly.   800
Then swift-footed Achilles spoke to Priam,
in a joking tone:

> "Sleep here outside, my dear old man,
> in case some Achaean counselor arrives.
> They always come to see me to make plans,
> as is our custom. If one of them saw you
> on this pitch black night, he might run off
> to tell Agamemnon, his people's shepherd.
> Then giving back the corpse might be delayed.
> But come, tell me—and speak truthfully—
> how many days do you require to bury   810
> godlike Hector, so I can stop that long

and keep the troops in check?"

                              Old godlike Priam
then said in answer to Achilles:

                              "If you're willing
for me to give lord Hector a full burial,
then, Achilles, as a personal favour,
there is something you could do for me.
You know how we're restricted to our city.
It's a long way to the mountains to get wood.
Besides, the Trojans are especially fearful.
We'll mourn Hector for nine days in our home.   820
On the tenth day we'll have his funeral.
Then there'll be a banquet for the people.
On the eleventh, we'll make his burial mound.
The twelfth day, if we must, we'll go to war."

Swift-footed Achilles then said to Priam:

                              "All right, old Priam, things will be arranged
as you request. I'll suspend the fighting
for the length of time you've asked for."

As he said this, Achilles took the old man's wrist
on his right hand, in case his heart was fearful.   830
So by that house on the porch they lay down to sleep,
Priam and his herald, both men of wisdom.
Achilles slept in a corner of his well-built hut,
with lovely Briseis stretched out there beside him.

Meanwhile, other gods and warrior charioteers,
all conquered by sweet sleep, slept the whole night through.
But slumber did not grip the Helper Hermes,
as he considered in his heart what he might do
to guide king Priam from the ships in secret,
without the strong guard at the gate observing.   840
So standing above Priam's head, he said to him:

"Old man, you're not expecting any harm,
as you sleep like this among your enemies,
since Achilles spared your life. Your dear son
is ransomed for that huge amount you paid.
But if Agamemnon, son of Atreus,
or all Achaeans learn that you are here,
those sons you've left behind will have to pay
a ransom three times greater for your life."

Hermes spoke. At his words, the old man grew afraid.   850
He woke up the herald. Hermes harnessed mules and horses,
then guided them himself quickly through the camp,
attracting no attention. But when they reached the ford
across the swirling river Xanthus, immortal Zeus' child,
Hermes left them and returned to high Olympus.

As Dawn spread her yellow robes over all the earth,
the two men drove their horses inside the city,
weeping and groaning. The mules pulled in the corpse.
No one noticed them, no man, no well-dressed woman,
except Cassandra, a girl as beautiful   860
as golden Aphrodite. She'd climbed up Pergamus.
She saw her father standing in his chariot,
together with his herald, the town crier.
In the mule cart she saw the corpse lying on the bier.
With a scream, Cassandra cried out to all the city:

            "See, men and women of Troy, come and see—
            look on Hector, if, while he was still alive,
            you would rejoice when he came back from war,
            for he was a great joy to all our city
            and its people."

                    At Cassandra's shout,   870
no man or woman was left unaffected.
There in the city all were overcome with grief
beyond anyone's control. Close to the gates,
they met Priam bringing home the body.
First Hector's dear wife and his noble mother,

550

tearing their hair, ran to the sturdy wagon,
trying to touch Hector's head. People crowded round,
all weeping. They would have stayed there by the gates,
shedding tears for Hector the entire day
until the sun went down, but from the chariot   880
the old man cried out to the crowd:

                              "Make way there—
let the mules get through. There'll be time enough,
once I've got him home, for everyone to weep."

At Priam's words, the crowd moved back, making room.
The wagon pushed on through. Once they'd got him home,
inside their great house, they laid him on a corded bed,
then placed singers there beside him, to lead their songs.
They sang a mournful funeral dirge. Then the women
began their wailing, led by white-armed Andromache,
who held in her arms the head of man-killing Hector.   890

     "My husband—you've lost your life so young,
     leaving me a widow in our home,
     with our son still an infant, the child
     born to you and me in our wretchedness.
     I don't think he'll grow up to adulthood.
     Before that, our city will all be destroyed.
     For you, who kept watch over for us, are dead.
     You used to protect our city, keeping
     its noble wives and little children safe.
     Now, soon enough, they'll all be carried off   900
     in hollow ships. I'll be there among them.
     And you, my child, you'll follow with me,
     to some place where you'll be put to work
     at menial tasks, slaving for a cruel master.
     Or else some Achaean man will grab your arm
     and throw you from the wall—a dreadful death—
     in his anger that Hector killed his brother,
     or his father, or his son. For Hector's hands
     made great numbers of Achaeans sink their teeth
     into the broad earth. In wretched warfare,   910

your father was not gentle. So in our city
they now weep for him. O Hector, what sorrow,
what untold grief you've laid upon your parents.
What painful sorrows will remain for me,
especially for me. As you were dying,
you didn't reach your hand out from the bed,
or give me some final words of wisdom,
something I could remember always,
night and day, as I continue my lament."

Andromache said this in tears. The women all wailed with her.   920
Then Hecuba took her turn in leading their laments:

"Hector, dearest by far of all my children,
loved by the gods, as well, when you were living.
Now, at your death, they still take care of you.
When swift Achilles took my other sons,
he'd ship them off across the boundless seas,
to Samos, or Imbros, or foggy Lemnos.
When his long-edged bronze took away your life,
he dragged you many times around the mound
for his comrade Patroclus, whom you killed.   930
Yet even so, he could not revive him.
Now you lie here in our house, fresh as dew,
like someone whom Apollo of the silver bow
has just come to and killed with gentle arrows."

As she spoke, Hecuba wept. She stirred them on
to endless lamentation. Helen was the third
to lead those women in their wailing:

"Hector—of all my husband's brothers,
you're by far the dearest to my heart.
My husband's godlike Alexander,   940
who brought me here to Troy. I wish I'd died
before that happened! This is the twentieth year
since I went away and left my native land,
but I've never heard a nasty word from you
or an abusive speech. In fact, if anyone

ever spoke rudely to me in the house—
one of your brothers or sisters, some brother's
well-dressed wife, or your mother—for your father
always was so kind, as if he were my own—
you'd speak out, persuading them to stop,   950
using your gentleness, your soothing words.
Now I weep for you and for my wretched self,
so sick at heart, for there's no one else
in spacious Troy who's kind to me and friendly.
They all look at me and shudder with disgust."

Helen spoke in tears. The huge crowd joined in their lament.
Then old Priam addressed his people:

                                        "You Trojans,
you must fetch some wood here to the city.
Don't let your hearts fear any ambush,
some crafty Achaean trick. For Achilles,   960
when he sent me back from the hollow ships,
gave me his word they'd not harm us
until the twelfth day dawns."

                                        Priam finished.
The people hitched up mules and oxen to their wagons
and then gathered before the city with all speed.
For nine days they brought in wood, an immense amount.
When the tenth dawn came, they brought brave Hector out,
then, all in tears, laid his corpse on top the funeral pyre.
They set it alight. When rose-fingered Dawn came up,
they gathered around that pyre of glorious Hector.   970
Once they'd all assembled there together,
first they doused the pyre with gleaming wine, every part
that fire's strength had touched. His brothers and comrades
collected Hector's ash-white bones, as they mourned him—
heavy tears running down their cheeks—and placed them
in a golden urn, wrapped in soft purple cloth.
They quickly set the urn down in a shallow grave,
covered it with large stones set close together,
then hurried to pile up the mound, posting sentries

on every side, in case well-armed Achaeans
attacked too soon. Once they'd piled up the mound,
they went back in, gathered together for a splendid feast,
all in due order, in Priam's house, king raised by Zeus.
And thus they buried Hector, tamer of horses.

Appendices

Glossary of People and Places

Map of the home states of some of the major
Achaean and Trojan Leaders

Map of the Area Around Troy

A Few Suggestions for Further Study

Glossary of People and Places

Below is a partial list including only the important names and a few others. For a complete list of all the names in the *Iliad*, together with a detailed glossary indicating where their names appear in the poem, please consult the following internet site:

http://www.mala.bc.ca/~johnstoi/homer/iliad_index.htm.

Achaea: mainland Greece.

Achaeans: collective name for the forces from Greece under Agamemnon, used interchangeably with the term **Argives** or **Danaans**.

Achilles: leader of the Myrmidons, part of Achaean army, son of Peleus and Thetis, often referred to as "son of Peleus" or "descendant of Aeacus."

Aeneas: major Trojan warrior, leader of Dardanians, son of Anchises and Aphrodite.

Agamemnon: king of Mycenae, son of Atreus, leader of Achaean forces, brother of Menelaus, commonly called "wide ruling" or "mighty."

Agenor: son of Antenor, Trojan warrior.

Ajax (1): son of Telamon, leader of forces from Salamis, greatest Achaean warrior after Achilles, known as the great Ajax or greater Ajax. **Ajax (2)**: son of Oïleus, leader of Locrian troops, the swift or lesser Ajax.

Alexander: another name for **Paris**.

Andromache: wife of Hector, daughter of Eëtion.

Antenor: senior Trojan counselor.

Aphrodite: divine daughter of Zeus and Hera, goddess of erotic love, a supporter of the Trojans.

Apollo: divine son of Zeus and Leto, a supporter of the Trojans.

Ares: son of Zeus, god of war, especially the destructive aspects, a supporter of the Trojans.

Argives: see **Achaeans**.

Argos (1): town in northern Peloponnese ruled by Diomedes. **Argos (2)**: a large area ruled by Agamemnon. **Argos (3)**: a general term for the homeland of Achaeans generally (i.e., mainland Greece and Peloponnese). **Argos (4)**: region in north-east Greece, part of the kingdom of Peleus (sometimes called Pelasgian Argos).

Artemis: goddess, daughter of Zeus and Hera, sister of Apollo, supporter of the Trojans.

Asteropaeus: alleged son of Pelagon, son of the river Axius and Periboea, Trojan warrior.

Astyanax: son of Hector and Andromache, an infant, also called **Scamandrius**.

Ate: divine daughter of Zeus, responsible for human and divine folly.

Athena: goddess daughter of Zeus, strong supporter of the Achaeans, commonly called "glittery eyed."

Atreus: king of Argos, son of Pelops, father of Agamemnon and Menelaus (known as the "sons of Atreus").

Automedon: Achaean warrior.

Boeotia: region of central Greece whose men are part of the Achaean forces.

Briseis: daughter of Briseus, captive awarded to Achilles.

Calchas: priest and interpreter of omens for Achaean army.

Cebriones: bastard son of Priam and brother of Hector.

Chryseis: young daughter of Chryses, captured by Achaeans.

Cronos: divine father of Zeus, overthrown by Zeus and kept imprisoned in Tartarus.

Danaans: see **Achaeans**.

Dardanians: people from around Troy, led by Aeneas.

Deïphobus: son of Priam, Trojan warrior.

Demeter: goddess of grain and food generally.

Diomedes: son of Tydeus, king of Argos, a younger warrior with the Achaeans.

Earthshaker: common epithet for Poseidon.

Eumelus: leader of Thessalian troops, part of the Achaean army.

Euryalus: a senior leader of the troops from the Argolid, an Achaean warrior.

Eurybates: one of the Achaean heralds.

Eurymedon: Achaean warrior, attendant on Agamemnon.

Eurypylus: leader of troops from parts of Thessaly, part of the Achaean army.

Glaucus: son of Hippolochus, leader of the Lycians (Trojan allies).

Hades: brother of Zeus and Poseidon, god of the dead.

Hector: leader of Trojan forces, son of Priam and Hecuba, often called "Hector of the shining helmet," or "man-killing Hector."

Hecuba: wife of Priam, mother of Hector (and others).

Helen: mortal child of Zeus, wife of Menelaus and later of Paris (Alexander).

Helenus: son of Priam, reader of omens for Trojans.

Hephaestus: divine son of Zeus and Hera, artisan god, crippled in his legs, supporter of the Achaeans.

Hera: divine wife and sister of Zeus, daughter of Cronos, frequently called "white armed" or "ox eyed," a strong supporter of the Achaeans.

Hercules: son of Zeus and Alcmene, legendary Greek hero, father of Tlepolemus.

Hermes: divine son of Zeus, often called "killer of Argus" or "Messenger."

Ida: a mountain near Troy.

Idaios: a Trojan herald.

Idomeneus: son of Deucalion, leader of Cretan forces, a senior commander in the Achaean forces.

Ilion: another name for **Troy**.

Iris: divine messenger of the gods.

Leto: goddess mother of Apollo and Artemis.

Lycia/Lycians: region of Asia Minor whose troops, led by Sarpedon and Glaucus, are allied with the Trojans.

Machaon: leader of troops from parts of Thessaly, a healer in the Achaean army.

Meges: son of Phyleus, leader of troops from Doulichium, part of the Achaean army.

Menelaus: son of Atreus, brother of Agamemnon, first husband of Helen of Troy, king of Sparta, a major figure in Achaean leadership.

Menestheus: leader of Athenian soldiers fighting with the Achaeans.

Meriones: an attendant on Idomeneus, part of the Cretan contingent in the Achaean forces.

Myrmidons: troops from Thessaly under the command of Achilles.

Nestor: king of Pylos, a senior warrior among Achaeans, called "the Geranian horseman."

Odysseus: king of Ithaca, major warrior for the Achaean forces, commonly called "resilient" and "resourceful" and "cunning."

Olympus: mountain in Greece where the major gods (the Olympians) live.

Ouranos: divine father of Cronos.

Pandarus: son of Lycaon, leader of troops from Zeleia, part of the Trojan forces.

Paris: son of Priam and Hecuba, brother of Hector, abductor of Helen from Menelaus, also called **Alexander.**

Patroclus: son of Menoetius, an Achaean warrior and special comrade of Achilles.

Peleus: father of Achilles.

Phoebus: see **Apollo.**

Phoenix: old companion and tutor of Achilles, an Achaean warrior.

Phthia: region in south Thessaly (in northern Greece), home of Achilles and his father Peleus.

Polydamas: a Trojan warrior.

Poseidon: major Olympian god (ruling the sea), brother of Zeus, commonly called "Earthshaker" or "Encircler of the Earth."

Priam: king of Troy, husband of Hecuba, father of Hector, Paris, and numerous others.

Sarpedon: son of Zeus and leader of the Lycians, Trojan allies.

Scaean Gates: the major gates through the Trojan walls.

Scamander: river outside Troy (also called the **Xanthus**), also the river god.

Scamandrius: see **Astyanax**.

Simoeis: river near Troy.

Sthenelus: one of the leaders of troops from the Argolid, a special comrade of Diomedes, an Achaean warrior.

Strife: goddess active in war, sister of Ares.

Talthybius: one of the Achaean heralds.

Terror: son of Ares, divine presence active in battle.

Teucer: bastard son of Telamon and hence brother to the greater Ajax, an Achaean warrior noted for his skill with a bow.

Thetis: divine sea nymph married to a mortal, Peleus, mother of Achilles.

Thrasymedes: son of Nestor, an Achaean warrior.

Tydeus: father of Diomedes.

Xanthus (1): one of Hector's horses. **Xanthus (2)**:Trojan warrior. **Xanthus (3)**: river in Lycia (Asia Minor). **Xanthus (4)**: river outside Troy, also called the **Scamander**, also the river god. **Xanthus (5)**: one of Achilles' horses.

Zeus: most powerful of the gods, commonly called "the son of Cronos," "cloud gatherer," "lord of the lightning bolt," "aegis-bearing," brother and husband of Hera, father of numerous gods and men.

The Area Around Troy

(Reprinted with kind permission of Carlos Parada of the Greek Mythology Link)

Map of Ancient Greek World

A Few Suggestions for Further Study

There are innumerable books and essays dealing with the *Iliad* and Homer. The brief list below includes some recommended titles for those wishing to explore Homer in more detail.

Howard Clarke, *Homer's Readers* (a very interesting study of the transmission and influence of the *Iliad* and *Odyssey*).

Ian Johnston, *Essays on Homer's Iliad*, available on line at the following site: http://www.mala.bc.ca/~johnstoi/homer/iliadessaystofc.htm. (a detailed look at the vision of life presented in the *Iliad*).

James M. Redfield, *Nature and Culture in the Iliad* (an influential modern study of Homer's epic).

Simone Weil, *The Iliad or The Poem of Force* (a classic study of the *Iliad*, still as eloquent as ever).

Michael Wood, *In Search of Troy* (a fascinating and easy-to-read account of the archeological work carried out to find Troy)

There are a number useful sites on the web including the Homer Home Page. This site can be found at the following address: http://www.gpc.edu/~shale/humanities/literature/world_literature/homer.ht ml. So there is no shortage of additional suggestions.

A recording of the complete translation contained in this book is available from Naxos Books, *The Iliad*, read by Anton Lesser (ISBN 9-626344-28-8), through the Naxos internet site: http://www.naxosaudiobooks.com/.